T0106321

My interest in Genealogy began many years before the Computer Age, when the only way to get information was to go to the Court House or the Parish Church, and pour over hand written documents, (Often in French) and slowly "back-track" through the years. My aunt, Mrs. Ruth Brewerton Robért compiled such a book in 1975, and some of her work is included here. I had always wanted to go deeper and farther, so after 21 years of research I compiled this comprehensive book of the Robért Family in Louisiana.

The

ROBÉRT FAMILY

OF

South Louisiana

1772 - 2009

Compiled by

Norman A. Robert

Order this book online at www.trafford.com
or email orders@trafford.com

Most Trafford titles are also available at major online book retailers.

© Copyright 2011 Norman A. Robért.
All rights reserved. No part of this publication may be reproduced, stored in a retrieval
system, or transmitted, in any form or by any means, electronic, mechanical, photocopying,
recording, or otherwise, without the written prior permission of the author.

Printed in the United States of America.

ISBN: 978-1-4269-7285-0 (sc)

Library of Congress Control Number: 2011910390

Trafford rev. 06/22/2011

 www.trafford.com

North America & international
toll-free: 1 888 232 4444 (USA & Canada)
phone: 250 383 6864 ♦ fax: 812 355 4082

Direct Descendants of

Jean Robért

and

Marianne Waguespack

Jean Robért
(1772 - 1815)

Son of **Mathieu Robért**
(?) - (1777)

and **Marie Catherine Menard**
(1750 - Bef-1820)

Marianne Waguespack
(1775 - AFT 1850)

Daughter of **Jean Louis Waguespack, Jr.**
(Abt-1731 - 1794)

and **Marie Magdelaine Edelmeire**
(1739 - 1830)

Introduction

by: Thomas J. Robert

WHO ARE WE ?

And how did we come to be ? The members of the families genealogically traced in this book number in the thousands. The Robért, Brou, Waguespack, Schexnayder, Faucheux, Folse, and Waggenspack's ancestors are all listed as they intermarry and expand their own family and then their children marry and intermarry. The consanguinity lines between the individuals and these families look like a large bowl of spaghetti, twisting and turning and surfacing in the most unexpected spots.

Some of these families can be traced back to the old world, but not all. We have been unable to find any European tie to the oldest Robért, (Mathieu). We do know he was living in New Orleans about 1771, and we began the Robért genealogy with him. How and when he arrived here may someday be found, perhaps in one of the folowing histories.

In 1717 John Law was given a 25 year concession to locate and transport emigrants to Louisiana. The city of New Orleans was founded a year later. In 1719 the first settlers, enticed by John Law, arrive in Louisiana, mainly from Germany. It is from this migration that most of the German Families listed above moved to Louisiana. At the same time ships continue to arrive from France also carrying French Citizens and officials and administrators for the colony.

Louisiana was well established and populated when the French ceded Canada to the British in 1763. Within two years Britain begins "cleansing" Arcadia of French Citizens. Large numbers of these exiles arrived in Louisiana in 1765, and more in the following year.

From whichever of these possibilities Mathieu did arrive, we do not know, but we do know that he married Marie Catherine Menard about 1770 in St. Charles Parish, Louisiana. He became a land owner on May 15, 1771 when he and Charles Robeau bought six arpents of land in St. Charles Parish. His land was located along the "German Coast" of the Mississippi River about 20 miles up river from New Orleans, near present day Hahnville. One of the covenants attached to the river bank land was a requirement that the land owner build and maintain a levee and road on the property along the river bank. He and Robeau were unable to meet this requirement and lost their property in July 1776.

Two of Mathieu's children married Waguespacks. His grandchildren married into the Faucheux and Schexnayder families. And, thus begins the constant intermarrying which continues to this day. But it is this close close relationship which allows these destitute families to survive. They combined their labor, knowledge, experience, fortitude and Faith in God, to carry them through unbelievable hardships. Only throug Family and Church were they able to sustain themselves.

We know that the first generation or two, in the Mathieu Robért line, lived and died in or near St. Charles Parish. We can surely surmise that they were totally absorbed into the "German Coast" families. He had 10 direct descendants by 1800. Seven of these are recorded as having been born and died in St. Charles Parish. It is most likely that the other three were also.

Very little is known about the actual life style and means of survival employed by these our forebears. We assume they were farming small plots of land, some they did own and some they farmed as sharecroppers, or perhaps rented. In the beginning they had no one to turn to, only the immediate family. They had no mechanical power of any kind. All work was done with muscle power, either your own or if you were fortunate, with an ox or mule. Mechanical power was far in the future, and it was heralded by the first steamboat which arrived in New Orleans in 1812. Railroads did not reach New Orleans until 1885. At the outset of the Civil War, there were still about 75 sugar mills in Louisiana which were using horses and mules to power the mills.

While it is no doubt true that the civil war with its utter and total destruction of all means of production in the Sugar Cane Belt caused a ruinous and lasting retardation in the ability of the small farming class to Mechanize. It is surprising how long it actually took. The year 1919 is viewed as the pivital year, the year when more of the farm work was done with tractors than was done with mules. Mules, however, did remain on the farm until the middle of the twentieth century.

It was due to the mandatory requirements of many strong hands and hearts that forced the communal effort of many families in a common goal of survival. As late as 1900 there were large numbers of families grouped together in abandoned antebellum homes and in the close by slave cabins. When Mathieu's grandson (Mathieu III) moved from Johnson Plantation (near Vacherie) to Soniat Plantation (near Harahan) in 1900, with him were his own family, his siblings and their families, at least three of his brothers-in-law, some of the Waguespacks and also the Schexnayders and their own families. There were over 20 seperate families working together planting rice and corn as cash crops. In addition they had garden plots for household use and the normal compliment of farm animals for fiber, feathers and food.

In 1903 Mathieu III and the Brou relatives and a few of the Waguespacks and the Shexnayders moved to Hermitage Plantation (near Darrow). They were here until 1911 when the Robért and Brou families separated and set out with their own families. The Robért clan went to Remy Plantation in St. James Parish, and stayed there until 1914.

iv

In 1915 and 1916 they were at Elise Plantation (near Modeste). The family groupings were getting smaller now, and in 1917 they moved to Orange Grove Plantation (at Burnside) for a two year stay. World War I had an effect on the close ties of the family, and some of the sons who had served in the war went off on their own. In 1920 Mathieu III died and Jean Paul, his youngest brother, became the head of the family.

It was Jean Paul (known as Pepere Paul or Cousin Paul) who brought the Robért family to Burnside in 1925 when he bought Donaldson Tract Plantation. With his wife of 50 years and five of his sons and an unmarried daughter, they all moved into one house on the original home plantation of Houmas House. He and his family had been moving every few years for all of his life and now he would stay put. He lived out his llong life at the (Tract). He was born in 1855 and was 95 when he died on December 7, 1950.

A nonstop stream of relatives visited "Pepere" during his time at Donaldson Tract and the closeness of the families was evident. The land was sold a few years after his death and the family members stayed in touch, but it was no longer the same. The Patriarch was gone.

Relatives

Some things appear to have always been. When I was asked by Mr. Bob Robért to write down how the Robért, Schexnayder, Waguespack, Brou and Folse were all related as a way of introducing the genealogical work published in this book, I just thought "some things appear to have always been". And further, why they migrated along the river as a network of families? Well, why does the sun come up every morning? Just always have and always will.

But upon closer examination, I think it appears to have gone back to the 1700s when Louisiana was in ins infancy. The colony of Louisiana was sparsely populated. One of those small settlements was along the Mississippi River in St. Charles Parish. In those days it was called "La Cote des Allemands" or the "German Coast". This is not to be confused with the present day Des Allemands. This "German Coast" was an area along the river between Luling, Hahnville, Taft and Killona. Those first inhabitants were living in a close-knit community where the survival of the settlement depended upon the survival of each family relying on a netwirk of families to simply survive. For survival, they also relied upon the Native Americans, who introduced them to Louisiana's climate, geography and wildlife.

Several unrelated opportunistic, hard-working, European couples settled on the "German Coast", those being:
> Mathieu Robért and Catherine Menard
> Joseph Waguespack and Anne Barbara Ackerman
> Pierre Brou and Marguerite Boyer
> Henry Albert Schexnayder and Magdalena Wiche

Amongst other families settling here were the Faucheux, Haydel, Troxclair, Folse, Loup and Champagne families. The spellings of a few of their names have now been morphed and Gallicized. But those bonds of frendship and family forged in the early pioneering days lasted for over 200 years. As time pressed onward those families remained very intimately related.

Mathieu Robért and Catherine Menard had a son named Jean Robért who married Marianne Waguespack. Marianne's brother, Andre Louis Waguespack married Julie Eugenie Robért, Also a child of Mathieu Robért and Catherine Menard.

Jean Robért and Marianne Waguespack had 8 known children, two of their three daughters married Schexnayder brothers. Three of their fove sons married Faucheux girls. The most significant to our family was Mathieu Robért, (named for his grandfather), who married Myrtile Antoinette Faucheux.

The double first cousins of the 8 children of Jean Robért and Marianne Waguespack were the 14 children of Andre Louis Waguespack and Julie Eugenie Robért. Of those 14 children, the oldest, Andre Evariste Waguespack married Arthemise Faucheux. It should be said that

Arthemise was the aunt of the above mentioned Myrtile Faucheux, married to Mathieu Robért. Now of the 14 children of Andre Louis Waguespack and Julie Eugenie Robért, three married first cousins on the Waguespack side of the family. Another three of the children married three of the children of Antoine Folse and Marie Eve Laiche. In the Folse family Another sister married a Brou, and three others married Waguespacks too. Confused yet?

Now the Andre Evariste Waguespack that married Arthemise Faucheux had 12 children, four married Waguespack cousins, two married Folse cousins, two Robért cousins and three others a Brou, Haydel and Champagne. Of those four that married Waguespack, two brothers, Florian and Florestant both married Julie Waguespacks! Those two "Julie" girls were born 16 days apart in January of 1837 and were double first cousins, both married Waguespacks who were cousins to them!!!

The youngest son of Andre Evariste Waguespack and Arthemise Faucheux was Alidore Waguespack. He was married to Delia Robért daughter of Mathieu Robért and Myrtile Faucheux, mentioned above. This Mathieu was the father of 11 children. Mathieu Jr. married twice leaving no offspring. His first wife, a first cousin, was Delia Faucheux and his second wife, a second cousin, was Nezelie Waguespack daughter of none other than Andre Evariste Waguespack and Arthemise Faucheux. Nezilie was the sister of Alidor Waguespack.

Mathieu Jr.'s brother, Septime Robért married his first cousin, Marie Schexnayder. Their mothers were both daughters of Louis Jean Faucheux and Francoise Roger. Septime and Marie had 8 children, three married Brou, two married Waguespacks, one married Zeringue and the other two did not marry.

The next son of Mathieu Robért and Myrtile Faucheux was Frumence Robért who married Euphrasie Bouy, not a relative. Frumence's five chikdren married very familiar names: 3rd cousin Borne, double 3rd cousin Waguespack, Hymel, 3rd cousin Brou and 1st cousin Robért.

The youngest son of Mathieu Robért and Myrtile Faucheux was Jean Paul Robért who married his half 2nd cousin Octavie Brou. Not to mention that Jean Paul's mother-in-law, Arthemise Waguespack Brou was his double 2nd cousin. Jean Paul Robért and Octavie Brou had 11 children. Three married Waggenspack siblings (their children became double 1st cousins), one married a 1st cousin, a Robért. It should now be mentioned that these three Waggenspack siblings were the children of Felix Waguespack and Amelie Waguespack. It was the sons of Felix that changed the spelling of Waguespack to Waggenspack. But needless to say, their Parents Felix and Amelie were 1st cousins, both grandchildren of Andre Louis Waguespack and Julie Eugenie Robért.

These families over the years moved up and down the Mississippi River, from St. Charles Parish westward to Bayou Lafourche and up river to St. John the Baptist Parish. Then back down to Jefferson Parish's Tchoupitoulas Plantation then up the river to St. James and Ascension Parishes. They split and rejoined one another, as they farmed sugar cane and lots of rice, which required lots of moves, meeting up again at different plantations along the river.

How joyous they must have been when they moved back to a plantation with a familiar bunch of cousins. With little opportunities to travel and nearly non-existent methods of easy transportation, they often married these relatives, some distantly related, some first cousins.

By this point you should be thorougly confused as to who is who. Robért, Waguespack, Brou, Schexnaydre, Folse, these names keep appearing over and over again. But regardless, descendants of the above are descendants of all, more than likely. Unless you are an experienced genealogist or even if you aren't, you probably were not able to follow much of the above, without at least charting it out on paper.

I am not trying to confuse anyone and neither was I trying to easily explain a complicated subject. What I am trying to convey in a few paragraphs cannot easily be done, as the cumbersome consanguinity of these families can best be understood, by doing the genealogy yourself or if you don't have time to, at least use this book. It should be a guide for the descendants of thie inter-related multi-generational Creole family network who for over 200 years lived and died along the mighty Mississippi River of South Louisiana.

Jay Michael Schexnaydre
October 27, 2004

Symbol Explanations

<   >   =   Alternate name or Alternate spelling

(   )   =   Nickname or pertinent information

+   =   Families with Children

*   =   Direct line to Jean Paul Robert and Marie Octavie Brou

**   =   Direct Line to Rene Waguespack and Marie Elmire Robért

***   =   Direct Line to Victor Waguespack and Marie Octavie Robért

Descendants of Jean Robért and Marianne Waguespack

Generation No. 1

1. Jean[2] Robért, *-*** (Mathieu[1]) was born Abt. 1772 in Ama, St. Charles Parish, Louisiana, USA, and died 15 July 1815 in St. Charles Parish, Louisiana[1]. He married **Marianne Waguespack, (minor)*- ***** Abt. 1789 in St. Charles Parish, Louisiana, daughter of Jean Waguespack and Marie Edelmaire. She was born 1775 in St. Charles Parish, Louisiana, and died Aft. 1850 in Ama, St. Charles Parish, Louisiana.

Children of Jean Robért and Marianne Waguespack are:

+	2	i.	**Marianne Melanie[3] Robért, born Abt. 1790 in St. Charles Parish, Louisiana; died in Louisiana.**
+	3	ii.	**Jean Robért II, born Abt. 1800 in St. Charles Parish, Louisiana.**
+	4	iii.	**Jean Louis Robért, born 1797 in St. Charles Parish, Louisiana; died 06 June 1851 in Taft, St. Charles Parish, Louisiana.**
+	5	iv.	**Norbert Robért, born 1803 in St. Charles Parish, Louisiana; died 1855 in Louisiana.**
+	6	v.	**Hubert Robért, Sr., born 1805 in St. Charles Parish, Louisiana; died 14 January 1865 in Destrehan, St. Charles Parish, Louisiana.**
	7	vi.	**Camille Robért, born Abt. 1807 in St. Charles Parish, Louisiana. She married Jean Baptiste Bertrand, Jr. 17 January 1832 in St. Charles Parish, Louisiana**[2]**; born 1800.**
	8	vii.	**Heloise Robért, born Abt. 1809 in St. Charles Parish, Louisiana; died 06 November 1844 in St. Charles Parish, Louisiana. She married Albert Schexnayder 30 October 1826 in Edgard, St. John the Baptist Parish, Louisiana**[3]**; born 1810 in St. John the Baptist , Louisiana; died in Louisiana.**
+	9	viii.	**Mathieu Robért, Sr. *- ***, born 1811 in St. Charles Parish, Louisiana; died 12 September 1855 in St. John the Baptist Parish, Louisiana.**

Generation No. 2

2. Marianne Melanie[3] Robért (Jean[2], Mathieu[1]) was born Abt. 1790 in St. Charles Parish, Louisiana, and died in Louisiana. She married **Epiphany <Tiffany> Schexnayder, Jr.** 05 November 1821 in St. John the Baptist Catholic

Church, Edgard, Louisiana[4], son of Epiphany Schexnayder and Lucy Haydel. He was born 1806 in St. John the Baptist Parish, Louisiana, and died in Louisiana.

Children of Marianne Robért and Epiphany Schexnayder are:

+ 10   i. **Emilien[4] Schexnayder, born 24 February 1829 in St. John the Baptist Parish, Louisiana; died 20 March 1878 in New Orleans, Orleans Parish, Louisiana.**

+ 11   ii. **Marcellin Schexnayder, born 1830 in St. John the Baptist Parish, Louisiana; died 09 December 1882 in St. John the Baptist Parish, Louisiana.**

   3. Jean[3] Robért II (Jean[2], Mathieu[1]) was born Abt. 1800 in St. Charles Parish, Louisiana. He married **(1) Eleanor Toups** 28 August 1820 in St. Charles Borromeo Catholic Church, Destrehan, Louisiana[4], daughter of Gaspard Toups and Genevieve Haydel. She was born 1807 in St. Charles Parish, Des Allemands, Louisiana, and died 15 November 1831 in Louisiana. He married **(2) Melanie <Melazie> Belsome** Abt. 1833.

Children of Jean Robért and Eleanor Toups are:

  12 i. **Genevieve Palmire[4] Robért, born 01 February 1823 in St. Charles Parish, Louisiana.**

  13 ii. **Marianne Esteve Robért, born 29 May 1825 in St. Charles Parish, Louisiana.**

  14 iii. **Estelle Robért, born 24 June 1826 in St. Charles Parish, Louisiana; died 13 October 1853 in St. Charles Parish, Louisiana.**

Child of Jean Robért and Melanie Belsome is:

+ 15   i. **Louis[4] Robért, born Abt. 1834 in St. Charles Parish, Louisiana; died Abt. 1856 in St. Charles Parish, Louisiana.**

   4. Jean Louis[3] Robért (Jean[2], Mathieu[1]) was born 1797 in St. Charles Parish, Louisiana, and died 06 June 1851 in Taft, St. Charles Parish, Louisiana. He married **(1) Isabelle Arceneaux** 05 November 1821 in St. Charles Borromeo Catholic Church, Destrehan, Louisiana[5], daughter of Jean Arceneaux and Charlotte Kinler. She was born Abt. 1801 in Louisiana, and died 25 October 1831 in Taft, St. Charles Parish, Louisiana. He married **(2) Erasie Kinler** 01 June 1835. He married **(3) Melanie Zeller** Abt. 1846. She was born 1826.

Children of Jean Robért and Isabelle Arceneaux are:

+ 16   i. **Jean Baptiste[4] Robért, born 1822 in St. Charles Parish, Louisiana; died 28 October 1883 in Ama, St. Charles Parish, Louisiana.**

  17 ii. **Odille Robért, born 1826 in St. Charles Parish, Louisiana; died October 1853 in St. Charles Parish, Louisiana.**

| 18 | iii. | Udger Robért, born 1829 in St. Charles Parish, Louisiana; died 1863 in Louisiana. He married Eugenie Maillard 30 December 1854 in St. Charles Borromeo Church, Destrahan, Louisiana. |

Children of Jean Robért and Melanie Zeller are:

+	19	i.	Emile[4] Robért, born Abt. 1847 in St. Charles Parish, Louisiana; died September 1859 in St. Charles Parish, Louisiana.
	20	ii.	Estelle Robért, born January 1849 in St. Charles Parish, Louisiana; died 23 March 1914 in St. Charles Parish, Louisiana. She married Kindler.
	21	iii.	Melanie Odile Robért, born 07 August 1851 in St. Charles Parish, Louisiana; died October 1853 in St. Charles Parish, Louisiana.

5. Norbert[3] Robért (Jean[2], Mathieu[1]) was born 1803 in St. Charles Parish, Louisiana, and died 1855 in Louisiana. He married **Amanda Leocadie Toledano** 20 March 1843 in St. Louis Cathedral, New Orleans, Orleans Parish, Louisiana[6], daughter of Jean Toledano and Hyancinthe Drouet. She was born 1824, and died 06 December 1899.

Children of Norbert Robért and Amanda Toledano are:

22	i.	Ernestine[4] Robért, born Abt. 1846.
23	ii.	Norbert Robért, Jr., born Abt. 1848.
24	iii.	Edward Robért, born Abt. 1854; died 12 February 1925. He married Aline Guillot.

6. Hubert[3] Robért, Sr. (Jean[2], Mathieu[1]) was born 1805 in St. Charles Parish, Louisiana, and died 14 January 1865 in Destrehan, St. Charles Parish, Louisiana. He married **Julie Faucheux** 09 February 1829 in St. Charles Borromeo Church, Destrahan, Louisiana[7]. She was born 1815 in St. Charles Parish, Louisiana, and died Bef. 1860 in St. Charles Parish, Louisiana.

Children of Hubert Robért and Julie Faucheux are:

25	i.	Hubert[4] Robért, Jr., born 1830 in St. Charles Parish, Louisiana.
26	ii.	Sosthine Robért, born 1834 in St. Charles Parish, Louisiana.
27	iii.	Jean Baptiste Robért, born 1837 in St. Charles Parish, Louisiana.
28	iv.	Alfred Robért, born 1839 in St. Charles Parish, Louisiana.
29	v.	Optime Robért, born 1844 in St. Charles Parish, Louisiana.

9. Mathieu[3] Robért, Sr. *- *** (Jean[2], Mathieu[1]) was born 1811 in St. Charles Parish, Louisiana[8], and died 12 September 1855 in St. John the Baptist Parish, Louisiana[8]. He married **Myrtilie Antoinette Faucheux** 15 July 1833 in Edgard, St. John the Baptist Parish, Louisiana[9], daughter of Pierre Faucheux and Francoise

Roger. She was born 17 June 1816 in Louisiana[10], and died 04 July 1860 in St. John the Baptist Parish, Louisiana[10].

Children of Mathieu Robért and Myrtille Faucheux are:

    30   i.   **Mathieu[4] Robért, Jr. (Yen-Yen)[10], born 16 January 1835 in St. John the Baptist Parish, Louisiana[10]; died 16 November 1920 in Darrow, Ascension Parish, Louisiana[11]. He married (1) Delia Felonise Faucheux 05 January 1856 in St. Charles Parish, Louisiana[12]; born 1839 in Louisiana; died 15 March 1862 in St. Charles Parish, Destrehan, Louisiana[13]. He married (2) Marie Nezile (Inezile) Waguespack[13] 08 October 1866 in Lafourche Parish, Louisiana[14]; born 18 March 1838 in Thibodaux, Lafourche Parish, Louisiana[15]; died 29 July 1915 in Elise Plantation, Ascension Parish, Louisiana.**

    31   ii.   **Etienne Robért, born December 1836 in St. John the Baptist Parish, Louisiana[15]; died 29 June 1838 in St. John the Baptist Parish, Louisiana[15].**

+ 32   iii.   **Septime Louis Robért, Sr., born 10 October 1838 in St. John the Baptist Parish, Louisiana; died in Louisiana.**

    33   iv.   **Marie Phelonise Robért, born Abt. 1839 in St. John the Baptist Parish, Louisiana; died 11 May 1872 in St. John the Baptist Parish, Louisiana.**

    34   v.   **Ursin Robért, born 14 September 1840 in St. John the Baptist Parish, Louisiana[16]; died 29 August 1855 in St. John the Baptist Parish, Louisiana[17].**

+ 35   vi.   **Jean Frumence Robért, ***, born 27 October 1842 in St. John the Baptist Parish, Louisiana; died 25 March 1901 in Donaldsonville, Ascension Parish, Louisiana.**

    36   vii.   **Sardos Robért, (Nonc P-P), born Abt. 1843 in St. John the Baptist Parish, Louisiana; died Abt. 1917 in Ascension Parish, Louisiana.**

    37   viii.   **Benoit Robért, born 12 October 1844 in St. John the Baptist Parish, Louisiana; died 28 December 1844 in St. John the Baptist Parish, Louisiana.**

+ 38   ix.   **Marie Antoinette Robért, born 17 April 1847 in St. John the Baptist Parish, Louisiana; died Bef. 1900 in St. John the Baptist Parish, Louisiana.**

    39   x.   **Palmire Marie Robért, born 31 August 1848 in St. John the Baptist Parish, Louisiana[18]; died 19 January 1852 in St. John the Baptist Parish, Louisiana.**

    40   xi.   **Pierre Amedee Robért, born 20 September 1851 in St. John the Baptist Parish, Louisiana[18]; died 18 June 1852 in St. John the Baptist Parish, Louisiana.**

+ 41   xii.   **Delia Marie Robért, born 08 May 1853 in St. John the Baptist Parish, Louisiana; died 29 October 1914 in Burnside, Ascension Parish, Louisiana.**

+ 42   xiii.   **Jean Paul Robért, *, born 26 July 1855 in Wallace, St. John the Baptist Parish, Louisiana; died 07 December 1950 in Burnside, Ascension Parish, Louisiana.**

10. Emilien[4] Schexnayder (Marianne Melanie[3] Robért, Jean[2], Mathieu[1]) was born 24 February 1829 in St. John the Baptist Parish, Louisiana, and died 20 March 1878 in New Orleans, Orleans Parish, Louisiana. He married **Nathalie Zeringue** 02 June 1855 in New Orleans, Orleans Parish, Louisiana[18]. She was born 22 March 1829, and died Unknown.

Child of Emilien Schexnayder and Nathalie Zeringue is:

+ 43   i.   **Louis Bartholomu[5] Schexnayder, born 1868 in Raceland, Lafourche Parish, Louisiana; died in Louisiana.**

11. Marcellin[4] Schexnayder (Marianne Melanie[3] Robért, Jean[2], Mathieu[1]) was born 1830 in St. John the Baptist Parish, Louisiana, and died 09 December 1882 in St. John the Baptist Parish, Louisiana. He married **Marie Azelie Haydel** 13 April 1850 in Edgard, St. John the Baptist Parish, Louisiana, daughter of Pierre Haydel and Clementine Faucheux. She was born 1836 in St John the Baptist Parish , Louisiana, and died 09 October 1883 in St. John the Baptist Parish, Louisiana.

Children of Marcellin Schexnayder and Marie Azelie Haydel are:

+ 44   i.   **Optime Joseph[5] Schexnayder, born 1860 in Vacherie, St. James Parish, Louisiana; died 08 April 1931 in Ascension Parish, Darrow,Louisiana.**
   45   ii.   **Alherry Joseph Schexnayder, born 10 November 1862.**
+ 46   iii.   **Emilien Joseph Schexnayder, born 03 October 1868.**
   47   iv.   **Marie Azelino Schexnayder, born 22 January 1872.**
   48   v.   **Hubert Joseph Schexnayder, born 18 February 1874; died 03 January 1916. He married Marie Elodie Granier 07 July 1894 in St. John the Baptist Church, Edgard, Louisiana.**
+ 49   vi.   **Gilbert Schexnayder.**

15. Louis[4] Robért (Jean[3], Jean[2], Mathieu[1]) was born Abt. 1834 in St. Charles Parish, Louisiana, and died Abt. 1856 in St. Charles Parish, Louisiana. He married **Adelaide Belsome** 20 March 1854 in St. Charles Parish , Louisiana[19], daughter of Philogen Belsome and Adelaide Toups. She was born 1837 in Ama, St. Charles Parish, Louisiana, and died 28 August 1918 in Ama, St. Charles Parish, Louisiana.

Child of Louis Robért and Adelaide Belsome is:

+ 50   i.   **Cecile[5] Robért, born November 1855 in St. Charles Parish, Louisiana; died 11 June 1914 in St. Charles Parish, Louisiana.**

16. Jean Baptiste⁴ Robért (Jean Louis³, Jean², Mathieu¹) was born 1822 in St. Charles Parish, Louisiana, and died 28 October 1883 in Ama, St. Charles Parish, Louisiana. He married **Marie Aimee Chalier,<Chaleur>** Abt. 1844 in St. Charles Borromeo Church, Destrahan, Louisiana, daughter of Pierre Chalier and Marie Rosalia Petit. She was born 12 March 1820 in Jefferson Parish, Louisiana, and died 12 May 1905 in Ama, St. Charles Parish, Louisiana.

Children of Jean Baptiste Robért and Marie Aimee Chalier are:

	51	i.	**Lawrence⁵ Robért, born January 1846 in St. Charles Parish, Louisiana; died 01 January 1930.**
+	52	ii.	**Amedee Robért, Sr., born 22 April 1848 in St. Charles Parish, Louisiana; died 23 May 1914 in Louisiana.**
+	53	iii.	**Floremond Robért, born 1850 in St. Charles Parish, Louisiana.**
+	54	iv.	**Rosemond Robért, born November 1851 in St. Charles Parish, Louisiana; died 23 December 1915 in St. Charles Parish, Louisiana.**
+	55	v.	**Theotine Robért, born 1853 in St. Charles Parish, Louisiana; died 20 August 1923 in Ama, St. Charles Parish, Louisiana.**
	56	vi.	**Anastasie Robért, born 1854 in St. Charles Parish, Louisiana; died 25 May 1863 in St. Charles Parish, Louisiana(Little red Church).**
	57	vii.	**Septime Robért, born 1856 in St. Charles Parish, Louisiana.**
+	58	viii.	**Estelle Sydleie Robért, born 1858 in St. Charles Parish, Louisiana.**
+	59	ix.	**Alcide Robért, born March 1861 in St. Charles Parish, Louisiana; died June 1942 in Ama, St. Charles Parish, Louisiana.**

19. Emile⁴ Robért (Jean Louis³, Jean², Mathieu¹) was born Abt. 1847 in St. Charles Parish, Louisiana, and died September 1859 in St. Charles Parish, Louisiana. He married **Julienne Bourgeois**.

Child of Emile Robért and Julienne Bourgeois is:

60	i.	**Hortense⁵ Robért. She married Toussaint Edouard Florent Breaux 05 June 1887 in St. James Catholic Church, St. James Parish, Louisiana; born 07 November 1854 in St. James Parish, Louisiana.**

32. Septime Louis⁴ Robért, Sr. (Mathieu³, Jean², Mathieu¹) was born 10 October 1838 in St. John the Baptist Parish, Louisiana, and died in Louisiana. He married **Marie Schexnayder** 26 January 1861 in Edgard, St. John the Baptist Parish, Louisiana[20], daughter of Louis Schexnayder and Marie Faucheux. She was born 1843 in St. John the Baptist Parish, Louisiana, and died in Louisiana.

Children of Septime Robért and Marie Schexnayder are:

61	i.	**Marie Oneilda⁵ Robért, born 21 August 1862 in St. John the**

Baptist Parish, Louisiana.

+ 62   ii.   **Willis Louis Mathieu Robért, born 10 July 1865 in St. John the Baptist Parish, Louisiana; died 28 January 1928 in Burnside, Ascension Parish, Louisiana.**

+ 63   iii.   **Jean Ursin Robért, born 14 June 1868 in St. John the Baptist Parish, Louisiana; died 13 August 1957 in Donaldsonville, Ascension Parish, Louisiana.**

+ 64   iv.   **Jeanne Clelie Robért, born 24 November 1869 in St. John the Baptist Parish, Louisiana; died Abt. 1905.**

+ 65   v.   **Marie Evelina Robért, born 16 May 1873 in St. John the Baptist Parish, Louisiana; died 10 November 1943 in Gramercy, St. James Parish, Louisiana.**

+ 66   vi.   **Myrtile Mathilde Marie Robért, born January 1875 in St. John the Baptist Parish, Louisiana; died 23 October 1909 in St. John the Baptist Parish, Louisiana.**

   67   vii.   **Anatole Robért, born 30 September 1875 in St. John the Baptist Parish, Louisiana; died 1918. She married Augustine Dardard 14 September 1895 in Lafourche Parish, Louisiana[21]; born Unknown; died Unknown.**

+ 68   viii.   **Septime Robért, Jr., born 23 January 1881 in St. John the Baptist Parish, Louisiana; died 28 July 1943 in Donaldsonville, Ascension Parish, Louisiana.**

35. Jean Frumence[4] Robért, * (Mathieu[3], Jean[2], Mathieu[1])** was born 27 October 1842 in St. John the Baptist Parish, Louisiana, and died 25 March 1901 in Donaldsonville, Ascension Parish, Louisiana. He married **Euphrasie Froiselee Bouy, (Tante Pay-Pay), *** 21 February 1867 in Edgard, St. John the Baptist Parish, Louisiana[22], daughter of Francois Bouy and Marianne Simon. She was born 04 March 1850 in St. John the Baptist Parish, Louisiana, and died 24 May 1929 in Donaldsonville, Ascension Parish, Louisiana.

Children of Jean Frumence Robért and Euphrasie Bouy are:

+ 69   i.   **Omèr Jean[5] Robért, Sr., born 29 May 1868 in Destrehan, St. Charles Parish, Louisiana; died 04 July 1945 in Donaldsonville, Ascension Parish, Louisiana.**

+ 70   ii.   **Marie Octavie Robért, ***, born 22 August 1869 in St.James Parish, Louisiana; died 04 June 1938 in Burnside, Ascension Parish, Louisiana.**

+ 71   iii.   **Wallace Jean Robért, Sr., born 27 February 1874 in Vacherie, St. James Parish, Louisiana; died 01 December 1942 in Donaldsonville, Ascension Parish, Louisiana.**

+ 72   iv.   **Marie Palmyre Robért, (Tee-Nannan), born 18 April 1876 in Vacherie, St. James Parish, Louisiana; died 25 April 1966 in Burnside, Ascension Parish, Louisiana.**

+ 73   v.   **Amedee Jean Robért, born 29 February 1880 in Vacherie, St.**

James Parish, Louisiana; died 09 October 1955 in Burnside, Ascension Parish, Louisiana.

38. Marie Antoinette[4] Robért (Mathieu[3], Jean[2], Mathieu[1]) was born 17 April 1847 in St. John the Baptist Parish, Louisiana, and died Bef. 1900 in St. John the Baptist Parish, Louisiana. She married **Floribert Pierre Schexnaydre,** * 23 November 1867 in Edgard, St. John the Baptist Parish, Louisiana[22], son of Benjamin Schexnayder and Clara Aubert. He was born 15 July 1847 in Edgard, St. John the Baptist Parish, Louisiana, and died 08 February 1939 in St. James Parish, Louisiana.

Children of Marie Antoinette Robért and Floribert Schexnaydre are:

74	i.	**Marie Louise Clara[5] Schexnaydre, born 27 August 1868 in Edgard, St. John the Baptist Parish, Louisiana; died Unknown. She married Richard Abadie Unknown.**
+ 75	ii.	**Sidney Schexnaydre, Sr., born 1872 in Edgard, St. John the Baptist Parish, Louisiana; died Abt. 1913.**
+ 76	iii.	**Henry Joseph Schexnaydre, Sr *, born 30 July 1872 in Edgard, St. John the Baptist Parish, Louisiana; died December 1936 in Ascension Parish, Louisiana.**
+ 77	iv.	**Albert Simon Schexnaydre, born 1874 in Edgard, St. John the Baptist Parish, Louisiana; died 28 December 1939 in Ascension Parish, Louisiana.**
78	v.	**Antonia Schexnaydre, (ya-ya), born 15 November 1877 in Edgard, St. John the Baptist Parish, Louisiana; died 29 February 1976 in Gonzales, Ascension Parish, Louisiana.**
79	vi.	**Olympe Schexnaydre,(may-yea), born 10 October 1881 in Edgard, St. John the Baptist Parish, Louisiana; died 05 April 1976 in Gonzales, Ascension Parish, Louisiana.**
+ 80	vii.	**Wilfred Joseph Schexnaydre, born 1886 in Edgard, St. John the Baptist Parish, Louisiana; died 1935 in Donaldsonville, Ascension Parish, Louisiana.**

41. Delia Marie[4] Robért (Mathieu[3], Jean[2], Mathieu[1]) was born 08 May 1853 in St. John the Baptist Parish, Louisiana[23], and died 29 October 1914 in Burnside, Ascension Parish, Louisiana. She married **Alidor Waguespack** 16 April 1873 in St. John the Baptiste Parish, Edgard, Louisiana[24], son of André Waguespack and Arthemise Faucheux. He was born 15 October 1848 in Thibodaux, Lafourche Parish, Louisiana, and died 1920 in Burnside, Ascension Parish, Louisiana.

Children of Delia Robért and Alidor Waguespack are:

+ 81	i.	**Marie Antoinette[5] Waguespack, born 10 September 1874 in Raceland, Lafourche Parish, Louisiana; died 1922.**
+ 82	ii.	**Myrtile Arthemise Waguespack, born 12 December 1876 in**

Raceland, Lafourche Parish, Louisiana; died 01 June 1967 in Metairie, Jefferson Parish, Louisiana.

+ 83   iii.   **André M. Waguespack**, born 26 May 1878 in Raceland, Lafourche Parish, Louisiana; died 04 August 1952 in Rodriguez Plantation, Donaldsonville, Louisiana.

+ 84   iv.   **Alice Marie Waguespack**, born 26 November 1879 in Raceland, Lafourche Parish, Louisiana; died 15 June 1972 in Orleans Parish, New Orleans, Orleans Parish, Louisiana.

   85   v.   **Alcee Waguespack**, born 18 December 1881 in Houma, Terrebonne Parish, Louisiana; died 09 February 1904 in Donaldsonville, Ascension Parish, Louisiana.

   86   vi.   **Wilhelm Jean Waguespack**, born 08 February 1883 in Raceland, Lafourche Parish, Louisiana; died 04 October 1974 in Donaldsonville, Ascension Parish, Louisiana. He married (1) Leontine Landry. He married (2) Leona Landry.

+ 87   vii.   **Wilson Pierre Waguespack**, born 21 October 1886 in Labadieville, Assumption Parish, Louisiana; died 11 April 1969.

   88   viii.   **Phelonise Cecile Therese Waguespack**, born 17 August 1888 in Thibodaux, Lafourche Parish, Louisiana; died 04 February 1963 in Raceland, Lafourche Parish, Louisiana. She married Hector Joseph Folse 23 April 1911; born 14 August 1884 in Thibodaux, Lafourche Parish, Louisiana; died 27 December 1973 in Raceland, Lafourche Parish, Louisiana.

   89   ix.   **Winna Waguespack**, born 09 October 1890; died 03 September 1966.

   90   x.   **Heno <Enougle> J. Waguespack**, born 15 August 1893 in Edgard, St. John the Baptist Parish, Louisiana; died 14 October 1972 in Donaldsonville, Ascension Parish, Louisiana. He married Hazel Comeaux 1946; born 11 September 1912; died 23 November 1975.

42. Jean Paul[4] Robért, * (Mathieu[3], Jean[2], Mathieu[1]) was born 26 July 1855 in Wallace, St. John the Baptist Parish, Louisiana[25], and died 07 December 1950 in Burnside, Ascension Parish, Louisiana. He married **Marie Octavie Brou,** * 05 February 1876 in Thibodaux, Lafourche Parish, Louisiana[26], daughter of Octave Brou and Arthemise Waguespack. She was born 15 February 1858 in Thibodaux, Lafourche Parish, Louisiana, and died 28 January 1935 in Burnside, Ascension Parish, Louisiana.

Children of Jean Paul Robért and Marie Octavie Brou are:

+ 91   i.   **Elmira Marie[5] Robért**, born 19 December 1876 in Wallace, St. John the Baptist Parish, Louisiana; died 15 November 1968 in Darrow, Ascension Parish, Louisiana.

+ 92   ii.   **Paula Cecile Robért, (Tow-Tow)**, born 22 November 1878 in Wallace, St. John the Baptist Parish, Louisiana; died 22 March 1950 in Burnside, Ascension Parish, Louisiana.

+	93	iii.	Joseph Olide Robért, (Do-Doot), born 25 November 1880 in Wallace, St. John the Baptist Parish, Louisiana; died 20 September 1956 in Darrow, Ascension Parish, Louisiana.
+	94	iv.	Leona Theresa Robért, (Na-Na), born 15 October 1882 in Wallace, St. John the Baptist Parish, Louisiana; died 07 October 1971 in Donaldsonville, Ascension Parish, Louisiana.
+	95	v.	Raoul Matthew Robért, born 31 March 1885 in Wallace, St. John the Baptist Parish, Louisiana; died 31 October 1931 in Burnside, Ascension Parish, Louisiana.
+	96	vi.	Clovis Jean Robért, born 23 February 1888 in Wallace, St. John the Baptist Parish, Louisiana; died 04 July 1966 in Burnside, Ascension Parish, Louisiana.
	97	vii.	Martha Philomene Robért, (Bot), born 28 February 1890 in Wallace, St. John the Baptist Parish, Louisiana[27]; died 20 July 1970 in Gonzales, Ascension Parish, Louisiana.
+	98	viii.	Remy Paul Robért, born 02 July 1892 in Wallace, St. John the Baptist Parish, Louisiana; died 11 December 1970 in New Orleans, Orleans Parish, Louisiana.
+	99	ix.	Octave Pierre Robért, born 22 August 1894 in Wallace, St. John the Baptist Parish, Louisiana; died 03 June 1955 in Burnside, Ascension Parish, Louisiana.
+	100	x.	Rene Benoit Robért, (Ne-Nall), born 21 February 1897 in Wallace, St. John the Baptist Parish, Louisiana; died 22 May 1983 in Burnside, Ascension Parish, Louisiana.
+	101	xi.	Roland Jacques Robért, Sr. (Pan-Am), born 15 April 1900 in Tchoupitoulas Plantation, Jefferson Parish, Louisiana; died 28 October 1958 in Burnside, Ascension Parish, Louisiana.

Generation No. 4

43. Louis Bartholomu[5] Schexnayder (Emilien[4], Marianne Melanie[3] Robért, Jean[2], Mathieu[1]) was born 1868 in Raceland, Lafourche Parish, Louisiana, and died in Louisiana. He married **Marie Honorine Zeringue** 10 October 1890, daughter of Andre Zeringue and Josephine Troxclair. She was born 1873 in Raceland, Lafourche Parish, Louisiana, and died in Louisiana.

Child of Louis Schexnayder and Marie Honorine Zeringue is:
| + | 102 | i. | Cecila[6] Schexnayder, born Abt. 1892 in Louisiana. |

44. Optime Joseph[5] Schexnayder (Marcellin[4], Marianne Melanie[3] Robért, Jean[2], Mathieu[1]) was born 1860 in Vacherie, St. James Parish, Louisiana, and died 08 April 1931 in Ascension Parish, Darrow, Louisiana. He married **(1) Anna Apolonia Granier** 23 December 1885, daughter of Pierre Granier and Armantine Sprengler. She was born 24 February 1868 in Vacherie, St. James Parish,

Louisiana, and died 12 July 1906 in Vacherie, St. James Parish, Louisiana. He married **(2) Marie Azelie Granier** 18 October 1907 in St. James Parish, Vacherie, Louisiana, daughter of Jean Granier and Theodelia Hotard. She was born 05 November 1876 in Vacherie, St. James Parish, Louisiana, and died 22 January 1939 in New Orleans, Orleans Parish, Louisiana.

Children of Optime Schexnayder and Anna Granier are:

103	i.	**Marcellin O[6] Schexnayder**, born 02 October 1886 in Vacherie, St. James Parish, Louisiana; died 16 December 1964 in New Roads, Point Coupee Parish, Louisiana. He married Marie Francesca (Frances) Torres 06 October 1908 in St. James Parish, Louisiana[28]; born 10 June 1886 in St. James Parish, Louisiana.
104	ii.	**Marie Marcelline Schexnayder**, born 13 September 1887 in Vacherie, St. James Parish, Louisiana.
105	iii.	**Pierre Roman Schexnayder**, born 23 August 1889 in Vacherie, St. James Parish, Louisiana.
+ 106	iv.	**Edwin Joseph Schexnayder**, born 06 June 1906 in Vacherie, St. James Parish, Louisiana; died 19 August 1971 in Baton Rouge, East Baton Rouge Parish, Louisiana.
107	v.	**Azelie Schexnayder**, born in Vacherie, St. James Parish, Louisiana.
108	vi.	**Orenia Schexnayder**, born in Vacherie, St. James Parish, Louisiana.
109	vii.	**Willis Schexnayder**, born in Vacherie, St. James Parish, Louisiana.

Child of Optime Schexnayder and Marie Azelie Granier is:

+ 110	i.	**Victor Joseph[6] Schexnayder,Sr.**, born 10 June 1908 in Vacherie, St. James Parish, Louisiana; died 27 March 1988 in Darrow, Ascension Parish, Louisiana.

46. Emilien Joseph[5] Schexnayder (Marcellin[4], Marianne Melanie[3] Robért, Jean[2], Mathieu[1]) was born 03 October 1868. He married **Marie Felicite Granier** 11 February 1888 in Vacherie, St. James Parish, Louisiana, daughter of Felix Granier and Odelie Hotard. She was born 15 October 1858 in Vacherie, St. James Parish, Louisiana, and died Unknown.

Child of Emilien Schexnayder and Marie Felicite Granier is:

+ 111	i.	**Jean Marcellin[6] Schexnayder, (Zoot)**, born 02 March 1889 in Vacherie, St. James Parish, Louisiana; died January 1969 in Vacherie, St. James Parish, Louisiana.

49. Gilbert[5] Schexnayder (Marcellin[4], Marianne Melanie[3] Robért, Jean[2], Mathieu[1]) He married **Marie Amazelie Autin**.

Child of Gilbert Schexnayder and Marie Amazelie Autin is:

> 112   i.   **Marcellin G.**[6] **Schexnayder**, born July 1887; died Unknown. He married Elia Falgoust 29 July 1914 in St. James Parish, Louisiana[28]; born Unknown; died Unknown.

50.   Cecile[5] **Robért** (Louis[4], Jean[3], Jean[2], Mathieu[1]) was born November 1855 in St. Charles Parish, Louisiana, and died 11 June 1914 in St. Charles Parish, Louisiana. She married **Rosemond Robért** 23 December 1876 in St. Charles Borromeo Church, Destrahan, Louisiana, son of Jean Baptiste Robért and Marie Aimee Chalier. He was born November 1851 in St. Charles Parish, Louisiana, and died 23 December 1915 in St. Charles Parish, Louisiana.

Children of Cecile Robért and Rosemond Robért are:

> + 113   i.   **Louis Luke**[6] **Robért**, born 21 November 1877 in St. Charles Parish, Louisiana; died 12 June 1948.
> + 114   ii.   **Edgar Robért**, born May 1879 in St. Charles Parish, Louisiana; died Aft. 1920 in St. Charles Parish, Louisiana.
>   115   iii. **Odette Robért**, born 11 July 1881 in St. Charles Parish, Louisiana; died 01 April 1966 in Louisiana.
>   116   iv.   **Adel Robért**, born October 1885 in St. Charles Parish, Louisiana; died 1900 in St. Charles Parish, Louisiana.
>   117   v.   **Victor Robért**, born July 1888 in St. Charles Parish, Louisiana; died 23 May 1917 in St. Tammany Parish, Louisiana.
> + 118   vi.   **Adele Marie Robért**, born 27 July 1892 in St. Charles Parish, Louisiana; died February 1975 in Luling, St. Charles Parish, Louisiana.
>   119   vii. **Pauline Robért**, born October 1892 in St. Charles Parish, Louisiana.
>   120   viii. **Optime Robért**, born January 1893 in St. Charles Parish, Louisiana.
>   121   ix.   **Octave Robért**, born January 1896 in St. Charles Parish, Louisiana.
>   122   x.   **Gustave Robért**, born October 1898 in St. Charles Parish, Louisiana.

52.   Amedee[5] **Robért, Sr.** (Jean Baptiste[4], Jean Louis[3], Jean[2], Mathieu[1]) was born 22 April 1848 in St. Charles Parish, Louisiana, and died 23 May 1914 in Louisiana. He married **Estelle Kinler** Abt. 1866 in St. Charles Borromeo Church, Destrehan, Louisiana. She was born May 1850 in St. Charles Parish, Louisiana.

Children of Amedee Robért and Estelle Kinler are:

> + 123   i.   **Amedee**[6] **Robért, Jr.**, born 19 June 1867 in St. Charles Parish, Louisiana; died 20 August 1933 in Jefferson Parish, Louisiana.

124	ii.	Adalbo Robért, born February 1870 in St. Charles Parish, Louisiana.
+	125	iii.	Eranbert Robert, born 1871 in St. Charles Parish, Louisiana; died 14 November 1958 in Louisiana.
	126	iv.	Joseph W. Robért, born 1873 in St. Charles Parish, Louisiana; died in St. Charles Parish, Louisiana.
	127	v.	Anastasia Robért, born 1875 in St. Charles Parish, Louisiana.
+	128	vi.	Delphine Robért, born 24 December 1876 in Ama, St. Charles Parish, Louisiana; died 10 June 1976 in Luling, St. Charles Parish Louisiana.
	129	vii.	Oneziford Robért, born February 1879 in St. Charles Parish, Louisiana.
	130	viii.	John Baptiste Robért, born December 1880 in St. Charles Parish, Louisiana.
+	131	ix.	Eugene Robért, born 01 April 1885 in St. Charles Parish, Louisiana; died 04 July 1953.
	132	x.	Estelle Marie Robért, born 22 January 1887 in St. Charles Parish, Louisiana. She married Louis John Lauve 17 June 1911 in Jefferson Parish, Louisiana.
+	133	xi.	Odile Robért, born April 1892 in St. Charles Parish, Louisiana.

53. Floremond⁵ Robért (Jean Baptiste⁴, Jean Louis³, Jean², Mathieu¹) was born 1850 in St. Charles Parish, Louisiana. He married **Lucia Friloux**.

Children of Floremond Robért and Lucia Friloux are:

	134	i.	Alphonse⁶ Robért, born 1884; died 1950.
+	135	ii.	Ernest Robért, born 15 September 1886 in Louisiana; died 27 February 1968 in Westwego, Jefferson Parish, Louisiana.
	136	iii.	Bertha Robért, born 1888 in Louisiana; died 1907 in Louisiana.
	137	iv.	Noelie Robért, born 1890 in Edgard, St. John the Baptist Parish, Louisiana; died 1970 in Louisiana.
	138	v.	Marie Robért, born 1893 in Louisiana; died 1950 in Louisiana.

54. Rosemond⁵ Robért (Jean Baptiste⁴, Jean Louis³, Jean², Mathieu¹) was born November 1851 in St. Charles Parish, Louisiana, and died 23 December 1915 in St. Charles Parish, Louisiana. He married **Cecile Robért** 23 December 1876 in St. Charles Borromeo Church, Destrahan, Louisiana, daughter of Louis Robért and Adelaide Belsome. She was born November 1855 in St. Charles Parish, Louisiana, and died 11 June 1914 in St. Charles Parish, Louisiana.

Children are listed above under (50) Cecile Robért.

55. Theotine⁵ Robért (Jean Baptiste⁴, Jean Louis³, Jean², Mathieu¹) was born 1853 in St. Charles Parish, Louisiana, and died 20 August 1923 in Ama, St.

Charles Parish, Louisiana. He married **Auguste Champagne** Abt. 1880 in St. Charles, Parish, Louisiana, daughter of Louis Champagne and Celamire Friloux. She was born 1856 in Ama, St. Charles Parish, Louisiana, and died 12 June 1915 in Ama, St. Charles Parish, Louisiana.

Child of Theotine Robért and Auguste Champagne is:

+ 139   i.   **James Theotine[6] Robért, born 27 January 1883 in St. James Parish, Louisiana; died 31 January 1949 in Reserve, St. John the Baptist Parish, Louisiana.**

58. Estelle Sydleie[5] Robért (Jean Baptiste[4], Jean Louis[3], Jean[2], Mathieu[1]) was born 1858 in St. Charles Parish, Louisiana. She married **George J. Friloux** 25 May 1882 in Holy Rosary Church, Hahnville, St. Charles Parish, Louisiana, son of Florent Friloux and Adelaide Belsome. He was born Abt. 1859 in St. Charles Parish, Louisiana.

Child of Estelle Robért and George Friloux is:

+ 140   i.   **Dennis J.[6] Friloux, born 07 November 1894 in Louisiana; died 09 February 1967 in Westwego, Jefferson Parish, Louisiana.**

59. Alcide[5] Robért (Jean Baptiste[4], Jean Louis[3], Jean[2], Mathieu[1]) was born March 1861 in St. Charles Parish, Louisiana, and died June 1942 in Ama, St. Charles Parish, Louisiana. He married **Georgina F. Robért** 1878. She was born March 1863, and died 27 May 1918 in St. Charles Parish, Louisiana.

Children of Alcide Robért and Georgina Robért are:

   141   i.   **George[6] Robért, born March 1883 in St. Charles Parish, Louisiana.**
   142   ii.   **Prudent Robért, born April 1886 in St. Charles Parish, Louisiana.**
   143   iii.   **Aleina Robért, born March 1888 in St. Charles Parish, Louisiana.**
   144   iv.   **Alida Robért, born 10 June 1890 in St. Charles Parish, Louisiana; died April 1977 in St. Charles Parish, Louisiana.**
   145   v.   **Oliver Robért, born January 1894 in St. Charles Parish, Louisiana.**
   146   vi.   **Philogene Robért, born 05 December 1897 in St. Charles Parish, Louisiana; died 15 August 1968 in St. Charles Parish, Louisiana.**

62. Willis Louis Mathieu[5] Robért (Septime Louis[4], Mathieu[3], Jean[2], Mathieu[1]) was born 10 July 1865 in St. John the Baptist Parish, Louisiana[29], and died 28 January 1928 in Burnside, Ascension Parish, Louisiana. He married **Albertine Brou, (Tante Bat)** 04 April 1893 in St. James Catholic Church, St. James, Louisiana[30], daughter of Octave Brou and Arthemise Waguespack. She was born 10 February 1864 in Raceland, Lafourche Parish, Louisiana, and died 31 October 1950 in Convent, St. James Parish, Louisiana.

Children of Willis Robért and Albertine Brou are:

147   i.   **Claudia M.[6] Robért, (Ba-Low), born 08 July 1895 in Jefferson Parish, Louisiana; died 12 March 1978 in New Orleans, Orleans Parish, Louisiana.**

148   ii.   **Lillian Theresa Robért, (Lil), born 02 February 1897 in Jefferson Parish, Louisiana; died 25 April 1975 in Convent, St. James Parish, Louisiana.**

149   iii.   **Albin Robért, (Nick), born 24 February 1899 in Tchoupitoulas Plantation, Jefferson Parish, Kenner, Louisiana; died 26 September 1967 in Convent, St. James Parish, Louisiana.**

150   iv.   **Rosine Philomene Robért, born 1903 in Ascension Parish, Louisiana; died 23 April 1951 in New Orleans, Orleans Parish, Louisiana.**

151   v.   **Armand Robért, born 28 April 1906 in St. Elmo Plantation, Darrow, Louisiana; died 13 May 1985 in Baton Rouge, East Baton Rouge Parish, Louisiana.**

63.   Jean Ursin[5] Robért (Septime Louis[4], Mathieu[3], Jean[2], Mathieu[1]) was born 14 June 1868 in St. John the Baptist Parish, Louisiana[31], and died 13 August 1957 in Donaldsonville, Ascension Parish, Louisiana. He married **Euphrosine Brou** 08 April 1893 in St. John the Baptist Parish, Louisiana[32], daughter of Octave Brou and Arthemise Waguespack. She was born 03 August 1871 in Raceland, Lafourche Parish, Louisiana, and died 14 May 1949 in Donaldsonville, Ascension Parish, Louisiana.

Children of Jean Ursin Robért and Euphrosine Brou are:

+   152   i.   **Raymond Simon[6] Robért, Sr., born 18 February 1894 in Edgard, St. John the Baptist Parish, Louisiana; died 29 June 1968 in Texas City, Texas.**

153   ii.   **Elyse J. Robért, born 1896 in Louisiana; died 1918 in Louisiana.**

+   154   iii.   **Benoit Robért, (Ben), born 28 January 1898 in Kenner, Jefferson Parish, Louisiana; died 27 October 1987 in Ascension Parish, Donaldsonville, Louisiana.**

+   155   iv.   **Edna Marie Robért, born 05 November 1900 in Kenner, Jefferson Parish, Louisiana; died 14 February 1988 in Convent, St. James Parish, Louisiana.**

156   v.   **Alfred A. Robért, born 1901 in Kenner, Jefferson Parish, Louisiana; died 28 June 1923 in Ascension Parish, Burnside, Louisiana.**

+   157   vi.   **Oliver Paul Robért, Sr. (Tucker), born 17 January 1905 in Kenner, Jefferson Parish, Louisiana; died 08 September 1972 in Baton Rouge, East Baton Rouge Parish, Louisiana.**

+   158   vii.   **Felecien Peter Robért, (Bill), born 09 June 1907 in Burnside, Ascension Parish, Louisiana; died 02 November 1976 in Thibodaux, Lafourche Parish, Louisiana.**

15

159 viii. Claire Robért, born 12 August 1909 in Hermatage Plantation, Darrow, Ascension Parish, Louisiana.

64. Jeanne Clelie[5] Robért (Septime Louis[4], Mathieu[3], Jean[2], Mathieu[1]) was born 24 November 1869 in St. John the Baptist Parish, Louisiana[33], and died Abt. 1905. She married **Francois Joseph Zeringue** 07 April 1894 in St. John the Baptist Catholic Church, Edgard, Louisiana[34], son of Norbert Zeringue and Celeste Brou. He was born 07 August 1858 in St. John the Baptist Parish, Louisiana, and died Abt. 1905.

Children of Jeanne Robért and Francois Zeringue are:

+ **160**   i. **Josepha Marie[6] Zeringue**, born 20 November 1899 in Louisiana; died 24 October 1990 in St. James Parish, Louisiana.
   161   ii. **Clelie Zeringue**, (BeBel). She married (1) Leon Waguespack; born Unknown. She married (2) Seraphin Mire 10 January 1900 in Lafourche Parish, Louisiana.
   162   iii. **Cleona Zeringue**.
   163   iv. **Leon Zeringue**.
   164   v. **Oneida Zeringue**, born 1903; died 1982.
   165   vi. **Fuicy Zeringue**, born Abt. 1897. He married Lena Marie Zeringue Unknown; born Unknown; died Unknown.

65. Marie Evelina[5] Robért (Septime Louis[4], Mathieu[3], Jean[2], Mathieu[1]) was born 16 May 1873 in St. John the Baptist Parish, Louisiana[35], and died 10 November 1943 in Gramercy, St. James Parish, Louisiana. She married **Prudent Waguespack** 18 May 1893 in St. John the Baptist Parish, Louisiana[36], son of Pierre Waguespack and Hortense Faucheux. He was born 21 October 1871 in Vacherie, St. James Parish, Louisiana, and died 06 November 1939 in Gramercy, St. James Parish, Louisiana.

Children of Marie Evelina Robért and Prudent Waguespack are:

   166   i. **Marie Aurelie[6] Waguespack**.
   167   ii. **Morris Waguespack**.
   168   iii. **Victoire Waguespack**.
+ **169**   iv. **Regina Victoria Waguespack**, born May 1894 in St. John the Baptist Parish, Louisiana; died 17 July 1985 in Gramercy, St. James Parish, Louisiana.
   170   v. **Aurelie Waguespack**, born January 1896 in St. John the Baptist Parish, Louisiana. She married Fernand Decarreau.

66. Myrtile Mathilde Marie[5] Robért (Septime Louis[4], Mathieu[3], Jean[2], Mathieu[1]) was born January 1875 in St. John the Baptist Parish, Louisiana, and died 23 October 1909 in St. John the Baptist Parish, Louisiana. She married **Rene**

Francois Brou, Sr. 16 April 1898 in St.John the Baptist Parish, Edgard, Louisiana[37], son of Octave Brou and Arthemise Waguespack. He was born 12 November 1872 in Raceland, Lafourche Parish, Louisiana, and died 31 August 1911 in Ascension Parish, Donaldsonville, Louisiana.

Children of Myrtile Robért and Rene Brou are:

> 171   i.   **Lucille[6] Brou, born 05 April 1902 in Jefferson Parish, Kenner, Louisiana; died January 1986 in Donaldsonville, Ascension Parish, Louisiana.**
>
> 172   ii.   **Antoine Paul Brou, born 14 November 1903 in Hermitage Plantation, Ascension Parish, Darrow, Louisiana.**
>
> 173   iii.   **Rene Francois Brou,Jr., born 03 October 1905 in Hermitage Plantation, Ascension Parish, Darrow, Louisiana; died 16 May 1936.**
>
> 174   iv.   **Delta Mary Brou, born 28 September 1907 in Hermitage Plantation, Ascension Parish, Darrow, Louisiana; died 31 January 1991 in St. Charles Parish, Destrehan, Louisiana.**

68. Septime[5] Robért, Jr. (Septime Louis[4], Mathieu[3], Jean[2], Mathieu[1]) was born 23 January 1881 in St. John the Baptist Parish, Louisiana, and died 28 July 1943 in Donaldsonville, Ascension Parish, Louisiana. He married **Alice Marie Waguespack** 18 September 1902 in Ascension Catholic Church, Donaldsonville, Louisiana, daughter of Alidor Waguespack and Delia Robért. She was born 26 November 1879 in Raceland, Lafourche Parish, Louisiana, and died 15 June 1972 in Orleans Parish, New Orleans, Orleans Parish, Louisiana.

Children of Septime Robért and Alice Waguespack are:

> 175   i.   **Stella[6] Robért, born 1919 in Ascension Parish, Louisiana. She married Preston Comeaux Unknown; born Unknown; died Unknown.**
>
> 176   ii.   **Magda M. Robért, born 1915 in Ascension Parish, Louisiana; died 15 June 1942 in Louisiana.**
>
> 177   iii.   **Valerie Robért, born 1906 in Ascension Parish, Louisiana. He married Odette Cire.**
>
> 178   iv.   **Cyril Robért, born 1911 in Ascension Parish, Louisiana.**

69. Omèr Jean[5] Robért, Sr. (Jean Frumence[4], Mathieu[3], Jean[2], Mathieu[1]) was born 29 May 1868 in Destrehan, St. Charles Parish, Louisiana, and died 04 July 1945 in Donaldsonville, Ascension Parish, Louisiana. He married **Marie Louise Borne, < Borise>** 09 April 1891 in Edgard, St.John the Baptiste Parish, Louisiana[37]. She was born July 1876, and died 24 August 1935 in Donaldsonville, Ascension Parish, Louisiana.

Children of Omèr Robért and Marie Louise Borne are:

+   179   i.   Libby[6] Robért, born 06 October 1895 in Louisiana; died 20 December 1966 in Livingston Parish, Denham Springs, Louisiana.

     180   ii.   Laura Robért, born November 1897 in Louisiana; died 1917. She married Sam Haydel.

+   181   iii. Palmire Robért, born 01 November 1899 in Louisiana; died 28 August 1989 in Ascension Parish, Donaldsonville, Louisiana.

+   182   iv.   Aline Robért, born Abt. 1902 in Edgard, St. John the Baptist Parish, Louisiana; died 28 October 1999 in Gonzales, Ascension Parish, Louisiana.

     183   v.   Therése Robért, born Abt. 1907 in Louisiana. She married Earnest Dupeire.

     184   vi.   Jean Omér Robért, Jr. (Noon), born 12 December 1910 in Louisiana; died 28 February 2004 in New Orleans, Orleans Parish, Louisiana[38]. He married Margaret; born Unknown.

     185   vii. Frumence Robért, born Abt. 1913 in Louisiana.

+   186   viii. Neola Marie Robért, born Abt. 1905 in Edgard, St. John the Baptist Parish, Louisiana; died 11 November 2003 in Abbeville, Vermillion Parish, Louisiana.

70. Marie Octavie[5] Robért, *** (Jean Frumence[4], Mathieu[3], Jean[2], Mathieu[1]) was born 22 August 1869 in St.James Parish, Louisiana[39], and died 04 June 1938 in Burnside, Ascension Parish, Louisiana. She married **Victor Lovincie Waguespack,***** 17 May 1887 in St. Philip Catholic Church, Vacherie, Louisiana[40], son of Hubert Waguespack and Josephine Waguespack. He was born 21 July 1865 in Raceland, Lafourche Parish, Louisiana, and died 01 October 1958 in Burnside, Ascension Parish, Louisiana.

Children of Marie Octavie Robért and Victor Waguespack are:

+   187   i.   Edgar Joseph[6] Waguespack, born 12 February 1888 in Vacherie, St. James Parish, Louisiana; died 15 September 1952 in Burnside, Ascension Parish , Louisiana.

+   188   ii.   Denise Marie Waguespack, born 04 October 1889 in Vacherie, St. James Parish, Louisiana; died 30 January 1968 in Luling, St. Charles Parish, Louisiana.

+   189   iii. Wallis Jean Waguespack, born 15 July 1891 in Edgard, St. John the Baptist Parish, Louisiana; died 07 October 1981 in Baton Rouge, East Baton Rouge Parish, Louisiana.

+   190   iv.   Elda Augustine Waguespack, born 28 August 1893 in Edgard, St. John the Baptist Parish, Louisiana; died 31 August 1958 in Destrehan, St. Charles Parish, Louisiana.

     191   v.   Stanley Paul Waguespack, born 11 November 1895 in Edgard, St. John the Baptist Parish, Louisiana; died 21 October 1918 in Europe, World War I.

+   192   vi.   Octave Pierre Waguespack, born 04 March 1898 in Edgard, St. John the Baptist Parish, Louisiana; died 19 July 1987 in Baton

Rouge, East Baton Rouge Parish, Louisiana.

+   193   vii.   **George Nicholas Waguespack, (Gee), born 11 September 1899 in Edgard, St. John the Baptist Parish, Louisiana; died 07 March 1978 in Baton Rouge General Hospital, Baton Rouge, Louisiana.**

+   194   viii.   **Delia Philomene Waguespack, born 23 October 1901 in Edgard, St. John the Baptist Parish, Louisiana; died 27 July 1986 in Donaldsonville, Ascension Parish, Louisiana.**

+   195   ix.   **Frumence Hubert Waguespack, born 23 October 1905 in Vacherie, St. James Parish, Louisiana; died 11 September 1997 in Gonzales, Ascension Parish, Louisiana.**

+   196   x.   **Clarence Anthony Waguespack, born 12 September 1908 in Edgard, St. John the Baptist Parish, Louisiana; died 28 February 1984 in Baton Rouge, East Baton Rouge Parish, Louisiana.**

71. Wallace Jean[5] Robért, Sr. (Jean Frumence[4], Mathieu[3], Jean[2], Mathieu[1]) was born 27 February 1874 in Vacherie, St. James Parish, Louisiana[41], and died 01 December 1942 in Donaldsonville, Ascension Parish, Louisiana. He married **Zelia Hymel** 26 April 1900 in Edgard, St. John the Baptist Parish, Louisiana[42]. She was born 1879, and died 1952.

Children of Wallace Robért and Zelia Hymel are:

    197   i.   **Bertice[6] Robért.**

    198   ii.   **Morris Robért, born 25 February 1902 in Louisiana; died March 1984 in Point Coupee Parish, Ventress, Louisiana.**

    199   iii.   **Winna Marie Robért, born 31 October 1903 in Edgard, St. John the Baptist Parish, Louisiana; died 25 October 1956 in New Orleans, Orleans Parish, Louisiana. She married Thomas W. Tamplain 28 November 1925; born 01 June 1899 in Mt. Airy, St. John the Baptist Parish, Louisiana; died 10 April 1966 in Garyville, St. John the Baptist Parish, Louisiana.**

+   200   iv.   **William Robért, born 1905; died 1941.**

+   201   v.   **Cecile Marie Robért, born 21 December 1907 in Burnside, Ascension Parish, Louisiana; died 25 February 2002 in St. James Parish, Louisiana.**

    202   vi.   **Gladys Robért, born Abt. 1910.**

+   203   vii.   **Jean Wallace Robért, Jr., born 30 August 1912 in Louisiana; died 01 May 1989 in Houma, Terrebonne Parish, Louisiana.**

+   204   viii.   **Maxie Robért, Sr., born 16 September 1914 in Donaldsonville, Ascension Parish, Louisiana; died 21 December 1980 in Donaldsonville, Ascension Parish, Louisiana.**

    205   ix.   **Mable Robért, born Abt. 1916.**

    206   x.   **Elma Robért, born Abt. 1919.**

+   207   xi.   **Lester Robért, born 19 April 1921 in Donaldsonville, Ascension Parish, Louisiana; died 2001 in Gonzales, Ascension Parish, Louisiana.**

72. Marie Palmyre[5] Robért, (Tee-Nannan) (Jean Frumence[4], Mathieu[3], Jean[2], Mathieu[1]) was born 18 April 1876 in Vacherie, St. James Parish, Louisiana[43], and died 25 April 1966 in Burnside, Ascension Parish, Louisiana. She married **Honore Augustin Brou, (Tee Parrain)** 18 February 1896 in St. Rosaire Catholic Church, St.Charles Parish, Louisiana[44], son of Octave Brou and Arthemise Waguespack. He was born 28 August 1868 in Raceland, Lafourche Parish, Louisiana, and died 27 March 1943 in Burnside, Ascension Parish, Louisiana.

Children of Marie Palmyre Robért and Honore Brou are:

      208   i.   **Robert Joseph[6] Brou**, born 24 January 1897 in Tchoupitoulas Plantation,Jefferson Parish, Kenner, Louisiana; died 16 November 1946 in Burnside, Ascension Parish, Louisiana.

+ 209   ii.   **Edith Marie Brou**, born 28 April 1899 in Tchoupitoulas Plantation, Jefferson Parish, Kenner, Louisiana; died 17 March 1995 in Ascension Parish, Sorrento, Louisiana.

      210   iii.   **Horace Joseph Brou**, born 24 April 1902 in Tchoupitoulas Plantation, Jefferson Parish, Kenner, Louisiana; died 08 February 1976 in Baton Rouge, East Baton Rouge Parish, Louisiana.

+ 211   iv.   **André Augustine Brou, Sr. (Cap)**, born 27 August 1904 in Hermitage Plantation, Ascension Parish, Darrow, Louisiana; died 15 January 1999 in Gonzales, Ascension Parish, Louisiana.

      212   v.   **Rita Philomene Brou**, born 10 October 1906 in Hermitage Plantation, Ascension Parish, Darrow, Louisiana; died 02 January 1993 in Ascension Parish, Sorrento, Louisiana.

      213   vi.   **Antoine Otto Brou**, born 31 January 1911 in Burnside, Ascension Parish, Louisiana; died 15 February 1911 in Burnside, Ascension Parish, Louisiana.

      214   vii.   **Therése Arthemese Goldie Brou**, born 19 September 1914 in Burnside, Ascension Parish, Louisiana.

      215 viii.   **Marie Elvie Brou**, born 30 December 1916 in Burnside, Ascension Parish, Louisiana.

73. Amedee Jean[5] Robért (Jean Frumence[4], Mathieu[3], Jean[2], Mathieu[1]) was born 29 February 1880 in Vacherie, St. James Parish, Louisiana[45], and died 09 October 1955 in Burnside, Ascension Parish, Louisiana. He married **Paula Cecile Robért, (Tow-Tow)** 13 November 1900 in Hancock County, Mississippi, daughter of Jean Paul Robért and Marie Octavie Brou. She was born 22 November 1878 in Wallace, St. John the Baptist Parish, Louisiana[45], and died 22 March 1950 in Burnside, Ascension Parish, Louisiana.

Child of Amedee Robért and Paula Robért is:

      216   i.   **Anne Marie[6] Robért, (Grand-Fille)**, born 05 December 1912 in Moll Plantation, (Remy) St.John the Baptiste Parish, Louisiana[46,47];

died 04 December 2003 in Baton Rouge, East Baton Rouge Parish, Louisiana.

75. Sidney[5] Schexnaydre, Sr. (Marie Antoinette[4] Robért, Mathieu[3], Jean[2], Mathieu[1]) was born 1872 in Edgard, St. John the Baptist Parish, Louisiana, and died Abt. 1913. He married **Myrtile Arthemise Waguespack** 05 April 1894 in Edgard, St. John the Baptist Parish, Louisiana, daughter of Alidor Waguespack and Delia Robért. She was born 12 December 1876 in Raceland, Lafourche Parish, Louisiana, and died 01 June 1967 in Metairie, Jefferson Parish, Louisiana.

Children of Sidney Schexnaydre and Myrtile Waguespack are:

217	i.	**Elodie[6] Schexnayder.**
+ 218	ii.	**Odile Schexnayder.**
219	iii.	**Antoinette Schexnayder**, born 14 July 1895; died 23 October 1918 in Donaldsonville, Ascension Parish, Louisiana.
220	iv.	**Rosa T. Schexnayder**, born 28 April 1898; died 10 July 1991 in Donaldsonville, Ascension Parish, Louisiana.
221	v.	**Zoe Suzanna Schexnayder**, born 11 August 1899; died 11 March 1916 in Donaldsonville, Ascension Parish, Louisiana.
222	vi.	**Sidney Schexnayder, Jr.**, born 14 February 1910 in Louisiana; died 13 September 2000 in Vermillion Parish, Louisiana. He married **Daisy Boudreaux.**

76. Henry Joseph[5] Schexnaydre, Sr * (Marie Antoinette[4] Robért, Mathieu[3], Jean[2], Mathieu[1]) was born 30 July 1872 in Edgard, St. John the Baptist Parish, Louisiana, and died December 1936 in Ascension Parish, Louisiana. He married **Marie Antoinette Waguespack** 09 August 1894 in Edgard, St. John the Baptist Parish, Louisiana[48], daughter of Alidor Waguespack and Delia Robért. She was born 10 September 1874 in Raceland, Lafourche Parish, Louisiana, and died 1922.

Children of Henry Schexnaydre and Marie Antoinette Waguespack are:

223	i.	**Bertha M.[6] Schexnaydre**, born 10 May 1895 in Louisiana; died August 1985 in St. James Parish, Convent, Louisiana.
+ 224	ii.	**Berthile Joseph Schexnaydre, Sr.** *, born 20 December 1896 in Louisiana; died 14 December 1953 in Burnside, Ascension Parish, Louisiana.
225	iii.	**Imelda Schexnaydre**, born 23 August 1897 in Louisiana; died May 1983 in St. Charles Parish, Destrehan, Louisiana.
226	iv.	**Delia Schexnaydre**, born 05 March 1900 in Louisiana; died Unknown.
227	v.	**Olide Schexnaydre**, born 03 February 1903 in Louisiana; died 24 November 1993 in St. James Parish, Convent, Louisiana. He married Neva Naquin; born 25 February 1906; died 25 February

		1987 in St. James Parish, Convent, Louisiana.
228	vi.	Ferducie F. Schexnaydre, born 06 February 1905 in Louisiana; died 24 March 1992 in St. James Parish, Convent, Louisiana.
229	vii.	Henry Schexnaydre, Jr., born 1907 in Louisiana; died 1918.
230	viii.	Oliva Schexnaydre, born 26 February 1908 in Louisiana; died June 1984 in St. James Parish, Convent, Louisiana.
231	ix.	Agnes Schexnaydre, born 22 September 1910 in Louisiana; died April 1992 in St. Charles Parish, Destrehan, Louisiana. She married Prudent Simon 20 January 1951; born Unknown; died Unknown.
232	x.	Effie Schexnaydre, born 11 September 1912 in Ascension Parish, Smoke Bend, Louisiana; died 23 January 1999 in St. James Parish, Convent, Louisiana.
+ 233	xi.	Julian Pierre Schexnaydre, Sr. (Zoo), born 02 November 1914 in Ascension Parish, Smoke Bend, Louisiana; died 29 November 1991 in Baton Rouge, East Baton Rouge Parish, Louisiana.
234	xii.	Alceé Schexnaydre, born 23 January 1917 in Louisiana; died September 1975 in St. James Parish, Convent, Louisiana. He married Lee Anna Rousseau.
+ 235	xiii.	Bernadette Marie Schexnaydre, born 23 September 1918 in Burnside, Ascension Parish, Louisiana; died 15 March 2009 in Baton Rouge, East Baton Rouge Parish, Louisiana.

77. Albert Simon[5] Schexnaydre (Marie Antoinette[4] Robért, Mathieu[3], Jean[2], Mathieu[1]) was born 1874 in Edgard, St. John the Baptist Parish, Louisiana[49], and died 28 December 1939 in Ascension Parish, Louisiana. He married **Cesaire Eva Haydel** 12 February 1898 in Edgard, St. John the Baptist Parish, Louisiana[50], daughter of Achille Haydel and Mathilde Waguespack. She was born 27 August 1874 in Vermillion Parish, Abbeville, Louisiana, and died 1958 in Ascension Parish, Louisiana.

Children of Albert Schexnaydre and Cesaire Haydel are:
+ 236	i.	Mathilda Valerie[6] Schexnaydre, born Abt. 1898 in Louisiana; died 14 December 1987 in Orleans Parish, New Orleans, Orleans Parish, Louisiana.
237	ii.	Dennis Thomas Schexnaydre, born Abt. 1901 in Louisiana; died Unknown. He married Leone Faucheux Unknown; born Abt. 1901; died Unknown.
+ 238	iii.	Cecile Marie Schexnaydre, born Abt. 1903 in St. Charles Parish,Taft, Louisiana; died 30 November 2001 in Vacherie, St. James Parish, Louisiana.
239	iv.	Ada Schexnaydre, born Abt. 1907 in Louisiana. She married Edmond Louviere 14 August 1940.
240	v.	Laurence Schexnaydre, born Abt. 1914 in Louisiana. She married Laurent Aubert; born Abt. 1910.

80. Wilfred Joseph⁵ Schexnaydre (Marie Antoinette⁴ Robért, Mathieu³, Jean², Mathieu¹) was born 1886 in Edgard, St. John the Baptist Parish, Louisiana, and died 1935 in Donaldsonville, Ascension Parish, Louisiana. He married **Anne Valerie Waguespack** 15 December 1910. She was born 1885, and died 1964.

Children of Wilfred Schexnaydre and Anne Waguespack are:

241	i.	**Anne⁶ Schexnaydre. She married Achille Roques.**
242	ii.	**Clara Schexnaydre. She married Richard Abadie 22 June 1939 in Union, St. James Parish, Louisiana.**
243	iii.	**Lee Schexnaydre, (Bill).**
244	iv.	**Loraine Schexnaydre.**
245	v.	**Rita Schexnaydre.**
246	vi.	**Wilfred J. Schexnaydre, Jr., born 1918; died 1977 in St. Charles Parish, Destrehan, Louisiana.**
247	vii.	**Bertin Schexnaydre, (Boo Boo), born 26 January 1918 in Louisiana; died 25 June 1992 in Louisiana. He married Ruth Decareaux; born 23 September 1925; died 09 November 1965 in St. James Parish, Louisiana.**
248	viii.	**Elise Marie Schexnaydre, born 01 March 1920; died 07 June 1999 in Mandevile, St. Tammany Parish, Louisiana. She married Newton Joseph Spitzfaden 17 August 1948 in Convent, St. James Parish, Louisiana; born 29 March 1917 in New Orleans, Orleans Parish, Louisiana; died 07 May 1981 in New Orleans, Orleans Parish, Louisiana.**
+ 249	ix.	**Oleus Schexnaydre, Sr., born 02 March 1922 in Burnside, Ascension Parish, Louisiana; died 03 February 2003 in St. James Parish, Louisiana.**

81. Marie Antoinette⁵ Waguespack (Delia Marie⁴ Robért, Mathieu³, Jean², Mathieu¹) was born 10 September 1874 in Raceland, Lafourche Parish, Louisiana, and died 1922. She married **Henry Joseph Schexnaydre, Sr** * 09 August 1894 in Edgard, St. John the Baptist Parish, Louisiana⁵⁰, son of Floribert Schexnaydre and Marie Antoinette Robért. He was born 30 July 1872 in Edgard, St. John the Baptist Parish, Louisiana, and died December 1936 in Ascension Parish, Louisiana.

Children are listed above under (76) Henry Joseph Schexnaydre, Sr *.

82. Myrtile Arthemise⁵ Waguespack (Delia Marie⁴ Robért, Mathieu³, Jean², Mathieu¹) was born 12 December 1876 in Raceland, Lafourche Parish, Louisiana, and died 01 June 1967 in Metairie, Jefferson Parish, Louisiana. She married Sidney Schexnaydre, Sr. 05 April 1894 in Edgard, St. John the Baptist Parish, Louisiana, son of Floribert Schexnaydre and Marie Antoinette Robért. He was born 1872 in Edgard, St. John the Baptist Parish, Louisiana, and died Abt. 1913.

Children are listed above under (75) Sidney Schexnaydre, Sr..

83. André M.[5] Waguespack (Delia Marie[4] Robért, Mathieu[3], Jean[2], Mathieu[1]) was born 26 May 1878 in Raceland, Lafourche Parish, Louisiana, and died 04 August 1952 in Rodriguez Plantation, Donaldsonville, Louisiana. He married **(1) Armentine Landry**. She was born 11 September 1878, and died 03 October 1916 in Donaldsonville, Ascension Parish, Louisiana. He married **(2) Hermine Folse**. She was born 1888 in Louisiana.

Children of André Waguespack and Armentine Landry are:
250	i.	**Andrea[6] Waguespack.**
251	ii.	**Carolyn Waguespack.**
252	iii.	**Paul Waguespack.**
253	iv.	**Timothy Waguespack.**
254	v.	**Stephen Waguespack.**

84. Alice Marie[5] Waguespack (Delia Marie[4] Robért, Mathieu[3], Jean[2], Mathieu[1]) was born 26 November 1879 in Raceland, Lafourche Parish, Louisiana, and died 15 June 1972 in Orleans Parish, New Orleans, Orleans Parish, Louisiana. She married **Septime Robért, Jr.** 18 September 1902 in Ascension Catholic Church, Donaldsonville, Louisiana, son of Septime Robért and Marie Schexnayder. He was born 23 January 1881 in St. John the Baptist Parish, Louisiana, and died 28 July 1943 in Donaldsonville, Ascension Parish, Louisiana.

Children are listed above under (68) Septime Robért, Jr..

87. Wilson Pierre[5] Waguespack (Delia Marie[4] Robért, Mathieu[3], Jean[2], Mathieu[1]) was born 21 October 1886 in Labadieville, Assumption Parish, Louisiana, and died 11 April 1969. He married **Annette Marie Hebert** 09 October 1912 in Ascension Catholic Church, Donaldsonville, Louisiana. She was born 1891, and died 1973.

Children of Wilson Waguespack and Annette Hebert are:
+	255	i.	**George[6] Waguespack, born in Donaldsonville, Ascension Parish, Louisiana.**
	256	ii.	**Georgette Marie Waguespack, born in Donaldsonville, Ascension Parish, Louisiana; died Unknown. She married Warren H. Gonzales.**
+	257	iii.	**Jerome Waguespack, (Jerry), born in Donaldsonville, Ascension Parish, Louisiana.**
+	258	iv.	**Leslie J. Waguespack, Sr., born Abt. 1919 in Donaldsonville, Ascension Parish, Louisiana; died 23 December 2009 in Framingham, Mass..**

259	v.	Marie Antoinette Waguespack, born in Donaldsonville, Ascension Parish, Louisiana.
+ 260	vi.	Vivian Waguespack, born in Donaldsonville, Ascension Parish, Louisiana.
+ 261	vii.	Wilson Waguespack, born in Donaldsonville, Ascension Parish, Louisiana.
+ 262	viii.	Alidore Joseph Waguespack, born 26 November 1916 in Donaldsonville, Ascension Parish, Louisiana; died 19 June 1996 in Donaldsonville, Ascension Parish, Louisiana.
+ 263	ix.	Leonard Waguespack, born 29 August 1921 in Stella Plantation, Donaldsonville, Louisiana; died 25 December 2004 in Chalmette, St. Bernard Parish, Louisiana.
264	x.	Heloise Marie Waguespack, born Abt. 1923 in Donaldsonville, Ascension Parish, Louisiana; died 27 December 2008 in Donaldsonville, Ascension Parish, Louisiana.

91. Elmira Marie[5] Robért (Jean Paul[4], Mathieu[3], Jean[2], Mathieu[1]) was born 19 December 1876 in Wallace, St. John the Baptist Parish, Louisiana[51], and died 15 November 1968 in Darrow, Ascension Parish, Louisiana. She married **Jacque Rene Waggenspack, ** 11 January 1902 in St. Mary Catholic Church,Kenner, Louisiana[51], son of Felix Waggenspack and Amelie<Emily> Waguespack. He was born 09 December 1867 in Raceland, Lafourche Parish, Louisiana[51], and died 20 December 1956 in Burnside, Ascension Parish, Louisiana.

Children of Elmira Robért and Jacque Waggenspack are:

+ 265	i.	Pauline Marie[6] Waggenspack, born 14 December 1902 in Kenner, Jefferson Parish, Louisiana; died 31 January 1997 in Gonzales, Ascension Parish, Louisiana.
266	ii.	Ruffin Joseph Waggenspack, (2-D), born 18 May 1905 in Kenner, Jefferson Parish, Louisiana; died 25 November 1971 in Darrow, Ascension Parish, Louisiana.
+ 267	iii.	Claude Francis X. Waggenspack, born 16 July 1907 in Pedescleaux Plantation, Ascension Parish, Donaldsonville, La.; died 20 August 1999 in Gonzales, Ascension Parish, Louisiana.
+ 268	iv.	James Berlin Waggenspack, (Bill), born 12 August 1910 in Baton Rouge, East Baton Rouge Parish, Louisiana; died 07 February 1987 in Baton Rouge, East Baton Rouge Parish, Louisiana.
269	v.	Percy Paul Waggenspack, born 30 June 1912 in Baton Rouge, East Baton Rouge Parish, Louisiana; died 29 June 1968 in Baton Rouge, East Baton Rouge Parish, Louisiana. He married Marie Carmen Mistretta 24 October 1955; born Unknown.
270	vi.	John Robert Waggenspack, born 21 March 1914 in Smoke Bend, Ascension Plantation, Ascension Parish, Louisiana; died 22 February 1941 in Darrow, Ascension Parish, Louisiana.
271	vii.	Juliette Theresa Waggenspack,(Ye-Yet), born 18 July 1915 in

Smoke Bend, Ascension Plantation, Ascension Parish, Louisiana; died 12 January 1966 in Gonzales, Ascension Parish, Louisiana. She married Alvin J. Chabaud 20 February 1950 in New Orleans, Orleans Parish, Louisiana; born 03 June 1916 in New Orleans, Orleans Parish, Louisiana; died 20 May 1995 in St. Gabriel, Iberville Parish, Louisiana.

+ 272   viii.   **Esther Ann Waggenspack, (Tay-Tay), born 12 October 1916 in Point Houmas, Donaldsonville, Ascension Parish, Louisiana; died 09 October 2002 in Baton Rouge, East Baton Rouge Parish, Louisiana.**

+ 273   ix.   **Francis Benoit Waggenspack, born 16 July 1918 in Modeste, Ascension Parish, Louisiana; died 25 May 2004 in Darrow, Ascension Parish, Louisiana.**

+ 274   x.   **Jeannette Marie Waggenspack, (Non-e), born 30 August 1920 in Modeste, Ascension Parish, Louisiana; died 17 March 1994 in St. Gabriel, Iberville Parish, Louisiana.**

275   xi.   **Rene Anthony Waggenspack, (Beebe), born 02 October 1922 in Modeste, Ascension Parish, Louisiana.** He married Janice Normae Noto 25 April 1981 in Our Lady of the Holy Rosary Church, St. Amant, Louisiana; born 03 April 1941 in Lake, Ascension Parish, Louisiana.

92.   Paula Cecile[5] Robért, (Tow-Tow) (Jean Paul[4], Mathieu[3], Jean[2], Mathieu[1]) was born 22 November 1878 in Wallace, St. John the Baptist Parish, Louisiana[52], and died 22 March 1950 in Burnside, Ascension Parish, Louisiana. She married **Amedee Jean Robért** 13 November 1900 in Hancock County, Mississippi, son of Jean Frumence Robért and Euphrasie Bouy. He was born 29 February 1880 in Vacherie, St. James Parish, Louisiana[52], and died 09 October 1955 in Burnside, Ascension Parish, Louisiana.

Child is listed above under (73) Amedee Jean Robért.

93.   Joseph Olide[5] Robért, (Do-Doot) (Jean Paul[4], Mathieu[3], Jean[2], Mathieu[1]) was born 25 November 1880 in Wallace, St. John the Baptist Parish, Louisiana[52], and died 20 September 1956 in Darrow, Ascension Parish, Louisiana. He married **Therése Waggenspack** 21 December 1903 in St. Mary Catholic Church, Kenner, Louisiana, daughter of Felix Waggenspack and Amelie<Emily> Waguespack. She was born 27 April 1878 in Houma, Terrebonne Parish, Louisiana[53], and died 12 December 1958 in Darrow, Ascension Parish, Louisiana.

Children of Joseph Robért and Therése Waggenspack are:
276   i.   **Rurick Anthony[6] Robért, born 01 March 1905 in St. Elmo Plantation, Darrow, Ascension Parish, Louisiana; died 03 November 1986 in Gonzales, Ascension Parish, Louisiana.**

+ 277 ii. Maude Marie Robért, born 19 March 1906 in St. Elmo Plantation, Darrow, Ascension Parish, Louisiana; died 12 May 2001 in Donaldsonville, Ascension Parish, Louisiana.

278 iii. Mae Thérèse Robért, (Manette), born 07 August 1907 in St. Elmo Plantation, Darrow, Ascension Parish, Louisiana; died 07 February 1993 in Gonzales, Ascension Parish, Louisiana.

+ 279 iv. Joseph Nemours Robért, (Jo Jo), born 10 October 1908 in St. Elmo Plantation, Darrow, Ascension Parish, Louisiana; died 29 August 1998 in Gonzales, Ascension Parish, Louisiana.

+ 280 v. Lynn Jude Robért, Sr. (Noon), born 21 February 1910 in St. Elmo Plantation, Darrow, Ascension Parish, Louisiana; died 03 May 1966 in Gonzales, Ascension Parish, Louisiana.

+ 281 vi. Felix John Robért, (Benny), born 03 October 1912 in Remy, St. James Parish, Louisiana; died 20 October 1986 in Donaldsonville, Ascension Parish, Louisiana.

+ 282 vii. Adele Ann Robért, born 22 October 1915 in Riverton Plantation, Burnside, Ascension Parish, Louisiana; died 12 August 1998 in New Orleans, Orleans Parish, Louisiana.

283 viii. Paul Robért,(infant), born January 1916 in Holen Solms, Ascension Parish, Louisiana; died January 1916 in Holen Solms, Ascension Parish, Louisiana.

284 ix. Charles Louis Robért, (Tellie), born 24 July 1917 in St. Elmo Plantation, Darrow, Ascension Parish, Louisiana; died 11 October 1996 in Gonzales, Ascension Parish, Louisiana.

+ 285 x. Dorothy Elizabeth Robért, (Fat), born 01 October 1919 in St. Elmo Plantation, Darrow, Ascension Parish, Louisiana; died 26 August 1987 in Gonzales, Ascension Parish, Louisiana.

286 xi. George Pierre Robért, (Toby), born 19 February 1921 in Burnside, Ascension Parish, Louisiana; died 20 June 2008 in Burnside, Ascension Parish, Louisiana.

94. Leona Theresa[5] Robért, (Na-Na) (Jean Paul[4], Mathieu[3], Jean[2], Mathieu[1]) was born 15 October 1882 in Wallace, St. John the Baptist Parish, Louisiana[54], and died 07 October 1971 in Donaldsonville, Ascension Parish, Louisiana. She married **Joseph Louis Rome, Sr.** *** 30 November 1909 in Donaldsonville, Ascension Parish, Louisiana, son of John Augustin Rome and Amanda Dugas. He was born 04 March 1881 in Ascension Parish, Louisiana, and died 17 March 1957 in Donaldsonville, Ascension Parish, Louisiana.

Children of Leona Robért and Joseph Louis Rome are:
+ 287 i. Louis Joseph[6] Rome, Jr., born 14 October 1910 in Hermitage Plantation, Darrow, Ascension Parish, Louisiana; died 29 September 2009 in Baton Rouge, East Baton Rouge Parish, Louisiana.

+ 288 ii. John Augustin Rome, Sr. (Gus), born 14 December 1911 in Donaldsonville, Ascension Parish, Louisiana; died 05 August

			1992 in Baton Rouge, East Baton Rouge Parish, Louisiana.
+	289	iii.	**Paul Robert Rome**, born 14 December 1911 in Donaldsonville, Ascension Parish, Louisiana; died 08 May 2000 in Destrehan, St. Charles Parish, Louisiana.
+	290	iv.	**O'Neil Francis Rome**, born 14 June 1913 in Donaldsonville, Ascension Parish, Louisiana; died 03 September 2000 in Baton Rouge, East Baton Rouge Parish, Louisiana.
	291	v.	**Lucille Marie Rome, (Lucy)**, born 06 August 1914 in Burnside, Ascension Parish, Louisiana; died 12 January 1994 in Baton Rouge, East Baton Rouge Parish, Louisiana.
+	292	vi.	**Lillian Theresa Rome**, born 27 August 1916 in Burnside, Ascension Parish, Louisiana; died 25 August 2009 in Baton Rouge, East Baton Rouge Parish, Louisiana.
+	293	vii.	**Ike Antoine Rome**, born 01 December 1917 in Burnside, Ascension Parish, Louisiana; died 13 May 1995 in Baton Rouge, East Baton Rouge Parish, Louisiana.
+	294	viii.	**Charles David Rome, (C.D.)**, born 14 March 1919 in Donaldsonville, Ascension Parish, Louisiana; died 21 November 1971 in Baton Rouge, East Baton Rouge Parish, Louisiana.
+	295	ix.	**Donald Joseph Rome, (Jug Head)**, born 08 February 1924 in Donaldsonville, Ascension Parish, Louisiana; died 30 November 2003 in Gulf Shores, Alabama.

95. Raoul Matthew[5] Robért (Jean Paul[4], Mathieu[3], Jean[2], Mathieu[1]) was born 31 March 1885 in Wallace, St. John the Baptist Parish, Louisiana[54], and died 31 October 1931 in Burnside, Ascension Parish, Louisiana. He married **Clara Ann Waggenspack** 1916 in Louisiana, daughter of Felix Waggenspack and Amelie<Emily> Waguespack. She was born 04 February 1887 in Montegut, Terrebonne Parish, Louisiana, and died 11 March 1934 in Burnside, Ascension Parish, Louisiana.

Children of Raoul Robért and Clara Waggenspack are:

+	296	i.	**James Joseph[6] Robért, Sr.**, born 09 October 1918 in Burnside, Ascension Parish, Louisiana; died 11 January 1981 in Rapides Parish, Alexandria, Louisiana.
+	297	ii.	**Amalie Marie Robért, (Toot)**, born 16 August 1924 in Burnside, Ascension Parish, Louisiana.

96. Clovis Jean[5] Robért (Jean Paul[4], Mathieu[3], Jean[2], Mathieu[1]) was born 23 February 1888 in Wallace, St. John the Baptist Parish, Louisiana, and died 04 July 1966 in Burnside, Ascension Parish, Louisiana. He married **Marie Bernadette Troxclair** 14 April 1920 in St. Hubert Catholic Church, Garyville, Louisiana, daughter of Noah Troxclair and Marie Pollet. She was born 15 May 1895 in Waggaman, Jefferson Parish, Louisiana, and died 18 August 1982 in Luling, St.

Charles Parish, Louisiana.

Children of Clovis Robért and Marie Troxclair are:

298   i.   **Noah Dominique[6] Robért, born 30 August 1923 in Burnside, Ascension Parish, Louisiana; died 27 June 2009 in Baton Rouge, East Baton Rouge Parish, Louisiana.**

299   ii.   **John Joseph Robért,(infant), born 18 November 1926 in Burnside, Ascension Parish, Louisiana; died 19 December 1926 in Burnside, Ascension Parish, Louisiana.**

300   iii.   **Thomas James Robért, born 25 October 1927 in Burnside, Ascension Parish, Louisiana. He married Saundra Frances Owens; born 17 November 1935 in Kansas City, Jackson County, Missouri.**

98. Remy Paul[5] Robért (Jean Paul[4], Mathieu[3], Jean[2], Mathieu[1]) was born 02 July 1892 in Wallace, St. John the Baptist Parish, Louisiana[55], and died 11 December 1970 in New Orleans, Orleans Parish, Louisiana. He married **Ethel Marie Landry** 20 November 1922 in Ascension Catholic Church, Donaldsonville, Louisiana, daughter of Olibert Landry and Ellen Marchand. She was born 15 July 1904 in Darrow, Ascension Parish, Louisiana, and died 18 April 1980 in Gonzales, Ascension Parish, Louisiana.

Children of Remy Robért and Ethel Landry are:

+   301   i.   **Hulin Joseph[6] Robért, born 26 December 1923 in Donaldson Tract Plantation, Burnside, Ascension Parish, Louisiana.**

+   302   ii.   **Cecil Paul Robért, Sr, born 31 October 1925 in Burnside, Ascension Parish, Louisiana; died 17 February 1976 in Baton Rouge, East Baton Rouge Parish, Louisiana.**

+   303   iii.   **Glenn Jacque Robért, born 23 June 1927 in Donaldson Tract Plantation, Burnside, Ascension Parish, Louisiana.**

+   304   iv.   **Mary Lois Robért, born 20 August 1929 in Donaldson Tract Plantation, Burnside, Ascension Parish, Louisiana.**

    305   v.   **Francis Farrel Robért, (infant), born 1933 in Burnside, Ascension Parish, Louisiana; died 1933 in Burnside, Ascension Parish, Louisiana.**

+   306   vi.   **Shelby Lawrence Robért, born 28 September 1934 in Burnside, Ascension Parish, Louisiana.**

    307   vii.   **Joyce Ann Robért, born 24 September 1943 in Donaldson Tract Plantation, Burnside, Ascension Parish, Louisiana; died 15 December 1952 in Burnside, Ascension Parish,Louisiana.**

99. Octave Pierre[5] Robért (Jean Paul[4], Mathieu[3], Jean[2], Mathieu[1]) was born 22 August 1894 in Wallace, St. John the Baptist Parish, Louisiana[55], and died 03 June 1955 in Burnside, Ascension Parish, Louisiana. He married **Elizabeth Ruth**

Brewerton 26 October 1925 in St. Anthony Catholic Church, Darrow, Louisiana, daughter of Joseph Brewerton and Caroline King. She was born 18 January 1904 in Burnside, Ascension Parish, Louisiana, and died 26 June 1998 in Donaldsonville, Ascension Parish, Louisiana.

Children of Octave Robért and Elizabeth Brewerton are:

+ 308 i. **Matthew Joseph[6] Robért, born 05 August 1926 in Donaldson Tract Plantation, Burnside, Ascension Parish, Louisiana; died 01 December 2001 in El Paso County, Colorado Springs, Colorado.**
+ 309 ii. **Robert Francis Robért, born 14 June 1928 in Donaldson Tract Plantation, Burnside, Ascension Parish, Louisiana.**
+ 310 iii. **Paul Gerard Robért, born 08 October 1930 in Donaldson Tract Plantation, Burnside, Ascension Parish, Louisiana; died 16 October 1983 in Mamou, Evangeline Parish, Louisiana.**
  311 iv. **Mary Elizabeth Robért,(Betty), born 06 January 1933 in Donaldson Tract Plantation, Burnside, Ascension Parish, Louisiana.**
+ 312 v. **John Marius Robért, Sr., born 13 January 1935 in Donaldson Tract Plantation, Burnside, Ascension Parish, Louisiana.**
+ 313 vi. **Carolyn Teresa Robért, (Ceyon), born 13 March 1937 in Donaldson Tract Plantation, Burnside, Ascension Parish, Louisiana.**
+ 314 vii. **Genevieve Martha Robért, born 28 December 1940 in Peytavin Plantation, Donaldsonville, Ascension Parish, Louisiana.**
+ 315 viii. **Marie Noelle Robért, born 28 December 1941 in Peytavin Plantation, Donaldsonville, Ascension Parish, Louisiana.**
+ 316 ix. **Peter Octave Robért, born 30 December 1944 in Petyavin Plantation, Donaldsonville, Ascension Parish, Louisiana.**

100. Rene Benoit[5] Robért, (Ne-Nall) (Jean Paul[4], Mathieu[3], Jean[2], Mathieu[1]) was born 21 February 1897 in Wallace, St. John the Baptist Parish, Louisiana[55], and died 22 May 1983 in Burnside, Ascension Parish, Louisiana. He married **Gladys Lucille Cointment, (Dee-Dee)** 12 January 1925 in Ascension Catholic Church, Donaldsonville, Louisiana, daughter of Jean Cointment and Marie Hermina Lafargue. She was born 07 January 1901 in Donaldsonville, Ascension Parish, Louisiana, and died 10 August 1990 in Gonzales, Ascension Parish, Louisiana.

Children of Rene Robért and Gladys Cointment are:

  317 i. **Infant[6] Robért, born 1926 in Donaldson Tract Plantation, Burnside, Ascension Parish, Louisiana; died 1926 in Donaldson Tract Plantation, Burnside, Ascension Parish, Louisiana.**
  318 ii. **Lionel Joseph Robért, born 22 July 1927 in Donaldson Tract Plantation, Burnside, Ascension Parish, Louisiana; died 02 November 2009 in Gonzales, Ascension Parish, Louisiana.**
+ 319 iii. **Carl James Robért, (Hubble), born 31 January 1929 in Donaldson Tract Plantation, Burnside, Ascension Parish, Louisiana.**

+ 320   iv. **Norman Anthony Robért, born 04 October 1931 in Clark Plantation, Burnside, Ascension Parish, Louisiana.**

101. Roland Jacques[5] Robért, Sr. (Pan-Am) (Jean Paul[4], Mathieu[3], Jean[2], Mathieu[1]) was born 15 April 1900 in Tchoupitoulas Plantation, Jefferson Parish, Louisiana[55], and died 28 October 1958 in Burnside, Ascension Parish, Louisiana. He married **Vallie Lucy Hernandez** 20 November 1936 in St. Agnes Catholic Church, Baton Rouge, Louisiana, daughter of Adam Hernandez and Carmelite Falcon. She was born 16 September 1912 in White Castle, Iberville Parish, Louisiana, and died 10 November 2001 in Baton Rouge, East Baton Rouge Parish, Louisiana.

Children of Roland Robért and Vallie Hernandez are:

+ 321   i. **Roland James[6] Robért, Jr. (Row), born 17 September 1937 in Baton Rouge, East Baton Rouge Parish, Louisiana.**
+ 322   ii. **Gayle Patrick Robért, born 06 September 1938 in Donaldsonville, Ascension Parish, Louisiana.**
+ 323   iii. **Harry Paul Robért, Sr., born 25 January 1941 in Donaldsonville, Ascension Parish, Louisiana.**
+ 324   iv. **Val Ann Robért, born 20 March 1942 in Donaldsonville, Ascension Parish, Louisiana.**
+ 325   v. **Alvin Joseph Robért, Sr. (Al), born 10 May 1946 in Baton Rouge, East Baton Rouge Parish, Louisiana.**
+ 326   vi. **Stephen Adam Robért, (Steve), born 04 September 1947 in Baton Rouge, East Baton Rouge Parish, Louisiana.**
+ 327   vii. **Donald Christopher Robért, (Don), born 01 January 1950 in Baton Rouge, East Baton Rouge Parish, Louisiana.**

Generation No. 5

102. Cecila[6] Schexnayder (Louis Bartholomu[5], Emilien[4], Marianne Melanie[3] Robért, Jean[2], Mathieu[1]) was born Abt. 1892 in Louisiana. She married **Rosney Waguespack, (Waggenspack)** Abt. 1912, son of Arthur Waguespack and Marie Faucheux. He was born 14 March 1890, and died September 1980 in Vacherie, St. James Parish, Louisiana.

Children of Cecila Schexnayder and Rosney Waguespack are:

328   i. **Cecilia[7] Waguespack, born 1913 in Vacherie, St. James Parish, Louisiana; died 06 June 2006 in Thibodaux, Lafourche Parish, Louisiana. She married Emile (Conoon) Faucheux.**
329   ii. **Bessie Marion Waguespack, born 1917 in Vacherie, St. James Parish, Louisiana; died 07 November 2009 in Gretna, Jefferson Parish, Louisiana. She married George J. Haydel, Sr.**
330   iii. **Mary Grace Waguespack, born 1918.**

331	iv.	Ethelyn Marie Waguespack, born 19 October 1921. She married Joseph Emile Troxclair, Jr. 18 March 1945; born 08 September 1917 in Louisiana.
332	v.	Anna Mae Waguespack, born 1922.
333	vi.	Mathilde Therese Waguespack, born 1923.
334	vii.	Honorine Waguespack, born 1924.
335	viii.	Romana Waguespack, born 1925.
336	ix.	Joseph Rosney Waguespack, born 1926.

106. Edwin Joseph[6] **Schexnayder** (Optime Joseph[5], Marcellin[4], Marianne Melanie[3] Robért, Jean[2], Mathieu[1]) was born 06 June 1906 in Vacherie, St. James Parish, Louisiana, and died 19 August 1971 in Baton Rouge, East Baton Rouge Parish, Louisiana. He married **Margie Clara Averett**, daughter of Louandy Averett and Mary Clayton.

Child of Edwin Schexnayder and Margie Averett is:

337	i.	**Edwin Joseph**[7] **Schexnayder, Jr.**, born 29 April 1939 in Baton Rouge, East Baton Rouge Parish, Louisiana; died 28 May 1995 in Alexandria, Rapides Parish, Louisiana.

110. Victor Joseph[6] **Schexnayder,Sr.** (Optime Joseph[5], Marcellin[4], Marianne Melanie[3] Robért, Jean[2], Mathieu[1]) was born 10 June 1908 in Vacherie, St. James Parish, Louisiana, and died 27 March 1988 in Darrow, Ascension Parish, Louisiana. He married **Marie Ursuline Martinez, (Seline)** Abt. 1928, daughter of Adam Martinez and Anna Kraemer. She was born 14 January 1912 in Vacherie, St. James Parish, Louisiana, and died 15 March 1999 in Gonzales, Ascension Parish, Louisiana.

Children of Victor Schexnayder and Marie Ursuline Martinez are:

	338	i.	**Alice Margaret**[7] **Schexnayder**, born 01 July 1929 in Ascension Parish, Louisiana. She married Kerney Sheets September 1948 in Darrow, Ascension Parish, Louisiana.
	339	ii.	Marie Donna Schexnayder, born 19 September 1931 in Burnside, Ascension Parish, Louisiana; died 17 September 1936 in Burnside, Ascension Parish, Louisiana.
+	340	iii.	Marie Beatrice Schexnayder, born 06 December 1934 in Darrow, Ascension Parish, Louisiana.
+	341	iv.	Victor Arnold Schexnayder, born 13 October 1937 in Burnside, Ascension Parish, Louisiana; died 11 July 2006.

111. Jean Marcellin[6] **Schexnayder, (Zoot)** (Emilien Joseph[5], Marcellin[4], Marianne Melanie[3] Robért, Jean[2], Mathieu[1]) was born 02 March 1889 in Vacherie, St. James Parish, Louisiana, and died January 1969 in Vacherie, St. James

Parish, Louisiana[56]. He married **Marie Erasie Simon** 30 June 1908, daughter of Jean Ruffin Simon and Marie Hermine Falgoust. She was born January 1891.

Children of Jean Marcellin Schexnayder and Marie Erasie Simon are:

342	i.	Claude[7] Schexnayder, born 27 June 1909 in Vacherie, St. James Parish, Louisiana; died December 1986 in Vacherie, St. James Parish, Louisiana.
343	ii.	Inette Schexnayder, born 26 January 1911 in St. James Parish, Vacherie Louisiana; died 11 February 2002 in St. James Parish, Vacherie Louisiana. She married Benoit V. Robichaux Unknown.
344	iii.	Genevieve Schexnayder, born Abt. 1913. She married Zatarain Unknown.
+ 345	iv.	Simon Joseph Schexnayder, born 28 August 1916 in Vacherie, St. James Parish, Louisiana; died 30 December 1984 in Vacherie, St. James Parish, Louisiana.

113. Louis Luke[6] Robért (Rosemond[5], Jean Baptiste[4], Jean Louis[3], Jean[2], Mathieu[1]) was born 21 November 1877 in St. Charles Parish, Louisiana, and died 12 June 1948. He married **Odalie Hymel** 1904 in New Orleans, Orleans Parish, Louisiana, daughter of Francois Hymel and Marie Troxler. She was born 11 September 1876 in New Orleans, Orleans Parish, Louisiana, and died 03 November 1954.

Children of Louis Robért and Odalie Hymel are:

346	i.	Mable[7] Robért, born 06 October 1905 in St. Charles Parish, Louisiana; died 28 May 1921 in Ama, St. Charles Parish, Louisiana.
347	ii.	Anaise Robért, born 27 December 1906 in St. Charles Parish, Louisiana; died 13 September 2003 in St. Charles Parish, Louisiana. She married John Gonzales 06 June 1929 in St. Charles Borromeo Church, Destrahan, Louisiana; born 03 May 1906 in Louisiana; died 01 April 1983.
348	iii.	Luke Robért, born 05 October 1908 in St. Charles Parish, Louisiana; died January 1982. He married Odile Petit 24 April 1937; born 18 October 1910; died 11 July 1989.
+ 349	iv.	Althea Adolphine Robért, born 17 June 1910 in St. Charles Parish, Louisiana; died 21 December 1995 in St. Charles Parish, Louisiana.
+ 350	v.	Lawrence Robért, born 17 November 1912 in St. Charles Parish, Louisiana; died 25 February 2007 in Luling, St. Charles Parish, Louisiana.
351	vi.	Hebert Robért, born 23 May 1915 in St. Charles Parish, Louisiana; died 23 December 1999 in Louisiana. He married Felicie Michel 07 July 1945; born 07 June 1921.
352	vii.	Vivian Cecilia Robért, born 07 January 1917 in St. Charles Parish,

Louisiana; died 17 September 1993 in Harvey, Jefferson Parish, Louisiana. She married Anatole Joseph Faucheux 06 February 1939 in St. Charles Borromeo Church, Destrahan, Louisiana; born 22 December 1913 in St. Charles Parish, Louisiana; died 06 August 1968 in Marrero, Jefferson Parish, Louisiana.

353   viii. Norbert Robért, born December 1919 in St. Charles Parish, Louisiana. He married (1) Emma Guidry 12 October 1946 in Louisiana; born 05 March 1924 in Louisiana; died June 1980. He married (2) Janelle LeBlanc 18 October 1980.

354   ix.   Lucien Augustin Robért, born 13 December 1921 in St. Charles Parish, Louisiana; died 18 April 2007 in New Orleans, Orleans Parish, Louisiana. He married Jeanne Songy 21 October 1943 in Louisiana; born 24 August 1923 in Louisiana; died 13 October 1999 in New Orleans, Orleans Parish, Louisiana.

114. Edgar[6] Robért (Rosemond[5], Jean Baptiste[4], Jean Louis[3], Jean[2], Mathieu[1]) was born May 1879 in St. Charles Parish, Louisiana, and died Aft. 1920 in St. Charles Parish, Louisiana. He married **Jeanne <unknown> Robért** 1899 in St. Charles Borromeo Church, Destrahan, Louisiana. She was born September 1880 in Louisiana, and died 1965.

Children of Edgar Robért and Jeanne Robért are:

355   i.   **Marie[7] Robért, (neice),** born April 1898 in St. Charles Parish, Louisiana.

+ 356   ii.   Leonie Robért, born 27 March 1900 in St. Charles Parish, Louisiana; died 25 June 1993 in Westwego, Jefferson Parish, Louisiana.

357   iii. Annie Robért, born 1904 in St. Charles Parish, Louisiana.

118. Adele Marie[6] Robért (Rosemond[5], Jean Baptiste[4], Jean Louis[3], Jean[2], Mathieu[1]) was born 27 July 1892 in St. Charles Parish, Louisiana, and died February 1975 in Luling, St. Charles Parish, Louisiana. She married **Lawrence Emelien Hymel** 20 December 1905 in St. Charles Borromeo Church, Destrahan, Louisiana, son of Francois Hymel and Marie Troxler. He was born 10 August 1882 in New Orleans, Orleans Parish, Louisiana, and died October 1978 in New Orleans, Orleans Parish, Louisiana.

Child of Adele Robért and Lawrence Hymel is:

358   i.   **Madeline Marie[7] Hymel,** born 06 January 1909 in New Orleans, Orleans Parish, Louisiana; died 28 April 2003 in Marrero, Jefferson Parish, Louisiana. She married John Joseph Farris; born in Silsbee, Texas.

123. Amedee[6] Robért, Jr. (Amedee[5], Jean Baptiste[4], Jean Louis[3], Jean[2], Mathieu[1]) was born 19 June 1867 in St. Charles Parish, Louisiana, and died 20 August 1933 in Jefferson Parish, Louisiana. He married **Honorine Champaigne** 19 June 1897 in St. Charles Borromeo Church, Destrahan, Louisiana. She was born January 1875 in St. Charles Parish, Louisiana.

Children of Amedee Robért and Honorine Champaigne are:

+ 359   i.   **Joseph[7] Robért, born 20 May 1899 in Ama, St. Charles Parish, Louisiana; died January 1999 in White Castle, Iberville Parish, Louisiana.**
   360   ii.   **Leah Robért, born 1901 in St. Charles Parish, Louisiana.**
   361   iii.   **Laura Robért, born 1903 in St. Charles Parish, Louisiana.**
   362   iv.   **Grace Robért, born 1909 in St. Charles Parish, Louisiana.**

125. Eranbert[6] Robért (Amedee[5], Jean Baptiste[4], Jean Louis[3], Jean[2], Mathieu[1]) was born 1871 in St. Charles Parish, Louisiana, and died 14 November 1958 in Louisiana. He married **Adelina Zeller** Abt. 1897 in Little Red Church, Destrehan, St. Charles Parish, Louisiana. She was born Abt. 1877 in Louisiana.

Child of Eranbert Robért and Adelina Zeller is:

+ 363   i.   **Dewey Joseph[7] Robért, born 31 May 1898 in Ama, St. Charles Parish, Louisiana; died 16 November 1930 in Ama, St. Charles Parish, Louisiana.**

128. Delphine[6] Robért (Amedee[5], Jean Baptiste[4], Jean Louis[3], Jean[2], Mathieu[1]) was born 24 December 1876 in Ama, St. Charles Parish, Louisiana, and died 10 June 1976 in Luling, St. Charles Parish Louisiana. She married **Joseph Author Zeringue** 10 January 1898 in Ama, St. Charles Parish, Louisiana, son of Jean Zeringue and Louise Troxler. He was born 02 October 1867 in Ama, St. Charles Parish, Louisiana, and died 12 December 1941 in Ama, St. Charles Parish, Louisiana.

Child of Delphine Robért and Joseph Zeringue is:

+ 364   i.   **Louisa Marie[7] Zeringue, born 04 November 1898 in Waggaman, Jefferson Parish, Louisiana; died 30 October 1976 in Luling, St. Charles Parish Louisiana.**

131. Eugene[6] Robért (Amedee[5], Jean Baptiste[4], Jean Louis[3], Jean[2], Mathieu[1]) was born 01 April 1885 in St. Charles Parish, Louisiana, and died 04 July 1953. He married **Alice Marie Lauve** 03 November 1909 in Waggaman, Jefferson Parish, Louisiana, daughter of Louis Lauve and Adonia Friloux. She was born 22 April 1887, and died 01 December 1953.

Children of Eugene Robért and Alice Lauve are:

      365   i.   **Anthony Wilson[7] Robért. He married Marie Mary Margiotta.**

+ 366   ii. **Eujene Joseph Robért.**

      367   iii. **Marti Luther Robért.**

+ 368   iv. **Harry Clay Robért, born 12 July 1912; died 14 March 1953.**

      369   v. **Beatrice Robért, born 14 November 1914; died 17 July 1987. She married Edgar Joseph Friloux 30 June 1932; born 31 October 1910; died 23 February 1983.**

      370   vi. **Horace Joseph Robért, born 02 July 1919; died 10 June 1932.**

      371 vii. **Murphy Vincent Robért, born 21 January 1923; died 05 January 1964. He married Living Durapau.**

133. Odile[6] Robért (Amedee[5], Jean Baptiste[4], Jean Louis[3], Jean[2], Mathieu[1]) was born April 1892 in St. Charles Parish, Louisiana. She married **Opphonse Ernest Robért**.

Child of Odile Robért and Opphonse Robért is:

      372   i.   **Effie[7] Robért.**

135. Ernest[6] Robért (Floremond[5], Jean Baptiste[4], Jean Louis[3], Jean[2], Mathieu[1]) was born 15 September 1886 in Louisiana, and died 27 February 1968 in Westwego, Jefferson Parish, Louisiana. He married **Sadie Lorio**, daughter of Lucien Lorio and Clorinne Friloux. She was born June 1895 in St. Charles Parish, Louisiana.

Children of Ernest Robért and Sadie Lorio are:

      373   i.   **Carl[7] Robért.**

      374   ii. **Dudley Robért.**

      375   iii. **Hilda Robért, born Abt. 1916.**

      376   iv. **Harold Robért, born Abt. 1918.**

      377   v. **Leona Robért, born Abt. 1921.**

      378   vi. **Ernest Francis Robért, born 19 February 1927 in Raceland, Lafourche Parish, Louisiana; died 06 August 1991 in Luling, St. Charles Parish, Louisiana. He married Helen Mae Fournier; born 11 June 1932 in Raceland, Lafourche Parish, Louisiana; died 29 September 2007 in Luling, St. Charles Parish, Louisiana.**

139. James Theotine[6] Robért (Theotine[5], Jean Baptiste[4], Jean Louis[3], Jean[2], Mathieu[1]) was born 27 January 1883 in St. James Parish, Louisiana, and died 31 January 1949 in Reserve, St. John the Baptist Parish, Louisiana. He married **Pearl Zeringue** 27 December 1913 in Holy Rosary Church, Taft, St. Charles Parish, Louisiana, daughter of Amillcar Zeringue and Calamire Friloux.

She was born 25 November 1889 in Louisiana, and died 05 October 1974 in Reserve, St. John the Baptist Parish, Louisiana.

Children of James Robért and Pearl Zeringue are:

379   i.   **Ruby[7] Robért, born 26 October 1914 in Ama, St. Charles Parish, Louisiana; died 01 May 1974 in New Orleans, Orleans Parish, Louisiana.**

+ 380   ii.   **Pearl Marguerite Robért, born 27 March 1916 in Ama, St. Charles Parish, Louisiana; died 11 December 1987 in Laplace, St. John the Baptist Parish, Louisiana.**

381   iii.   **Roselie Marie Robért, born 17 February 1918 in St. John the Baptist Parish, Louisiana. She married Alden Bienvenu; born 09 May 1920 in Louisiana; died July 1982 in St. John the Baptist Parish, Louisiana.**

+ 382   iv.   **Beatrice Marie Robért, born 27 December 1919 in St. John the Baptist Parish, Louisiana; died in Louisiana.**

383   v.   **Emma Mae Robért, born 02 May 1921 in St. John the Baptist Parish, Louisiana; died 1974. She married Andrew Bourgeois, Sr.; born 16 November 1920 in Louisiana.**

384   vi.   **James Robért, born 14 November 1922 in St. John the Baptist Parish, Louisiana; died 09 February 1947 in St. John the Baptist Parish, Louisiana.**

385   vii.   **Marion Robért, born 15 March 1924 in St. John the Baptist Parish, Louisiana; died 20 November 1943 in Honolulu, Hawaii.**

386   viii.   **Ray Robért, born 25 June 1925 in St. John the Baptist Parish, Louisiana; died 04 October 2005 in Gramercy, St. James Parish, Louisiana.**

140. Dennis J.[6] Friloux (Estelle Sydleie[5] Robért, Jean Baptiste[4], Jean Louis[3], Jean[2], Mathieu[1]) was born 07 November 1894 in Louisiana, and died 09 February 1967 in Westwego, Jefferson Parish, Louisiana. He married **Leonie Robért**, daughter of Edgar Robért and Jeanne Robért. She was born 27 March 1900 in St. Charles Parish, Louisiana, and died 25 June 1993 in Westwego, Jefferson Parish, Louisiana.

Child of Dennis Friloux and Leonie Robért is:

387   i.   **Winfield Joseph[7] Friloux, born 28 April 1921 in Louisiana. He married Eunice Norma Marie Savoie 17 August 1946; born 29 August 1926 in Des Allemands, St. Charles Parish, Louisiana; died 09 February 1995.**

152. Raymond Simon[6] Robért, Sr. (Jean Ursin[5], Septime Louis[4], Mathieu[3], Jean[2], Mathieu[1]) was born 16 February 1894 in Edgard, St. John the Baptist Parish, Louisiana, and died 29 June 1968 in Texas City, Texas. He married

Bertha Bourgeois 03 February 1920 in St. Michael Catholic Church, Convent, Louisiana.

Children of Raymond Robért and Bertha Bourgeois are:

388	i.	Joyce[7] Robért.
389	ii.	Lloyd Robért.
390	iii.	Raymond Simon Robért, Jr..
391	iv.	Rivis Robért.
392	v.	Charles Robért.
393	vi.	Gardon Robért.

154. Benoit[6] Robért, (Ben) (Jean Ursin[5], Septime Louis[4], Mathieu[3], Jean[2], Mathieu[1]) was born 28 January 1898 in Kenner, Jefferson Parish, Louisiana, and died 27 October 1987 in Ascension Parish, Donaldsonville, Louisiana. He married **Elise Agnes Cire** 10 February 1926 in Ascension Catholic Church, Donaldsonville, Louisiana, daughter of Willis Cire and Agnes Jambois. She was born 09 October 1899 in Donaldsonville, Ascension Parish, Louisiana, and died 27 January 1969 in Ascension Parish, Donaldsonville, Louisiana.

Children of Benoit Robért and Elise Cire are:

+	394	i.	**Curtis[7] Robért,** born 05 February 1927 in Ascension Plantation, Mc Call, Louisiana; died 04 September 1997 in Ascension Parish, Donaldsonville, Louisiana.
+	395	ii.	**Irby Paul Robért,** born 20 May 1928 in Ascension Parish, Louisiana.
+	396	iii.	**Herman Anthony Robért, Sr.,** born 02 May 1930 in Ascension Parish, Louisiana.
+	397	iv.	**Marian Theresa Robért,** born 31 July 1931 in Ascension Parish, Louisiana.
+	398	v.	**Bernard Francis Robért, Sr.,** born 06 December 1933 in Ascension Parish, Louisiana.
+	399	vi.	**Eugene Thomas Robért, Sr.,** born 10 September 1936 in Ascension Parish, Louisiana.
+	400	vii.	**Clara Ann Robért,** born 18 December 1938 in Ascension Parish, Louisiana.
+	401	viii.	**Agnes Robért,** born 12 November 1940 in Ascension Parish, Louisiana.

155. Edna Marie[6] Robért (Jean Ursin[5], Septime Louis[4], Mathieu[3], Jean[2], Mathieu[1]) was born 05 November 1900 in Kenner, Jefferson Parish, Louisiana[57], and died 14 February 1988 in Convent, St. James Parish, Louisiana. She married **Octave Pierre Waguespack** 07 February 1923 in Donaldsonville, Ascension Parish, Louisiana, son of Victor Waguespack and Marie Octavie Robért. He was born 04 March 1898 in Edgard, St. John the Baptist Parish, Louisiana[57], and died

19 July 1987 in Baton Rouge, East Baton Rouge Parish, Louisiana.

Children of Edna Robért and Octave Waguespack are:

+ 402   i.   **Godfrey Joseph[7] Waguespack, born 01 December 1923 in Burnside, Ascension Parish, Louisiana.**

+ 403   ii.   **Larry Pierre Waguespack, Sr., born 14 October 1925 in Burnside, Ascension Parish, Louisiana.**

    404   iii.   **Myrtle Marie Waguespack, born 13 June 1928 in Burnside, Ascension Parish, Louisiana.**

+ 405   iv.   **Gertrude Ann Waguespack, born 10 August 1930 in Burnside, Ascension Parish, Louisiana.**

+ 406   v.   **Barbara Rita Waguespack, born 24 July 1933 in Burnside, Ascension Parish, Louisiana.**

+ 407   vi.   **Genevieve Waguespack, born 15 February 1936 in Burnside, Ascension Parish, Louisiana.**

+ 408   vii.   **Jacqueline Marie Waguespack, born 12 September 1939 in Burnside, Ascension Parish, Louisiana.**

157. Oliver Paul[6] Robért, Sr. (Tucker) (Jean Ursin[5], Septime Louis[4], Mathieu[3], Jean[2], Mathieu[1]) was born 17 January 1905 in Kenner, Jefferson Parish, Louisiana, and died 08 September 1972 in Baton Rouge, East Baton Rouge Parish, Louisiana. He married **Mary Myrthee Doran** 01 February 1932 in Ascension Catholic Church, Donaldsonville, Louisiana, daughter of Daniel Doran and Mary Rodrigue. She was born 22 August 1912 in Donaldsonville, Ascension Parish, Louisiana, and died 11 January 1993 in Baton Rouge, East Baton Rouge Parish, Louisiana.

Children of Oliver Robért and Mary Doran are:

+ 409   i.   **Oliver Paul[7] Robért, Jr., born 21 December 1932 in Donaldsonville, Ascension Parish, Louisiana.**

+ 410   ii.   **Doran J. Robért, born 02 November 1935 in Donaldsonville, Ascension Parish, Louisiana; died in Baton Rouge, East Baton Rouge Parish, Louisiana.**

+ 411   iii.   **Dale Thomas Robért, Sr., born 26 September 1937 in Donaldsonville, Ascension Parish, Louisiana; died 16 December 2007 in Baton Rouge, East Baton Rouge Parish, Louisiana.**

+ 412   iv.   **Clinton Joseph Robért, born 26 August 1941 in Donaldsonville, Ascension Parish, Louisiana.**

+ 413   v.   **Charles Earl Robért, Sr., born 22 December 1943 in Donaldsonville, Ascension Parish, Louisiana.**

    414   vi.   **David Paul Robért.**

158. Felecien Peter[6] Robért, (Bill) (Jean Ursin[5], Septime Louis[4], Mathieu[3], Jean[2], Mathieu[1]) was born 09 June 1907 in Burnside, Ascension Parish,

Louisiana, and died 02 November 1976 in Thibodaux, Lafourche Parish, Louisiana. He married **Edmonde Marie Rayne, (Dee)** 23 November 1938, daughter of H.M. Rayne and Lucille Songy.

Children of Felecien Robért and Edmonde Rayne are:

+ 415   i.   **Daniel Steven[7] Robért, born 03 September 1939 in Thibodaux, Lafourche Parish, Louisiana.**
    416   ii.   **Linda Raye Robért, born 21 February 1951 in Thibodaux, Lafourche Parish, Louisiana.**
+ 417   iii.   **Rose Marie Robért, born 21 February 1951 in Thibodaux, Lafourche Parish, Louisiana.**
+ 418   iv.   **David Paul Robért, born in Thibodaux, Lafourche Parish, Louisiana.**

160.   Josepha Marie[6] Zeringue (Jeanne Clelie[5] Robért, Septime Louis[4], Mathieu[3], Jean[2], Mathieu[1]) was born 20 November 1899 in Louisiana, and died 24 October 1990 in St. James Parish, Louisiana. She married **Marcel Troxclair** 27 July 1921 in Norco, St.Charles Parish, Louisiana, son of Noah Troxclair and Marie Pollet. He was born 19 January 1901 in Waggaman, Louisiana, and died 19 October 1990 in St.James Parish, Louisiana.

Children of Josepha Zeringue and Marcel Troxclair are:

+ 419   i.   **Mariam[7] Troxclair, born 03 October 1924 in New Orleans, Orleans Parish, Louisiana; died 08 October 2000 in Mount Airy, St. John the Baptist Parish, Louisiana.**
+ 420   ii.   **Adlice Marie Troxclair, born 12 December 1926 in New Orleans, Orleans Parish, Louisiana.**
+ 421   iii.   **Sherman Joseph Troxclair, born 18 December 1928 in New Orleans, Orleans Parish, Louisiana; died 21 November 2005 in Lutcher, St. James Parish, Louisiana.**
    422   iv.   **Davis P. Troxclair, (Slack), born 19 October 1930 in New Orleans, Orleans Parish, Louisiana; died 27 September 2004 in Metairie, Jefferson Parish, Louisiana. He married Thelma M. Krotz 16 August 1969 in St. Anthony Catholic Church, Krotz Springs, Louisiana; born 16 June 1928 in Krotz Springs, St. Landry Parish, Louisiana; died 03 June 2003 in Metairie, Jefferson Parish, Louisiana.**
+ 423   v.   **Bessie Troxclair, born 19 April 1935 in New Orleans, Orleans Parish, Louisiana.**

169.   Regina Victoria[6] Waguespack (Marie Evelina[5] Robért, Septime Louis[4], Mathieu[3], Jean[2], Mathieu[1]) was born May 1894 in St. John the Baptist Parish, Louisiana, and died 17 July 1985 in Gramercy, St. James Parish, Louisiana. She married **Albert Paul Zeringue** 11 February 1915 in Louisiana, son of Jean

Zeringue and Marie Aubert. He was born 25 November 1893 in St. John the Baptist Parish, Louisiana, and died 23 May 1961 in Baton Rouge, East Baton Rouge Parish, Louisiana.

Children of Regina Waguespack and Albert Zeringue are:

424   i.   **Aline Cecile[7] Zeringue, born 03 November 1919 in Modeste, Ascension Parish, Louisiana; died 08 October 2004 in Donaldsonville, Ascension Parish, Louisiana. She married Bernard Benjamine Becnel, Sr. 21 May 1941 in St. James Parish, Louisiana; born 22 May 1918 in St. James Parish, Louisiana; died 30 December 1971 in Donaldsonville, Ascension Parish, Louisiana.**

425   ii.   **Therese Marie Zeringue, born 26 August 1917 in Port Barre, Iberville Parish, Louisiana; died 11 May 1955 in St. James Parish, Louisiana. She married Antoine Royley Folse 18 September 1941 in St. James Catholic Church, St. James Parish, Louisiana; born 05 September 1913 in Fairmont, West Virginia; died 07 March 2001 in Dalton, Ohio.**

179. Libby[6] Robért (Omèr Jean[5], Jean Frumence[4], Mathieu[3], Jean[2], Mathieu[1]) was born 06 October 1895 in Louisiana, and died 20 December 1966 in Livingston Parish, Denham Springs, Louisiana. He married **Stella Ourso**.

Children of Libby Robért and Stella Ourso are:

426   i.   **Ethelyne[7] Robért.**
427   ii.   **Gwendalyne Robért.**

181. Palmire[6] Robért (Omèr Jean[5], Jean Frumence[4], Mathieu[3], Jean[2], Mathieu[1]) was born 01 November 1899 in Louisiana, and died 28 August 1989 in Ascension Parish, Donaldsonville, Louisiana. She married **Clemil Joseph Brou** 22 April 1918 in St. Anthony Catholic Chapel, Darrow, Louisiana, son of Clement Brou and Eugenie Folse. He was born 19 December 1894 in Jefferson Parish, Kenner, Louisiana, and died 23 December 1947 in New Orleans, Orleans Parish, Louisiana.

Children of Palmire Robért and Clemil Brou are:

428   i.   **Marjorie Rita[7] Brou, (Sr. Margaret), born 31 December 1919 in Burnside, Ascension Parish, Louisiana; died 18 March 2003 in Baton Rouge, East Baton Rouge Parish, Louisiana.**

+ 429   ii.   **Joseph Clemil Brou, born 20 February 1921 in Burnside, Ascension Parish, Louisiana; died 04 August 1986 in Grand Isle, Louisiana.**

+ 430   iii. **Warren Jude Brou,Sr., born 26 February 1923 in Burnside, Ascension Parish, Louisiana; died 20 February 1996 in**

Donaldsonville, Ascension Parish, Louisiana.

+ 431   iv.   **Marie Therése Brou**, born 16 August 1924 in Burnside, Ascension Parish, Louisiana.

+ 432   v.   **Harold James Brou**, born 21 October 1926 in Ascension Plantation, McCall, Louisiana.

+ 433   vi.   **Grace Mary Brou**, born 14 April 1928 in Ascension Plantation, McCall, Louisiana.

+ 434   vii.   **Dale John Brou**, born 25 August 1930 in Ascension Plantation, McCall, Louisiana.

+ 435   viii.   **Joan Mae Brou**, born 23 March 1932 in Ascension Plantation, McCall, Louisiana.

    436   ix.   **Lynn Anthony Brou**, born 16 December 1933 in Ascension Plantation, McCall, Louisiana. He married Michelle Juliana Donlin 19 December 1970.

+ 437   x.   **Kenneth Paul Brou**, born 25 August 1936 in Ascension Plantation, McCall, Louisiana.

+ 438   xi.   **Margaret Ann Brou**, born 16 March 1940 in Chatham Plantation, Hohen Solms, Louisiana.

182. Aline[6] Robért (Omèr Jean[5], Jean Frumence[4], Mathieu[3], Jean[2], Mathieu[1]) was born Abt. 1902 in Edgard, St. John the Baptist Parish, Louisiana, and died 28 October 1999 in Gonzales, Ascension Parish, Louisiana. She married **Marcel Jean Brou** 17 January 1922 in Gonzales, Ascension Parish, Louisiana, son of Faustin Brou and Eugenie Waguespack. He was born 21 June 1900 in Jefferson Parish, Kenner, Louisiana, and died 03 March 1976 in Gonzales, Ascension Parish, Louisiana.

Children of Aline Robért and Marcel Brou are:

    439   i.   **Audrey M.[7] Brou**, born 24 February 1923 in Burnside, Ascension Parish, Louisiana; died 20 June 1995 in Gonzales, Ascension Parish, Louisiana. She married Irwin Anthony Waggenspack, (Finny) 14 July 1947 in Louisiana; born 08 August 1921 in Ascension Parish, Louisiana; died 13 July 2004 in Gonzales, Ascension Parish, Louisiana.

+ 440   ii.   **Rowena Theresa Brou**, born 08 July 1924 in Burnside, Ascension Parish, Louisiana.

+ 441   iii.   **Marcelle Theresa Brou**, born 18 January 1928 in McCall, Louisiana.

186. Neola Marie[6] Robért (Omèr Jean[5], Jean Frumence[4], Mathieu[3], Jean[2], Mathieu[1]) was born Abt. 1905 in Edgard, St. John the Baptist Parish, Louisiana, and died 11 November 2003 in Abbeville, Vermillion Parish, Louisiana. She married **Leonard Clement LeBlanc, Sr.** 1922, son of Michael LeBlanc and Elmier Dugas. He was born 21 November 1900 in Smoke Bend, Ascension Parish, Louisiana, and died 12 July 1975 in Sorrento, Ascension Parish, Louisiana.

Children of Neola Robért and Leonard LeBlanc are:

442   i.   **Marie Louise[7] LeBlanc, born Abt. 1924 in Ascension Parish, Louisiana. She married Charles L. Dirks.**

443   ii.   **Rosemary LeBlanc, born Abt. 1924 in Ascension Parish, Louisiana. She married Tosy Sandoz.**

444   iii.   **Leonard LeBlanc, Jr., born Abt. 1925 in Ascension Parish, Louisiana. He married Jeanette.**

445   iv.   **Michael Paul LeBlanc, born Abt. 1928 in Ascension Parish, Louisiana.**

446   v.   **Leonas LeBlanc, born Abt. 1929 in Ascension Parish, Louisiana. She married William D. Fortner.**

187. Edgar Joseph[6] Waguespack (Marie Octavie[5] Robért, ***, Jean Frumence[4], Mathieu[3], Jean[2], Mathieu[1]) was born 12 February 1888 in Vacherie, St. James Parish, Louisiana, and died 15 September 1952 in Burnside, Ascension Parish , Louisiana. He married **Irma Caillet** 17 September 1907 in St. John the Baptist Parish, Louisiana, daughter of Paul Caillet and Apolantine Duhe. She was born 20 March 1887 in St. Charles Parish, Louisiana, and died 07 November 1970 in Burnside, Ascension Parish , Louisiana.

Children of Edgar Waguespack and Irma Caillet are:

447   i.   **Laurence Marie[7] Waguespack, born 09 August 1908 in Burnside, Ascension Parish, Louisiana; died 10 August 1924 in Burnside, Ascension Parish, Louisiana.**

448   ii.   **Nolan Joseph Waguespack, born 22 December 1909 in Ben Hur Plantation, South of Baton Rouge, Louisiana; died 28 May 1985 in Convent, St. James Parish, Louisiana. He married Vivian Leah Oubre 23 January 1934; born 07 October 1910 in Convent, St. James Parish, Louisiana; died 24 April 1994.**

449   iii.   **Rudy Paul Antoine Waguespack, born 27 November 1912 in Burnside, Ascension Parish, Louisiana; died 16 November 2005 in Gonzales, Ascension Parish, Louisiana.**

450   iv.   **Cecile Ruth Waguespack, (infant), born 13 September 1915 in Burnside, Ascension Parish, Louisiana; died 16 November 1915 in Burnside, Ascension Parish, Louisiana.**

451   v.   **Bernie Noel Waguespack, born 25 December 1916 in Burnside, Ascension Parish, Louisiana; died 14 August 1998 in Donaldsonville, Ascension Parish, Louisiana. He married Dolores Grace Acosta, (To-Lou) 04 April 1951 in Ascension Catholic Church, Donaldsonville, Louisiana; born 24 November 1927 in Donaldsonville, Ascension Parish, Louisiana; died 02 March 1998 in Donaldsonville, Ascension Parish, Louisiana.**

452   vi.   **Elgie Mae Waguespack, born 10 December 1918 in Burnside, Ascension Parish, Louisiana.**

+ 453 vii. Edgar Joseph Waguespack, Jr.(E.J.), born 13 August 1920 in Burnside, Ascension Parish, Louisiana; died July 2008 in Gonzales, Ascension Parish, Louisiana.

454 viii. Majel Ann Waguespack, born 14 September 1923 in Burnside, Ascension Parish, Louisiana; died 12 January 1924 in Burnside, Ascension Parish, Louisiana.

188. Denise Marie[6] Waguespack (Marie Octavie[5] Robért, ***, Jean Frumence[4], Mathieu[3], Jean[2], Mathieu[1]) was born 04 October 1889 in Vacherie, St. James Parish, Louisiana, and died 30 January 1968 in Luling, St. Charles Parish, Louisiana. She married **Cyril Antoine Caillet, Sr.** 05 February 1917 in St. James Parish, Convent, Louisiana, son of Paul Caillet and Apolantine Duhe. He was born 15 June 1890 in St. Charles Parish, Louisiana, and died 08 October 1966 in Hahnville, St. Charles Parish, Louisiana.

Children of Denise Waguespack and Cyril Caillet are:
+ 455 i. Leola Sophie[7] Caillet, born 07 December 1917 in Bayou Goula, Iberville Parish, Louisiana; died 02 September 1975 in Luling, St. Charles Parish, Louisiana.

+ 456 ii. Lois Marie Caillet, born 20 April 1919 in Edgard, St. John the Baptist Parish, Louisiana.

+ 457 iii. Florence Elizabeth Caillet, born 19 November 1921 in Burnside, Ascension Parish, Louisiana.

+ 458 iv. Helene Caillet, born 10 December 1922.

+ 459 v. Hazel Theresa Caillet, born 12 August 1924 in Killona, St. Charles Parish, Louisiana; died 07 January 1985 in Narco, Louisiana.

+ 460 vi. Cyril Anthony Caillet, Jr., born 23 November 1925 in Killona, St. Charles Parish, Louisiana.

+ 461 vii. Paul Victor Caillet, (P.V.), born 20 March 1928 in Taft, St. Charles Parish, Louisiana.

+ 462 viii. Odell Francis Caillet, born 04 January 1930 in Killona, St. Charles Parish, Louisiana.

+ 463 ix. Shirley Mae Caillet, born 23 November 1931 in Killona, St. Charles Parish, Louisiana.

+ 464 x. Muriel Ann Caillet, born 08 April 1934 in Killona, St. Charles Parish, Louisiana.

189. Wallis Jean[6] Waguespack (Marie Octavie[5] Robért, ***, Jean Frumence[4], Mathieu[3], Jean[2], Mathieu[1]) was born 15 July 1891 in Edgard, St. John the Baptist Parish, Louisiana, and died 07 October 1981 in Baton Rouge, East Baton Rouge Parish, Louisiana. He married **Edna Marie Decareaux** 07 April 1915 in St. James Parish, Convent, Louisiana[58], daughter of Charles Decareaux and Alminda Pollet. She was born 31 August 1895 in St. James Parish, Paulina, Louisiana, and died 06 February 1985 in Baton Rouge, East Baton Rouge Parish,

Louisiana.

Children of Wallis Waguespack and Edna Decareaux are:

+ 465   i.   **Stanford John[7] Waguespack, born 28 April 1916 in St. James Parish, Gramercy, Louisiana; died 02 November 1999 in Gonzales, Ascension Parish, Louisiana.**

+ 466   ii.   **Wallis J. Waguespack, Jr., born 05 August 1918 in Ascension Parish, Burnside, Louisiana; died 24 July 1998 in Ascension Parish, Gonzales, Louisiana.**

+ 467   iii.   **Stanley Paul Waguespack, (Da-Da), born 15 December 1920 in Burnside, Ascension Parish, Louisiana.**

+ 468   iv.   **Seymour Raymond Waguespack, born 30 August 1923 in Burnside, Ascension Parish, Louisiana; died 14 May 1984 in Baton Rouge, East Baton Rouge Parish, Louisiana.**

+ 469   v.   **Lenora Theresa Waguespack, born 03 August 1925 in Ascension Parish ,Burnside, Louisiana; died 18 November 2005 in Baton Rouge, East Baton Rouge Parish, Louisiana.**

+ 470   vi.   **Ola Mae Rita Waguespack, born 13 February 1928 in Burnside, Ascension Parish, Louisiana.**

+ 471   vii.   **Mercedes Ann Waguespack, born 10 February 1930 in Burnside, Ascension Parish, Louisiana; died 13 August 1987 in Violet, St. Bernard Parish, Louisiana.**

190. Elda Augustine[6] Waguespack (Marie Octavie[5] Robért, ***, Jean Frumence[4], Mathieu[3], Jean[2], Mathieu[1]) was born 28 August 1893 in Edgard, St. John the Baptist Parish, Louisiana, and died 31 August 1958 in Destrehan, St. Charles Parish, Louisiana. She married **Ernest Haydel** 04 April 1915 in St. James Parish, Convent, Louisiana, son of Pierre Haydel and Martha Hymel. He was born 12 November 1891 in Edgard, St. John the Baptist Parish, Louisiana, and died 25 March 1964 in Destrehan, St. Charles Parish, Louisiana.

Children of Elda Waguespack and Ernest Haydel are:

+ 472   i.   **Jessie Joseph[7] Haydel, born 19 March 1916.**

+ 473   ii.   **Jennie Marie Haydel, born 09 January 1918 in Edgard, St. John the Baptist Parish, Louisiana; died Unknown in Narco, Louisiana.**

   474   iii.   **Rita Theresa Haydel, born 1920; died 09 February 1933 in St. John the Baptist Parish, Louisiana.**

+ 475   iv.   **Antoine Ernest Haydel, born 23 September 1924 in St. Charles Parish, Sellers, Louisiana (New Sarpy, La.).**

192. Octave Pierre[6] Waguespack (Marie Octavie[5] Robért, ***, Jean Frumence[4], Mathieu[3], Jean[2], Mathieu[1]) was born 04 March 1898 in Edgard, St. John the Baptist Parish, Louisiana[58], and died 19 July 1967 in Baton Rouge, East Baton Rouge Parish, Louisiana. He married **Edna Marie Robért** 07 February

1923 in Donaldsonville, Ascension Parish, Louisiana, daughter of Jean Ursin Robért and Euphrosine Brou. She was born 05 November 1900 in Kenner, Jefferson Parish, Louisiana[59], and died 14 February 1988 in Convent, St. James Parish, Louisiana.

Children are listed above under (155) Edna Marie Robért.

193. George Nicholas[6] Waguespack, (Gee) (Marie Octavie[5] Robért, ***, Jean Frumence[4], Mathieu[3], Jean[2], Mathieu[1]) was born 11 September 1899 in Edgard, St. John the Baptist Parish, Louisiana, and died 07 March 1978 in Baton Rouge General Hospital, Baton Rouge, Louisiana. He married **Pauline Marie Waggenspack** 05 February 1923 in St. Mary Catholic Church ,Union, St. James Parish, Louisiana, daughter of Jacque Waggenspack and Elmira Robért. She was born 14 December 1902 in Kenner, Jefferson Parish, Louisiana, and died 31 January 1997 in Gonzales, Ascension Parish, Louisiana.

Children of George Waguespack and Pauline Waggenspack are:

476	i.	**Jackie[7] Waguespack,(infant), born 23 January 1924 in Burnside, Ascension Parish, Louisiana; died 23 January 1924 in Burnside, Ascension Parish, Louisiana.**
+ 477	ii.	**Gerald Marie Waguespack, born 14 January 1925 in Burnside, Ascension Parish, Louisiana; died 20 January 1985 in Baton Rouge, East Baton Rouge Parish, Louisiana.**
+ 478	iii.	**Richard Waguespack, born 28 April 1927 in Burnside, Ascension Parish, Louisiana.**
479	iv.	**Jacquelyn Waguespack,(infant), born 12 March 1929 in Burnside, Ascension Parish, Louisiana; died 12 March 1929 in Burnside, Ascension Parish, Louisiana.**
+ 480	v.	**George Ann Waguespack, born 19 May 1932 in Burnside, Ascension Parish, Louisiana.**

194. Delia Philomene[6] Waguespack (Marie Octavie[5] Robért, ***, Jean Frumence[4], Mathieu[3], Jean[2], Mathieu[1]) was born 23 October 1901 in Edgard, St. John the Baptist Parish, Louisiana, and died 27 July 1986 in Donaldsonville, Ascension Parish, Louisiana. She married **Clement Anthony Brou** 27 February 1924 in St. Anthony Chapel, Darrow, Louisiana, son of Clement Brou and Eugenie Folse. He was born 05 September 1901 in Tchoupitoulas Plantation, Kenner, Louisiana, and died 12 March 1976 in Donaldsonville, Ascension Parish, Louisiana.

Children of Delia Waguespack and Clement Brou are:

+ 481	i.	**Thelma Marie[7] Brou, born 30 November 1925 in Ascension Plantation, Donaldsonville, Ascension Parish, Louisiana; died 06 August 2000 in Ascension Parish, Donaldsonville, Louisiana.**

482	ii.	Hubert Joseph Brou, Fr., born 26 January 1928 in Ascension Plantation, Mc Call, Louisiana; died 24 March 1997 in Baton Rouge, East Baton Rouge Parish, Louisiana.
+ 483	iii.	Doris Therése Brou, born 20 August 1930 in Ascension Plantation, Mc Call, Louisiana.
+ 484	iv.	Joyce Ann Brou, born 26 October 1932 in Ascension Plantation, Mc Call, Louisiana.
485	v.	Marvin Anthony Brou, born 03 August 1935 in Ascension Plantation, Mc Call, Louisiana; died 17 March 1956 in Chatham Plantation, Hohen Solms, Louisiana.
+ 486	vi.	Paul Charles Brou, born 26 March 1940 in Chatham Plantation, Hohen Solms, Louisiana.

195. Frumence Hubert[6] Waguespack (Marie Octavie[5] Robért, ***, Jean Frumence[4], Mathieu[3], Jean[2], Mathieu[1]) was born 23 October 1905 in Vacherie, St. James Parish, Louisiana, and died 11 September 1997 in Gonzales, Ascension Parish, Louisiana. He married **Ivy Ann Brou** 12 February 1934 in St. Francis Assissi Catholic Church, Smoke Bend, Louisiana, daughter of Octave Brou and Molda Rome. She was born 03 July 1915 in Orange Grove Plantation, Burnside, Ascension Parish, Louisiana, and died 01 October 1999 in Ascension Parish, Gonzales, Louisiana.

Children of Frumence Waguespack and Ivy Brou are:

+ 487	i.	Leroy Joseph[7] Waguespack, born 16 June 1935 in Modeste, Louisiana; died 26 November 1994 in New Orleans, Orleans Parish, Louisiana.
+ 488	ii.	Clyde Paul Waguespack, born 25 April 1937 in Donaldsonville, Ascension Parish, Louisiana.
+ 489	iii.	Kerry Gerard Waguespack, born 15 November 1942 in Donaldsonville, Ascension Parish, Louisiana.
+ 490	iv.	Galyn Thomas Waguespack, born 07 March 1945 in Burnside, Ascension Parish, Louisiana.
+ 491	v.	Ivy Joseph Waguespack, born 08 February 1946 in Donaldsonville, Ascension Parish, Louisiana.

196. Clarence Anthony[6] Waguespack (Marie Octavie[5] Robért, ***, Jean Frumence[4], Mathieu[3], Jean[2], Mathieu[1]) was born 12 September 1908 in Edgard, St. John the Baptist Parish, Louisiana, and died 28 February 1984 in Baton Rouge, East Baton Rouge Parish, Louisiana. He married **Patricia Waggenspack** 29 January 1940 in St. Anthony Chapel, Darrow, Louisiana, daughter of Willis Waggenspack and Julia Landry. She was born 18 October 1913 in Baton Rouge, East Baton Rouge Parish, Louisiana, and died 21 August 2001 in Gonzales, Ascension Parish, Louisiana.

Children of Clarence Waguespack and Patricia Waggenspack are:

+ 492   i.   **Cathy Marie[7] Waguespack, born 27 June 1941 in Donaldsonville, Ascension Parish, Louisiana.**

+ 493   ii.   **Brenda Ann Waguespack, born 15 July 1942 in Donaldsonville, Ascension Parish, Louisiana.**

+ 494   iii.   **Daryl Joseph Waguespack, born 30 October 1945 in Donaldsonville, Ascension Parish, Louisiana.**

+ 495   iv.   **Joel Anthony Waguespack, born 11 January 1949 in Donaldsonville, Ascension Parish, Louisiana.**

+ 496   v.   **Janel Mary Waguespack, born 27 June 1952 in Donaldsonville, Ascension Parish, Louisiana.**

200. William[6] Robért (Wallace Jean[5], Jean Frumence[4], Mathieu[3], Jean[2], Mathieu[1]) was born 1905, and died 1941. He married **Marie Dugas** Unknown in Donaldsonville, Ascension Parish, Louisiana. She was born Abt. 1910.

Children of William Robért and Marie Dugas are:

497   i.   **Carmen[7] Robért, born Abt. 1931 in Ascension Parish, Donaldsonville, Louisiana. She married (1) Cecil J. Oubre; born Unknown; died Unknown. She married (2) A. C. Hymel Abt. 1965 in Donaldsonville, Ascension Parish, Louisiana; born Unknown in Ascension Parish, Louisiana.**

498   ii.   **Willie A. Robért, born Unknown in Ascension Parish, Donaldsonville, Louisiana.**

201. Cecile Marie[6] Robért (Wallace Jean[5], Jean Frumence[4], Mathieu[3], Jean[2], Mathieu[1]) was born 21 December 1907 in Burnside, Ascension Parish, Louisiana, and died 25 February 2002 in St. James Parish, Louisiana. She married **Leopold Jean Zeringue** 18 January 1928 in Ascension Catholic Church, Donaldsinville, Louisiana, son of Jean Zeringue and Marie Aubert. He was born 20 August 1913 in Louisiana, and died 17 August 1990.

Children of Cecile Robért and Leopold Zeringue are:

499   i.   **Roland[7] Zeringue, born 1927.**

500   ii.   **Doris Zeringue, born 1929.**

501   iii.   **Living Zeringue.**

203. Jean Wallace[6] Robért, Jr. (Wallace Jean[5], Jean Frumence[4], Mathieu[3], Jean[2], Mathieu[1]) was born 30 August 1912 in Louisiana, and died 01 May 1989 in Houma, Terrebonne Parish, Louisiana. He married **Marjorie Capello**, daughter of Ernest Capello and Carmelite Babin. She was born 05 June 1916 in Ascension Parish, Donaldsonville, Louisiana, and died 07 August 2003 in Ascension Parish, Gonzales, Louisiana.

Children of Jean Wallace Robért and Marjorie Capello are:

502	i.	**Cheryl**[7] **Robért.**	
503	ii.	**Shelby Robért.**	
504	iii.	**Roland Robért.**	

204. Maxie[6] **Robért, Sr.** (Wallace Jean[5], Jean Frumence[4], Mathieu[3], Jean[2], Mathieu[1]) was born 16 September 1914 in Donaldsonville, Ascension Parish, Louisiana, and died 21 December 1980 in Donaldsonville, Ascension Parish, Louisiana. He married **Ethel Schexnayder**, daughter of Romain Schexnayder and Agalice Martinez. She was born 22 October 1923 in Donaldsonville, Ascension Parish, Louisiana, and died 01 June 2003 in Donaldsonville, Ascension Parish, Louisiana.

Children of Maxie Robért and Ethel Schexnayder are:

505	i.	**Maxie**[7] **Robért, Jr..**
506	ii.	**Leroy Robért.**
507	iii.	**Ronald Robért.**
508	iv.	**Shirline Robért.**
509	v.	**Carolyn Robért.**
510	vi.	**Juanita Robért.**

207. Lester[6] **Robért** (Wallace Jean[5], Jean Frumence[4], Mathieu[3], Jean[2], Mathieu[1]) was born 19 April 1921 in Donaldsonville, Ascension Parish, Louisiana, and died 2001 in Gonzales, Ascension Parish, Louisiana. He married **Dorothy Elizabeth Robért, (Fat)** 07 August 1946 in Darrow, Ascension Parish, Louisiana, daughter of Joseph Robért and Therése Waggenspack. She was born 01 October 1919 in St. Elmo Plantation, Darrow, Ascension Parish, Louisiana, and died 26 August 1987 in Gonzales, Ascension Parish, Louisiana.

Children of Lester Robért and Dorothy Robért are:

+	511	i.	**Renell Joseph**[7] **Robért, born 06 November 1947 in Donaldsonville, Ascension Parish, Louisiana.**
+	512	ii.	**Phyllis Anne Robért, born 25 November 1948 in Donaldsonville, Ascension Parish, Louisiana.**
+	513	iii.	**Dale Anthony Robért, born 13 March 1951 in Donaldsonville, Ascension Parish, Louisiana.**
+	514	iv.	**Faryl Charles Robért, born 28 July 1953 in Donaldsonville, Ascension Parish, Louisiana.**
	515	v.	**Rickey John Robért, born 06 September 1955 in Donaldsonville, Ascension Parish, Louisiana. He married Rebecca Lambert 04 May 1979 in Holy Rosary Catholic Church, St. Amant, Ascension Parish, Louisiana; born 27 December 1960 in Baton Rouge, East Baton Rouge Parish, Louisiana.**

+ 516 vi. **Kirk David Robért, born 23 May 1957 in Donaldsonville, Ascension Parish, Louisiana.**

+ 517 vii. **Keeley Paul Robért, born 19 November 1959 in Donaldsonville, Ascension Parish, Louisiana.**

209. Edith Marie[6] Brou (Marie Palmyre[5] Robért, (Tee-Nannan), Jean Frumence[4], Mathieu[3], Jean[2], Mathieu[1]) was born 28 April 1899 in Tchoupitoulas Plantation, Jefferson Parish, Kenner, Louisiana, and died 17 March 1995 in Ascension Parish, Sorrento, Louisiana. She married **Berthile Joseph Schexnaydre, Sr.** * 22 January 1920 in St Anthont Chapel, Darrow, Louisiana, son of Henry Schexnaydre and Marie Antoinette Waguespack. He was born 20 December 1896 in Louisiana, and died 14 December 1953 in Burnside, Ascension Parish, Louisiana.

Children of Edith Brou and Berthile Schexnaydre are:

 518 i. **Bianca[7] Schexnaydre, born 18 February 1921; died 20 July 1934 in Burnside, Ascension Parish, Louisiana.**

 519 ii. **Nolte Pierre Schexnaydre, born 29 January 1924. He married Agnes Lillian Martine 06 April 1974; born Unknown.**

+ 520 iii. **Vernon Schexnaydre, (Coon), born 22 November 1925 in Burnside, Ascension Parish, Louisiana.**

+ 521 iv. **Berthile Joseph Schexnaydre, Jr. (Bert), born 25 May 1927 in Burnside, Ascension Parish, Louisiana.**

 522 v. **Earl Joseph Schexnaydre, born 25 March 1929 in Burnside, Ascension Parish, Louisiana; died 02 November 1959 in Burnside, Ascension Parish, Louisiana.**

 523 vi. **Dolores Edith Schexnaydre,(Doe-Doe), born 26 September 1930 in Burnside, Ascension Parish, Louisiana.**

+ 524 vii. **Ione Theresa Schexnaydre, born 03 June 1932 in Burnside, Ascension Parish, Louisiana.**

+ 525 viii. **Clyde Thaddeus Schexnaydre, born 29 October 1933 in Burnside, Ascension Parish, Louisiana; died 25 March 2003 in Ascension Parish, Sorrento, Louisiana.**

 526 ix. **Kenneth Schexnaydre, (Ke-Ken), born 12 November 1934 in Burnside, Ascension Parish, Louisiana.**

 527 x. **Katheleen Schexnaydre, born 12 November 1934 in Burnside, Ascension Parish, Louisiana; died 12 November 1934 in Burnside, Ascension Parish, Louisiana.**

+ 528 xi. **Edith Marie Schexnaydre, (Bo-Boot), born 16 December 1936 in Burnside, Ascension Parish, Louisiana; died 29 October 2001 in Ascension Parish, Donaldsonville, Louisiana.**

+ 529 xii. **Dayton Schexnaydre, born 16 January 1939 in Burnside, Ascension Parish, Louisiana.**

+ 530 xiii. **Lyle Schexnaydre, born 20 August 1941 in Burnside, Ascension Parish, Louisiana.**

531   xiv. Elaine Rita Schexnaydre.

211. André Augustine[6] Brou, Sr. (Cap) (Marie Palmyre[5] Robért, (Tee-Nannan), Jean Frumence[4], Mathieu[3], Jean[2], Mathieu[1]) was born 27 August 1904 in Hermitage Plantation, Ascension Parish, Darrow, Louisiana, and died 15 January 1999 in Gonzales, Ascension Parish, Louisiana. He married **Rose Elizabeth Cire** in St. Francis of Assissi Church, Smoke Bend, Louisiana, daughter of Willis Cire and Agnes Jambois. She was born 09 April 1905 in Donaldsonville, Ascension Parish, Louisiana, and died 29 October 1970 in Donaldsonville, Ascension Parish, Louisiana.

Children of André Brou and Rose Cire are:
+   532   i. **Ronald Paul[7] Brou, Sr., born 04 October 1929 in McCall, Ascension Parish, Louisiana; died 11 June 2008 in Denham Springs, Livingston Parish, Louisiana.**
+   533   ii. **Goldie Marie Brou, (Giggle), born 06 March 1931 in McCall, Ascension Parish, Louisiana.**
     534   iii. **André Augustine Brou, Jr. (Mickey), born 08 October 1936 in Burnside, Ascension Parish, Louisiana.**

218. Odile[6] Schexnayder (Sidney[5] Schexnaydre, Sr., Marie Antoinette[4] Robért, Mathieu[3], Jean[2], Mathieu[1]) She married **Louis Parr.**

Child of Odile Schexnayder and Louis Parr is:
     535   i. **Mary Karen[7] Parr.**

224. Berthile Joseph[6] Schexnaydre, Sr. * (Henry Joseph[5], Marie Antoinette[4] Robért, Mathieu[3], Jean[2], Mathieu[1]) was born 20 December 1896 in Louisiana, and died 14 December 1953 in Burnside, Ascension Parish, Louisiana. He married **Edith Marie Brou** 22 January 1920 in St Anthont Chapel, Darrow, Louisiana, daughter of Honore Brou and Marie Palmyre Robért. She was born 28 April 1899 in Tchoupitoulas Plantation, Jefferson Parish, Kenner, Louisiana, and died 17 March 1995 in Ascension Parish, Sorrento, Louisiana.

Children are listed above under (209) Edith Marie Brou.

233. Julian Pierre[6] Schexnaydre, Sr. (Zoo) (Henry Joseph[5], Marie Antoinette[4] Robért, Mathieu[3], Jean[2], Mathieu[1]) was born 02 November 1914 in Ascension Parish, Smoke Bend, Louisiana, and died 29 November 1991 in Baton Rouge, East Baton Rouge Parish, Louisiana. He married **Glory Mary Letulle 28 January 1950 in St. Michael Catholic Church, Convent, Louisiana. She** was born 16 April 1921 in St. James Parish, Central, Louisiana.

Children of Julian Schexnaydre and Glory Letulle are:
+ 536   i.   **Julian Pierre[7] Schexnaydre, Jr., born 28 November 1950 in Ascension Parish, Donaldsonville, Louisiana.**
+ 537   ii. **Roberta Ann Schexnaydre, born 29 May 1953 in Tezcuco Plantation, Burnside, Ascension Parish, Louisiana.**
  538   iii. **Marlene Marie Schexnaydre, born 06 February 1956 in Tezcuco Plantation, Burnside, Ascension Parish, Louisiana.**
+ 539   iv. **Connie Theresa Schexnaydre, born 14 January 1960 in St. James Parish, Lutcher, Louisiana.**

235. Bernadette Marie[6] Schexnaydre (Henry Joseph[5], Marie Antoinette[4] Robért, Mathieu[3], Jean[2], Mathieu[1]) was born 23 September 1918 in Burnside, Ascension Parish, Louisiana, and died 15 March 2009 in Baton Rouge, East Baton Rouge Parish, Louisiana. She married **Martin Carville Hellouin, Dr..** He was born Unknown.

Children of Bernadette Schexnaydre and Martin Hellouin are:
  540   i.   **Mitzi[7] Hellouin.**
  541   ii. **Amy Hellouin.**
  542   iii. **Carl Hellouin.**
  543   iv. **Brent Hellouin, Sr..**

236. Mathilda Valerie[6] Schexnaydre (Albert Simon[5], Marie Antoinette[4] Robért, Mathieu[3], Jean[2], Mathieu[1]) was born Abt. 1898 in Louisiana, and died 14 December 1987 in Orleans Parish, New Orleans, Orleans Parish, Louisiana. She married **Emile T. Waguespack** Abt. 1917 in Louisiana, son of Emile Waguespack and Antonia Waguespack. He was born 24 August 1898 in Louisiana, and died April 1963 in Louisiana.

Children of Mathilda Schexnaydre and Emile Waguespack are:
  544   i.   **Madeleine[7] Waguespack, died in Lumperton, Mississippi.**
+ 545   ii. **Laura Marie Waguespack, born 03 October 1917 in Louisiana; died 03 May 2005 in Baton Rouge, East Baton Rouge Parish, Louisiana.**
  546   iii. **Daniel Waguespack, born 30 July 1918 in Burnside, Ascension Parish, Louisiana; died 19 September 1998 in Metairie, Jefferson Parish, Louisiana.**
+ 547   iv. **Leroy Waguespack, born 1920 in Lafourche Parish, Louisiana; died 14 September 2002 in Louisiana.**
  548   v.   **Marguerite Waguespack, born 09 December 1921 in Louisiana; died 06 February 2001 in Jefferson Parish, Louisiana.**

238. Cecile Marie[6] Schexnaydre (Albert Simon[5], Marie Antoinette[4] Robért, Mathieu[3], Jean[2], Mathieu[1]) was born Abt. 1903 in St. Charles Parish,Taft, Louisiana, and died 30 November 2001 in Vacherie, St. James Parish, Louisiana. She married **Francis Waguespack** 10 February 1925 in St. Mary Catholic Church, Union , Louisiana, son of Leonard Waguespack and Alice Monier. He was born 1896 in St.James Parish, Louisiana.

Children of Cecile Schexnaydre and Francis Waguespack are:

549	i.	**Shirley Philomine[7] Waguespack, born Abt. 1927 in Louisiana; died 18 December 2007 in Lutcher, St. James Parish, Louisiana. She married George Henry Waguespack, Sr.; born 30 July 1926 in Vacherie, St. James Parish, Louisiana; died 17 October 2001 in Thibodaux, Lafourche Parish, Louisiana.**
550	ii.	**Alan Michael Waguespack, born 1945; died 1967. He married (1) Living. He married (2) Living Waguespack; born Unknown. He married (3) Mary Ellen Waguespack Abt. 1967; born Abt. 1946.**

249. Oleus[6] Schexnaydre, Sr. (Wilfred Joseph[5], Marie Antoinette[4] Robért, Mathieu[3], Jean[2], Mathieu[1]) was born 02 March 1922 in Burnside, Ascension Parish, Louisiana, and died 03 February 2003 in St. James Parish, Louisiana. He married **Rosa Faucheux** Unknown.

Children of Oleus Schexnaydre and Rosa Faucheux are:

551	i.	**Timothy[7] Schexnaydre.**
552	ii.	**Marie Schexnaydre.**
553	iii.	**Oleus Schexnaydre, Jr. (Rusty). He married Carla Anderman.**
554	iv.	**Lorain Schexnaydre. She married Dennis Landry, (Poncho).**

255. George[6] Waguespack (Wilson Pierre[5], Delia Marie[4] Robért, Mathieu[3], Jean[2], Mathieu[1]) was born in Donaldsonville, Ascension Parish, Louisiana. He married **Emma Dell Marie LeBouef**.

Children of George Waguespack and Emma LeBouef are:

555	i.	**George David[7] Waguespack, died 29 November 2009 in St. Amant, Ascension Parish, Louisiana. He married Alison Petermann.**
556	ii.	**Anne Marie Waguespack.**
557	iii.	**Glenn Michael Waguespack.**

257. Jerome[6] Waguespack, (Jerry) (Wilson Pierre[5], Delia Marie[4] Robért, Mathieu[3], Jean[2], Mathieu[1]) was born in Donaldsonville, Ascension Parish, Louisiana. He married **Earlene Callegan**

Children of Jerome Waguespack and Earlene Callegan are:

558   i.   Jan[7] Waguespack.
559   ii. Jeri Waguespack.

258. Leslie J.[6] Waguespack, Sr. (Wilson Pierre[5], Delia Marie[4] Robért, Mathieu[3], Jean[2], Mathieu[1]) was born Abt. 1919 in Donaldsonville, Ascension Parish, Louisiana, and died 23 December 2009 in Framingham, Mass.. He married **Catherine A. Moore** Abt. 1949. She was born in Bolton, Texas.

Child of Leslie Waguespack and Catherine Moore is:
560   i.   **Leslie J.[7] Waguespack, Jr.. He married Blanche Marie Iglinsky.**

260. Vivian[6] Waguespack (Wilson Pierre[5], Delia Marie[4] Robért, Mathieu[3], Jean[2], Mathieu[1]) was born in Donaldsonville, Ascension Parish, Louisiana. She married **Lawrence Joseph Landry**.

Child of Vivian Waguespack and Lawrence Landry is:
+   561   i.   **Annette[7] Landry.**

261. Wilson[6] Waguespack (Wilson Pierre[5], Delia Marie[4] Robért, Mathieu[3], Jean[2], Mathieu[1]) was born in Donaldsonville, Ascension Parish, Louisiana. He married **Marjorie Mary Waguespack**.

Children of Wilson Waguespack and Marjorie Waguespack are:
562   i.   **Marian[7] Waguespack.**
563   ii. **Donna Waguespack.**
564   iii. **Sandry (Sandy) Waguespack.**
565   iv. **Cynthia (Cindy) Waguespack.**

262. Alidore Joseph[6] Waguespack (Wilson Pierre[5], Delia Marie[4] Robért, Mathieu[3], Jean[2], Mathieu[1]) was born 26 November 1916 in Donaldsonville, Ascension Parish, Louisiana, and died 19 June 1996 in Donaldsonville, Ascension Parish, Louisiana. He married **Claire Marie Torres**. She was born in Vacherie, St. James Parish, Louisiana.

Children of Alidore Waguespack and Claire Torres are:
566   i.   **Dennis[7] Waguespack. He married Catheline Richard.**
567   ii. **Nanette Waguespack.**

263. Leonard[6] Waguespack (Wilson Pierre[5], Delia Marie[4] Robért, Mathieu[3], Jean[2], Mathieu[1]) was born 29 August 1921 in Stella Plantation, Donaldsonville, Louisiana, and died 25 December 2004 in Chalmette, St. Bernard Parish,

Louisiana. He married **Gertrude Cieutat**.

Children of Leonard Waguespack and Gertrude Cieutat are:

+ 568   i.   **Gayle Anne[7] Waguespack, born Unknown in New Orleans, Louisiana.**
   569   ii.   **Leonard James Waguespack, born Unknown in New Orleans, Louisiana.**
+ 570   iii.   **Wendy Waguespack, born Unknown in New Orleans, Louisiana.**
   571   iv.   **Carl Waguespack, born Unknown in New Orleans, Orleans Parish, Louisiana. He married Trudy Nelson; born Unknown in New Orleans, Orleans Parish, Louisiana.**

265. Pauline Marie[6] Waggenspack (Elmira Marie[5] Robért, Jean Paul[4], Mathieu[3], Jean[2], Mathieu[1]) was born 14 December 1902 in Kenner, Jefferson Parish, Louisiana, and died 31 January 1997 in Gonzales, Ascension Parish, Louisiana. She married **George Nicholas Waguespack, (Gee)** 05 February 1923 in St. Mary Catholic Church ,Union, St. James Parish, Louisiana, son of Victor Waguespack and Marie Octavie Robért. He was born 11 September 1899 in Edgard, St. John the Baptist Parish, Louisiana, and died 07 March 1978 in Baton Rouge General Hospital, Baton Rouge, Louisiana.

Children are listed above under (193) George Nicholas Waguespack, (Gee).

267. Claude Francis X.[6] Waggenspack (Elmira Marie[5] Robért, Jean Paul[4], Mathieu[3], Jean[2], Mathieu[1]) was born 16 July 1907 in Pedescleaux Plantation, Ascension Parish, Donaldsonville, La., and died 20 August 1999 in Gonzales, Ascension Parish, Louisiana. He married **Irma Marie Oubre** 16 July 1945 in St. Stephens, New Orleans, Orleans Parish, Louisiana, daughter of Felix Oubre and Eugenie Bourgeois. She was born 03 November 1909 in Convent, St. James Parish, Louisiana, and died 15 December 1993 in Darrow, Ascension Parish, Louisiana.

Child of Claude Waggenspack and Irma Oubre is:

+ 572   i.   **Kay Marie[7] Waggenspack, born 15 September 1948 in Donaldsonville, Ascension Parish, Louisiana.**

268. James Berlin[6] Waggenspack, (Bill) (Elmira Marie[5] Robért, Jean Paul[4], Mathieu[3], Jean[2], Mathieu[1]) was born 12 August 1910 in Baton Rouge, East Baton Rouge Parish, Louisiana, and died 07 February 1987 in Baton Rouge, East Baton Rouge Parish, Louisiana. He married **Mary Ann Melancon** 14 December 1948 in Darrow, Ascension Parish, Louisiana, daughter of Emile Melancon and Marie Martine. She was born 10 August 1925 in Burnside, Ascension Parish, Louisiana, and died 16 November 1991 in Darrow, Ascension Parish, Louisiana.

Children of James Waggenspack and Mary Melancon are:

573   i.   **James Joseph[7] Waggenspack, born 03 October 1949 in East Baton Rouge Parish, Baton Rouge, La..**

+ 574   ii.   **Paul John Waggenspack, born 22 November 1952 in East Baton Rouge Parish, Baton Rouge, La..**

575   iii.   **Jan Marie Waggenspack, born 02 March 1955 in East Baton Rouge Parish, Baton Rouge, La..**

+ 576   iv.   **Lee Jude Waggenspack, born 03 March 1958 in Baton Rouge, East Baton Rouge Parish, Louisiana.**

+ 577   v.   **Judy Ann Waggenspack, born 13 May 1966 in Lutcher, St. James Parish, Louisiana; died 15 March 1993 in Gonzales, Ascension Parish, Louisiana.**

272. Esther Ann[6] Waggenspack, (Tay-Tay) (Elmira Marie[5] Robért, Jean Paul[4], Mathieu[3], Jean[2], Mathieu[1]) was born 12 October 1916 in Point Houmas, Donaldsonville, Ascension Parish, Louisiana, and died 09 October 2002 in Baton Rouge, East Baton Rouge Parish, Louisiana. She married **Thomas J. Rauch, Jr.** 21 December 1951 in Darrow, Ascension Parish, Louisiana, son of Thomas Rauch and Margaret Bulliany. He was born 14 March 1917 in New Orleans, Orleans Parish, Louisiana, and died 03 March 1982 in Baton Rouge, East Baton Rouge Parish, Louisiana.

Children of Esther Waggenspack and Thomas Rauch are:

+ 578   i.   **Thomas J.[7] Rauch III, born 23 June 1953 in Baton Rouge, East Baton Rouge Parish, Louisiana.**

+ 579   ii.   **Myra Margaret Rauch, born 18 January 1955 in Baton Rouge, East Baton Rouge Parish, Louisiana.**

580   iii.   **Elizabeth Ann Rauch, born 14 March 1958 in Baton Rouge, East Baton Rouge Parish, Louisiana.**

273. Francis Benoit[6] Waggenspack (Elmira Marie[5] Robért, Jean Paul[4], Mathieu[3], Jean[2], Mathieu[1]) was born 16 July 1918 in Modeste, Ascension Parish, Louisiana, and died 25 May 2004 in Darrow, Ascension Parish, Louisiana. He married **Marie Beatrice Schexnayder** 16 November 1957 in Darrow, Ascension Parish, Louisiana, daughter of Victor Schexnayder and Marie Ursuline Martinez. She was born 06 December 1934 in Darrow, Ascension Parish, Louisiana.

Child of Francis Waggenspack and Marie Schexnayder is:

+ 581   i.   **LaMarylis Ann[7] Waggenspack, born 13 September 1958 in Baton Rouge, Louisiana.**

274. Jeannette Marie[6] Waggenspack, (Non-e) (Elmira Marie[5] Robért,

Jean Paul[4], Mathieu[3], Jean[2], Mathieu[1]) was born 30 August 1920 in Modeste, Ascension Parish, Louisiana, and died 17 March 1994 in St. Gabriel, Iberville Parish, Louisiana. She married **Verney Etienne Becnel** 22 November 1945 in Ascension Parish, Darrow, Louisiana, son of Alcee Becnel and Nomie Friche. He was born 20 September 1913 in St. Gabriel, Louisiana, and died 02 July 1996 in St. Gabriel, Louisiana.

Children of Jeannette Waggenspack and Verney Becnel are:

+ 582   i.   **Marlene Marie[7] Becnel, born 04 September 1946.**
    583   ii.   **Randy Joseph Becnel,(infant), born 19 September 1949 in East Baton Rouge Parish, Baton Rouge, La.; died 19 September 1949 in East Baton Rouge Parish, Baton Rouge, La..**
+ 584   iii.   **Ronny John Becnel, born 24 November 1950 in East Baton Rouge Parish, Baton Rouge, La..**
    585   iv.   **Verney E. Becnel,Jr., born 07 December 1953 in East Baton Rouge Parish, Baton Rouge, La..**
    586   v.   **Matthew Becnel,(infant), born 14 February 1955 in East Baton Rouge Parish, Baton Rouge, La.; died 14 February 1955 in East Baton Rouge Parish, Baton Rouge, La..**
    587   vi.   **Michael Becnel,(infant), born 14 February 1955 in East Baton Rouge Parish, Baton Rouge, La.; died 14 February 1955 in East Baton Rouge Parish, Baton Rouge, La..**
+ 588   vii.   **Wade Benedict Becnel, born 30 October 1957 in East Baton Rouge Parish, Baton Rouge, La..**

277. Maude Marie[6] Robért (Joseph Olide[5], Jean Paul[4], Mathieu[3], Jean[2], Mathieu[1]) was born 19 March 1906 in St. Elmo Plantation, Darrow, Ascension Parish, Louisiana, and died 12 May 2001 in Donaldsonville, Ascension Parish, Louisiana. She married **Nicholas Dominic Milano** 05 July 1933 in Darrow, Ascension Parish, Louisiana, son of Frank Milano and Marie Varisni. He was born 31 October 1900 in Donaldsonville, Ascension Parish, Louisiana, and died 14 December 1977 in Donaldsonville, Ascension Parish, Louisiana.

Children of Maude Robért and Nicholas Milano are:

+ 589   i.   **Sybil Stanilaus[7] Milano, born 19 November 1935 in Donaldsonville, Ascension Parish, Louisiana.**
+ 590   ii.   **Paul Anthony Milano, born 17 December 1936 in Donaldsonville, Ascension Parish, Louisiana.**
+ 591   iii.   **Janice Ann Milano, born 09 November 1938 in Darrow, Ascension Parish, Louisiana; died 13 July 2007 in Thibodaux, Lafourche Parish, Louisiana.**
+ 592   iv.   **Myrna Marie Milano, born 02 July 1940 in Donaldsonville, Ascension Parish, Louisiana.**

279. Joseph Nemours[6] Robért, (Jo Jo) (Joseph Olide[5], Jean Paul[4], Mathieu[3], Jean[2], Mathieu[1]) was born 10 October 1908 in St. Elmo Plantation, Darrow, Ascension Parish, Louisiana, and died 29 August 1998 in Gonzales, Ascension Parish, Louisiana. He married **Annie Bellish, (Dinah)** 18 February 1938 in Sacred Heart Catholic Church, Baton Rouge, East Baton Rouge Parish, Louisiana, daughter of Steve Bellish and Ida Davis. She was born 15 November 1916 in Tunica, West Feliciana Parish, Louisiana.

Children of Joseph Robért and Annie Bellish are:

+ 593   i.   **Joe Anne[7] Robért, born 05 December 1938 in Donaldsonville, Ascension Parish, Louisiana.**
+ 594   ii.   **Fay Marie Robért, born 02 September 1941 in Donaldsonville, Ascension Parish, Louisiana.**
+ 595   iii.   **Frances Elizabeth Robért, born 27 December 1943 in Donaldsonville, Ascension Parish, Louisiana.**
+ 596   iv.   **Joseph Reginald Robért, (Reggie), born 28 January 1945 in Donaldsonville, Ascension Parish, Louisiana.**
+ 597   v.   **Terry Jude Robért, born 28 July 1948 in Gonzales, Ascension Parish, Louisiana.**

280. Lynn Jude[6] Robért, Sr. (Noon) (Joseph Olide[5], Jean Paul[4], Mathieu[3], Jean[2], Mathieu[1]) was born 21 February 1910 in St. Elmo Plantation, Darrow, Ascension Parish, Louisiana, and died 03 May 1966 in Gonzales, Ascension Parish, Louisiana. He married **Mildred Gautreau** 16 April 1958 in Gonzales, Ascension Parish, Louisiana, daughter of Henry Gautreau and Emma Bellish. She was born 05 March 1929 in New Orleans, Orleans Parish, Louisiana.

Child of Lynn Robért and Mildred Gautreau is:

+ 598   i.   **Lynn Jude[7] Robért, Jr., born 25 January 1959 in Baton Rouge, East Baton Rouge Parish, Louisiana.**

281. Felix John[6] Robért, (Benny) (Joseph Olide[5], Jean Paul[4], Mathieu[3], Jean[2], Mathieu[1]) was born 03 October 1912 in Remy, St. James Parish, Louisiana, and died 20 October 1986 in Donaldsonville, Ascension Parish, Louisiana. He married **Lurienne Rhoton** 17 December. She was born 1913, and died 1968.

Child of Felix Robért and Lurienne Rhoton is:

    599   i.   **Linda[7] Robért.**

282. Adele Ann[6] Robért (Joseph Olide[5], Jean Paul[4], Mathieu[3], Jean[2], Mathieu[1]) was born 22 October 1915 in Riverton Plantation, Burnside, Ascension

Parish, Louisiana, and died 12 August 1998 in New Orleans, Orleans Parish, Louisiana. She married **Stanley Robert Babin** 13 January 1941 in Ascension Parish, Darrow, Louisiana, son of Raliegh Babin and Bertha Landry. He was born 30 June 1909 in East St. Louis, Illinois, and died 13 March 1976 in New Orleans, Orleans Parish, Louisiana.

Children of Adele Robért and Stanley Babin are:

+ 600   i.   **Lynne Mary[7] Babin, born 19 September 1942 in New Orleans, Orleans Parish, Louisiana; died 24 August 1999 in New Orleans, Orleans Parish, Louisiana.**
+ 601   ii.   **Stanley Joseph Babin, born 25 August 1944 in New Orleans, Orleans Parish, Louisiana.**
+ 602   iii.   **Kenneth Anthony Babin, born 09 December 1946 in New Orleans, Orleans Parish, Louisiana.**
+ 603   iv.   **Leslie Ann Babin, born 03 February 1948 in New Orleans, Orleans Parish, Louisiana.**
+ 604   v.   **Barbara Elizabeth Babin, born 04 August 1951 in Marrero, Jefferson Parish, Louisiana.**

285. Dorothy Elizabeth[6] Robért, (Fat) (Joseph Olide[5], Jean Paul[4], Mathieu[3], Jean[2], Mathieu[1]) was born 01 October 1919 in St. Elmo Plantation, Darrow, Ascension Parish, Louisiana, and died 26 August 1987 in Gonzales, Ascension Parish, Louisiana. She married **Lester Robért** 07 August 1946 in Darrow, Ascension Parish, Louisiana, son of Wallace Robért and Zelia Hymel. He was born 19 April 1921 in Donaldsonville, Ascension Parish, Louisiana, and died 2001 in Gonzales, Ascension Parish, Louisiana.

Children are listed above under (207) Lester Robért.

287. Louis Joseph[6] Rome, Jr. (Leona Theresa[5] Robért, (Na-Na), Jean Paul[4], Mathieu[3], Jean[2], Mathieu[1]) was born 14 October 1910 in Hermitage Plantation, Darrow, Ascension Parish, Louisiana, and died 29 September 2009 in Baton Rouge, East Baton Rouge Parish, Louisiana. He married **Annabel Mary Dugas** 26 December 1934 in Donaldsonville, Ascension Parish, Louisiana, daughter of Henry Dugas and Loretta Montecino. She was born 09 October 1912 in Smoke Bend, Ascension Parish, Louisiana, and died 14 December 1994 in Baton Rouge, East Baton Rouge Parish, Louisiana.

Children of Louis Rome and Annabel Dugas are:

+ 605   i.   **Robert Louis[7] Rome, born 08 March 1936 in Donaldsonville, Ascension Parish, Louisiana.**
+ 606   ii.   **Ronald Richard Rome, born 08 March 1936 in Donaldsonville, Ascension Parish, Louisiana.**
+ 607   iii.   **Judith Anne Rome, born 22 April 1938 in Donaldsonville, Ascension Parish, Louisiana.**

+   608   iv.   **Eleanor Loretta Rome, born 06 September 1940 in Donaldsonville, Ascension Parish, Louisiana.**

288. John Augustin[6] Rome, Sr. (Gus) (Leona Theresa[5] Robért, (Na-Na), Jean Paul[4], Mathieu[3], Jean[2], Mathieu[1]) was born 14 December 1911 in Donaldsonville, Ascension Parish, Louisiana, and died 05 August 1992 in Baton Rouge, East Baton Rouge Parish, Louisiana. He married **Signa M. Gonzales, (Patsy)** 23 September 1946 in Baton Rouge, East Baton Rouge Parish, Louisiana. She was born 22 September 1915 in Baton Rouge, East Baton Rouge Parish, Louisiana, and died 27 March 1998 in Baton Rouge, East Baton Rouge Parish, Louisiana.

Children of John Rome and Signa Gonzales are:

     609   i.   **John Augustin[7] Rome, Jr., born 03 February 1949. He married Laura Nell Glynn 10 October 1981.**
+   610   ii. **Signa Mathieu Rome, born 04 December 1952 in Baton Rouge, East Baton Rouge Parish, Louisiana.**

289. Paul Robert[6] Rome (Leona Theresa[5] Robért, (Na-Na), Jean Paul[4], Mathieu[3], Jean[2], Mathieu[1]) was born 14 December 1911 in Donaldsonville, Ascension Parish, Louisiana, and died 08 May 2000 in Destrehan, St. Charles Parish, Louisiana. He married **Loretta Cecile Dugas** 18 September 1935 in Donaldsonville, Ascension Parish, Louisiana, daughter of Henry Dugas and Loretta Montecino. She was born 06 March 1914 in Smoke Bend, Ascension Parish, Louisiana, and died 19 May 1987 in La Place, St. John the Baptist Parish, Louisiana.

Children of Paul Rome and Loretta Dugas are:

+   611   i.   **Suzanne P.[7] Rome, born 25 March 1938 in Donaldsonville, Ascension Parish, Louisiana.**
+   612   ii.   **Alice Marie Rome, born 08 June 1941 in Donaldsonville, Ascension Parish, Louisiana.**
+   613   iii. **Eileen Mary Rome, born 16 February 1944 in New Orleans, Orleans Parish, Louisiana.**
+   614   iv.   **John Paul Rome, Sr., born 16 January 1946 in New Orleans, Orleans Parish, Louisiana.**
+   615   v.   **Michael H. Rome, born 18 July 1952 in New Orleans, Orleans Parish, Louisiana.**

290. O'Neil Francis[6] Rome (Leona Theresa[5] Robért, (Na-Na), Jean Paul[4], Mathieu[3], Jean[2], Mathieu[1]) was born 14 June 1913 in Donaldsonville, Ascension Parish, Louisiana, and died 03 September 2000 in Baton Rouge, East Baton Rouge Parish, Louisiana. He married **Annie Day LeBlanc** 06 November 1939 in

Donaldsonville, Ascension Parish, Louisiana, daughter of Waldon LeBlanc and Annie Parenton. She was born 09 November 1915 in Donaldsonville, Ascension Parish, Louisiana, and died 09 December 2000 in Baton Rouge, East Baton Rouge Parish, Louisiana.

Children of O'Neil Rome and Annie LeBlanc are:

+ 616   i.   **O'Neil Francis[7] Rome,Jr., born 27 July 1941 in Baton Rouge, East Baton Rouge Parish, Louisiana.**
+ 617   ii.   **Elizabeth Day Rome, born 27 November 1943 in Donaldsonville, Ascension Parish, Louisiana.**
   618   iii.   **Richard Charles Rome, born 14 November 1945 in Donaldsonville, Ascension Parish, Louisiana.**

292. Lillian Theresa[6] Rome (Leona Theresa[5] Robért, (Na-Na), Jean Paul[4], Mathieu[3], Jean[2], Mathieu[1]) was born 27 August 1916 in Burnside, Ascension Parish, Louisiana, and died 25 August 2009 in Baton Rouge, East Baton Rouge Parish, Louisiana. She married **Robert Courtland Blanchard, Sr.** 10 September 1940 in Donaldsonville, Ascension Parish, Louisiana, son of Joseph Blanchard and Edith Beatty. He was born 10 September 1915 in Donaldsonville, Ascension Parish, Louisiana, and died 30 July 2001 in Donaldsonville, Ascension Parish, Louisiana.

Children of Lillian Rome and Robert Blanchard are:

+ 619   i.   **Robert Courtland[7] Blanchard, Jr., born 28 December 1941 in Donaldsonville, Ascension Parish, Louisiana.**
+ 620   ii.   **Lillian Theresa Blanchard, born 20 July 1944 in Donaldsonville, Ascension Parish, Louisiana.**
+ 621   iii.   **Madeline Marie Blanchard, born 31 March 1947 in Donaldsonville, Ascension Parish, Louisiana.**

293. Ike Antoine[6] Rome (Leona Theresa[5] Robért, (Na-Na), Jean Paul[4], Mathieu[3], Jean[2], Mathieu[1]) was born 01 December 1917 in Burnside, Ascension Parish, Louisiana, and died 13 May 1995 in Baton Rouge, East Baton Rouge Parish, Louisiana. He married **Ruby Oschwald** 25 November 1940 in Donaldsonville, Ascension Parish, Louisiana, daughter of Charles Oschwald and Annette Dugas. She was born 04 October 1921 in Donaldsonville, Ascension Parish, Louisiana, and died 25 May 1986 in Baton Rouge, East Baton Rouge Parish, Louisiana.

Children of Ike Rome and Ruby Oschwald are:

+ 622   i.   **Kathy[7] Rome, born 25 May 1942 in Donaldsonville, Ascension Parish, Louisiana.**
   623   ii.   **Donovan Rome, born 11 September 1949 in Baton Rouge, East Baton Rouge Parish, Louisiana. He married Sue Stephens; born**

294. Charles David[6] Rome, (C.D.) (Leona Theresa[5] Robért, (Na-Na), Jean Paul[4], Mathieu[3], Jean[2], Mathieu[1]) was born 14 March 1919 in Donaldsonville, Ascension Parish, Louisiana, and died 21 November 1971 in Baton Rouge, East Baton Rouge Parish, Louisiana. He married **Alice May Naquin** 05 July 1942 in Donaldsonville, Ascension Parish, Louisiana, daughter of Villier Naquin and Bessie Hebert. She was born 09 August 1920 in Donaldsonville, Ascension Parish, Louisiana, and died 23 August 1999 in Houston, Texas.

Children of Charles Rome and Alice Naquin are:

+ 624   i.   **Cynthia[7] Rome, born 30 January 1944.**
+ 625   ii. **Carolyn Rome, born 30 August 1949.**

295. Donald Joseph[6] Rome, (Jug Head) (Leona Theresa[5] Robért, (Na-Na), Jean Paul[4], Mathieu[3], Jean[2], Mathieu[1]) was born 08 February 1924 in Donaldsonville, Ascension Parish, Louisiana, and died 30 November 2003 in Gulf Shores, Alabama. He married **Melba L. Dunham** 15 January 1959. She was born 23 April 1934.

Children of Donald Rome and Melba Dunham are:

+ 626   i.   **Christopher Paul[7] Rome, born 26 November 1959 in Lake Charles, Calcasieu Parish, Louisiana.**
+ 627   ii. **Teresa Ann Rome, born 30 December 1960 in Lake Charles, Calcasieu Parish, Louisiana.**
+ 628   iii. **Joy Elizabeth Rome, born 08 July 1962 in Lake Charles, Calcasieu Parish, Louisiana.**
  629   iv. **Edith Reneè Rome, born 24 October 1963 in Lake Charles, Calcasieu Parish, Louisiana.**
  630   v. **Gregory Allen Rome, born 01 June 1966 in Luling, St. Charles Parish, Louisiana.**

296. James Joseph[6] Robért, Sr. (Raoul Matthew[5], Jean Paul[4], Mathieu[3], Jean[2], Mathieu[1]) was born 09 October 1918 in Burnside, Ascension Parish, Louisiana, and died 11 January 1981 in Rapides Parish, Alexandria, Louisiana. He married **Mary Jewell Taylor** 14 March 1940, daughter of William Taylor and Mary Laplace. She was born 09 September 1921 in Port Gibson, Mississippi, and died 25 January 1992 in St. Landry Parish, Opelousas, Louisiana.

Children of James Robért and Mary Taylor are:

+ 631   i.   **James Joseph[7] Robért, Jr. Dr., born 02 January 1941 in Union, St. James Parish, Louisiana.**

+	632	ii.	Raoul William Robért, Sr., born 24 August 1942 in Donaldsonville, Ascension Parish, Louisiana.
+	633	iii.	Mary Bobbye Robért, born 14 December 1943 in New Roads, Pointe Coupee Parish, Louisiana.
	634	iv.	John Taylor Robért, born 13 June 1945 in Donaldsonville, Ascension Parish, Louisiana.
	635	v.	Jeffery Paul Robért, born 17 September 1956 in Opelousas, St. Landry Parish, Louisiana. He married Mary Frances Woods Wheat 23 April 1983.

297. Amalie Marie[6] **Robért, (Toot)** (Raoul Matthew[5], Jean Paul[4], Mathieu[3], Jean[2], Mathieu[1]) was born 16 August 1924 in Burnside, Ascension Parish, Louisiana. She married **Anthony Mumphrey** 23 April 1948 in Ascension Parish, Darrow, Louisiana, son of Joseph Mumphrey and Lena Yenni. He was born 09 October 1921 in St. Charles Parish, St. Rose, Louisiana.

Children of Amalie Robért and Anthony Mumphrey are:

	636	i.	Linda Marie[7] Mumphrey, born 18 February 1949.
	637	ii.	Peggy Jane Mumphrey, born 19 March 1950. She married David Gregg Broussard Unknown.
+	638	iii.	Joseph Scott Mumphrey, born 19 December 1951.
+	639	iv.	Robbie Anne Mumphrey, born 08 October 1953.
	640	v.	Ray Anthony Mumphrey, born 23 April 1957. He married Verna Louise Dupre' 20 December 1978.
	641	vi.	Terri Gerilyn Mumphrey, born 08 September 1960. She married Gerald Anthony Fuselier 15 April 1983.
	642	vii.	Michael Louis Mumphrey, born 28 June 1962. He married Kaprice Ann Miller 06 August 1983; born 26 April 1964.
	643	viii.	Robért Neil Mumphrey, born 19 September 1969 in Eunice, Louisiana.

301. Hulin Joseph[6] **Robért** (Remy Paul[5], Jean Paul[4], Mathieu[3], Jean[2], Mathieu[1]) was born 26 December 1923 in Donaldson Tract Plantation, Burnside, Ascension Parish, Louisiana. He married **Elizabeth Adele Stewart** 16 May 1953 in Our Lady of Lourdes Catholic Church, New Orleans, Orleans Parish, Louisiana, daughter of Seymour Stewart and Marie DeJohn. She was born 10 January 1930.

Children of Hulin Robért and Elizabeth Stewart are:

+	644	i.	Robin Andrea[7] Robért, born 06 March 1954 in New Orleans, Orleans Parish, Louisiana.
+	645	ii.	David Bernard Robért, born 08 April 1955 in New Orleans, Orleans Parish, Louisiana.
+	646	iii.	Nancy Claire Robért, born 12 March 1956 in New Orleans, Orleans Parish, Louisiana.

647	iv.	Philip Stewart Robért, born 24 November 1961 in Hammond,Tangipahoa Parish, Louisiana.
648	v.	Michael Emile Robért, (lived only 16 hours), born 16 February 1963 in Hammond,Tangipahoa Parish, Louisiana; died 16 February 1963 in New Orleans, Orleans Parish, Louisiana.
649	vi.	Martha Marie Robért, born 01 June 1964 in Hammond,Tangipahoa Parish, Louisiana.
+ 650	vii.	Nolan Jacques Robért, born 07 March 1966 in Hammond,Tangipahoa Parish, Louisiana.
+ 651	viii.	Remy Pierre Robért, born 08 September 1967 in Hammond, Tangipahoa Parish, Louisiana.

302. Cecil Paul[6] Robért, Sr (Remy Paul[5], Jean Paul[4], Mathieu[3], Jean[2], Mathieu[1]) was born 31 October 1925 in Burnside, Ascension Parish, Louisiana, and died 17 February 1976 in Baton Rouge, East Baton Rouge Parish, Louisiana. He married **Betty Ann LeBlanc** 11 August 1952 in Ascension Catholic Church, Donaldsonville, Louisiana, daughter of Waldon LeBlanc and Melanie Faucheux. She was born 17 February 1934 in Donaldsonville, Ascension Parish, Louisiana.

Children of Cecil Robért and Betty LeBlanc are:

+ 652	i.	Cecil Paul[7] Robért, Jr., born 13 August 1954 in Donaldsonville, Ascension Parish, Louisiana.
653	ii.	Mary Catherine Robért, born 07 August 1957 in Donaldsonville, Ascension Parish, Louisiana.
654	iii.	Jane Ann Marie Robért, born 13 January 1960 in Donaldsonville, Ascension Parish, Louisiana.
+ 655	iv.	Waldon Charles Robért, born 30 December 1961 in Donaldsonville, Ascension Parish, Louisiana.
+ 656	v.	Penny Elizabeth Robért, born 25 March 1963 in Donaldsonville, Ascension Parish, Louisiana.
657	vi.	Jeffrey Joseph Robért, born 30 December 1964 in Donaldsonville, Ascension Parish, Louisiana. He married Charlene Ann Burch 21 March 1992 in Country Club, Baton Rouge, Louisiana; born 08 August 1957 in Bogalusa, Washington Parish, Louisiana.
+ 658	vii.	Natalie Marie Robért, born 09 November 1967 in Donaldsonville, Ascension Parish, Louisiana.

303. Glenn Jacque[6] Robért (Remy Paul[5], Jean Paul[4], Mathieu[3], Jean[2], Mathieu[1]) was born 23 June 1927 in Donaldson Tract Plantation, Burnside, Ascension Parish, Louisiana. He married **Lena Gloria Mistretta** 09 June 1949 in Donaldsonville, Ascension Parish, Louisiana. She was born 23 June 1929 in Ascension Parish, Donaldsonville , Louisiana.

Children of Glenn Robért and Lena Mistretta are:

+ 659 i. Alan Joseph[7] Robért, born 03 November 1950 in Ascension Parish, Donaldsonville, Louisiana.
+ 660 ii. Glenna Marie Robért, born 28 June 1954 in Ascension Parish, Donaldsonville, Louisiana.
  661 iii. Roy Michael Robért, born 13 March 1957 in Ascension Parish, Donaldsonville, Louisiana. He married Laurie Shrider 15 February 1992 in Savanna, Ga..
  662 iv. Randal James Robért, born 30 January 1962 in Ascension Parish, Donaldsonville, Louisiana. He married Jane Gonzales 12 January 1991 in St. Amant, Ascension Parish, Louisiana.

304. Mary Lois[6] Robért (Remy Paul[5], Jean Paul[4], Mathieu[3], Jean[2], Mathieu[1]) was born 20 August 1929 in Donaldson Tract Plantation, Burnside, Ascension Parish, Louisiana. She married **Mervin J. Simoneaux** 27 October 1948 in Ascension Parish, Darrow, Louisiana, son of Milton Simoneaux and Louise Landry. He was born 17 October 1924 in Ascension Parish, Donaldsonville, Louisiana.

Children of Mary Robért and Mervin Simoneaux are:
+ 663 i. Robert Lynn[7] Simoneaux, born 23 August 1949 in Ascension Parish, Donaldsonville, Louisiana.
+ 664 ii. Bruce James Simoneaux, born 26 February 1951 in Ascension Parish, Donaldsonville, Louisiana.
+ 665 iii. Jill Elaine Simoneaux, born 07 September 1954 in Baton Rouge, East Baton Rouge Parish, Louisiana.
  666 iv. Brian Alvin Simoneaux, born 12 April 1956 in Baton Rouge, East Baton Rouge Parish, Louisiana. He married Janet Muller 28 January 1984.
+ 667 v. Guy Remy Simoneaux, born 13 January 1958 in Baton Rouge, East Baton Rouge Parish, Louisiana.
  668 vi. Wade Michael Simoneaux, born 03 August 1960 in Baton Rouge, East Baton Rouge Parish, Louisiana. He married Bridget Lisa Landry 10 July 1987; born 13 March 1964.

306. Shelby Lawrence[6] Robért (Remy Paul[5], Jean Paul[4], Mathieu[3], Jean[2], Mathieu[1]) was born 28 September 1934 in Burnside, Ascension Parish, Louisiana. He married **Betty Carole Cicero** 05 September 1959, daughter of Samuel Cicero and Beulah Soulier.

Children of Shelby Robért and Betty Cicero are:
+ 669 i. Shelly Lauren[7] Robért, born 17 January 1961 in Baton Rouge, East Baton Rouge Parish, Louisiana.
+ 670 ii. Todd Justin Robért, born 13 August 1962 in Baton Rouge, East Baton Rouge Parish, Louisiana.

+ 671   iii.   **Boyd Houston Joseph Robért, born 24 September 1963 in Baton Rouge, East Baton Rouge Parish, Louisiana.**

+ 672   iv.   **Barry Steele Robért, born 24 September 1963 in Baton Rouge, East Baton Rouge Parish, Louisiana.**

308. Matthew Joseph[6] Robért (Octave Pierre[5], Jean Paul[4], Mathieu[3], Jean[2], Mathieu[1]) was born 05 August 1926 in Donaldson Tract Plantation, Burnside, Ascension Parish, Louisiana, and died 01 December 2001 in El Paso County, Colorado Springs, Colorado. He married **Dorothea Henrietta LaTorre** 16 December 1952 in Ascension Parish, Darrow, Louisiana, daughter of Harry LaTorre and Adeline Oelkers. She was born Unknown in Charleston, South Carolina.

Children of Matthew Robért and Dorothea LaTorre are:

673   i.   **Mark Eugene[7] Robért, born 03 January 1955 in Birkenfeld, Germany. He met Laura Lynne Ahlander March 1996 in Pasadena, California; born 15 November 1957 in Modesto, California.**

674   ii.   **Dru Marie Robért, born 01 May 1956 in Landstuhl, West Germany. She married (1) David Joseph Solomon 28 October 1985; born Unknown. She married (2) Leopold Michael Ablicki 09 October 1999; born 28 January 1950 in Holyoke, Massachusetts.**

675   iii.   **Douglas Joseph Robért, born 25 July 1957 in Houma, Terrebonne Parish, Louisiana.**

+ 676   iv.   **Juliette Anne Robért, born 13 March 1959 in Montgomery, Alabama.**

+ 677   v.   **Charles Herbert Robért, born 27 July 1960 in Montgomery, Alabama.**

309. Robert Francis[6] Robért (Octave Pierre[5], Jean Paul[4], Mathieu[3], Jean[2], Mathieu[1]) was born 14 June 1928 in Donaldson Tract Plantation, Burnside, Ascension Parish, Louisiana. He married **Winnnie Mae Veillon** 10 January 1959 in St. Anne Church, Mamou, Evangeline Parish, Louisiana, daughter of Tanzy Veillon and Lovella Isreal. She was born 17 July 1936 in Reddell, Evangeline Parish, Louisiana.

Children of Robert Robért and Winnnie Veillon are:

+ 678   i.   **Marcie Ann[7] Robért, born 23 August 1960 in Baton Rouge, East Baton Rouge Parish, Louisiana.**

+ 679   ii.   **Donna Marie Robért, born 26 March 1962 in Baton Rouge, East Baton Rouge Parish, Louisiana.**

+ 680   iii.   **Gregory Michael Robért, born 18 June 1963 in Baton Rouge, East Baton Rouge Parish, Louisiana.**

+ 681   iv.   **Gary Jerome Robért, born 20 May 1965 in Baton Rouge, East Baton Rouge Parish, Louisiana.**

+ 682   v.   **Anthony Luke Robért, born 15 February 1970 in Baton Rouge, East Baton Rouge Parish, Louisiana.**

310. Paul Gerard[6] Robért (Octave Pierre[5], Jean Paul[4], Mathieu[3], Jean[2], Mathieu[1]) was born 08 October 1930 in Donaldson Tract Plantation, Burnside, Ascension Parish, Louisiana, and died 16 October 1983 in Mamou, Evangeline Parish, Louisiana. He married **Ouida Nell LaHaye** 29 August 1959 in Mamou, Evangeline Parish, Louisiana, daughter of J. LaHaye and Thelma Guillory. She was born 23 November 1937 in Mamou, Evangeline Parish, Louisiana.

Child of Paul Robért and Ouida LaHaye is:

+ 683   i.   **Marie Ouida[7] Robért, born 25 June 1960 in Lafayette, Lafayette Parish, Louisiana.**

312. John Marius[6] Robért, Sr. (Octave Pierre[5], Jean Paul[4], Mathieu[3], Jean[2], Mathieu[1]) was born 13 January 1935 in Donaldson Tract Plantation, Burnside, Ascension Parish, Louisiana. He married **Priscilla Lane Shows** 19 November 1960 in St. Isidore Catholic Church, Baker, East Baton Rouge Parish, Louisiana, daughter of Auber Shows and Maud Brashear. She was born 21 September 1939 in Baton Rouge, East Baton Rouge Parish, Louisiana.

Children of John Robért and Priscilla Shows are:

+ 684   i.   **John Marius[7] Robért, Jr., born 31 August 1961 in Baton Rouge, East Baton Rouge Parish, Louisiana.**
+ 685   ii.   **Dana Elizabeth Robért, born 19 February 1963 in Baton Rouge, East Baton Rouge Parish, Louisiana.**
+ 686   iii.   **Christopher James Robért, Sr., born 21 September 1964 in Baton Rouge, East Baton Rouge Parish, Louisiana.**
   687   iv.   **Michael Octave Robért, born 31 October 1967 in Baton Rouge, East Baton Rouge Parish, Louisiana.**
+ 688   v.   **Rebecca Ann Robért, born 21 August 1971 in Baton Rouge, East Baton Rouge Parish, Louisiana.**
+ 689   vi.   **Jennifer Marie Robért, born 22 April 1974 in Baton Rouge, East Baton Rouge Parish, Louisiana.**
+ 690   vii.   **Matthew Paul Robért, born 24 May 1977 in Baton Rouge, East Baton Rouge Parish, Louisiana.**
   691   viii.   **Rachel Maria Robért, born 15 July 1983 in Baton Rouge, East Baton Rouge Parish, Louisiana.**

313. Carolyn Teresa[6] Robért, (Ceyon) (Octave Pierre[5], Jean Paul[4], Mathieu[3], Jean[2], Mathieu[1]) was born 13 March 1937 in Donaldson Tract Plantation, Burnside, Ascension Parish, Louisiana. She married **Dr. Carol Burton McCauley, M.D.** 01 August 1959 in St. Anthony Catholic Church, Darrow,

Louisiana, son of Nealy McCauley and Agnes Vidrine. He was born 14 October 1934 in Ville Platte, Evangeline Parish, Louisiana.

Children of Carolyn Robért and Carol McCauley are:

+ 692   i.   **Sharon Elizabeth[7] McCauley, born 12 June 1960 in Shreveport, Caddo Parish, Louisiana.**

+ 693   ii.   **Bryan Edward McCauley, born 25 December 1961 in Ville Platte, Evangeline Parish, Louisiana.**

    694   iii.   **Catherine McCauley, born 26 December 1964 in Richmond, Virginia. She married Raymond Leonard Voskamp III 04 July 2004 in Colleyville, Texas; born 07 June 1959 in Kansas City, Kansas.**

314. Genevieve Martha[6] Robért (Octave Pierre[5], Jean Paul[4], Mathieu[3], Jean[2], Mathieu[1]) was born 28 December 1940 in Peytavin Plantation, Donaldsonville, Ascension Parish, Louisiana. She married **Clarence Auguste Landry, (Gus)** 03 March 1962 in St. Anthony Catholic Chapel, Darrow, Louisiana, son of Emile Landry and Laure Dugas. He was born 28 October 1939 in Golden Meadow, Lafourche Parish, Louisiana.

Children of Genevieve Robért and Clarence Landry are:

    695   i.   **Amy Ruth[7] Landry, born 14 March 1963 in Baton Rouge, East Baton Rouge Parish, Louisiana; died 18 August 1975 in Baton Rouge, East Baton Rouge Parish, Louisiana.**

    696   ii.   **Duane Joseph Landry, born 19 September 1964 in Baton Rouge, East Baton Rouge Parish, Louisiana; died 18 December 1996 in Donaldsonville, Ascension Parish, Louisiana.**

+ 697   iii.   **Brent David Landry, born 16 November 1967 in Baton Rouge, East Baton Rouge Parish, Louisiana.**

+ 698   iv.   **Pierre Auguste Landry, born 22 April 1969 in Baton Rouge, East Baton Rouge Parish, Louisiana.**

+ 699   v.   **Jeanne Marie Landry, born 15 September 1972 in Baton Rouge, East Baton Rouge Parish, Louisiana.**

315. Marie Noelle[6] Robért (Octave Pierre[5], Jean Paul[4], Mathieu[3], Jean[2], Mathieu[1]) was born 28 December 1941 in Peytavin Plantation, Donaldsonville, Ascension Parish, Louisiana. She married **Cleo Joseph Hebert, Jr.** 01 December 1962 in Darrow, Ascension Parish, Louisiana, son of Cleo Hebert and Marie Milano. He was born 02 September 1938 in Donaldsonville, Ascension Parish, Louisiana, and died 21 September 2002 in Donaldsonville, Ascension Parish, Louisiana.

Children of Marie Robért and Cleo Hebert are:

+ 700   i.   **Dean Gregory[7] Hebert, born 21 December 1967 in Baton Rouge, East Baton Rouge Parish, Louisiana.**

| 701 | ii. | Jeffery Paul Hebert, born 01 April 1970 in Baton Rouge, East Baton Rouge Parish, Louisiana. |
| + 702 | iii. | Cliff Michael Hebert, born 15 September 1971 in Baton Rouge, East Baton Rouge Parish, Louisiana. |

316. Peter Octave[6] Robért (Octave Pierre[5], Jean Paul[4], Mathieu[3], Jean[2], Mathieu[1]) was born 30 December 1944 in Petyavin Plantation, Donaldsonville, Ascension Parish, Louisiana. He married **(1) Marcia Matranga, (Divorced)** 25 May 1968 in Christ the King Chapel, LSU, Baton Rouge, Louisiana, daughter of Joseph Matranga and Mildred Davis. She was born 15 August 1946 in New Orleans, Orleans Parish, Louisiana. He married **(2) Constance Lorraine Seymour** 06 May 1978 in Gonzales, Ascension Parish, Louisiana, daughter of Edward Seymour and Jamie Parker. She was born 21 August 1946 in Vicksburg, Mississippi.

Child of Peter Robért and Marcia Matranga is:

| + 703 | i. | Jean-Paul Josef[7] Robért, Sr., born 13 December 1968 in Huntsville, Alabama. |

Children of Peter Robért and Constance Seymour are:

704	i.	Victor Edward[7] Dardin, (adopted), born 04 October 1967 in Dalton, Georgia. He married Jennifer Buss 08 February 2003 in Blanche, Tennessee.
+ 705	ii.	Dana Shea Dardin, (adopted), born 30 November 1974 in Tallahassee, Florida.
+ 706	iii.	Sarah Elizabeth Robért, born 16 January 1980 in Huntsville, Alabama.
707	iv.	Erin Ruth Robért, born 23 March 1982 in Huntsville, Alabama. She married Matthew Alan Kahanic 09 September 2005 in Huntsville, Alabama; born 04 April 1980 in Buffalo, New York.
708	v.	Ashley Marie Robért, born 19 July 1984 in Huntsville, Alabama.
709	vi.	Catherine Ann Robért, born 26 October 1987 in Huntsville, Alabama.

319. Carl James[6] Robért, (Hubble) (Rene Benoit[5], Jean Paul[4], Mathieu[3], Jean[2], Mathieu[1]) was born 31 January 1929 in Donaldson Tract Plantation, Burnside, Ascension Parish, Louisiana. He married **George Ann Waguespack** 12 February 1953 in St. Anthony Catholic Church, Darrow, Louisiana, daughter of George Waguespack and Pauline Waggenspack. She was born 19 May 1932 in Burnside, Ascension Parish, Louisiana.

Children of Carl Robert and George Ann Waguespack are:

| + 710 | i. | Renée Geralyn[7] Robért, born 24 March 1954 in Gonzales, |

69

Ascension Parish, Louisiana.

+ 711 ii. **Mitzi Marie Robért, born 21 May 1955 in Gonzales, Ascension Parish, Louisiana.**

+ 712 iii. **Mona Ann Robért, born 07 November 1956 in Gonzales, Ascension Parish, Louisiana.**

+ 713 iv. **Jaime Terése Robért, born 10 November 1958 in Gonzales, Ascension Parish, Louisiana.**

+ 714 v. **Danny Gerard Robért, born 14 February 1962 in Baton Rouge, East Baton Rouge Parish, Louisiana.**

+ 715 vi. **Suzanne Marie Robért, born 16 June 1964 in Baton Rouge, East Baton Rouge Parish, Louisiana.**

320. Norman Anthony[6] Robért (Rene Benoit[5], Jean Paul[4], Mathieu[3], Jean[2], Mathieu[1]) was born 04 October 1931 in Clark Plantation, Burnside, Ascension Parish, Louisiana. He married **Beryl Jane Ducote** 01 February 1964 in St. Mary Catholic Church, Cottonport, Louisiana, daughter of Joseph Ducote and Viola McDonald. She was born 07 November 1933 in Cottonport, Avoyelles Parish, Louisiana.

Children of Norman Robért and Beryl Ducote are:

716 i. **Lane Anthony[7] Robért, born 15 March 1965 in Baton Rouge, East Baton Rouge Parish, Louisiana.**

717 ii. **Jeffery Paul Robért, born 04 September 1966 in Baton Rouge, East Baton Rouge Parish, Louisiana.**

321. Roland James[6] Robért, Jr. (Row) (Roland Jacques[5], Jean Paul[4], Mathieu[3], Jean[2], Mathieu[1]) was born 17 September 1937 in Baton Rouge, East Baton Rouge Parish, Louisiana. He married **Catherine Louisa Hoover** 05 November 1960 in St. Stephens Catholic Church, New Orleans, Orleans Parish, Louisiana. She was born 23 August 1941 in Orleans Parish, New Orleans, Orleans Parish, Louisiana.

Children of Roland Robért and Catherine Hoover are:

+ 718 i. **Roland James[7] Robért III, born 23 October 1961 in Baton Rouge, East Baton Rouge Parish, Louisiana.**

+ 719 ii. **Michael Joseph Robért, Sr., born 25 September 1962 in Baton Rouge, East Baton Rouge Parish, Louisiana.**

+ 720 iii. **Adam Paul Robért, Sr., born 02 January 1964 in Baton Rouge, East Baton Rouge Parish, Louisiana.**

+ 721 iv. **Thomas Jude Robért, born 29 January 1966 in Baton Rouge, East Baton Rouge Parish, Louisiana.**

+ 722 v. **Larry Denis Robért, Sr., born 14 November 1968.**

322. Gayle Patrick⁶ Robért (Roland Jacques⁵, Jean Paul⁴, Mathieu³, Jean², Mathieu¹) was born 06 September 1938 in Donaldsonville, Ascension Parish, Louisiana. He married **(1) Myrna Marie Melancon** 21 January 1961 in St. Theresa Catholic Church, Gonzales, Louisiana, daughter of Dawson Melancon and Odile Delatte. She was born 28 February 1939 in Livingston Parish, Louisiana, and died 19 June 1979 in Houston, Texas (Buried in Gonzales, Louisiana). He married **(2) Jeannie Arlene Sanders** 09 August 1980 in Gonzales, Ascension Parish, Louisiana, daughter of Jack Sanders and Isla Courtney. She was born 20 November 1950 in La Salle Parish, Olla, Louisiana.

Children of Gayle Robért and Myrna Melancon are:
   723   i.   **Chad Patrick⁷ Robért, born 14 October 1961 in Baton Rouge, East Baton Rouge Parish, Louisiana.**
   724   ii. **Kevin Paul Robért, born 26 September 1962 in Baton Rouge, East Baton Rouge Parish, Louisiana.**
 + 725   iii. **Kandis Ann Robért, born 26 September 1962 in Baton Rouge, East Baton Rouge Parish, Louisiana.**
 + 726   iv. **Gina Monique Robért, born 22 October 1964 in Baton Rouge, East Baton Rouge Parish, Louisiana.**
   727   v.   **Bridget Marie Robért, born 18 July 1967 in Baton Rouge, East Baton Rouge Parish, Louisiana.**

Children of Gayle Robért and Jeannie Sanders are:
   728   i.   **Courtney Blake⁷ Robért, born 17 August 1981 in Baton Rouge, East Baton Rouge Parish, Louisiana.**
   729   ii. **Jake Vincent Robért, born 21 December 1987 in Baton Rouge, East Baton Rouge Parish, Louisiana.**

323. Harry Paul⁶ Robért, Sr. (Roland Jacques⁵, Jean Paul⁴, Mathieu³, Jean², Mathieu¹) was born 25 January 1941 in Donaldsonville, Ascension Parish, Louisiana. He married **Jeanne Marie Morris** 13 September 1976 in Woodville, Mississippi, daughter of David Morris and Vina Gaspard. She was born 16 October 1946 in Brooklyn, New York.

Children of Harry Robért and Jeanne Morris are:
   730   i.   **Harry Paul⁷ Robért, Jr., born 26 May 1977 in Baton Rouge, East Baton Rouge Parish, Louisiana.**
   731   ii. **Taylor Morris Robért, born 25 October 1978 in Baton Rouge, East Baton Rouge Parish, Louisiana.**
   732   iii. **Wesley David Robért, born 25 August 1981 in Baton Rouge, East Baton Rouge Parish, Louisiana.**

324. Val Ann⁶ Robért (Roland Jacques⁵, Jean Paul⁴, Mathieu³, Jean²,

Mathieu[1]) was born 20 March 1942 in Donaldsonville, Ascension Parish, Louisiana. She married **(1) Ray E. Holder**.   She met **(2) Woodson Harvey,Jr.** 09 June 1962 in St. Anthony Catholic Chapel, Darrow, Louisiana, son of Woodson Harvey and Eula De Rouen. He was born 28 February 1941.

Children of Val Ann Robért and Woodson Harvey are:
+ 733   i.   **Woodson[7] Harvey III, born 20 March 1963 in Baton Rouge, East Baton Rouge Parish, Louisiana.**
+ 734   ii.   **Robert Doyle Harvey, born 25 February 1964 in Baton Rouge, East Baton Rouge Parish, Louisiana.**
+ 735   iii. **Wynn Traylor Harvey, born 18 July 1966 in Houston, Texas.**
+ 736   iv.   **Valerie Ann Harvey, born 16 September 1968 in Opelousas, St. Landry Parish, Louisiana.**
+ 737   v.   **George Brian Harvey, born 17 August 1970 in Opelousas, St. Landry Parish, Louisiana.**

325. Alvin Joseph[6] Robért, Sr. (Al) (Roland Jacques[5], Jean Paul[4], Mathieu[3], Jean[2], Mathieu[1]) was born 10 May 1946 in Baton Rouge, East Baton Rouge Parish, Louisiana. He married **Sherri Theresa Opperman** 21 January 1975, daughter of Ernest Opperman and Laura Seymour. She was born 22 August 1953 in Vicksburg, Mississippi.

Children of Alvin Robért and Sherri Opperman are:
738   i.   **Alvin Joseph[7] Robért,Jr., born 29 July 1975 in Baton Rouge, East Baton Rouge Parish, Louisiana. He married Monica Lynn Hebert 04 August 2001 in Burnside, Ascension Parish, Louisiana; born 22 January 1976 in Baton Rouge, East Baton Rouge Parish, Louisiana.**
739   ii.   **Jamie Marie Robért, born 09 May 1977 in Baton Rouge, East Baton Rouge Parish, Louisiana.**
740   iii. **Joel Michael Robért, born 24 November 1980 in Baton Rouge, East Baton Rouge Parish, Louisiana. He married Amanda Gwen Zimmerman 27 May 2006 in Baton Rouge, East Baton Rouge Parish, Louisiana; born 05 December 1985 in Baton Rouge, East Baton Rouge Parish, Louisiana.**

326. Stephen Adam[6] Robért, (Steve) (Roland Jacques[5], Jean Paul[4], Mathieu[3], Jean[2], Mathieu[1]) was born 04 September 1947 in Baton Rouge, East Baton Rouge Parish, Louisiana. He married **Randi Ann Mire** 10 July 1968 in St. Theresa Catholic Church, Gonzales, Louisiana. She was born 07 March 1948 in Baton Rouge, East Baton Rouge Parish, Louisiana.

Children of Stephen Robért and Randi Mire are:
741   i.   **Keith Brian[7] Robért, born 21 February 1969 in Lafayette Parish,**

Lafayette, Louisiana.

742   ii.   **Stephanie Ann Robért, born 24 May 1977 in Baton Rouge, East Baton Rouge Parish, Louisiana.**

327. Donald Christopher[6] Robért, (Don) (Roland Jacques[5], Jean Paul[4], Mathieu[3], Jean[2], Mathieu[1]) was born 01 January 1950 in Baton Rouge, East Baton Rouge Parish, Louisiana. He married **Michele Clare Waguespack** 19 October 1968 in Woodville, Mississippi, daughter of Michael Waguespack and Loyce LeBlanc. She was born 09 February 1949 in Donaldsonville, Ascension Parish, Louisiana.

Children of Donald Robért and Michele Waguespack are:

+   743   i.   **Michelle Christy[7] Robért, born 21 November 1969 in Baton Rouge, East Baton Rouge Parish, Louisiana.**

+   744   ii.   **Amanda Clare Robért, born 09 February 1980 in Baton Rouge, East Baton Rouge Parish, Louisiana.**

     745   iii.   **Jacques Christopher Robért, born 19 August 1984 in Baton Rouge, East Baton Rouge Parish, Louisiana.**

Generation No. 6

340. Marie Beatrice[7] Schexnayder (Victor Joseph[6], Optime Joseph[5], Marcellin[4], Marianne Melanie[3] Robért, Jean[2], Mathieu[1]) was born 06 December 1934 in Darrow, Ascension Parish, Louisiana. She married **Francis Benoit Waggenspack** 16 November 1957 in Darrow, Ascension Parish, Louisiana, son of Jacque Waggenspack and Elmira Robért. He was born 16 July 1918 in Modeste, Ascension Parish, Louisiana, and died 25 May 2004 in Darrow, Ascension Parish, Louisiana.

Child is listed above under (273) Francis Benoit Waggenspack.

341. Victor Arnold[7] Schexnayder (Victor Joseph[6], Optime Joseph[5], Marcellin[4], Marianne Melanie[3] Robért, Jean[2], Mathieu[1]) was born 13 October 1937 in Burnside, Ascension Parish, Louisiana, and died 11 July 2006. He married **Carolyn Gomez**.

Children of Victor Schexnayder and Carolyn Gomez are:

    746   i.   **Kim[8] Schexnayder.**
    747   ii.   **Kevin Mark Schexnayder.**
    748   iii. **Kent Schexnayder.**
    749   iv. **Kelley Schexnayder.**

345. Simon Joseph[7] Schexnayder (Jean Marcellin[6], Emilien Joseph[5],

Marcellin[4], Marianne Melanie[3] Robért, Jean[2], Mathieu[1]) was born 28 August 1916 in Vacherie, St. James Parish, Louisiana, and died 30 December 1984 in Vacherie, St. James Parish, Louisiana. He married **Antoinette Falgoust**.

Children of Simon Schexnayder and Antoinette Falgoust are:

750	i.	**Mary Ann[8] Schexnayder.**
751	ii.	**Clara Belle Schexnayder.**
752	iii.	**Rose Schexnayder.**
753	iv.	**Claire Schexnayder.**
754	v.	**Gerrard (Jerry) Schexnayder.**

349. Althea Adolphine[7] Robért (Louis Luke[6], Rosemond[5], Jean Baptiste[4], Jean Louis[3], Jean[2], Mathieu[1]) was born 17 June 1910 in St. Charles Parish, Louisiana, and died 21 December 1995 in St. Charles Parish, Louisiana. She married **Hubert Robért** 30 September 1939 in St. Charles Borromeo Church, Destrahan, Louisiana. He was born 17 October 1910, and died 17 November 1959.

Children of Althea Robért and Hubert Robért are:

755	i.	**Clifford[8] Robért.**
756	ii.	**James Robért.**
757	iii.	**Janet Robért.**
758	iv.	**Living Robért. She married Glynn Joseph Zeringue 15 October 1960; born 15 October 1938; died 13 January 2006 in Luling, St. Charles Parish, Louisiana.**

350. Lawrence[7] Robért (Louis Luke[6], Rosemond[5], Jean Baptiste[4], Jean Louis[3], Jean[2], Mathieu[1]) was born 17 November 1912 in St. Charles Parish, Louisiana, and died 25 February 2007 in Luling, St. Charles Parish, Louisiana. He married **Eunice Gaubert** 13 January 1940, daughter of Ambrose Gaubert and Leah Zeringue. She was born 17 November 1915 in Lafourche Parish, Louisiana.

Child of Lawrence Robért and Eunice Gaubert is:

+ 759	i.	**Ralph Joseph[8] Robért, born 08 December 1942 in Ama, St. Charles Parish, Louisiana; died 12 October 2007 in Luling, St. Charles Parish, Louisiana.**

356. Leonie[7] Robért (Edgar[6], Rosemond[5], Jean Baptiste[4], Jean Louis[3], Jean[2], Mathieu[1]) was born 27 March 1900 in St. Charles Parish, Louisiana, and died 25 June 1993 in Westwego, Jefferson Parish, Louisiana. She married **Dennis J. Friloux**, son of George Friloux and Estelle Robért. He was born 07 November 1894 in Louisiana, and died 09 February 1967 in Westwego, Jefferson Parish, Louisiana.

Child is listed above under (140) Dennis J. Friloux.

359. Joseph[7] Robért (Amedee[6], Amedee[5], Jean Baptiste[4], Jean Louis[3], Jean[2], Mathieu[1]) was born 20 May 1899 in Ama, St. Charles Parish, Louisiana, and died January 1999 in White Castle, Iberville Parish, Louisiana. He married **Odette Mury** Abt. 1922, daughter of Charles Mury and Marie Becnel. She was born 20 February 1904 in Ama, St. Charles Parish, Louisiana, and died September 1992 in White Castle, Iberville Parish, Louisiana.

Children of Joseph Robért and Odette Mury are:
760	i.	**Floyd[8] Robért, born 1924 in Ama, St. Charles Parish, Louisiana.**
761	ii.	**Gerald Robért, born February 1925 in Ama, St. Charles Parish, Louisiana.**
762	iii.	**Warren F. Robért, born 05 December 1926 in Ama, St. Charles Parish, Louisiana; died 24 January 1999 in Baton Rouge, East Baton Rouge Parish, Louisiana. He married Mary Jean Mayerhoff; died January 1999 in Baton Rouge, East Baton Rouge Parish, Louisiana.**

363. Dewey Joseph[7] Robért (Eranbert[6], Amedee[5], Jean Baptiste[4], Jean Louis[3], Jean[2], Mathieu[1]) was born 31 May 1898 in Ama, St. Charles Parish, Louisiana, and died 16 November 1930 in Ama, St. Charles Parish, Louisiana. He married **Martha Bridgitte Ford** 23 July 1925 in Taft, St. Charles Parish, Louisiana, daughter of James Ford and Henrietta Toups. She was born 26 March 1908 in Lafourche Parish, Louisiana, and died 26 February 1940 in New Orleans, Orleans Parish, Louisiana.

Children of Dewey Robért and Martha Ford are:
763	i.	**Living[8] Robért. He married Living Meliet.**
764	ii.	**Living Robért. She married Living Blanchard.**
765	iii.	**Living Robért. She married Living Favre.**

364. Louisa Marie[7] Zeringue (Delphine[6] Robért, Amedee[5], Jean Baptiste[4], Jean Louis[3], Jean[2], Mathieu[1]) was born 04 November 1898 in Waggaman, Jefferson Parish, Louisiana, and died 30 October 1976 in Luling, St. Charles Parish Louisiana. She married **Joseph Patrick Ford** 07 October 1922 in Taft, St. Charles Parish, Louisiana, son of James Ford and Henrietta Toups. He was born 03 March 1896 in Thibodaux, Lafourche Parish, Louisiana, and died 03 August 1986 in New Orleans, Orleans Parish, Louisiana.

Children of Louisa Zeringue and Joseph Ford are:
766	i.	**Living[8] Ford.**

| 767 | ii. | Living Ford. |
| 768 | iii. | Charles Joseph Ford, born 04 April 1932 in Boutte, St. Charles Parish, Louisiana; died 01 June 1932 in Boutte, St. Charles Parish, Louisiana. |

366. Eujene Joseph[7] Robért (Eugene[6], Amedee[5], Jean Baptiste[4], Jean Louis[3], Jean[2], Mathieu[1]) He married **Marie Ory**.

Children of Eujene Robért and Marie Ory are:
769	i.	Alice[8] Robért.
770	ii.	Ashley Robért.
771	iii.	Eddie Robért.
772	iv.	Vernon Robért.
773	v.	Myron Robért.
774	vi.	Maybelle Robért.
775	vii.	Casandra Robért.
776	viii.	Patrick Robért.
777	ix.	Ben Robért.

368. Harry Clay[7] Robért (Eugene[6], Amedee[5], Jean Baptiste[4], Jean Louis[3], Jean[2], Mathieu[1]) was born 12 July 1912, and died 14 March 1953. He married **Myrtle Kenny**.

Children of Harry Robért and Myrtle Kenny are:
| 778 | i. | Living[8] Robért. |
| 779 | ii. | Living Robért. |

380. Pearl Marguerite[7] Robért (James Theotine[6], Theotine[5], Jean Baptiste[4], Jean Louis[3], Jean[2], Mathieu[1]) was born 27 March 1916 in Ama, St. Charles Parish, Louisiana, and died 11 December 1987 in Laplace, St. John the Baptist Parish, Louisiana. She married **Wharton Armand LeBlanc**, son of Hypolite LeBlanc and Ruphena Longmire. He was born 11 April 1917 in Reserve, St. John the Baptist Parish, Lousiana.

Children of Pearl Robért and Wharton LeBlanc are:
780	i.	Wharton Armand[8] LeBlanc, Jr..
781	ii.	Robert LeBlanc.
782	iii.	Susan LeBlanc.

382. Beatrice Marie[7] Robért (James Theotine[6], Theotine[5], Jean Baptiste[4], Jean Louis[3], Jean[2], Mathieu[1]) was born 27 December 1919 in St. John the Baptist Parish, Louisiana, and died in Louisiana. She married **Charles Horace Maurin**,

Jr.. He was born 09 May 1920.

Children of Beatrice Robért and Charles Maurin are:
- 783   i.   **Mary Beatrice[8] Maurin, born in Louisiana.**
- 784   ii.   **Charles Maurin, III., born 04 December 1946 in Louisiana; died 21 February 1993 in Louisiana.**
- 785   iii.   **Robert Patrick Maurin, born 30 November 1959 in Reserve, St. John the Baptist Parish, Lousiana; died 13 December 1959 in Reserve, St. John the Baptist Parish, Lousiana.**

394. Curtis[7] Robért (Benoit[6], Jean Ursin[5], Septime Louis[4], Mathieu[3], Jean[2], Mathieu[1]) was born 05 February 1927 in Ascension Plantation, Mc Call, Louisiana, and died 04 September 1997 in Ascension Parish, Donaldsonville, Louisiana. He married **Ella Faustene Landry** Unknown in Air Force Base, Lake Charles, Louisiana. She was born 10 April 1927, and died Unknown.

Child of Curtis Robért and Ella Landry is:
- 786   i.   **Charlene Lucy[8] Robért, born 03 September 1961 in Air Force Base, Lake Charles, Louisiana; died Unknown. She married Peter Palermo 24 September 1983 in Donaldsonville, Ascension Parish, Louisiana; born Unknown; died Unknown.**

395. Irby Paul[7] Robért (Benoit[6], Jean Ursin[5], Septime Louis[4], Mathieu[3], Jean[2], Mathieu[1]) was born 20 May 1928 in Ascension Parish, Louisiana. He married **Jacquline Marie Milano** 26 November 1952, daughter of Mike Milano and Lucy Mesina. She was born Abt. 1932, and died Unknown.

Children of Irby Robért and Jacquline Milano are:
- 787   i.   **Susan Marie[8] Robért, born 12 March 1954. She married Hugh Alphonso Freeze 27 May 1978; born Unknown.**
- 788   ii.   **Bruce Paul Robért, born 07 December 1955 in Donaldsonville, Ascension Parish, Louisiana. He married Claire Cecilia Becnel 20 August 1976 in St. Francis of Assisi Catholic Church, Smoke Bend, Louisiana; born Unknown.**
- 789   iii.   **Marcia Ann Robért, born 06 November 1958. She married Steven Modica 29 June 1981; born Unknown.**
- 790   iv.   **Gwendolyn Therese Robért, born 11 October 1960.**

396. Herman Anthony[7] Robért, Sr. (Benoit[6], Jean Ursin[5], Septime Louis[4], Mathieu[3], Jean[2], Mathieu[1]) was born 02 May 1930 in Ascension Parish, Louisiana. He married **Jacqueline Ann Landry** 09 May 1953 in Ascension Catholic Church, Donaldsonville, Louisiana, daughter of Milburn Landry and Myrtis Harp. She was born Unknown, and died Unknown.

Children of Herman Robért and Jacqueline Landry are:

791   i.   **Herman Anthony[8] Robért, Jr.,** born 14 October 1954. He married **Rosemary Thompson;** born Unknown.

792   ii.   **Myrtis Agnes Robért,** born 02 October 1956. She married **Louis Hill Marix** 24 February 1978; born Unknown.

793   iii.   **Denise Marie Robért,** born 09 January 1959. She married **James Joseph Hidalgo** 24 June 1977; born Unknown.

397. Marian Theresa[7] Robért (Benoit[6], Jean Ursin[5], Septime Louis[4], Mathieu[3], Jean[2], Mathieu[1]) was born 31 July 1931 in Ascension Parish, Louisiana. She married **Sam J. Guercio, Sr. (Blue)** 07 May 1952 in Ascension Catholic Church, Donaldsonville, Louisiana. He was born Unknown, and died Unknown.

Children of Marian Robért and Sam Guercio are:

794   i.   **Brenda Theresa[8] Guercio,** born 09 March 1953 in Iberville Parish, White Castle, Louisiana. She married **Felix Joseph Joffrion** 07 January 1972 in Our Lady of Prompt Succor Church, White Castle, Louisiana; born Unknown.

795   ii.   **Marilyn Ann Guercio,** born 01 July 1954 in Iberville Parish, White Castle, Louisiana. She married (1) **Randell Clement Leglue** 29 January 1979; born Unknown. She married (2) **Johnny Joseph Zeringue** 14 November 1980.

796   iii.   **Maria Guercio,** born 12 June 1955 in Iberville Parish, White Castle, Louisiana. She married **Earnest Joseph LeBlanc** 25 November 1977; born Unknown.

797   iv.   **Sam Joseph Guercio, Jr.,** born 29 August 1956 in Iberville Parish, White Castle, Louisiana. He married (1) **Belvas Lynn Hanson** 19 December 1975; born Unknown. He married (2) **Rita Lynn Marino** 06 November 1987.

798   v.   **Camella Catherine Guercio,** born 12 February 1958 in Iberville Parish, White Castle, Louisiana. She married **Patrick Joseph Landry** 14 November 1986; born Unknown.

799   vi.   **Luke H. Guercio,** born 13 July 1959 in Iberville Parish, White Castle, Louisiana. He married (1) **Rebecca Geralyn Medine** 07 April 1978; born Unknown. He married (2) **Arlene Marie Landry** 26 June 1987.

800   vii.   **Russell Joseph Guercio,** born 05 January 1963 in Iberville Parish, White Castle, Louisiana. He married **Stacy Ann Barlow** 03 August 1990; born Unknown.

801   viii.   **Marian Theresa Guercio,** born 29 September 1964 in Iberville Parish, White Castle, Louisiana. She married **Todd Christopher Doiron** 11 March 1988; born Unknown.

398. Bernard Francis[7] Robért, Sr. (Benoit[6], Jean Ursin[5], Septime Louis[4], Mathieu[3], Jean[2], Mathieu[1]) was born 06 December 1933 in Ascension Parish, Louisiana. He married **(1) Josephine Guercio** 01 September 1954. She was born Unknown, and died Unknown. He married **(2) Barbera Stephens** 23 October 1986.

Children of Bernard Robért and Josephine Guercio are:

   802   i. **Maria Theresa[8] Robért, born 07 September 1964. She married Jules Peterson 20 December 1985; born Unknown.**

   803   ii. **Bernard Francis Robért, Jr., born 30 December 1965. He married Kim Stewart Unknown; born Unknown.**

   804   iii. **Michael Jude Robért, born 13 September 1967.**

399. Eugene Thomas[7] Robert, Sr. (Benoit[6], Jean Ursin[5], Septime Louis[4], Mathieu[3], Jean[2], Mathieu[1]) was born 10 September 1936 in Ascension Parish, Louisiana. He married **Alice Bergeron** 27 June 1959, daughter of John Bergeron and Marie Landry. She was born Unknown, and died Unknown.

Children of Eugene Robért and Alice Bergeron are:

   805   i. **Eugene Thomas[8] Robért, Jr., born 19 July 1960.**

   806   ii. **Cheryl Ann Robért, born 24 February 1964.**

400. Clara Ann[7] Robért (Benoit[6], Jean Ursin[5], Septime Louis[4], Mathieu[3], Jean[2], Mathieu[1]) was born 18 December 1938 in Ascension Parish, Louisiana. She married **Jeddy Joseph LeBlanc, Sr.** 30 December 1961. He was born Unknown, and died Unknown.

Children of Clara Robért and Jeddy LeBlanc are:

   807   i. **Jeddy Joseph[8] LeBlanc, Jr., born 20 January 1963.**

   808   ii. **Vicki Lyn LeBlanc, born 27 July 1965. She married William Allen Pierce August 1986; born Unknown.**

   809   iii. **Darren LeBlanc, born 12 January 1969.**

401. Agnes[7] Robért (Benoit[6], Jean Ursin[5], Septime Louis[4], Mathieu[3], Jean[2], Mathieu[1]) was born 12 November 1940 in Ascension Parish, Louisiana. She married **Roy Daigle** 29 December 1962. He was born Unknown, and died Unknown.

Children of Agnes Robért and Roy Daigle are:

   810   i. **Terri[8] Daigle, born 02 March 1964. She married Joe Cavalier 25 July 1986; born Unknown.**

   811   ii. **Dana Daigle, born 31 March 1967.**

812   iii.   **Chrystal Daigle, born 07 August 1968. She married Rob Boudreaux 27 December 1986; born Unknown.**

402. Godfrey Joseph[7] Waguespack (Octave Pierre[6], Marie Octavie[5] Robért, ***, Jean Frumence[4], Mathieu[3], Jean[2], Mathieu[1]) was born 01 December 1923 in Burnside, Ascension Parish, Louisiana. He married **Rose Lee Mitchell** 29 January 1951 in St. Mary Chapel, Union Louisiana, daughter of Fred Mitchell and Victoria Cox. She was born 13 August 1932.

Children of Godfrey Waguespack and Rose Lee Mitchell are:
813   i.   **Deborah Lee[8] Waguespack, born 29 October 1951.**
814   ii.   **Leslie Ann Waguespack, born 29 July 1953.**
815   iii.   **Fran Cabrini Waguespack, born 21 July 1956.**
816   iv.   **Godfrey Joseph Waguespack, Jr, born 13 March 1958.**
817   v.   **Dana Marie Waguespack, born 03 May 1961.**

403. Larry Pierre[7] Waguespack, Sr. (Octave Pierre[6], Marie Octavie[5] Robért, ***, Jean Frumence[4], Mathieu[3], Jean[2], Mathieu[1]) was born 14 October 1925 in Burnside, Ascension Parish, Louisiana. He married **Marie Edna Bercegeay** 22 February 1949 in St. Theresa Catholic Church, Gonzales, Louisiana, daughter of Linden Bercegeay and Edith Braud. She was born 12 October 1930.

Children of Larry Waguespack and Marie Bercegeay are:
+ 818   i.   **Sharon Ann[8] Waguespack, born 16 March 1950 in Burnside, Ascension Parish, Louisiana.**
+ 819   ii.   **Rebecca Marie Waguespack, born 28 September 1951 in Burnside, Ascension Parish, Louisiana.**
+ 820   iii.   **Amy Marie Waguespack, born 29 August 1953 in Burnside, Ascension Parish, Louisiana.**
+ 821   iv.   **Susan Mary Waguespack, born 21 December 1954 in Burnside, Ascension Parish, Louisiana.**
+ 822   v.   **Ryan Joseph Waguespack, born 10 January 1956 in Burnside, Ascension Parish, Louisiana.**
+ 823   vi.   **Nanette Marie Waguespack, born 26 February 1957 in Burnside, Ascension Parish, Louisiana.**
+ 824   vii.   **Larry P. Waguespack, Jr., born 03 November 1958 in St. James Parish, Lutcher, Louisiana.**
    825   viii.   **Laura Ann Waguespack, born 28 November 1959 in Burnside, Ascension Parish, Louisiana.**
+ 826   ix.   **Chad Anthony Waguespack, born 28 June 1961 in Burnside, Ascension Parish, Louisiana.**

405. Gertrude Ann[7] Waguespack (Octave Pierre[6], Marie Octavie[5] Robért,

***, Jean Frumence[4], Mathieu[3], Jean[2], Mathieu[1]) was born 10 August 1930 in Burnside, Ascension Parish, Louisiana. She married **Medford William Magill.** 22 December 1955 in St. Anthony Catholic Chapel, Darrow, Louisiana, son of George Magill and Nellie Foster. He was born 15 January 1930 in Henderson, Missouri.

Children of Gertrude Waguespack and Medford Magill. are:

827   i.   **William Medford[8] Magill, born 21 November 1956 in Ascension Parish, Gonzales, Louisiana. He married Wendy Rose Breard 29 February 1992 in Christ the King Chapel, LSU Campus, Baton Rouge, Louisiana; born Unknown.**

828   ii.   **Victoria Ann Magill, born 17 July 1958 in Gonzales, Ascension Parish, Louisiana. She married Stephen Joseph Compagna 02 October 1982 in Our Lady of Mercy Catholic Church, Baton Rouge, Louisiana; born Unknown.**

829   iii.   **Paul Pierre Magill, born 05 November 1960 in Lutcher, Louisiana.**

406. Barbara Rita[7] Waguespack (Octave Pierre[6], Marie Octavie[5] Robért, ***, Jean Frumence[4], Mathieu[3], Jean[2], Mathieu[1]) was born 24 July 1933 in Burnside, Ascension Parish, Louisiana. She married **Milton Keller, Jr.** 22 January 1953 in St. Anthony Catholic Chapel, Darrow, Louisiana, son of Milton Keller and Elda Breaux. He was born 17 November 1929.

Children of Barbara Waguespack and Milton Keller are:

830   i.   **Pamela Ann[8] Keller, born 05 December 1953; died 13 October 1960.**

+ 831   ii.   **Cynthia Ann Keller, born 14 November 1954.**

+ 832   iii.   **Timothy Joseph Keller, born 02 October 1956.**

+ 833   iv.   **Patrick James Keller, born 18 September 1957.**

+ 834   v.   **Phyllis Ann Keller, born 22 January 1960.**

+ 835   vi.   **Blain Anthony Keller, born 16 February 1962.**

+ 836   vii.   **Jennifer Ann Keller, born 12 November 1964.**

837   viii.   **David Paul Keller, born 08 October 1966; died 26 August 1984.**

407. Genevieve[7] Waguespack (Octave Pierre[6], Marie Octavie[5] Robért, ***, Jean Frumence[4], Mathieu[3], Jean[2], Mathieu[1]) was born 15 February 1936 in Burnside, Ascension Parish, Louisiana. She married **Vincent Joseph Sotile, (Beazy)** 22 November 1956 in St. Anthony Catholic Chapel, Darrow, Louisiana, son of Vincent Sotile and Marie Montalbano. He was born 31 August 1935.

Children of Genevieve Waguespack and Vincent Sotile are:

+ 838   i.   **Wendy Ann[8] Sotile, born 12 February 1958 in Donaldsonville, Ascension Parish, Louisiana.**

839   ii.   **Lisa Marie Sotile, born 01 July 1960 in Donaldsonville, Ascension**

Parish, Louisiana. She married David Francis Rowell 13 June 1987 in Cathederal of Christ the King, Atlanta, Georgia; born 04 November 1959.

840   iii.   Vincent Joseph Sotile, Jr., born 14 November 1962 in Donaldsonville, Ascension Parish, Louisiana. He married Stephanie Bryant Nethery 17 November 1990 in Independent Presbyterian Church, Memphis, Tennessee; born Unknown.

+ 841   iv.   Monica Lynne Sotile, born 09 May 1966 in Donaldsonville, Ascension Parish, Louisiana.

408. Jacqueline Marie[7] Waguespack (Octave Pierre[6], Marie Octavie[5] Robért, ***, Jean Frumence[4], Mathieu[3], Jean[2], Mathieu[1]) was born 12 September 1939 in Burnside, Ascension Parish, Louisiana. She married **Bryan Joseph Guillot,Sr.** 07 February 1959 in St. Mary Catholic Church, Union, Louisiana, son of Bryan Guillot and Louise Caballero. He was born 11 May 1937.

Children of Jacqueline Waguespack and Bryan Guillot are:

842   i.   Bryan Joseph[8] Guillot, Jr., born 27 March 1960. He married (1) Kathleen Rose Canatella 27 November 1981 in St. Michael Catholic Church, Convent, Louisiana; born Unknown. He married (2) Romney Brantley 01 October 1988 in New Orleans, Orleans Parish, Louisiana.

843   ii.   Diane Marie Guillot, born 15 August 1961 in Lutcher, Louisiana. She married Eric Charles Weimer 08 June 1985 in St. Patrick Catholic Church, Baton Rouge, Louisiana.

+ 844   iii.   Robin Marie Guillot, born 10 September 1962.

845   iv.   Michael Joseph Guillot, (infant), born 14 October 1963; died 15 October 1963.

846   v.   Michelle Marie Guillot, born 01 April 1965. She married James Joseph Brien, Jr. 29 August 1987 in St. Patrick Catholic Church, Baton Rouge, Louisiana; born Unknown.

+ 847   vi.   Julie Marie Guillot, born 21 February 1967 in Baton Rouge, East Baton Rouge Parish, Louisiana.

848   vii.   Keith Joseph Guillot, born 21 September 1971 in Thibodaux, Lafourche Parish, Louisiana.

409. Oliver Paul[7] Robért, Jr. (Oliver Paul[6], Jean Ursin[5], Septime Louis[4], Mathieu[3], Jean[2], Mathieu[1]) was born 21 December 1932 in Donaldsonville, Ascension Parish, Louisiana. He married **Terry Lynn Townes** 24 April 1965 in Holy Name of Jesus, West Palm Beach, Florida. She was born Unknown.

Children of Oliver Robért and Terry Townes are:

849   i.   Kevin James[8] Robért, born 31 December 1965 in Baton Rouge, East Baton Rouge Parish, Louisiana. He married Joy Caryl Smith

21 April 1989 in St. Theresa Catholic Church, Gonzales, Louisiana; born Unknown.

850   ii.   **Jennifer Ann Robért**, born 23 September 1967 in Baton Rouge, East Baton Rouge Parish, Louisiana.

851   iii.   **David Raymond Robért**, born 20 March 1970 in Baton Rouge, East Baton Rouge Parish, Louisiana.

410. Doran J.[7] Robért (Oliver Paul[6], Jean Ursin[5], Septime Louis[4], Mathieu[3], Jean[2], Mathieu[1]) was born 02 November 1935 in Donaldsonville, Ascension Parish, Louisiana, and died in Baton Rouge, East Baton Rouge Parish, Louisiana. He married **Dorothy Lea Martin** 09 December 1955 in Our Lady of Mercy Catholic Church, Baton Rouge, Louisiana, daughter of Allen Martin and Hilda Sellers.

Children of Doran Robért and Dorothy Martin are:

852   i.   **Karen Lynn[8] Robért**, born 05 January 1957 in Baton Rouge, East Baton Rouge Parish, Louisiana; died Unknown in Hewitt, Texas. She married John Steven Fell 04 August 1979 in Christ the King Chapel, LSU Campus, Baton Rouge, Louisiana; born Unknown.

853   ii.   **Jan Elizabeth Robért**, born 17 October 1960 in Baton Rouge, East Baton Rouge Parish, Louisiana; died Unknown in Baton Rouge, East Baton Rouge Parish, Louisiana. She married Warren Joseph Aymond 16 February 1980 in St. George Catholic Church, Baton Rouge, Louisiana; born Unknown.

854   iii.   **Gayle Renee Robért**, born 29 May 1965 in Baton Rouge, East Baton Rouge Parish, Louisiana; died Unknown in Brusly, Louisiana. She married Fred Joseph Tassin 15 September 1984 in St. George Catholic Church, Baton Rouge, Louisiana; born Unknown.

411. Dale Thomas[7] Robért, Sr. (Oliver Paul[6], Jean Ursin[5], Septime Louis[4], Mathieu[3], Jean[2], Mathieu[1]) was born 26 September 1937 in Donaldsonville, Ascension Parish, Louisiana, and died 16 December 2007 in Baton Rouge, East Baton Rouge Parish, Louisiana. He married **Barbara Ann Martin** 07 July 1956 in Our Lady of Mercy Catholic Church, Baton Rouge, Louisiana, daughter of Allen Martin and Hilda Sellers.

Children of Dale Robért and Barbara Martin are:

855   i.   **Dale Thomas[8] Robért, Jr.**, born 07 September 1957 in Baton Rouge, East Baton Rouge Parish, Louisiana.

856   ii.   **Katherine Ann Robért**, born 08 January 1958 in Baton Rouge, East Baton Rouge Parish, Louisiana; died 08 January 1958 in Baton Rouge, East Baton Rouge Parish, Louisiana.

857   iii.   Pamela Sue Robért, born 04 March 1959 in Baton Rouge, East Baton Rouge Parish, Louisiana; died in Gonzales, Louisiana. She

married (1) Douglas Ellis Talbot 16 April 1977 in St. George Catholic Church, Baton Rouge, Louisiana. She married (2) Joseph Thomas Stephens 22 November 1985 in St. George Catholic Church, Baton Rouge, Louisiana; born Unknown.

858   iv.   Linda Lea Robért, born 04 February 1960 in Baton Rouge, East Baton Rouge Parish, Louisiana; died in Baton Rouge, East Baton Rouge Parish, Louisiana. She married Duane Armond Thibeau 02 February 1980 in St. George Catholic Church, Baton Rouge, Louisiana.

859   v.   Michael Joseph Robért, born 13 January 1961 in Baton Rouge, East Baton Rouge Parish, Louisiana; died in Baton Rouge, East Baton Rouge Parish, Louisiana. He married Kristina Ellen White 11 August 1985 in St. George Catholic Church, Baton Rouge, Louisiana.

860   vi.   Mark Wayne Robért, born 01 March 1962 in Baton Rouge, East Baton Rouge Parish, Louisiana. He married Karen Patricia Landry 14 August 1982 in St. George Catholic Church, Baton Rouge, Louisiana.

412. Clinton Joseph[7] Robért (Oliver Paul[6], Jean Ursin[5], Septime Louis[4], Mathieu[3], Jean[2], Mathieu[1]) was born 26 August 1941 in Donaldsonville, Ascension Parish, Louisiana. He married **Glenda Ann Blades** 31 May 1969 in St. Anthony Catholic Church, Baton Rouge, Louisiana, daughter of Abraham Blades and Marie Gregoire.

Child of Clinton Robért and Glenda Blades is:

861   i.   Cherie Ann[8] Robért, born 14 January 1973 in Baton Rouge, East Baton Rouge Parish, Louisiana. She married Jason David Taylor 28 April 1955 in St. Alphonsus Catholic Church, Greenwell Springs, Louisiana.

413. Charles Earl[7] Robért, Sr. (Oliver Paul[6], Jean Ursin[5], Septime Louis[4], Mathieu[3], Jean[2], Mathieu[1]) was born 22 December 1943 in Donaldsonville, Ascension Parish, Louisiana. He married **Thechla Rita Cangelosia** 29 May 1965 in Ascension Catholic Church, Donaldsonville, Louisiana.

Children of Charles Robért and Thechla Cangelosia are:

862   i.   Donna Theresa[8] Robért, born 18 June 1966; died Unknown in East Baton Rouge Parish, Baton Rouge, La.. She married Randy Blackwell 22 June 1984 in Villa Del Rey Church of God, Baton Rouge, Louisiana.

863   ii.   Charles Earl Robért, Jr., born 29 February 1968 in East Baton Rouge Parish, Baton Rouge, La.; died Unknown in East Baton Rouge Parish, Baton Rouge, La..

864	iii.	Michelle Renee Robért, born 11 September 1970 in Baton Rouge, East Baton Rouge Parish, Louisiana; died Unknown in Baton Rouge, East Baton Rouge Parish, Louisiana.
865	iv.	Anthony Paul Robért, born 19 December 1972 in Baton Rouge, East Baton Rouge Parish, Louisiana.
866	v.	Angelele Monique Robért, born 28 September 1974 in Baton Rouge, East Baton Rouge Parish, Louisiana.

415. Daniel Steven[7] Robért (Felecien Peter[6], Jean Ursin[5], Septime Louis[4], Mathieu[3], Jean[2], Mathieu[1]) was born 03 September 1939 in Thibodaux, Lafourche Parish, Louisiana. He married **Betty Anne Brignac** Unknown. She was born Unknown.

Children of Daniel Robért and Betty Brignac are:

867	i.	Kay Ann[8] Robért, born 11 July 1964 in Thibodaux, Lafourche Parish, Louisiana; died Unknown in Lafourche Parish, Galliano, Louisiana. She married Kenneth Lefort 27 May 1988; born Unknown.
868	ii.	Keith Michael Robért, born Unknown in Thibodaux, Lafourche Parish, Louisiana. He married Hope Ann Guidry 04 June 1988; born Unknown.
869	iii.	Guy Robért, born Unknown in Thibodaux, Lafourche Parish, Louisiana.

417. Rose Marie[7] Robért (Felecien Peter[6], Jean Ursin[5], Septime Louis[4], Mathieu[3], Jean[2], Mathieu[1]) was born 21 February 1951 in Thibodaux, Lafourche Parish, Louisiana. She married **Elmo Andrew Soignet** 06 April 1967 in St. Joseph Catholic Church, Thibodaux, Louisiana. He was born Unknown.

Children of Rose Robért and Elmo Soignet are:

| 870 | i. | Elmo[8] Soignet.. He married Deborah Theriot 23 December 1988 in Thibodaux, Lafourche Parish, Louisiana. |
| 871 | ii. | Robin Marie Soignet, born Unknown. |

418. David Paul[7] Robért (Felecien Peter[6], Jean Ursin[5], Septime Louis[4], Mathieu[3], Jean[2], Mathieu[1]) was born in Thibodaux, Lafourche Parish, Louisiana. He married **Hazel Maddock**. She was born Unknown.

Children of David Robért and Hazel Maddock are:

| 872 | i. | Jody[8] Robért. |
| 873 | ii. | Amy Robért. |

419. Mariam[7] Troxclair (Josepha Marie[6] Zeringue, Jeanne Clelie[5] Robért, Septime Louis[4], Mathieu[3], Jean[2], Mathieu[1]) was born 03 October 1924 in New Orleans, Orleans Parish, Louisiana, and died 08 October 2000 in Mount Airy, St. John the Baptist Parish, Louisiana. She married **(1) Irving P. Champagne** 12 December 1945. He was born 04 January 1922, and died 06 September 1965. She married **(2) Hewitt Patrick Robért, (Jap)** 03 November 1973. He was born 05 January 1928.

Children of Mariam Troxclair and Irving Champagne are:
874	i.	Dianne[8] Champagne, (Dee).
875	ii.	Paula Ann Champagne.
876	iii.	Paul Champagne.
877	iv.	Larry Champagne, (Specks).

Children of Mariam Troxclair and Hewitt Robért are:
878	i.	Loretta[8] Robért.
879	ii.	Pat Robért.
880	iii.	Willie Robért.

420. Adlice Marie[7] Troxclair (Josepha Marie[6] Zeringue, Jeanne Clelie[5] Robért, Septime Louis[4], Mathieu[3], Jean[2], Mathieu[1]) was born 12 December 1926 in New Orleans, Orleans Parish, Louisiana. She married **Edgar Joseph Waguespack, Jr.(E.J.)** 19 April 1949 in St. Anthony Chapel, Darrow, Ascension Parish, Louisiana, son of Edgar Waguespack and Irma Caillet. He was born 13 August 1920 in Burnside, Ascension Parish, Louisiana, and died July 2008 in Gonzales, Ascension Parish, Louisiana.

Children of Adlice Troxclair and Edgar Waguespack are:
	881	i.	Barry Joseph[8] Waguespack, born 19 April 1950 in Donaldsonville, Ascension Parish, Louisiana. He married (1) Mildred Hargrave. He married (2) Mary Jane Anderson 06 August 1972. He married (3) Sue T. Smith 11 November 1978.
+	882	ii.	Nelda Ann Waguespack, born 30 September 1951 in Donaldsonville, Ascension Parish, Louisiana.
+	883	iii.	Judy Marie Waguespack, born 16 February 1953 in Donaldsonville, Ascension Parish, Louisiana.
	884	iv.	Connie Theresa Waguespack, (infant), born 19 January 1954 in Donaldsonville, Ascension Parish, Louisiana; died 31 March 1954 in Burnside, Ascension Parish, Louisiana.
+	885	v.	Arlene Lucy Waguespack, born 23 February 1955 in Burnside, Ascension Parish, Louisiana.
+	886	vi.	Marvin Peter Waguespack, born 18 July 1956.
+	887	vii.	Jason Paul Waguespack, born 18 September 1957 in Lutcher, St. James Parish, Louisiana.

+ 888   viii.   **Jessie Jude Waguespack**, born 29 September 1959 in Lutcher, St. James Parish, Louisiana.

+ 889   ix.   **Elise Rita Waguespack**, born 07 November 1961 in Lutcher, Louisiana.

421. Sherman Joseph[7] Troxclair (Josepha Marie[6] Zeringue, Jeanne Clelie[5] Robért, Septime Louis[4], Mathieu[3], Jean[2], Mathieu[1]) was born 18 December 1928 in New Orleans, Orleans Parish, Louisiana, and died 21 November 2005 in Lutcher, St. James Parish, Louisiana. He married **Shirlie Borne** 12 October 1957 in Lutcher, St. James Parish, Louisiana, daughter of Edward Borne and Dora Benoit. She was born 20 July 1931 in Remy, St. James Parish, Louisiana, and died 20 June 2008 in Lutcher, St. James Parish, Louisiana.

Child of Sherman Troxclair and Shirlie Borne is:

+ 890   i.   **Donny J.[8] Troxclair**, born 24 August 1958 in Lutcher, St. James Parish, Louisiana.

423. Bessie[7] Troxclair (Josepha Marie[6] Zeringue, Jeanne Clelie[5] Robért, Septime Louis[4], Mathieu[3], Jean[2], Mathieu[1]) was born 19 April 1935 in New Orleans, Orleans Parish, Louisiana. She married **Anthony Gayle Poche, Sr. (Dr.)** 16 August 1958. He was born 17 April 1931, and died 27 April 2000 in St. James Parish, Convent, Louisiana.

Children of Bessie Troxclair and Anthony Poche are:

891   i.   **Claire Elizabeth[8] Poche**, born 14 October 1959. She married Jean Chachere 06 January 1990; born 17 April 1931.

892   ii.   **Anthony Gayle Poche, Jr.**, born 17 April 1961; died 02 May 1981 in St. James Parish, Convent, Louisiana.

893   iii.   **Adele Frances Poche**, born 26 November 1962.

429. Joseph Clemil[7] Brou (Palmire[6] Robért, Omèr Jean[5], Jean Frumence[4], Mathieu[3], Jean[2], Mathieu[1]) was born 20 February 1921 in Burnside, Ascension Parish, Louisiana, and died 04 August 1986 in Grand Isle, Louisiana. He married **Elinor Margaret Eliassen** 16 March 1946 in Church of St. Clement, S.Ozone Park, N. Y., daughter of William Eliassen and Inga Ingerbretsen. She was born Unknown.

Children of Joseph Brou and Elinor Eliassen are:

894   i.   **James Joseph[8] Brou**, born 25 January 1947 in Donaldsonville, Ascension Parish, Louisiana. He married Jo Ann Bonvillian 24 May 1969 in Thibodaux, Lafourche Parish, Louisiana; born Unknown.

895   ii.   **Gregory Michael Brou**, born 18 December 1948 in Donaldsonville,

Ascension Parish, Louisiana. He married Rebecca Ann Hill 23 August 1969 in First Presb. Church, Luling, Louisiana; born Unknown.

896   iii.   **Alan John Brou**, born 10 September 1954 in Luling, Louisiana. He married Janice Mary Breaux 10 June 1977 in St. Anthony Catholic Church, Luling, Louisiana; born Unknown.

897   iv.   **Cheryl Ann Brou**, born 20 January 1961 in New Orleans, Orleans Parish, Louisiana. She married Denis John Mahler 01 August 1986 in Luling, Louisiana; born Unknown.

898   v.   **Gordon William Brou**, born 19 August 1963 in New Orleans, Orleans Parish, Louisiana.

430. Warren Jude[7] Brou,Sr. (Palmire[6] Robért, Omèr Jean[5], Jean Frumence[4], Mathieu[3], Jean[2], Mathieu[1]) was born 26 February 1923 in Burnside, Ascension Parish, Louisiana, and died 20 February 1996 in Donaldsonville, Ascension Parish, Louisiana. He married **Jean Anna Benson** 31 August 1946 in Cathederal of Immaculate Conception, Syracuse, N. Y., daughter of John Benson and Bertha Graves. She was born Unknown.

Children of Warren Brou and Jean Benson are:

899   i.   **Karen Ann[8] Brou**, born 28 December 1947 in Donaldsonville, Ascension Parish, Louisiana. She married Ronald Munro Mills 20 July 1968 in Ethel, Louisiana; born Unknown.

900   ii.   **Glenn Stephen Brou**, born 16 June 1949 in Donaldsonville, Ascension Parish, Louisiana. He married Joyce Marie Cormier 18 November 1972 in St. Lawrence, Mowata, Louisiana; born Unknown.

901   iii.   **Warren Jude Brou, Jr.**, born 28 September 1950 in White Castle, Iberville Parish, Louisiana. He married Cynthia Ann Delaune 17 November 1973 in Our Lady of Prompt Succor Church, White Castle, Louisiana; born Unknown.

902   iv.   **Linda Marie Brou**, born 05 May 1952 in White Castle, Iberville Parish, Louisiana. She married Cedric Jude Delaune 27 June 1981 in Donaldsonville, Ascension Parish, Louisiana; born Unknown.

903   v.   **Marie Noel Brou**, born 25 December 1958 in White Castle, Iberville Parish, Louisiana. She married Donald Kay Payton 02 January 1982 in St. Francis of Assisi Catholic Church, Smoke Bend, Louisiana; born Unknown.

431. Marie Therése[7] Brou (Palmire[6] Robért, Omèr Jean[5], Jean Frumence[4], Mathieu[3], Jean[2], Mathieu[1]) was born 16 August 1924 in Burnside, Ascension Parish, Louisiana. She married **Alton Joseph Richard** 22 January 1950 in St. Francis of Assisi Catholic Church, Smoke Bend, Louisiana, son of Clebert Richard and Clelie Daigle. He was born Unknown.

Children of Marie Brou and Alton Richard are:

904   i.   **Rhonda Margaret**[8] **Richard**, born 29 January 1951 in Iberville Parish, White Castle, Louisiana; died Unknown in Baton Rouge, East Baton Rouge Parish, Louisiana. She married Kenneth Wayne Altazin 03 June 1983 in West Baton Rouge Parish, Port Allen, Louisiana; born Unknown.

905   ii.   **Dawn Elizabeth Richard**, born 13 October 1954 in Iberville Parish, White Castle, Louisiana. She married Dallas James Ballmer 21 January 1995 in Lake Tahoe, Nevada; born Unknown.

906   iii.   **Mark Rory Richard**, born 11 December 1955 in Iberville Parish, White Castle, Louisiana.

907   iv.   **Robyn Ann Richard**, born 25 January 1960 in Iberville Parish, White Castle, Louisiana. She married (1) Martin Joseph Reed 18 March 1981 in Lafayette, Louisiana; born Unknown. She married (2) Keith Michael Cedotal 05 October 1985 in White Castle, Louisiana.

432. Harold James[7] **Brou** (Palmire[6] Robért, Omèr Jean[5], Jean Frumence[4], Mathieu[3], Jean[2], Mathieu[1]) was born 21 October 1926 in Ascension Plantation, McCall, Louisiana. He married **Catherine Jane Babin** 07 September 1957 in Iberville Parish, White Castle, Louisiana, daughter of Herbert Babin and Mary Supple. She was born Unknown.

Children of Harold Brou and Catherine Babin are:

908   i.   **Denise Marie**[8] **Brou**, born 28 November 1958 in Iberville Parish, White Castle, Louisiana. She married Adrian Ellis Fitzgerald 21 July 1990 in Christ the King Chapel, LSU Campus, Baton Rouge, Louisiana; born Unknown.

909   ii.   **John Robért Brou**, born 11 March 1960 in Iberville Parish, White Castle, Louisiana. He married Kathleen Elizabeth Kracht 22 August 1987 in Baton Rouge, East Baton Rouge Parish, Louisiana; born Unknown.

910   iii.   **Paula Jane Brou**, born 27 October 1961 in Ibervile Parish, White Castle, Louisiana. She married Andrew Paul Matherne 18 June 1983 in St. John the Baptiste Catholic Church, Brusly, Louisiana; born Unknown.

911   iv.   **Michelle Margaret Brou**, born 05 August 1964 in Iberville Parish, White Castle, Louisiana. She married (1) James Martin Tabor 22 May 1987 in West Baton Rouge Parish, Port Allen, Louisiana; born Unknown. She married (2) Charles Henry Allen 03 June 1994 in West Baton Rouge Parish, Port Allen, Louisiana; born Unknown.

433. Grace Mary[7] **Brou** (Palmire[6] Robért, Omèr Jean[5], Jean Frumence[4],

Mathieu[3], Jean[2], Mathieu[1]) was born 14 April 1928 in Ascension Plantation, McCall, Louisiana. She married **Stanford John Waguespack** 17 February 1947 in Ascension Parish, St. Francis Assissi Catholic Church, Smoke Bend, Louisiana, son of Wallis Waguespack and Edna Decareaux. He was born 28 April 1916 in St. James Parish, Gramercy, Louisiana, and died 02 November 1999 in Gonzales, Ascension Parish, Louisiana.

Children of Grace Brou and Stanford Waguespack are:

+ 912　　i. **Catherine[8] Waguespack, born 08 October 1948 in Donaldsonville, Ascension Parish, Louisiana.**
+ 913　　ii. **Kevin John Waguespack, born 21 December 1949 in Donaldsonville, Ascension Parish, Louisiana.**
  914　　iii. **Duane Joseph Waguespack, born 21 August 1953 in Donaldsonville, Ascension Parish, Louisiana. He married Pam Plauche 13 October 1984; born 11 May 1958.**
  915　　iv. **Hollis Mark Waguespack, born 08 October 1954 in Donaldsonville, Ascension Parish, Louisiana.**
+ 916　　v. **Marjorie Mary Waguespack, born 17 August 1961 in Lutcher, Louisiana.**

434. Dale John[7] Brou (Palmire[6] Robért, Omèr Jean[5], Jean Frumence[4], Mathieu[3], Jean[2], Mathieu[1]) was born 25 August 1930 in Ascension Plantation, McCall, Louisiana. He married **Phyllis Ellen Brown** 17 August 1957 in Shriever, Louisiana, daughter of James Brown and Florence Alexander.

Children of Dale Brou and Phyllis Brown are:

  917　　i. **Deborah Lin[8] Brou, born 10 January 1959 in Thibodaux, Lafourche Parish, Louisiana. She married Robért Jacque Kinler 21 October 1978 in St. Anthony Catholic Church, Luling, Louisiana.**
  918　　ii. **Donald James Brou, born 28 November 1959 in Thibodaux, Lafourche Parish, Louisiana. He married Davlynn Ann Candies 15 March 1980 in St. Gertrude Church, Des Allemand, Louisiana.**
  919　　iii. **Jeffrey John Brou, born 07 June 1963 in Thibodaux, Lafourche Parish, Louisiana. He married Tina Marie Landeche 09 May 1986 in St. Anthony Catholic Church, Luling, Louisiana.**

435. Joan Mae[7] Brou (Palmire[6] Robért, Omèr Jean[5], Jean Frumence[4], Mathieu[3], Jean[2], Mathieu[1]) was born 23 March 1932 in Ascension Plantation, McCall, Louisiana. She married **Sam Acosta** 27 November 1958 in Iberville Parish, White Castle, Louisiana, son of Andrew Agosta and Lucy Sciortino. He was born Abt. 1925 in Iberville Parish, White Castle, Louisiana, and died 09 March 2000 in Baton Rouge, East Baton Rouge Parish, Louisiana.

Children of Joan Brou and Sam Acosta are:

920	i.	Lucie Janelle[8] Agosta, born 23 January 1960 in White Castle, Louisiana.
921	ii.	Andrew Rene Agosta, born 03 January 1961 in White Castle, Louisiana.
922	iii.	Adrian Anthony Agosta, born 30 August 1962 in White Castle, Louisiana.

437. Kenneth Paul[7] Brou (Palmire[6] Robért, Omèr Jean[5], Jean Frumence[4], Mathieu[3], Jean[2], Mathieu[1]) was born 25 August 1936 in Ascension Plantation, McCall, Louisiana. He married **Martha Ann McLaughlin** 23 February 1963 in Army Base, Seoul, Korea, daughter of Richard McLaughlin and Marie Till.

Children of Kenneth Brou and Martha McLaughlin are:

923	i.	Laura Marie[8] Brou, born 11 September 1964 in East Baton Rouge Parish, Baton Rouge, La..
924	ii.	Julie Claire Brou, born 29 June 1966 in East Baton Rouge Parish, Baton Rouge, La..
925	iii.	Elaine Gail Brou, born 30 April 1969 in East Baton Rouge Parish, Baton Rouge, La..

438. Margaret Ann[7] Brou (Palmire[6] Robért, Omèr Jean[5], Jean Frumence[4], Mathieu[3], Jean[2], Mathieu[1]) was born 16 March 1940 in Chatham Plantation, Hohen Solms, Louisiana. She married **Vincent Paul Pizzolato** 02 June 1962 in St. Francis of Assisi Catholic Church, Smoke Bend, Louisiana, son of Paul Pizzolato and Virginia Sotile.

Children of Margaret Brou and Vincent Pizzolato are:

926	i.	Monica Christine[8] Pizzolato, born 06 May 1963 in East Baton Rouge Parish, Baton Rouge, La.. She married Gerald Francis Flood, (Jerry) 15 June 1990 in St. Patrick Catholic Church, Baton Rouge, Louisiana.
927	ii.	Elizabeth Diane Pizzolato, born 02 February 1965 in East Baton Rouge Parish, Baton Rouge, La.. She married Michael David Diez 19 January 1985 in St. Patrick Catholic Church, Baton Rouge, Louisiana.
928	iii.	Paul Joseph Pizzolato, born 27 July 1967 in East Baton Rouge Parish, Baton Rouge, La.; died Unknown in East Baton Rouge Parish, Baton Rouge, La.. He married Torrie Juanita Shepherd 19 March 1993 in St. Aloysius Catholic Church, Baton Rouge, Louisiana.
929	iv.	Anne Marie Pizzolato, born 24 May 1973 in East Baton Rouge Parish, Baton Rouge, La.. She married Joseph Victor Binder 11 August 1995 in St. Patrick Catholic Church, Baton Rouge, Louisiana.

440. Rowena Theresa[7] Brou (Aline[6] Robért, Omèr Jean[5], Jean Frumence[4], Mathieu[3], Jean[2], Mathieu[1]) was born 08 July 1924 in Burnside, Ascension Parish, Louisiana. She married **Robért McClelland** 13 April 1950 in St. Michael Catholic Church, Convent, Louisiana.

Children of Rowena Brou and Robért McClelland are:

930	i.	**Michael[8] McClelland.**
931	ii.	**Robért B. McClelland, born 23 June 1951 in Lafayette, Louisiana. He married Brenda Pitre 25 August 1973.**
932	iii.	**Richard Scott McClelland, born 24 November 1954 in Lafayette, Louisiana. He married Betty Courville 06 July 1985.**
933	iv.	**Mary Elizabeth McClelland, born 14 November 1957 in Lafayette, Louisiana. She married Harold Murrell 04 April 1985.**
934	v.	**Neal McClelland, born 29 December 1966 in Lafayette, Louisiana. He married Catherine Viator 02 June 1995 in St. Peter Catholic Church, New Iberia, Louisiana.**

441. Marcelle Theresa[7] Brou (Aline[6] Robért, Omèr Jean[5], Jean Frumence[4], Mathieu[3], Jean[2], Mathieu[1]) was born 18 January 1928 in McCall, Louisiana. She married **John Stanley Woosley** 05 February 1948 in Baton Rouge, East Baton Rouge Parish, Louisiana.

Child of Marcelle Brou and John Woosley is:

935	i.	**Michael J.[8] Woosley, born 19 January 1949 in Baton Rouge, East Baton Rouge Parish, Louisiana. He married Cathy J. Blanchard 31 January 1970.**

452. Elgie Mae[7] Waguespack (Edgar Joseph[6], Marie Octavie[5] Robért, ***, Jean Frumence[4], Mathieu[3], Jean[2], Mathieu[1]) was born 10 December 1918 in Burnside, Ascension Parish, Louisiana. She married **Edward Louis LeBlanc** 10 May 1949 in St. Anthony Chapel, Darrow, Louisiana. He was born 13 November 1915 in Baton Rouge, East Baton Rouge Parish, Louisiana, and died 02 September 1991 in Donaldsonville, Ascension Parish, Louisiana.

Children of Elgie Mae Waguespack and Edward LeBlanc are:

+	936	i.	**Gene Gerald[8] LeBlanc, born 27 February 1951 in Donaldsonville, Ascension Parish, Louisiana.**
+	937	ii.	**Glyn Edward LeBlanc, born 03 May 1955 in Donaldsonville, Ascension Parish, Louisiana.**
+	938	iii.	**Gerilyn Marie LeBlanc, born 17 November 1956 in Donaldsonville, Ascension Parish, Louisiana.**
+	939	iv.	**Kerilyn Mary LeBlanc, born 17 November 1956 in Donaldsonville,**

Ascension Parish, Louisiana.

940   v.   **Dwain Joseph LeBlanc.**

453. Edgar Joseph[7] Waguespack, Jr.(E.J.) (Edgar Joseph[6], Marie Octavie[5] Robért, ***, Jean Frumence[4], Mathieu[3], Jean[2], Mathieu[1]) was born 13 August 1920 in Burnside, Ascension Parish, Louisiana, and died July 2008 in Gonzales, Ascension Parish, Louisiana. He married **Adlice Marie Troxclair** 19 April 1949 in St. Anthony Chapel, Darrow, Ascension Parish, Louisiana, daughter of Marcel Troxclair and Josepha Zeringue. She was born 12 December 1926 in New Orleans, Orleans Parish, Louisiana.

Children are listed above under (420) Adlice Marie Troxclair.

455. Leola Sophie[7] Caillet (Denise Marie[6] Waguespack, Marie Octavie[5] Robért, ***, Jean Frumence[4], Mathieu[3], Jean[2], Mathieu[1]) was born 07 December 1917 in Bayou Goula, Iberville Parish, Louisiana, and died 02 September 1975 in Luling, St. Charles Parish, Louisiana. She married **John Williams Madere** 06 November 1954 in St. Charles Parish, Taft, Louisiana. He was born June 1919 in Luling, St. Charles Parish, Louisiana.

Children of Leola Caillet and John Madere are:

941   i.   **Joan Ann[8] Madere, born 21 February 1956 in New Orleans, Orleans Parish, Louisiana.**

942   ii.   **Marlene Ann Madere, born 20 February 1957 in New Orleans, Orleans Parish, Louisiana. She married Kevin Matherne 19 August 1977; born 12 November 1957.**

943   iii.   **Lynn Terese Madere, born 24 August 1958 in New Orleans, Orleans Parish, Louisiana.**

944   iv.   **June Mary Madere, born 10 February 1962 in Luling, St. Charles Parish, Louisiana.**

456. Lois Marie[7] Caillet (Denise Marie[6] Waguespack, Marie Octavie[5] Robért, ***, Jean Frumence[4], Mathieu[3], Jean[2], Mathieu[1]) was born 20 April 1919 in Edgard, St. John the Baptist Parish, Louisiana. She married **Irby Telesphore Baudouin, Jr.** 19 September 1942 in Holy Rosary Church, Taft, Louisiana. He was born 30 April 1917 in St. Charles Parish, Luling, Louisiana.

Children of Lois Caillet and Irby Baudouin are:

+   945   i.   **Lois Margaret[8] Baudouin, born 27 September 1943 in Orleans Parish, New Orleans, Orleans Parish, Louisiana.**

+   946   ii.   **Catherine Mary Baudouin, born 07 October 1948.**

+   947   iii.   Irby T. Baudouin, born 18 January 1953 in Orleans Parish, New Orleans, Orleans Parish, Louisiana.

948   iv.   **Jane Frances Baudouin, born 21 August 1954 in Orleans Parish,**

New Orleans, Orleans Parish, Louisiana.

949   v. **Gary Michael Baudouin, born 13 August 1957 in Orleans Parish, New Orleans, Orleans Parish, Louisiana. He married Anne Elizabeth Fournet 10 August 1979 in Baton Rouge, East Baton Rouge Parish, Louisiana.**

457. Florence Elizabeth[7] Caillet (Denise Marie[6] Waguespack, Marie Octavie[5] Robért, ***, Jean Frumence[4], Mathieu[3], Jean[2], Mathieu[1]) was born 19 November 1921 in Burnside, Ascension Parish, Louisiana. She married **Antoine Sidney Madere, Sr.** 26 December 1949 in St. Charles Parish, Taft, Louisiana. He was born 14 June 1924 in St. Charles Parish, Hahnville, Louisiana, and died 20 March 1978.

Children of Florence Caillet and Antoine Madere are:

950   i. **Antoine Sidney[8] Madere, Jr., born 08 March 1952 in Luling, Louisiana. He married Carol McNicoll 08 August 1981; born 24 December 1958.**

951   ii. **Mary Elizabeth Madere, born 10 October 1954. She married Raymond Nebel 04 January 1975; born 24 July 1953.**

952   iii. **Judith Ann Madere, born 15 December 1958 in Luling, Louisiana. She married Craig Michael Matherne 19 June 1981; born 31 January 1956.**

953   iv. **William Joseph Madere, born 24 October 1961 in Luling, Louisiana.**

458. Helene[7] Caillet (Denise Marie[6] Waguespack, Marie Octavie[5] Robért, ***, Jean Frumence[4], Mathieu[3], Jean[2], Mathieu[1]) was born 10 December 1922. She married **Donald Michael Baudouin, Sr.** 05 September 1946. He was born 28 December 1924.

Children of Helene Caillet and Donald Baudouin are:

954   i. **Donald Michael[8] Baudouin, Jr, born 06 July 1947. He married Ima Lorene Russell 24 September 1980.**

+ 955   ii. **Patricia Maria Baudouin, born 25 September 1949.**

+ 956   iii. **Gregory Thomas Baudouin, born 25 May 1954.**

+ 957   iv. **Georgia Helene Baudouin, born 07 February 1958.**

459. Hazel Theresa[7] Caillet (Denise Marie[6] Waguespack, Marie Octavie[5] Robért, ***, Jean Frumence[4], Mathieu[3], Jean[2], Mathieu[1]) was born 12 August 1924 in Killona, St. Charles Parish, Louisiana, and died 07 January 1985 in Narco, Louisiana. She married **Walter Edgar Millet, Jr.** 03 July 1948. He was born 26 December 1922 in Reserve, St. John the Baptist Parish , Louisiana.

Children of Hazel Caillet and Walter Millet are:

+ 958   i.   **Walter Edgar[8] Millet, III, born 01 January 1950 in New Orleans, Orleans Parish, Louisiana.**

+ 959   ii.   **Emily Clair Millet, born 26 March 1952 in New Orleans, Orleans Parish, Louisiana.**

+ 960   iii.   **Philip Alan Millet, born 03 February 1953 in New Orleans, Orleans Parish, Louisiana.**

     961   iv.   **Ivan George Millet, born 09 May 1954 in New Orleans, Orleans Parish, Louisiana.**

+ 962   v.   **Theresa Agnes Millet, born 30 May 1955 in New Orleans, Orleans Parish, Louisiana.**

+ 963   vi.   **Lester James Millet, born 02 April 1957 in New Orleans, Orleans Parish, Louisiana.**

+ 964   vii.   **Martha Louise Millet, born 30 December 1958 in New Orleans, Orleans Parish, Louisiana.**

460. Cyril Anthony[7] Caillet, Jr. (Denise Marie[6] Waguespack, Marie Octavie[5] Robért, ***, Jean Frumence[4], Mathieu[3], Jean[2], Mathieu[1]) was born 23 November 1925 in Killona, St. Charles Parish, Louisiana. He married **Carole Claire Brady** 31 July 1951 in Holy Rosary Catholic Church, Taft, Louisiana. She was born 24 August 1927 in St. Charles Parish,Taft, Louisiana.

Children of Cyril Caillet and Carole Brady are:

     965   i.   **David Anthony[8] Caillet, born 30 August 1952 in New Orleans, Orleans Parish, Louisiana. He married Brenda Lynn Foerster 30 July 1977 in Our Lady of Perpetual Help, Belle Chasse, Louisiana; born 13 May 1956 in New Orleans, Orleans Parish, Louisiana.**

     966   ii.   **Mary Claire Caillet, born 27 August 1954 in New Orleans, Orleans Parish, Louisiana.**

     967   iii.   **Charles Joseph Caillet, born 06 May 1957 in New Orleans, Orleans Parish, Louisiana.**

     968   iv.   **Edward Anthony Caillet, born 28 August 1961 in New Orleans, Orleans Parish, Louisiana.**

461. Paul Victor[7] Caillet, (P.V.) (Denise Marie[6] Waguespack, Marie Octavie[5] Robért, ***, Jean Frumence[4], Mathieu[3], Jean[2], Mathieu[1]) was born 20 March 1928 in Taft, St. Charles Parish, Louisiana. He married **Gwendolyn Bernice Fahrig** 13 October 1951 in Holy Rosary Catholic Church, Taft, Louisiana. She was born 07 January 1930 in St. Louis, Missouri.

Children of Paul Caillet and Gwendolyn Fahrig are:

     969   i.   **Paula Ruth[8] Caillet, born 09 July 1952 in New Orleans, Orleans Parish, Louisiana.**

     970   ii.   **Helen Denise Caillet, born 06 August 1954 in Greenville, South**

Carolina. She married David Hillburn 19 July 1980; born 03 February 1952.

971   iii.   **Lowell Paul Caillet**, born 19 February 1956 in New Orleans, Orleans Parish, Louisiana; died 01 February 1958 in Taft, St. Charles Parish, Louisiana.

972   iv.   **Paul Christian Caillet**, born 11 July 1958 in New Orleans, Orleans Parish, Louisiana.

973   v.   **Frances Ellen Caillet**, born 06 February 1961 in New Orleans, Orleans Parish, Louisiana. She married Emile Dupre 28 May 1983; born 03 June 1961.

974   vi.   **Peggy Jo Caillet**, born 01 October 1965 in New Orleans, Orleans Parish, Louisiana.

462. Odell Francis[7] Caillet (Denise Marie[6] Waguespack, Marie Octavie[5] Robért, ***, Jean Frumence[4], Mathieu[3], Jean[2], Mathieu[1]) was born 04 January 1930 in Killona, St. Charles Parish, Louisiana. He married **Jeanne Florence Brou** 01 October 1955 in St. Charles Parish, Luling, Louisiana. She was born 23 November 1931 in Evergreen Plantation.

Children of Odell Caillet and Jeanne Brou are:

975   i.   **Mary Joan[8] Caillet**, born 20 August 1957 in New Orleans, Orleans Parish, Louisiana. She married Russel Cortez Smith 19 May 1978 in Luling, Louisiana.

976   ii.   **Edward Gerard Caillet**, born 19 May 1959 in New Orleans, Orleans Parish, Louisiana; died 19 May 1959 in New Orleans, Orleans Parish, Louisiana.

463. Shirley Mae[7] Caillet (Denise Marie[6] Waguespack, Marie Octavie[5] Robért, ***, Jean Frumence[4], Mathieu[3], Jean[2], Mathieu[1]) was born 23 November 1931 in Killona, St. Charles Parish, Louisiana. She married **Howard Lambert** 01 November 1956. He was born 08 November 1921.

Children of Shirley Caillet and Howard Lambert are:

977   i.   **Marie Louise[8] Lambert**, born 05 January 1958. She married Thomas Sylvester.

978   ii.   **Howard Joseph Lambert, Jr.**, born 09 April 1959.

979   iii.   **Mark Timothy Lambert**, born 19 November 1960; died 08 July 1988 in AMI Medical Center, Gonzales, Louisiana.

980   iv.   **Raymond Paul Lambert**, born 23 November 1963.

464. Muriel Ann[7] Caillet (Denise Marie[6] Waguespack, Marie Octavie[5] Robért, ***, Jean Frumence[4], Mathieu[3], Jean[2], Mathieu[1]) was born 08 April 1934 in Killona, St. Charles Parish, Louisiana. She married **Emmett Allen Foxworth, Sr.**

19 March 1957. He was born 09 September 1934 in Foxworth, Mississippi.

Children of Muriel Caillet and Emmett Foxworth are:
981   i.   **Emmet Allen[8] Foxworth, born 28 November 1957 in New Orleans, Orleans Parish, Louisiana.**
982   ii.   **Steven Glen Foxworth, born 11 March 1959 in New Orleans, Orleans Parish, Louisiana.**
983   iii.   **Tammy Ann Foxworth, born 22 September 1962 in Thibodaux, Lafourche Parish, Louisiana.**

465. Stanford John[7] Waguespack (Wallis Jean[6], Marie Octavie[5] Robért, ***, Jean Frumence[4], Mathieu[3], Jean[2], Mathieu[1]) was born 28 April 1916 in St. James Parish, Gramercy, Louisiana, and died 02 November 1999 in Gonzales, Ascension Parish, Louisiana. He married **Grace Mary Brou** 17 February 1947 in Ascension Parish, St. Francis Assissi Catholic Church, Smoke Bend, Louisiana, daughter of Clemil Brou and Palmire Robért. She was born 14 April 1928 in Ascension Plantation, McCall, Louisiana.

Children are listed above under (433) Grace Mary Brou.

466. Wallis J.[7] Waguespack, Jr. (Wallis Jean[6], Marie Octavie[5] Robért, ***, Jean Frumence[4], Mathieu[3], Jean[2], Mathieu[1]) was born 05 August 1918 in Ascension Parish, Burnside, Louisiana, and died 24 July 1998 in Ascension Parish, Gonzales, Louisiana. He married **Mary Elizabeth Fandel, (Nookie)** 24 May 1942. She was born 22 August 1919.

Child of Wallis Waguespack and Mary Fandel is:
+   984   i.   **Wallis J.[8] Waguespack, III, born 18 July 1947.**

467. Stanley Paul[7] Waguespack, (Da-Da) (Wallis Jean[6], Marie Octavie[5] Robért, ***, Jean Frumence[4], Mathieu[3], Jean[2], Mathieu[1]) was born 15 December 1920 in Burnside, Ascension Parish, Louisiana. He married **Marie Carmelite Peytavin** 09 July 1949 in St. Mary Catholic Church, Union, Louisiana. She was born 06 December 1929 in St. James Parish, Union, Louisiana.

Children of Stanley Waguespack and Marie Peytavin are:
+   985   i.   **Westley Paul[8] Waguespack, Sr., born 15 January 1953.**
   986   ii.   **Claire Marie Waguespack, born 22 January 1955.**
   987   iii.   **Rodney John Waguespack, born 05 April 1956.**
   988   iv.   **Linda Judith Waguespack, born 25 February 1962.**
   989   v.   **Bernard Joseph Waguespack, born 17 September 1968.**

468. Seymour Raymond[7] Waguespack (Wallis Jean[6], Marie Octavie[5] Robért, ***, Jean Frumence[4], Mathieu[3], Jean[2], Mathieu[1]) was born 30 August 1923 in Burnside, Ascension Parish, Louisiana, and died 14 May 1984 in Baton Rouge, East Baton Rouge Parish, Louisiana. He married **Catherine Alice Troxclair** 31 October 1953 in St. Charles Borromeo Church, Destrehan, Louisiana, daughter of Noah Troxclair and Eliska Simon. She was born 01 April 1935.

Children of Seymour Waguespack and Catherine Troxclair are:

- + 990   i.   **Tanya Ann[8] Waguespack, born 23 October 1954.**
- + 991   ii.   **Karen Ann Waguespack, born 29 December 1955.**
- + 992   iii.   **Michelle Marie Waguespack, born 19 April 1957.**
- + 993   iv.   **Alice Marie Waguespack, born 29 November 1959.**
-    994   v.   **Seymour Raymond Waguespack, Jr., born 20 August 1961. He married Cheryl Ann Crews 20 April 1985 in St. Michael Catholic Church, Convent, Louisiana; born 20 January 1964.**
- + 995   vi.   **Kurt Dominic Waguespack, born 01 September 1963.**
-    996   vii.   **Steve Paul Waguespack, born 02 January 1970.**

469. Lenora Theresa[7] Waguespack (Wallis Jean[6], Marie Octavie[5] Robért, ***, Jean Frumence[4], Mathieu[3], Jean[2], Mathieu[1]) was born 03 August 1925 in Ascension Parish ,Burnside, Louisiana, and died 18 November 2005 in Baton Rouge, East Baton Rouge Parish, Louisiana. She married **Joseph Garland Dornier** 11 April 1948 in St. Mary Chapel, Union,St. James Parish, Louisiana. He was born 19 May 1920.

Child of Lenora Waguespack and Joseph Dornier is:

- + 997   i.   **Christine Anne[8] Dornier, born 15 September 1949.**

470. Ola Mae Rita[7] Waguespack (Wallis Jean[6], Marie Octavie[5] Robért, ***, Jean Frumence[4], Mathieu[3], Jean[2], Mathieu[1]) was born 13 February 1928 in Burnside, Ascension Parish, Louisiana. She married **Berthile Joseph Schexnaydre, Jr. (Bert)** 07 June 1948 in St. Mary Chapel, Union Louisiana, son of Berthile Schexnaydre and Edith Brou. He was born 25 May 1927 in Burnside, Ascension Parish, Louisiana.

Children of Ola Mae Waguespack and Berthile Schexnaydre are:

- + 998   i.   **Lynette Marie[8] Schexnaydre, born 24 June 1949 in Ascension Parish, Burnside, Louisiana; died 26 January 2006 in Orleans Parish, New Orleans, Orleans Parish, Louisiana.**
- + 999   ii.   **Craig Joseph Schexnaydre, born 28 July 1951.**
- + 1000   iii.   **Myles Michael Schexnaydre, born 02 December 1954.**
- + 1001   iv.   **Kim Marie Schexnaydre, born 15 May 1957.**

+ 1002   v.   Jeffery Joseph Schexnaydre, born 18 July 1958.
  1003   vi.   Boyd Joseph Schexnaydre, born 05 February 1962 in Burnside, Ascension Parish, Louisiana. He married (1) Stacie Elise Wilson 07 September 1985 in St. Gerard Majella Catholic Church, Baton Rouge, Louisiana; born 16 June 1962. He married (2) Steffi Braud 11 January 1992 in Recreation Crnter, Gonzales, Louisiana.

471. Mercedes Ann⁷ Waguespack (Wallis Jean⁶, Marie Octavie⁵ Robért, ***, Jean Frumence⁴, Mathieu³, Jean², Mathieu¹) was born 10 February 1930 in Burnside, Ascension Parish, Louisiana, and died 13 August 1987 in Violet, St. Bernard Parish, Louisiana. She married **John Joseph Canatella** 01 March 1951 in St. Mary Chapel, Union Louisiana. He was born 14 August 1929, and died 09 January 1987 in Orleans Parish, New Orleans, Orleans Parish, Louisiana.

Children of Mercedes Waguespack and John Canatella are:
+ 1004   i.   John Joseph⁸ Canatella, Jr., born 10 November 1953.
+ 1005   ii.   Todd James Canatella, born 06 September 1955.
+ 1006   iii. Cheryl Ann Canatella, born 26 November 1957.

472. Jessie Joseph⁷ Haydel (Elda Augustine⁶ Waguespack, Marie Octavie⁵ Robért, ***, Jean Frumence⁴, Mathieu³, Jean², Mathieu¹) was born 19 March 1916. He married **Doris Catherine Anne LeBlanc** 04 September 1941 in St. Charles Borromeo Church, Destrehan, Louisiana. She was born 01 August 1919 in Labadieville, Louisiana.

Child of Jessie Haydel and Doris LeBlanc is:
+ 1007   i.   Kenneth⁸ Haydel, born 21 July 1951 in New Orleans, Orleans Parish, Louisiana.

473. Jennie Marie⁷ Haydel (Elda Augustine⁶ Waguespack, Marie Octavie⁵ Robért, ***, Jean Frumence⁴, Mathieu³, Jean², Mathieu¹) was born 09 January 1918 in Edgard, St. John the Baptist Parish, Louisiana, and died Unknown in Narco, Louisiana. She married **John August Maggiore** 25 January 1936. He was born 12 October 1912, and died 17 February 1979 in Destrehan, Louisiana.

Children of Jennie Haydel and John Maggiore are:
  1008   i.   August John⁸ Maggiore, born 11 October 1937; died 17 February 1979.
  1009   ii.   Ernest Joseph Maggiore, born 31 December 1942 in New Orleans, Orleans Parish, Louisiana.

475. Antoine Ernest⁷ Haydel (Elda Augustine⁶ Waguespack, Marie Octavie⁵

Robért, ***, Jean Frumence[4], Mathieu[3], Jean[2], Mathieu[1]) was born 23 September 1924 in St. Charles Parish, Sellers, Louisiana (New Sarpy, La.). He married **Mary Migliore** 01 June 1947 in St. Charles Borromeo Church, Destrehan, Louisiana. She was born 06 February 1927 in St. Charles Parish, St. Rose, Louisiana.

Children of Antoine Haydel and Mary Migliore are:

1010	i.	Craig David[8] Haydel, born 08 October 1948 in Baton Rouge, East Baton Rouge Parish, Louisiana.
1011	ii.	Chris Haydel, Rev., born 08 October 1948 in Baton Rouge, East Baton Rouge Parish, Louisiana.

477. Gerald Marie[7] Waguespack (George Nicholas[6], Marie Octavie[5] Robért, ***, Jean Frumence[4], Mathieu[3], Jean[2], Mathieu[1]) was born 14 January 1925 in Burnside, Ascension Parish, Louisiana, and died 20 January 1985 in Baton Rouge, East Baton Rouge Parish, Louisiana. He married **Marian Troxclair, (Sis)** 04 October 1952 in Our Lady of Prompt Succor Church, White Castle, Louisiana, daughter of Maurice Troxclair and Georgine Rome. She was born 10 March 1926 in St. James Parish, Louisiana.

Children of Gerald Waguespack and Marian Troxclair are:

	1012	i.	**Gerald M.[8] Waguespack, Jr.(infant), born 23 May 1953 in Baton Rouge, East Baton Rouge Parish, Louisiana; died 24 May 1953 in Burnside, Ascension Parish, Louisiana.**
+	1013	ii.	**Gerald Jude Waguespack, born 17 July 1954 in Gonzales, Ascension Parish, Louisiana.**
+	1014	iii.	**Georgene Marie Waguespack, born 10 December 1955.**
+	1015	iv.	**Nevil Ann Waguespack, born 10 January 1957 in Gonzales, Ascension Parish, Louisiana.**
+	1016	v.	**Paula Ann Waguespack, born 29 July 1958.**
+	1017	vi.	**Roberta Therese Waguespack, born 08 October 1960.**
	1018	vii.	**Durward Gerald Waguespack, born 03 October 1962. He married (1) Connie Marie Conner, (Divorced) 01 March 1986 in St. Michael Catholic Church, Convent, Louisiana. He married (2) Penny Jarreau December 2005 in New Roads, Point Coupee Parish, Louisiana; born 20 October 1963.**

478. Richard[7] Waguespack (George Nicholas[6], Marie Octavie[5] Robért, ***, Jean Frumence[4], Mathieu[3], Jean[2], Mathieu[1]) was born 28 April 1927 in Burnside, Ascension Parish, Louisiana. He married **Myrtle Marie Gautreau** 01 September 1949 in St. Theresa Catholic Church, Gonzales, Louisiana, daughter of Henry Gautreau and Emma Bellish. She was born 12 November 1930 in New Orleans, Orleans Parish, Louisiana.

Children of Richard Waguespack and Myrtle Gautreau are:

1019	i.	Richard P.[8] Waguespack, Jr. (Woody), born 21 January 1951 in Gonzales, Ascension Parish, Louisiana; died 21 July 1966 in Ascension Parish, Louisiana.
+ 1020	ii.	Adrian Charles Waguespack, born 16 February 1952 in Gonzales, Ascension Parish, Louisiana.
+ 1021	iii.	Michael Curtis Waguespack, born 30 June 1953 in Gonzales, Ascension Parish, Louisiana.
+ 1022	iv.	Rhonda Faye Waguespack, born 02 November 1954 in Gonzales, Ascension Parish, Louisiana.
+ 1023	v.	Bonnie Ann Waguespack, born 30 July 1957 in Gonzales, Ascension Parish, Louisiana.
+ 1024	vi.	George Keith Waguespack, born 20 March 1961 in Lutcher, St. James Parish, Louisiana.
+ 1025	vii.	Kelli Jean Waguespack, born 02 November 1970 in Baton Rouge, East Baton Rouge Parish, Louisiana.

480. George Ann[7] Waguespack (George Nicholas[6], Marie Octavie[5] Robért, ***, Jean Frumence[4], Mathieu[3], Jean[2], Mathieu[1]) was born 19 May 1932 in Burnside, Ascension Parish, Louisiana. She married **Carl James Robért, (Hubble)** 12 February 1953 in St. Anthony Catholic Church, Darrow, Louisiana, son of Rene Robért and Gladys Cointment. He was born 31 January 1929 in Donaldson Tract Plantation, Burnside, Ascension Parish, Louisiana.

Children are listed above under (319) Carl James Robért, (Hubble).

481. Thelma Marie[7] Brou (Delia Philomene[6] Waguespack, Marie Octavie[5] Robért, ***, Jean Frumence[4], Mathieu[3], Jean[2], Mathieu[1]) was born 30 November 1925 in Ascension Plantation, Donaldsonville, Ascension Parish, Louisiana, and died 06 August 2000 in Ascension Parish, Donaldsonville, Louisiana. She married **Edward Lawless Michel** 02 August 1947 in St. Francis of Assissi Catholic Church, Smoke Bend, Louisiana, son of Arthur Michel and Irene Lawless. He was born 16 August 1924 in Donaldsonville, Ascension Parish, Louisiana, and died 03 March 1999 in Donaldsonville, Ascension Parish, Louisiana.

Children of Thelma Brou and Edward Michel are:
+ 1026	i.	Edward Arthur[8] Michel, born 04 May 1948 in Donaldsonville, Ascension Parish, Louisiana.
1027	ii.	Stephen Michael Michel, born 13 December 1949 in Donaldsonville, Ascension Parish, Louisiana. He married Helena Ann Berthelot 12 August 1972 in St. Joseph Catholic Church, Pierre Part, Louisiana; born 30 July 1951 in Assumption Parish, Pierre Part, Louisiana.

483. Doris Therése[7] Brou (Delia Philomene[6] Waguespack, Marie Octavie[5]

Robért, ***, Jean Frumence[4], Mathieu[3], Jean[2], Mathieu[1]) was born 20 August 1930 in Ascension Plantation, Mc Call, Louisiana. She married **Raymond Francois Blanchard** 11 April 1953 in St. Francis Assissi Catholic Church, Smoke Bend, Louisiana. He was born 08 August 1926 in Belle Rose, Louisiana.

Children of Doris Brou and Raymond Blanchard are:

- \+ 1028 i. Donna Marie[8] Blanchard, born 18 June 1954 in Donaldsonville, Ascension Parish, Louisiana; died Unknown in Belle Rose, Louisiana.
- \+ 1029 ii. Constance Anne Blanchard, born 11 July 1955 in Donaldsonville, Ascension Parish, Louisiana.
- \+ 1030 iii. Julie Therese Blanchard, born 08 February 1957 in Donaldsonville, Ascension Parish, Louisiana; died Unknown in Assumption Parish, Napoleonville. Louisiana.
- \+ 1031 iv. Lauren Claire Blanchard, born 12 February 1960 in Donaldsonville, Ascension Parish, Louisiana; died Unknown in Houma, Louisiana.
- \+ 1032 v. Marvin Clay Blanchard, born 13 September 1961 in Donaldsonville, Ascension Parish, Louisiana; died Unknown in Assumption Parish, Napoleonville. Louisiana.

484. Joyce Ann[7] Brou (Delia Philomene[6] Waguespack, Marie Octavie[5] Robért, ***, Jean Frumence[4], Mathieu[3], Jean[2], Mathieu[1]) was born 26 October 1932 in Ascension Plantation, Mc Call, Louisiana. She married **Herbert Joseph Danos** 27 February 1954 in St. Francis Assissi Catholic Church, Smoke Bend, Louisiana, son of Joseph Danos and Inez Grabert. He was born 22 June 1929.

Children of Joyce Brou and Herbert Danos are:

- 1033 i. Jerome Paul[8] Danos, born 07 March 1957 in Raceland, Lafourche Parish, Louisiana. He married Betty Borne 07 August 1982 in St. Phillip Church, Vacherie, Louisiana; born 07 September in Vacherie, Louisiana.
- \+ 1034 ii. Joseph Charles Danos, born 10 June 1958 in Raceland, Lafourche Parish, Louisiana.
- 1035 iii. Jane Marie Danos, born 17 May 1960 in Raceland, Lafourche Parish, Louisiana. She married Russell D. Carithers 14 June 1986 in St. Aloysius Catholic Church, Baton Rouge, Louisiana; born Unknown.
- 1036 iv. Jacqueline Marie Danos, born 01 April 1963 in Raceland, Lafourche Parish, Louisiana. She married Les Rhodes Unknown in Houston, Texas; born Unknown.
- 1037 v. John Herbert Danos, born 24 May 1966 in Raceland, Lafourche Parish, Louisiana. He married Melissa Ann Arceneaux 11 October 1991 in St. Louis Catholic Church, Houma, Louisiana; born Unknown.
- 1038 vi. Joy Noella Danos, born 10 September 1969 in Raceland,

Lafourche Parish, Louisiana. She married Dale Joseph Fremin, Jr. 10 July 1993 in St. Charles Borromeo Church, Thibodaux, Louisiana; born Unknown.

486. Paul Charles[7] Brou (Delia Philomene[6] Waguespack, Marie Octavie[5] Robért, ***, Jean Frumence[4], Mathieu[3], Jean[2], Mathieu[1]) was born 26 March 1940 in Chatham Plantation, Hohen Solms, Louisiana. He married **Barbara Ann Zeringue** 19 June 1962 in St. Francis Assissi Catholic Church, Smoke Bend, Louisiana, daughter of Leon Zeringue and Evelyn Amedee. She was born 08 February 1942 in Donaldsonville, Ascension Parish, Louisiana.

Children of Paul Brou and Barbara Zeringue are:

1039	i.	**Sharon Elizabeth[8] Brou, born 30 April 1963 in Anniston, Alabama. She married Edward Scott Tonseth 26 November 1988 in Christ King Catholic Church, Oklahoma City, Oklahoma; born Unknown.**
1040	ii.	**Leslie Marie Brou, born 21 September 1964 in New Orleans, Orleans Parish, Louisiana. She married (1) Victor Salas 22 September 1990 in Christ the King Catholic Church, Oklahoma City, Oklahoma; born Unknown. She married (2) Eric Stanley Shaffer 14 January 1995 in St. Rita Catholic Church, Dallas, Texas; born Unknown.**
1041	iii.	**Renée Claire Brou, born 13 October 1965 in New Orleans, Orleans Parish, Louisiana; died 15 October 1965 in New Orleans, Orleans Parish, Louisiana.**
1042	iv.	**Dana Michelle Brou, born 13 June 1967 in New Orleans, Orleans Parish, Louisiana. She married Ronald Austin Hill 26 May 1991 in Christ the King Catholic Church, Oklahoma City, Oklahoma; born Unknown.**
1043	v.	**David Paul Brou, born 05 January 1970 in New Orleans, Orleans Parish, Louisiana.**
1044	vi.	**Jennifer Leigh Brou, born 22 July 1971 in New Orleans, Orleans Parish, Louisiana; died Unknown in Oklahoma City, Oklahoma. She married David James Thielke 21 July 1995 in Christ the King Catholic Church, Oklahoma City, Oklahoma; born Unknown.**

487. Leroy Joseph[7] Waguespack (Frumence Hubert[6], Marie Octavie[5] Robért, ***, Jean Frumence[4], Mathieu[3], Jean[2], Mathieu[1]) was born 16 June 1935 in Modeste, Louisiana, and died 26 November 1994 in New Orleans, Orleans Parish, Louisiana. He married **Shirly Ann Bourque** 20 August 1956 in St. Theresa Catholic Church, Gonzales, Louisiana. She was born 21 December 1938.

Children of Leroy Waguespack and Shirly Bourque are:

| 1045 | i. | **Denise Marie[8] Waguespack, born 22 May 1957 in Donaldsonville,** |

Ascension Parish, Louisiana. She married Edmond Wade Shows 22 November 1986 in Vacherie, St. James Parish, Louisiana; born Unknown.

1046   ii.   Donna Marie Waguespack, born 14 May 1959 in Lutcher, Louisiana. She married George Joseph Shaheen, Jr. 22 November 1986 in St. James Catholic Church, St. James, Louisiana; born Unknown.

+   1047   iii.   Dawn Marie Waguespack, born 07 April 1961 in Lutcher, Louisiana.

1048   iv.   Leroy Joseph Waguespack, Jr., born 26 May 1964 in Lutcher, Louisiana.

488. Clyde Paul[7] Waguespack (Frumence Hubert[6], Marie Octavie[5] Robért, ***, Jean Frumence[4], Mathieu[3], Jean[2], Mathieu[1]) was born 25 April 1937 in Donaldsonville, Ascension Parish, Louisiana. He married **Doris Jumonville** 09 February 1957 in St. Mary Catholic Church, Convent, Louisiana. She was born 07 April 1937.

Children of Clyde Waguespack and Doris Jumonville are:

+   1049   i.   Vickie Ann[8] Waguespack, born 12 April 1959 in Lutcher, Louisiana.

+   1050   ii.   Trudi Marie Waguespack, born 14 December 1959 in Lutcher, Louisiana.

+   1051   iii.   Monica Ann Waguespack, born 29 August 1962 in Lutcher, Louisiana.

1052   iv.   Clyde Paul Waguespack, Jr., born 16 July 1966 in Lutcher, Louisiana.

1053   v.   Neal Anthony Waguespack, born 13 July 1967 in Lutcher, Louisiana. He married Paula A. Dornier 01 July 1988 in St. Anthony Catholic Chapel, Darrow, Louisiana; born Unknown.

489. Kerry Gerard[7] Waguespack (Frumence Hubert[6], Marie Octavie[5] Robért, ***, Jean Frumence[4], Mathieu[3], Jean[2], Mathieu[1]) was born 15 November 1942 in Donaldsonville, Ascension Parish, Louisiana. He married **Mercedean Marie Lessard** 07 July 1962 in Christ the King Chapel, LSU Campus, Baton Rouge, Louisiana. She was born 18 January 1944.

Children of Kerry Waguespack and Mercedean Lessard are:

+   1054   i.   Kerry Ann[8] Waguespack, born 07 February 1963.

1055   ii.   Kirk Patrick Waguespack, born 21 August 1964 in Lutcher, Louisiana.

1056   iii.   Kim Marie Waguespack, born 26 December 1967 in Lutcher, Louisiana.

490. Galyn Thomas[7] Waguespack (Frumence Hubert[6], Marie Octavie[5] Robért, ***, Jean Frumence[4], Mathieu[3], Jean[2], Mathieu[1]) was born 07 March 1945 in Burnside, Ascension Parish, Louisiana. He married **Michele Elaine Boustany** 16 May 1970 in Lafayette, Louisiana. She was born 26 November 1945.

Children of Galyn Waguespack and Michele Boustany are:
| 1057 | i. | **Christi Lynn[8] Waguespack, born 23 September 1974 in Baton Rouge, East Baton Rouge Parish, Louisiana.** |
| 1058 | ii. | **April Marie Waguespack, born 25 April 1982 in Baton Rouge, East Baton Rouge Parish, Louisiana.** |

491. Ivy Joseph[7] Waguespack (Frumence Hubert[6], Marie Octavie[5] Robért, ***, Jean Frumence[4], Mathieu[3], Jean[2], Mathieu[1]) was born 08 February 1946 in Donaldsonville, Ascension Parish, Louisiana. He married **Marilyn Marie Arceneaux** 28 July 1973 in St. Mary Catholic Church, Convent, Louisiana. She was born 23 July 1954.

Children of Ivy Waguespack and Marilyn Arceneaux are:
1059	i.	**Jennifer Lynn[8] Waguespack, born 24 December 1975 in Baton Rouge, East Baton Rouge Parish, Louisiana.**
1060	ii.	**Brad Michael Waguespack, born 05 July 1979 in Baton Rouge, East Baton Rouge Parish, Louisiana.**
1061	iii.	**Devon Michele Waguespack, born 01 February 1984 in Baton Rouge, East Baton Rouge Parish, Louisiana.**

492. Cathy Marie[7] Waguespack (Clarence Anthony[6], Marie Octavie[5] Robért, ***, Jean Frumence[4], Mathieu[3], Jean[2], Mathieu[1]) was born 27 June 1941 in Donaldsonville, Ascension Parish, Louisiana. She married **John Wayne Lanoux, Sr.** 04 July 1964 in St. Mary Catholic Chapel, Union, Louisiana. He was born 20 April 1941 in Gonzales, Ascension Parish, Louisiana.

Children of Cathy Waguespack and John Lanoux are:
+	1062	i.	**Stacy Louise[8] Lanoux, born 05 September 1965 in Baton Rouge, East Baton Rouge Parish, Louisiana.**
	1063	ii.	**Shelly Marie Lanoux, born 30 December 1966 in Baton Rouge, East Baton Rouge Parish, Louisiana.**
	1064	iii.	**Simone Lanoux, born 06 May 1969 in Baton Rouge, East Baton Rouge Parish, Louisiana.**
	1065	iv.	**John Wayne Lanoux, Jr., born 17 July 1973 in Baton Rouge, East Baton Rouge Parish, Louisiana.**

493. Brenda Ann[7] Waguespack (Clarence Anthony[6], Marie Octavie[5] Robért,

***, Jean Frumence[4], Mathieu[3], Jean[2], Mathieu[1]) was born 15 July 1942 in Donaldsonville, Ascension Parish, Louisiana. She married **Donald Ray Harelson** 31 December 1961 in St. Mary Catholic Church, Union, Louisiana. He was born 26 March 1941.

Children of Brenda Waguespack and Donald Harelson are:
+   1066   i.   **Wade Anthony[8] Harelson, born 21 October 1962.**
    1067   ii. **Jody Robért Harelson, born 17 April 1964 in Baton Rouge, East Baton Rouge Parish, Louisiana.**
    1068   iii. **Glen Thomas Harelson, born 13 October 1965 in Baton Rouge, East Baton Rouge Parish, Louisiana.**
    1069   iv. **Gary Paul Harelson, born 09 December 1966 in Baton Rouge, East Baton Rouge Parish, Louisiana.**

494. Daryl Joseph[7] Waguespack (Clarence Anthony[6], Marie Octavie[5] Robért, ***, Jean Frumence[4], Mathieu[3], Jean[2], Mathieu[1]) was born 30 October 1945 in Donaldsonville, Ascension Parish, Louisiana. He married **Mary Alice Simon** 14 January 1967 in St. Mary Catholic Chapel, Union, Louisiana. She was born 29 January 1948.

Children of Daryl Waguespack and Mary Simon are:
    1070   i.   **Donovan[8] Waguespack, born 29 November 1967 in Baton Rouge, East Baton Rouge Parish, Louisiana.**
    1071   ii. **Nicole Waguespack, born 10 September 1969 in Baton Rouge, East Baton Rouge Parish, Louisiana.**
    1072   iii. **Dal Jeremy Waguespack, born 19 July 1974 in Baton Rouge, East Baton Rouge Parish, Louisiana.**

495. Joel Anthony[7] Waguespack (Clarence Anthony[6], Marie Octavie[5] Robért, ***, Jean Frumence[4], Mathieu[3], Jean[2], Mathieu[1]) was born 11 January 1949 in Donaldsonville, Ascension Parish, Louisiana. He married **Sherry A. Pailette** 02 April 1971 in St. Anthony Catholic Chapel, Darrow, Louisiana. She was born 07 May 1952.

Children of Joel Waguespack and Sherry Pailette are:
    1073   i.   **Shane Anthony[8] Waguespack, born 03 November 1971 in Baton Rouge, East Baton Rouge Parish, Louisiana.**
    1074   ii. **Joell Marie Waguespack, born 24 October 1974 in Baton Rouge, East Baton Rouge Parish, Louisiana.**

496. Janel Mary[7] Waguespack (Clarence Anthony[6], Marie Octavie[5] Robért, ***, Jean Frumence[4], Mathieu[3], Jean[2], Mathieu[1]) was born 27 June 1952 in Donaldsonville, Ascension Parish, Louisiana. She married **Lionel Vincent Porta**

25 August 1973 in St. Michael Catholic Church, Convent, Louisiana. He was born 14 August 1950.

Children of Janel Waguespack and Lionel Porta are:

  1075   i.   Randal Jude[8] Porta, born 16 April 1977 in Baton Rouge, East Baton Rouge Parish, Louisiana.
  1076   ii. Resa Lynn Porta, born 09 July 1980 in Baton Rouge, East Baton Rouge Parish, Louisiana.

511.   Renell Joseph[7] Robért (Lester[6], Wallace Jean[5], Jean Frumence[4], Mathieu[3], Jean[2], Mathieu[1]) was born 06 November 1947 in Donaldsonville, Ascension Parish, Louisiana. He married **Karen Elizabeth Cascio** 07 July 1972 in Amite Baptist Church, Denham Springs, Livingston Parish, Louisiana, daughter of Paul Cascio and Mary Garrison. She was born 28 June 1950 in Baton Rouge, East Baton Rouge Parish, Louisiana, and died 26 December 2008 in Baton Rouge, East Baton Rouge Parish, Louisiana.

Children of Renell Robért and Karen Cascio are:

  1077   i.   **Robyn Elizabeth[8] Robért, born 20 December 1978 in Baton Rouge, East Baton Rouge Parish, Louisiana. She married Brian Dale Miller 01 March 2003 in Amite Baptist Church, Denham Springs, Louisiana.**
  1078   ii. **Rebecca Elise Robért, born 10 October 1984 in Baton Rouge, East Baton Rouge Parish, Louisiana.**

512.   Phyllis Anne[7] Robért (Lester[6], Wallace Jean[5], Jean Frumence[4], Mathieu[3], Jean[2], Mathieu[1]) was born 25 November 1948 in Donaldsonville, Ascension Parish, Louisiana. She married **John Part** 27 December 1969 in Darrow, Ascension Parish, Louisiana, son of Stafford Part and Evelyn St. Blanc. He was born 09 May 1948 in New Orleans, Orleans Parish, Louisiana.

Children of Phyllis Robért and John Part are:

  + 1079   i.   **Shandra Anne[8] Part, born 23 March 1971 in Panama City, Florida.**
     1080   ii. **Leslie Therése Part, born 30 November 1973 in Donaldsonville, Ascension Parish, Louisiana. She married Brenen Hebert 18 October 1996 in St. Amant, Ascension Parish, Louisiana.**
     1081   iii. **Jodey Lynne Part, born 10 March 1978 in Baton Rouge, East Baton Rouge Parish, Louisiana. She married Paul Bruno 28 June 2002 in Dutchtown, Ascension Parish, Louisiana.**

513.   Dale Anthony[7] Robért (Lester[6], Wallace Jean[5], Jean Frumence[4], Mathieu[3], Jean[2], Mathieu[1]) was born 13 March 1951 in Donaldsonville, Ascension Parish, Louisiana. He married **Joan Karen Sherrwood, (Divorced)** 26 August

1972 in Gonzales, Ascension Parish, Louisiana, daughter of H. Sherrwood and Louise Bowles. She was born 05 July 1954 in Shaw, Mississippi.

Children of Dale Robért and Joan Sherrwood are:

1082   **i.   Cheryl[8] Robért, born 02 March 1977 in Baton Rouge, East Baton Rouge Parish, Louisiana.**

1083   **ii. Aaron Paul Robért, born 25 September 1973 in Baton Rouge, East Baton Rouge Parish, Louisiana. He married Kristy Gallagher 15 September 2006 in Las Vegas Nevada.**

1084   **iii. Stephanie Robért, born 01 October 1974 in Baton Rouge, East Baton Rouge Parish, Louisiana. She married Brett Williams 28 February 2003 in Prairieville, Ascension Parish, Louisiana.**

514. Faryl Charles[7] Robért (Lester[6], Wallace Jean[5], Jean Frumence[4], Mathieu[3], Jean[2], Mathieu[1]) was born 28 July 1953 in Donaldsonville, Ascension Parish, Louisiana. He married **Mona Roussel** 15 October 1982 in Hester, St. James Parish, Louisiana, daughter of Sheldon Roussel and Lois St.Pierre. She was born 15 January 1956 in Convent, St. James Parish, Louisiana.

Children of Faryl Robért and Mona Roussel are:

1085   **i.   Kristy Ann[8] Robért, born 09 September 1984 in Baton Rouge, East Baton Rouge Parish, Louisiana.**

1086   **ii. Jeremy Paul Robért, born 01 May 1988 in Baton Rouge, East Baton Rouge Parish, Louisiana.**

1087   **iii. Colby Charles Robért, born 03 November 1990 in Baton Rouge, East Baton Rouge Parish, Louisiana.**

516. Kirk David[7] Robért (Lester[6], Wallace Jean[5], Jean Frumence[4], Mathieu[3], Jean[2], Mathieu[1]) was born 23 May 1957 in Donaldsonville, Ascension Parish, Louisiana. He married **Susan Montagnino** 05 November 1999 in Las Vegas, Nevada, daughter of Nicholas Montagnino and Anna Alello. She was born 14 September 1956 in Baton Rouge, East Baton Rouge Parish, Louisiana.

Children of Kirk Robért and Susan Montagnino are:

1088   **i.   David Ryan[8] Robért, born 11 February 1980 in Baton Rouge, East Baton Rouge Parish, Louisiana. He married Nancy Parsons 24 February 2001.**

1089   **ii. Nathan Paul Robért, born 03 December 1981 in Baton Rouge, East Baton Rouge Parish, Louisiana. He married Ester Tannehill 30 December 2000 in Baton Rouge, East Baton Rouge Parish, Louisiana.**

1090   **iii. Joshua Blake Robért, born 13 November 1984 in Baton Rouge, East Baton Rouge Parish, Louisiana.**

1091   **iv. Kelly Leann Millican, born 26 May 1983 in Baton Rouge, East**

Baton Rouge Parish, Louisiana.

517. Keeley Paul[7] Robért (Lester[6], Wallace Jean[5], Jean Frumence[4], Mathieu[3], Jean[2], Mathieu[1]) was born 19 November 1959 in Donaldsonville, Ascension Parish, Louisiana. He married **Mary Elizabeth Napoli** 28 June 1980 in Baton Rouge, East Baton Rouge Parish, Louisiana, daughter of Charles Napoli and Grace Jones. She was born 01 August 1961 in Baton Rouge, East Baton Rouge Parish, Louisiana.

Children of Keeley Robért and Mary Napoli are:

1092	i.	**Brittney Leigh[8] Robért, born 29 May 1983 in Baton Rouge, East Baton Rouge Parish, Louisiana.**
1093	ii.	**Michael Paul Robért, born 04 December 1985 in Baton Rouge, East Baton Rouge Parish, Louisiana.**

520. Vernon[7] Schexnaydre, (Coon) (Berthile Joseph[6], Henry Joseph[5], Marie Antoinette[4] Robért, Mathieu[3], Jean[2], Mathieu[1]) was born 22 November 1925 in Burnside, Ascension Parish, Louisiana. He married **Barbara Bourgeois** 23 August 1952, daughter of Joseph Bourgeois and Elizabeth Mire. She was born Unknown.

Children of Vernon Schexnaydre and Barbara Bourgeois are:

+	1094	i.	**Kent Alan[8] Schexnaydre, born 21 May 1953 in Baton Rouge, East Baton Rouge Parish, Louisiana.**
	1095	ii.	**Ellen Claire Schexnaydre, born 19 October 1954 in Donaldsonville, Ascension Parish, Louisiana. She married Lyle Dixon Unknown; born Unknown.**
	1096	iii.	**Lorna Mary Schexnaydre, born 19 November 1955 in Donaldsonville, Ascension Parish, Louisiana. She married Craig Gautreaux Unknown; born Unknown.**
	1097	iv.	**Lamar Schexnaydre, born 21 May 1957 in Donaldsonville, Ascension Parish, Louisiana. He married Cathy Hedberg Unknown; born Unknown.**
	1098	v.	**Angela Ann Schexnaydre, born 13 August 1959 in Donaldsonville, Ascension Parish, Louisiana. She married Kenny John LeBlanc 15 September 1978; born Unknown.**
	1099	vi.	**Iris Joan Schexnaydre, born 06 March 1963 in Baton Rouge, East Baton Rouge Parish, Louisiana. She married James Morgan; born Unknown.**
	1100	vii.	**Verna Agnes Schexnaydre, born 16 December 1963 in Baton Rouge, East Baton Rouge Parish, Louisiana. She married Randy Weimer Unknown; born Unknown.**
	1101	viii.	**James Maurice Schexnaydre, born 28 February 1964 in Baton Rouge, East Baton Rouge Parish, Louisiana.**

1102   ix.   Larry Joseph Schexnaydre, born 29 April 1966 in Baton Rouge, East Baton Rouge Parish, Louisiana.

521. Berthile Joseph[7] Schexnaydre, Jr. (Bert) (Berthile Joseph[6], Henry Joseph[5], Marie Antoinette[4] Robért, Mathieu[3], Jean[2], Mathieu[1]) was born 25 May 1927 in Burnside, Ascension Parish, Louisiana. He married **Ola Mae Rita Waguespack** 07 June 1948 in St. Mary Chapel, Union Louisiana, daughter of Wallis Waguespack and Edna Decareaux. She was born 13 February 1928 in Burnside, Ascension Parish, Louisiana.

Children are listed above under (470) Ola Mae Rita Waguespack.

524. Ione Theresa[7] Schexnaydre (Berthile Joseph[6], Henry Joseph[5], Marie Antoinette[4] Robért, Mathieu[3], Jean[2], Mathieu[1]) was born 03 June 1932 in Burnside, Ascension Parish, Louisiana. She married **Ruffin Joseph LeBlanc** 02 August 1958, son of Clebert LeBlanc and Alida Achée. He was born 25 December 1919 in Point Coupee Parish, LaBarre, Louisiana, and died 17 June 2001 in Burnside, Ascension Parish, Louisiana.

Children of Ione Schexnaydre and Ruffin LeBlanc are:

1103   i.   **Lori Therese[8] LeBlanc, born 01 November 1959. She married Kenneth Ridgdell 28 January 1984; born Unknown.**

1104   ii.   **Alida Marie LeBlanc, born 12 February 1961. She married Jeffrey Dean Lewis Unknown; born Unknown.**

1105   iii.   **Kyle Joseph LeBlanc, born 22 February 1963. He married Cynthia Renée Wilcher 25 November 1985; born Unknown.**

1106   iv.   **Lydia Ann LeBlanc, born 05 July 1964. She married Joseph Neal Odom 31 August 1985; born Unknown.**

1107   v.   **Hope Elizabeth LeBlanc, born 10 November 1965.**

1108   vi.   **Marcia Leigh LeBlanc, born 31 March 1967. She married William Spears 05 November 1988; born Unknown.**

1109   vii.   **Keith Gerard LeBlanc, born 29 December 1970.**

525. Clyde Thaddeus[7] Schexnaydre (Berthile Joseph[6], Henry Joseph[5], Marie Antoinette[4] Robért, Mathieu[3], Jean[2], Mathieu[1]) was born 29 October 1933 in Burnside, Ascension Parish, Louisiana, and died 25 March 2003 in Ascension Parish, Sorrento, Louisiana. He married **Marie Louise Jumonville** 16 June 1963, daughter of Adolphe Jumonville and Louise Trabeaux.

Children of Clyde Schexnaydre and Marie Jumonville are:

1110   i.   **Blaine Thaddeus[8] Schexnaydre, born 08 April 1964. He married Jane.**

1111   ii.   **Stacey Marie Schexnaydre, born 21 September 1967.**

528. Edith Marie[7] **Schexnaydre, (Bo-Boot)** (Berthile Joseph[6], Henry Joseph[5], Marie Antoinette[4] Robért, Mathieu[3], Jean[2], Mathieu[1]) was born 16 December 1936 in Burnside, Ascension Parish, Louisiana, and died 29 October 2001 in Ascension Parish, Donaldsonville, Louisiana. She married **Claude Bourg, Jr.** 26 April 1958 in St. Anthony Chapel, Darrow, Louisiana, son of Claude Bourg and Georgine Gros. He was born 10 December 1934 in Ascension Parish, Donaldsonville, Louisiana, and died 28 September 2004 in Ascension Parish, Donaldsonville, Louisiana.

Children of Edith Schexnaydre and Claude Bourg are:

1112	i.	**Bambi Ann**[8] **Bourg,** born 22 May 1959 in Donaldsonville, Ascension Parish, Louisiana. She married Charles LeBlanc 04 December 1981 in Ascension Catholic Church, Donaldsonville, Louisiana; born Unknown.
1113	ii.	**Brad Paul Bourg,** born 29 June 1960 in Donaldsonville, Ascension Parish, Louisiana. He married Malea Rachel Roy 19 October 1990 in Sacred Heart Catholic Church, Baton Rouge, Louisiana; born Unknown.
1114	iii.	**Bertile Joseph Bourg,** born 13 July 1963 in Donaldsonville, Ascension Parish, Louisiana.
1115	iv.	**Brennan Michael Bourg,** born 21 October 1964 in Donaldsonville, Ascension Parish, Louisiana.

529. Dayton[7] **Schexnaydre** (Berthile Joseph[6], Henry Joseph[5], Marie Antoinette[4] Robért, Mathieu[3], Jean[2], Mathieu[1]) was born 16 January 1939 in Burnside, Ascension Parish, Louisiana. He married **Carmen Marie Daigle** 15 April 1961, daughter of Francis Daigle and Carmen Tregre.

Children of Dayton Schexnaydre and Carmen Daigle are:

1116	i.	**Dale Anthony**[8] **Schexnaydre,** born 08 July 1962. He married Deanie Wright 24 June 1989; born Unknown.
1117	ii.	**Carmen Ann Schexnaydre,** born 31 October 1963. She married Neil Ramber 04 April 1992; born Unknown.
1118	iii.	**Diane Marie Schexnaydre,** born 03 December 1965. She married Kelly McGovern 07 September 1991; born Unknown.
1119	iv.	**Guy Grancis Schexnaydre,** born 09 January 1967. He married Tinna Lopinto 19 January 1991; born Unknown.
1120	v.	**Neal Joseph Schexnaydre,** born 11 September 1970 in Donaldsonville, Ascension Parish, Louisiana. He married Judy Elizabeth Sagona 02 September 1994 in Ascension Catholic Church, Donaldsonville, Louisiana; born Unknown.
1121	vi.	**Chris Michael Schexnaydre,** born 26 December 1972.
1122	vii.	Brian Thomas Schexnaydre, born 11 October 1983. He married Jeanette Marie Bourgeois; born May 1983 in Baton Rouge, East

530. Lyle[7] **Schexnaydre** (Berthile Joseph[6], Henry Joseph[5], Marie Antoinette[4] Robért, Mathieu[3], Jean[2], Mathieu[1]) was born 20 August 1941 in Burnside, Ascension Parish, Louisiana. He married **Frankie Foster** 04 February 1961, daughter of Claude Foster and Ella Antie. She was born Unknown.

Children of Lyle Schexnaydre and Frankie Foster are:

1123	i.	**Troy Michael**[8] **Schexnaydre, born 28 November 1961. He married Terry Riley Unknown; born Unknown.**
1124	ii.	**Tab Andrew Schexnaydre, born 13 October 1962; died 14 October 1962.**
1125	iii.	**Terri Lynne Schexnaydre, born 29 July 1964.**
1126	iv.	**Clint Michael Schexnaydre, born 20 February 1966.**
1127	v.	**Lance Paul Schexnaydre, born 22 August 1969.**

532. Ronald Paul[7] **Brou, Sr.** (André Augustine[6], Marie Palmyre[5] Robért, (Tee-Nannan), Jean Frumence[4], Mathieu[3], Jean[2], Mathieu[1]) was born 04 October 1929 in McCall, Ascension Parish, Louisiana, and died 11 June 2008 in Denham Springs, Livingston Parish, Louisiana.

Children of Ronald Paul Brou, Sr. are:

1128	i.	**Ronald Paul**[8] **Brou, Jr., born 28 December 1954.**
1129	ii.	**Sybil Brou.**

533. Goldie Marie[7] **Brou, (Giggle)** (André Augustine[6], Marie Palmyre[5] Robért, (Tee-Nannan), Jean Frumence[4], Mathieu[3], Jean[2], Mathieu[1]) was born 06 March 1931 in McCall, Ascension Parish, Louisiana. She married **Murray Edward Stevens** 18 August 1951 in St. Anthony Catholic Chapel, Darrow, Louisiana, son of Murray Stevens and Eura Bahm. He was born 07 July 1929 in Orleans Parish, New Orleans, Orleans Parish, Louisiana, and died 12 May 1992 in Baton Rouge, East Baton Rouge Parish, Louisiana.

Children of Goldie Brou and Murray Stevens are:

1130	i.	**Patrice Marie**[8] **Stevens, born 06 May 1952 in Donaldsonville, Ascension Parish, Louisiana. She married James Randall Aiken 27 July 1974 in St. Joseph Cathederal, Baton Rouge, Louisiana.**
1131	ii.	**Mark Alvin Stevens, born 20 November 1954 in Donaldsonville, Ascension Parish, Louisiana. He married Christine Herman 03 July 1981.**
1132	iii.	**Greg Patrick Stevens, born 18 August 1956 in Donaldsonville, Ascension Parish, Louisiana.**
1133	iv.	**Blake Edwards Stevens, born 08 July 1959 in Fort Smith,**

Arkansas.

536. Julian Pierre[7] Schexnaydre,Jr. (Julian Pierre[6], Henry Joseph[5], Marie Antoinette[4] Robért, Mathieu[3], Jean[2], Mathieu[1]) was born 28 November 1950 in Ascension Parish, Donaldsonville, Louisiana. He married **Cindy Olive Simoneaux** 30 May 1975 in St. Theresa Catholic Church, Gonzales, Louisiana. She was born 17 August 1956 in St. Charles Parish, Luling, Louisiana.

Children of Julian Schexnaydre and Cindy Simoneaux are:

1134	i.	**Jay Michael[8] Schexnaydre, born 12 May 1979 in Baton Rouge, East Baton Rouge Parish, Louisiana.**
1135	ii.	**Kip J. Schexnaydre, born 25 February 1982 in Baton Rouge, East Baton Rouge Parish, Louisiana.**
1136	iii.	**Dirk P. Schexnaydre, born 28 January 1985 in Baton Rouge, East Baton Rouge Parish, Louisiana.**

537. Roberta Ann[7] Schexnaydre (Julian Pierre[6], Henry Joseph[5], Marie Antoinette[4] Robért, Mathieu[3], Jean[2], Mathieu[1]) was born 29 May 1953 in Tezcuco Plantation, Burnside, Ascension Parish, Louisiana. She married **Terry Gail Dubois** 23 January 1976 in Gonzales, Ascension Parish, Louisiana, son of Julius Dubois and Edna Garner. He was born 23 January 1948 in Texas.

Children of Roberta Schexnaydre and Terry Dubois are:

| 1137 | i. | **Todd[8] Dubois, born 19 July 1979 in Baton Rouge, East Baton Rouge Parish, Louisiana.** |
| 1138 | ii. | **Meché Ann Dubois, born 31 August 1981 in Baton Rouge, East Baton Rouge Parish, Louisiana.** |

539. Connie Theresa[7] Schexnaydre (Julian Pierre[6], Henry Joseph[5], Marie Antoinette[4] Robért, Mathieu[3], Jean[2], Mathieu[1]) was born 14 January 1960 in St. James Parish, Lutcher, Louisiana. She married **Patrick Jude Frederic** 25 June 1988 in St. James Parish, Central, Louisiana. He was born 19 January 1961 in St. James Parish, Central, Louisiana.

Child of Connie Schexnaydre and Patrick Frederic is:

| 1139 | i. | **Crystal Michelle[8] Schexnaydre, born 16 September 1981 in Baton Rouge, East Baton Rouge Parish, Louisiana.** |

545. Laura Marie[7] Waguespack (Mathilda Valerie[6] Schexnaydre, Albert Simon[5] Marie Antoinette[4] Robért, Mathieu[3], Jean[2], Mathieu[1]) was born 03 October 1917 in Louisiana, and died 03 May 2005 in Baton Rouge, East Baton Rouge Parish, Louisiana. She married **Newell Roy Boudreaux** Abt. 1939 in

Louisiana. He was born 02 February 1918 in St. James Parish, and died 03 November 1991 in Convent, St. James Parish, Louisiana.

Children of Laura Waguespack and Newell Boudreaux are:
  1140   i.   **Melvin[8] Boudreaux, died 03 May 2005 in Louisiana.**
  1141   ii. **Tilda Boudreaux, died in Gonzales, Ascension Parish, Louisiana.**

547. Leroy[7] Waguespack (Mathilda Valerie[6] Schexnaydre, Albert Simon[5], Marie Antoinette[4] Robért, Mathieu[3], Jean[2], Mathieu[1]) was born 1920 in Lafourche Parish, Louisiana, and died 14 September 2002 in Louisiana. He married **Mae Merancia Chauvin** 09 July 1941 in Lafourche Parish, Louisiana, daughter of Albert Chauvin and Merancia Waguespack. She was born Abt. 1919 in Lafourche Parish, Louisiana, and died 14 September 2002 in Beaumont, Texas.

Children of Leroy Waguespack and Mae Chauvin are:
  1142   i.   **Gerald[8] Waguespack, died 14 September 2002 in Lafourche Parish, Louisiana.**
  1143   ii. **Joyce Waguespack, died in Plano, Texas. She married Leland Leblanc; died in Plano, Texas.**

561. Annette[7] Landry (Vivian[6] Waguespack, Wilson Pierre[5], Delia Marie[4] Robért, Mathieu[3], Jean[2], Mathieu[1]) She married **Louis Joseph Zeringue**, son of Louis Zeringue and Jeanne LeBlanc.

Children of Annette Landry and Louis Zeringue are:
  1144   i.   **Maureen[8] Zeringue.**
  1145   ii.   **Alce Ann Zeringue.**
  1146   iii. **Lisa Marie Zeringue.**
  1147   iv.   **Mark Zeringue.**
  1148   v.   **Lynette Zeringue.**

568. Gayle Anne[7] Waguespack (Leonard[6], Wilson Pierre[5], Delia Marie[4] Robért, Mathieu[3], Jean[2], Mathieu[1]) was born Unknown in New Orleans, Louisiana. She married **Gary Terwilliger** Unknown. He was born Unknown in Smithfield, Virginia.

Child of Gayle Waguespack and Gary Terwilliger is:
  1149   i.   **Martin Wall[8] Terwilliger, born Unknown in Smithfield, Virginia.**

570. Wendy[7] Waguespack (Leonard[6], Wilson Pierre[5], Delia Marie[4] Robért, Mathieu[3], Jean[2], Mathieu[1]) was born Unknown in New Orleans, Louisiana. She married **Paul Ivey** Unknown. He was born Unknown in Baton Rouge, Louisiana.

Child of Wendy Waguespack and Paul Ivey is:

    1150   i.   **Justin Paul**[8] **Ivey, born Unknown in Baton Rouge, Louisiana.**

572. Kay Marie[7] **Waggenspack** (Claude Francis X.[6], Elmira Marie[5] Robért, Jean Paul[4], Mathieu[3], Jean[2], Mathieu[1]) was born 15 September 1948 in Donaldsonville, Ascension Parish, Louisiana. She married **Donald Russel Smith** 02 August 1969, son of Lee Smith and Inez Slay. He was born 12 January 1944 in Meridian, Mississippi.

Children of Kay Waggenspack and Donald Smith are:

    1151   i.   **Adrian R.**[8] **Smith, born 12 May 1973 in Baton Rouge, East Baton Rouge Parish, Louisiana.**

    1152   ii.   **Lauren Marie Smith, born 18 August 1976 in Baton Rouge, East Baton Rouge Parish, Louisiana.**

    1153 iii.   **Gretchen Kay Smith, born 24 July 1978 in Baton Rouge, East Baton Rouge Parish, Louisiana.**

574. Paul John[7] **Waggenspack** (James Berlin[6], Elmira Marie[5] Robért, Jean Paul[4], Mathieu[3], Jean[2], Mathieu[1]) was born 22 November 1952 in East Baton Rouge Parish, Baton Rouge, La.. He married **Ann Marie Gadel** 15 July 1978, daughter of Warren Gadel and Bernadine Spahn. She was born 29 December 1951 in New Orleans, Orleans Parish, Louisiana.

Children of Paul Waggenspack and Ann Gadel are:

    1154   i.   **Scott Joseph**[8] **Waggenspack, born 10 March 1981 in East Baton Rouge Parish, Baton Rouge, La..**

    1155   ii.   **Susan Marie Waggenspack, born 10 May 1982 in East Baton Rouge Parish, Baton Rouge, La..**

    1156 iii.   **Christopher Paul Waggenspack, born 20 July 1984 in East Baton Rouge Parish, Baton Rouge, La..**

576. Lee Jude[7] **Waggenspack** (James Berlin[6], Elmira Marie[5] Robért, Jean Paul[4], Mathieu[3], Jean[2], Mathieu[1]) was born 03 March 1958 in Baton Rouge, East Baton Rouge Parish, Louisiana. He married **Alice Marie Waguespack** 29 April 1981 in St. Mary Catholic Church, Union, Louisiana, daughter of Seymour Waguespack and Catherine Troxclair. She was born 29 November 1959.

Children of Lee Waggenspack and Alice Waguespack are:

    1157   i.   **Katie Marie**[8] **Waggenspack, born 03 December 1981 in Baton Rouge, East Baton Rouge Parish, Louisiana.**

    1158   ii.   **Kevin Joseph Waggenspack, born 28 February 1984 in Baton Rouge, East Baton Rouge Parish, Louisiana.**

577. Judy Ann[7] Waggenspack (James Berlin[6], Elmira Marie[5] Robért, Jean Paul[4], Mathieu[3], Jean[2], Mathieu[1]) was born 13 May 1966 in Lutcher, St. James Parish, Louisiana, and died 15 March 1993 in Gonzales, Ascension Parish, Louisiana. She married **James Paul Aucoin,Jr.** 03 March 1984 in St. Jules Catholic Church, Belle Rose, Louisiana, son of James Aucoin and Theresa Medine. He was born 13 November 1965 in White Castle, Louisiana.

Child of Judy Waggenspack and James Aucoin is:
 1159   i.   **Kimberly Lynn[8] Aucoin, born 01 October 1984 in East Baton Rouge Parish, Baton Rouge, La..**

578. Thomas J.[7] Rauch III (Esther Ann[6] Waggenspack, (Tay-Tay), Elmira Marie[5] Robért, Jean Paul[4], Mathieu[3], Jean[2], Mathieu[1]) was born 23 June 1953 in Baton Rouge, East Baton Rouge Parish, Louisiana. He married **Charmaine.**

Child of Thomas Rauch and Charmaine is:
 1160   i.   **Andrew[8] Rauch.**

579. Myra Margaret[7] Rauch (Esther Ann[6] Waggenspack, (Tay-Tay), Elmira Marie[5] Robért, Jean Paul[4], Mathieu[3], Jean[2], Mathieu[1]) was born 18 January 1955 in Baton Rouge, East Baton Rouge Parish, Louisiana. She married **Stephen Yates Landry** 22 June 1974, son of Louis Landry and Dorothy Yates. He was born 21 July 1953.

Children of Myra Rauch and Stephen Landry are:
 1161   i.   **Brandon Yates[8] Landry, born 20 September 1985 in Baton Rouge, East Baton Rouge Parish, Louisiana.**
 1162   ii. **Leah Michelle Landry, born 22 May 1988 in Baton Rouge, East Baton Rouge Parish, Louisiana.**

581. LaMarylis Ann[7] Waggenspack (Francis Benoit[6], Elmira Marie[5] Robért, Jean Paul[4], Mathieu[3], Jean[2], Mathieu[1]) was born 13 September 1958 in Baton Rouge, Louisiana. She married **Danny Keith Taylor** 15 November 1980 in St. Theresa Church , Gonzales, Louisiana. He was born 26 March 1958.

Children of LaMarylis Waggenspack and Danny Taylor are:
 1163   i.   **Brad Keith[8] Taylor, born 27 April 1986.**
 1164   ii. **Adam Waggenspack Taylor, born 20 July 1989.**
 1165   iii. **Mark Daniel Taylor, born 25 March 1992.**

582. Marlene Marie[7] Becnel (Jeannette Marie[6] Waggenspack, (Non-e), Elmira Marie[5] Robért, Jean Paul[4], Mathieu[3], Jean[2], Mathieu[1]) was born 04 September 1946. She married **Charley Joseph Bourgeois** 25 September 1971 in St. Gabriel, Iberville Parish, Louisiana, son of Felix Bourgeois and Flossie Bergeron.

Children of Marlene Becnel and Charley Bourgeois are:
1166	i.	**Mathew Charles[8] Bourgeois, born 21 February 1973 in Silver Springs, Maryland.**
1167	ii.	**Bryan Patrick Bourgeois, born 21 January 1977 in New Orleans, Orleans Parish, Louisiana.**
1168	iii.	**Michelle Renee Bourgeois, born 23 May 1980 in Shreveport, Caddo Parish, Louisiana.**

584. Ronny John[7] Becnel (Jeannette Marie[6] Waggenspack, (Non-e), Elmira Marie[5] Robért, Jean Paul[4], Mathieu[3], Jean[2], Mathieu[1]) was born 24 November 1950 in East Baton Rouge Parish, Baton Rouge, La.. He married **Lettie Harp** 20 June 1982, daughter of Bruce Harp and Sally Thibodeaux. She was born 21 June 1958.

Child of Ronny Becnel and Lettie Harp is:
1169	i.	**Ashley Claire[8] Becnel, born Unknown; Adopted child.**

588. Wade Benedict[7] Becnel (Jeannette Marie[6] Waggenspack, (Non-e), Elmira Marie[5] Robért, Jean Paul[4], Mathieu[3], Jean[2], Mathieu[1]) was born 30 October 1957 in East Baton Rouge Parish, Baton Rouge, La.. He married **Jan Reneau Whatley** 02 August 1986 in Alabama, daughter of Verlis Reneau. She was born 02 July 1956.

Children of Wade Becnel and Jan Whatley are:
1170	i.	**Lindsay[8] Whatley, born 26 June.**
1171	ii.	**Scarlett Whatley, born 26 August.**

589. Sybil Stanilaus[7] Milano (Maude Marie[6] Robért, Joseph Olide[5], Jean Paul[4], Mathieu[3], Jean[2], Mathieu[1]) was born 19 November 1935 in Donaldsonville, Ascension Parish, Louisiana. She married **Jon Anthony Savoie** 02 June 1955 in Ascension Catholic Church, Donaldsonville, Louisiana, son of Felix Savoie and Winnie Hebert. He was born 16 November 1934 in Donaldsonville, Ascension Parish, Louisiana.

Children of Sybil Milano and Jon Savoie are:
+ 1172	i.	**Lisa Marie[8] Savoie, born 22 September 1956 in New Orleans,**

Orleans Parish, Louisiana.

+ 1173   ii.   Jon Anthony Savoie,Jr, born 05 July 1958 in New Orleans, Orleans Parish, Louisiana.

+ 1174   iii.   Daniel Nicholas Savoie, born 04 April 1960 in New Orleans, Orleans Parish, Louisiana.

+ 1175   iv.   Michelle Ann Savoie, born 27 June 1961 in New Orleans, Orleans Parish, Louisiana.

+ 1176   v.   Stephanie Jo Savoie, born 30 October 1962 in New Orleans, Orleans Parish, Louisiana.

+ 1177   vi.   Pamela Joan Savoie, born 29 April 1964 in New Orleans, Orleans Parish, Louisiana.

590. Paul Anthony[7] Milano (Maude Marie[6] Robért, Joseph Olide[5], Jean Paul[4], Mathieu[3], Jean[2], Mathieu[1]) was born 17 December 1936 in Donaldsonville, Ascension Parish, Louisiana. He married **Wanda Oubre** 01 October 1960 in Darrow, Ascension Parish, Louisiana, daughter of Wilbert Oubre and Camilla Landry. She was born 07 December 1942 in Donaldsonville, Ascension Parish, Louisiana.

Children of Paul Milano and Wanda Oubre are:

+ 1178   i.   Mona Marie[8] Milano, born 27 September 1961 in Paincourtville, Assumption Parish, Louisiana.

   1179   ii.   Kim Ann Milano, born 17 December 1964 in Paincourtville, Assumption Parish, Louisiana.

+ 1180   iii.   Rae Anne Milano, born 10 September 1967 in Donaldsonville, Ascension Parish, Louisiana.

+ 1181   iv.   Nicholas Wilbert Milano, born 08 September 1971 in Baton Rouge, East Baton Rouge Parish, Louisiana.

591. Janice Ann[7] Milano (Maude Marie[6] Robért, Joseph Olide[5], Jean Paul[4], Mathieu[3], Jean[2], Mathieu[1]) was born 09 November 1938 in Darrow, Ascension Parish, Louisiana, and died 13 July 2007 in Thibodaux, Lafourche Parish, Louisiana. She married **Byron Joseph Thiac** 11 April 1956 in Donaldsonville, Ascension Parish, Louisiana, son of Emile Thiac and Laura Brant. He was born 19 March 1937.

Children of Janice Milano and Byron Thiac are:

+ 1182   i.   Melissa Lee[8] Thiac, born 27 May 1957 in Frankfurt, Germany.

+ 1183   ii.   Cindy Marie Thiac, born 19 November 1958 in Thibodaux, Lafourche Parish, Louisiana.

+ 1184   iii.   Peggy Jo Thiac, born 15 March 1960 in Thibodaux, Lafourche Parish, Louisiana.

   1185   iv.   Julie Lynn Thiac, born 02 August 1961 in Thibodaux, Lafourche Parish, Louisiana. She married Michael Ng 02 December 2006 in

Thibodaux, Lafourche Parish, Louisiana.
+ 1186   v.   **Mary Beth Thiac, born 23 November 1963 in Thibodaux, Lafourche Parish, Louisiana.**
+ 1187   vi.   **Timothy Paul Thiac, born 12 May 1965 in Thibodaux, Lafourche Parish, Louisiana.**

592. Myrna Marie[7] Milano (Maude Marie[6] Robért, Joseph Olide[5], Jean Paul[4], Mathieu[3], Jean[2], Mathieu[1]) was born 02 July 1940 in Donaldsonville, Ascension Parish, Louisiana. She married **(1) Frederic John Anderson** 11 February 1961 in Ascension Catholic Church, Donaldsonville, Louisiana, son of Nolan Anderson and Stella Gravois. He was born 09 August 1940 in New Orleans, Orleans Parish, Louisiana, and died 09 May 1986 in West Baton Rouge Parish, Port Allen, Louisiana. She married **(2) H. Paul DuBois** 31 August 1991 in Christ the Redeemer Church, Thibodaux, Lafourche Parish, Louisiana, son of Davis DuBois and Rita Bernard. He was born 11 October 1939 in Houma, Terrebonne Parish, Louisiana.

Children of Myrna Milano and Frederic Anderson are:
+ 1188   i.   **Jamie Lynne[8] Anderson, born 07 January 1962 in Paincourtville, Assumption Parish, Louisiana.**
+ 1189   ii.   **Frederic (Fritz) Anderson, born 05 September 1964 in Paincourtville, Assumption Parish, Louisiana.**
+ 1190   iii.   **David Jerome Anderson, born 11 June 1967 in Donaldsonville, Ascension Parish, Louisiana.**
   1191   iv.   **Jason Paul Anderson, born 10 June 1970 in Donaldsonville, Ascension Parish, Louisiana.**
+ 1192   v.   **Jessica Therese Anderson, born 08 August 1980 in Baton Rouge, East Baton Rouge Parish, Louisiana.**

593. Joe Anne[7] Robért (Joseph Nemours[6], Joseph Olide[5], Jean Paul[4], Mathieu[3], Jean[2], Mathieu[1]) was born 05 December 1938 in Donaldsonville, Ascension Parish, Louisiana. She married **George Louis Cox, Jr.** 17 August 1957 in St. Anthony Chapel, Darrow, Ascension Parish, Louisiana, son of George Cox and Mae Barbier.

Children of Joe Anne Robért and George Cox are:
   1193   i.   **Barth Louis[8] Cox, born 29 June 1958. He married Toue Foss 05 May 1982.**
   1194   ii.   **Janeen Anne Cox, born 23 June 1960. She married Ronald Rodrigue 19 December 1981.**
   1195   iii.   **Jedd Joseph Cox, born 04 February 1962.**
   1196   iv.   **Penny Marie Cox, born 04 November 1963.**
   1197   v.   **Thad Jude Cox, born 08 March 1965.**

594. Fay Marie[7] Robért (Joseph Nemours[6], Joseph Olide[5], Jean Paul[4], Mathieu[3], Jean[2], Mathieu[1]) was born 02 September 1941 in Donaldsonville, Ascension Parish, Louisiana. She married **Ralph John Babin** 24 November 1960 in St. Theresa Catholic Church, Gonzales, Louisiana, son of Pellum Babin and Mildred Alexander. He was born 17 December 1940 in Duplessis, Ascension Parish, Louisiana.

Children of Fay Robért and Ralph Babin are:

+ 1198   i.   **Daria Ann[8] Babin, born 23 October 1962 in Baton Rouge, East Baton Rouge Parish, Louisiana; died 13 September 2004 in Baton Rouge, East Baton Rouge Parish, Louisiana.**
+ 1199   ii.   **Blaise Anthony Babin, born 04 June 1964 in Baton Rouge, East Baton Rouge Parish, Louisiana.**
+ 1200   iii.   **Steven Paul Babin, born 07 October 1969 in Baton Rouge, East Baton Rouge Parish, Louisiana.**

595. Frances Elizabeth[7] Robért (Joseph Nemours[6], Joseph Olide[5], Jean Paul[4], Mathieu[3], Jean[2], Mathieu[1]) was born 27 December 1943 in Donaldsonville, Ascension Parish, Louisiana. She married **J. Ferrel Sheets** 07 July 1962 in St. Theresa Catholic Church, Gonzales, Ascension Parish, Louisiana, son of Nolan Sheets and Ruth Arceneaux. He was born 07 December 1941 in New Orleans, Orleans Parish, Louisiana.

Children of Frances Robért and J. Sheets are:

+ 1201   i.   **Kari Marie[8] Sheets, born 11 November 1963 in Gonzales, Ascension Parish, Louisiana.**
   1202   ii.   **Sandy Theresa Sheets, born 26 October 1964 in Gonzales, Ascension Parish, Louisiana. She married Scott Shaddinger 06 June 1986; born Unknown.**
   1203   iii.   **Robin Michelle Sheets, born 11 May 1967 in Gonzales, Ascension Parish, Louisiana. She married Russell Bourque 22 January 1988.**
   1204   iv.   **Anne Marie Sheets, born 30 September 1968 in Gonzales, Ascension Parish, Louisiana.**
   1205   v.   **Damian Michael Sheets, born 30 September 1968 in Gonzales, Ascension Parish, Louisiana.**

596. Joseph Reginald[7] Robért, (Reggie) (Joseph Nemours[6], Joseph Olide[5], Jean Paul[4], Mathieu[3], Jean[2], Mathieu[1]) was born 28 January 1945 in Donaldsonville, Ascension Parish, Louisiana. He married **Rosalind Rita Braud** 28 April 1974 in St. John the Evangelist Catholic Church, Prairieville, Ascension Parish, Louisiana, daughter of Elton Braud and Viola LeBlanc. She was born 26 January 1952 in Baton Rouge, East Baton Rouge Parish, Louisiana.

Children of Joseph Robért and Rosalind Braud are:
1206   i.   **Rachel Lynn[8] Robért, born 29 January 1976 in Baton Rouge, East Baton Rouge Parish, Louisiana. She married Shane Michael King 19 October 2004; born 08 November 1973.**
+ 1207   ii. **Russell Joseph Robért, born 28 March 1980 in Baton Rouge, East Baton Rouge Parish, Louisiana.**
1208   iii. **Randall Paul Robért, born 28 July 1983 in Baton Rouge, East Baton Rouge Parish, Louisiana.**

597. Terry Jude[7] Robért (Joseph Nemours[6], Joseph Olide[5], Jean Paul[4], Mathieu[3], Jean[2], Mathieu[1]) was born 28 July 1948 in Gonzales, Ascension Parish, Louisiana. He married **Brenda Ann Martin** 20 June 1970 in Immaculate Heart of Mary Catholic Church, Crowley, Acadia Parish, Louisiana, daughter of Benoit Martin and Duiby Breaux. She was born 31 March 1949 in Crowley, Acadia Parish, Louisiana.

Children of Terry Robért and Brenda Martin are:
1209   i.   **Kimberly Ann[8] Robért, born 19 April 1971 in Gonzales, Ascension Parish, Louisiana. She married Michael Odell 09 July 1993 in St. Theresa Catholic Church, Gonzales, Ascension Parish, Louisiana.**
1210   ii. **Toni Therese Robért, born 11 May 1972 in Gonzales, Ascension Parish, Louisiana. She married Gregory Joseph Swanson 21 March 1992 in The Cabin, Burnside,(c/o 1st Baptist Church of Gonzales), Ascension Parish, Louisiana.**
+ 1211   iii. **Brian Paul Robért, born 21 November 1974 in Gonzales, Ascension Parish, Louisiana.**
1212   iv. **Jeffery Michael Robért, born 17 February 1978 in East Baton Rouge Parish, Baton Rouge, Louisiana. He married Janelle 06 May 2000 in Gatlenburg, Sevier County, Tennessee.**

598. Lynn Jude[7] Robért, Jr. (Lynn Jude[6], Joseph Olide[5], Jean Paul[4], Mathieu[3], Jean[2], Mathieu[1]) was born 25 January 1959 in Baton Rouge, East Baton Rouge Parish, Louisiana. He married **Rebecca Bennett** 09 October 1981 in Baton Rouge, East Baton Rouge Parish, Louisiana, daughter of Frederick Bennett and Lillian Roussell. She was born 20 November 1957 in Bogalusa, Washington Parish, Louisiana.

Children of Lynn Robért and Rebecca Bennett are:
1213   i.   **Sheree Michelle[8] Robért, born 16 January 1979 in Bogalusa, Washington Parish, Louisiana.**
1214   ii. **Louis Wayne Robért, born 11 March 1982 in Baton Rouge, East Baton Rouge Parish, Louisiana. He married Kayla Williamson 25 August 2001 in Lake Charles, Calcasieu Parish, Louisiana.**
1215   iii. **Matthew Lynn Robért, born 15 May 1983 in Baton Rouge, East**

600. Lynne Mary[7] **Babin** (Adele Ann[6] Robért, Joseph Olide[5], Jean Paul[4], Mathieu[3], Jean[2], Mathieu[1]) was born 19 September 1942 in New Orleans, Orleans Parish, Louisiana, and died 24 August 1999 in New Orleans, Orleans Parish, Louisiana. She married **Joseph Paul Guistiniano** 22 June 1961 in St. Anthony Catholic Church, Gretna, Louisiana, son of Joseph Guistiniana and Ora Peltier. He was born 06 April 1939 in New Orleans, Orleans Parish, Louisiana.

Children of Lynne Babin and Joseph Guistiniano are:

1216	i.	**Erin Theresa**[8] **Guistiniano, born 04 October 1962 in Marrero, Jefferson Parish, Louisiana.**
1217	ii.	**Joseph Paul Guistiniano,Jr., born 18 January 1964 in Marrero, Jefferson Parish, Louisiana; died 20 January 1964 in Marrero, Jefferson Parish, Louisiana.**
1218	iii.	**Anthony Jude Guistiniano, born 18 January 1964 in Marrero, Jefferson Parish, Louisiana; died 20 January 1964 in Marrero, Jefferson Parish, Louisiana.**
1219	iv.	**Todd Gerald Guistiniano, born 05 December 1964 in Marrero, Jefferson Parish, Louisiana. He married Donna Lynn Eckert 23 July 1988.**
1220	v.	**Blaine Nicholas Guistiniano, born 24 February 1969 in Marrero, Jefferson Parish, Louisiana.**
1221	vi.	**Robin Jude Guistiniano, born 09 September 1972 in Marrero, Jefferson Parish, Louisiana.**

601. Stanley Joseph[7] **Babin** (Adele Ann[6] Robért, Joseph Olide[5], Jean Paul[4], Mathieu[3], Jean[2], Mathieu[1]) was born 25 August 1944 in New Orleans, Orleans Parish, Louisiana. He married **Patricia Smith** 29 May 1965 in St. Anthony Catholic Church, Gretna, Louisiana, daughter of Roland Smith and Rose Rome. She was born Unknown in New Orleans, Orleans Parish, Louisiana.

Children of Stanley Babin and Patricia Smith are:

+	1222	i.	**Denise Ann**[8] **Babin, born 24 February 1966 in Marrero, Jefferson Parish, Louisiana.**
	1223	ii.	**Wade Joseph Babin, born 20 September 1967 in Marrero, Jefferson Parish, Louisiana.**
	1224	iii.	**Blake Anthony Babin, born 09 August 1988 in New Orleans, Orleans Parish, Louisiana.**

602. Kenneth Anthony[7] **Babin** (Adele Ann[6] Robért, Joseph Olide[5], Jean Paul[4], Mathieu[3], Jean[2], Mathieu[1]) was born 09 December 1946 in New Orleans, Orleans Parish, Louisiana. He married **Beverly Ann Hill** 07 October

1972 in St. Anthony Catholic Church, Gretna, Louisiana, daughter of David Hill and Anne Bianchini. She was born 19 May 1951 in New Orleans, Orleans Parish, Louisiana.

Children of Kenneth Babin and Beverly Hill are:

1225   i.   **Casey Jude[8] Babin, born 02 June 1974 in Marrero, Jefferson Parish, Louisiana.**

1226   ii.   **Ashlie Ann Babin, born 07 December 1977 in Marrero, Jefferson Parish, Louisiana.**

1227   iii.   **Kenneth Anthony Babin, Jr., born 24 August 1982 in Marrero, Jefferson Parish, Louisiana.**

603. Leslie Ann[7] Babin (Adele Ann[6] Robért, Joseph Olide[5], Jean Paul[4], Mathieu[3], Jean[2], Mathieu[1]) was born 03 February 1948 in New Orleans, Orleans Parish, Louisiana. She married **Elmo Bergeron, Jr.** 03 February 1968 in St. Anthony Catholic Church, Gretna, Louisiana, son of Elmo Bergeron and Iris Dufore. He was born 16 October 1948 in New Orleans, Orleans Parish, Louisiana.

Children of Leslie Babin and Elmo Bergeron are:

1228   i.   **Brandi Jude[8] Bergeron, born 25 October 1973 in Marrero, Jefferson Parish, Louisiana.**

1229   ii.   **Brett Elizabeth Bergeron, born 24 November 1979 in Marrero, Jefferson Parish, Louisiana.**

604. Barbara Elizabeth[7] Babin (Adele Ann[6] Robért, Joseph Olide[5], Jean Paul[4], Mathieu[3], Jean[2], Mathieu[1]) was born 04 August 1951 in Marrero, Jefferson Parish, Louisiana. She married **Pat Joseph DiGiovanni** 04 November 1972 in St. Anthony Catholic Church, Gretna, Louisiana.

Children of Barbara Babin and Pat DiGiovanni are:

1230   i.   **Kori Jude[8] DiGiovanni, born 11 January 1977 in Marrero, Jefferson Parish, Louisiana.**

1231   ii.   **Pat Joseph DiGiovanni, Jr., born 19 July 1978 in Marrero, Jefferson Parish, Louisiana.**

605. Robert Louis[7] Rome (Louis Joseph[6], Leona Theresa[5] Robért, (Na-Na), Jean Paul[4], Mathieu[3], Jean[2], Mathieu[1]) was born 08 March 1936 in Donaldsonville, Ascension Parish, Louisiana. He married **Estelle Marie LeBlanc** 29 April 1967 in Holy Family Catholic Church, Port Allen, Louisiana, daughter of Lloyd LeBlanc and Rosina Echelard. She was born 11 July 1943 in Baton Rouge, East Baton Rouge Parish, Louisiana.

Children of Robert Rome and Estelle LeBlanc are:

+ 1232   i.   **Suzette Estelle[8] Rome, born 05 September 1968 in Baton Rouge, East Baton Rouge Parish, Louisiana.**

+ 1233   ii.   **Byron Robert Rome, born 04 September 1970 in Baton Rouge, East Baton Rouge Parish, Louisiana.**

+ 1234   iii.   **Carey Louis Rome, born 08 March 1972 in Baton Rouge, East Baton Rouge Parish, Louisiana.**

+ 1235   iv.   **Gregg Lawrence Rome, born 09 February 1975 in Baton Rouge, East Baton Rouge Parish, Louisiana.**

606. Ronald Richard[7] Rome (Louis Joseph[6], Leona Theresa[5] Robért, (Na-Na), Jean Paul[4], Mathieu[3], Jean[2], Mathieu[1]) was born 08 March 1936 in Donaldsonville, Ascension Parish, Louisiana. He married **Margaret Frances Robichaux** 21 August 1965 in St. Aloysuis Catholic Church, Baton Rouge, East Baton Rouge Parish, Louisiana, daughter of Lloyd Robichaux and Myrle Landry. She was born 27 March 1941 in Montegut, Terrebonne Parish, Louisiana.

Children of Ronald Rome and Margaret Robichaux are:

+ 1236   i.   **Michelle Margaret[8] Rome, born 13 March 1967 in Baton Rouge, East Baton Rouge Parish, Louisiana.**

+ 1237   ii.   **Aimee Cecile Rome, born 02 December 1968 in Baton Rouge, East Baton Rouge Parish, Louisiana.**

607. Judith Anne[7] Rome (Louis Joseph[6], Leona Theresa[5] Robért, (Na-Na), Jean Paul[4], Mathieu[3], Jean[2], Mathieu[1]) was born 22 April 1938 in Donaldsonville, Ascension Parish, Louisiana. She married **Paul Taggart Barber** 30 July 1960 in Sacred Heart Church, Baton Rouge, East Baton Rouge Parish, Louisiana, son of Aubrey Barber and Annie Guillory. He was born 28 July 1938 in Baton Rouge, East Baton Rouge Parish, Louisiana.

Children of Judith Rome and Paul Barber are:

+ 1238   i.   **Paul Taggart[8] Barber, Jr., born 05 May 1961 in Baton Rouge, East Baton Rouge Parish, Louisiana.**

+ 1239   ii.   **Madalyn Monique Barber, born 08 February 1963 in Baton Rouge, East Baton Rouge Parish, Louisiana.**

   1240   iii.   **Stephen Michael Barber,(infant), born 11 July 1965 in Baton Rouge, East Baton Rouge Parish, Louisiana; died 11 July 1965 in Baton Rouge, East Baton Rouge Parish, Louisiana.**

   1241   iv.   **Anna Michael Barber,(infant), born 19 January 1971 in Baton Rouge, East Baton Rouge Parish, Louisiana; died 19 January 1971 in Baton Rouge, East Baton Rouge Parish, Louisiana.**

+ 1242   v.   **Patrick Hillard Barber, born 27 September 1971 in Baton Rouge, East Baton Rouge Parish, Louisiana.**

608. Eleanor Loretta[7] Rome (Louis Joseph[6], Leona Theresa[5] Robért, (Na-Na), Jean Paul[4], Mathieu[3], Jean[2], Mathieu[1]) was born 06 September 1940 in Donaldsonville, Ascension Parish, Louisiana. She married **Herman Finley Sockrider, Jr.** 01 August 1959 in Baton Rouge, East Baton Rouge Parish, Louisiana, son of Herman Sockrider and Julia Davis. He was born 26 October 1938 in Lake Charles, Calcasieu Parish, Louisiana.

Children of Eleanor Rome and Herman Sockrider are:
	1243	i.	**Keith Brian[8] Sockrider, born 09 May 1960 in Baton Rouge, East Baton Rouge Parish, Louisiana.**
+	1244	ii.	**Steven Louis Sockrider, born 09 April 1963 in Baton Rouge, East Baton Rouge Parish, Louisiana.**
+	1245	iii.	**Gary Wayne Sockrider, born 08 October 1965 in Shreveport, Caddo Parish, Louisiana.**
+	1246	iv.	**Christopher Sean Sockrider, born 25 October 1970 in Shreveport, Caddo Parish, Louisiana.**

610. Signa Mathieu[7] Rome (John Augustin[6], Leona Theresa[5] Robért, (Na-Na), Jean Paul[4], Mathieu[3], Jean[2], Mathieu[1]) was born 04 December 1952 in Baton Rouge, East Baton Rouge Parish, Louisiana. She married **Joseph Edward Casagrande, Jr.** 07 August 1982, son of Joseph Casagrande and Marion Nierhaus. He was born 11 March 1956 in St. Louis, Missouri.

Children of Signa Rome and Joseph Casagrande are:
| | 1247 | i. | **Jeffrey Joseph[8] Casagrande, born 25 October 1984 in Baton Rouge, East Baton Rouge Parish, Louisiana.** |
| | 1248 | ii. | **Ashley Nicole Casagrande, born 18 March 1991 in Baton Rouge, East Baton Rouge Parish, Louisiana.** |

611. Suzanne P.[7] Rome (Paul Robert[6], Leona Theresa[5] Robért, (Na-Na), Jean Paul[4], Mathieu[3], Jean[2], Mathieu[1]) was born 25 March 1938 in Donaldsonville, Ascension Parish, Louisiana. She married **Leon Laiche** 03 January 1959. He was born 09 June 1936.

Children of Suzanne Rome and Leon Laiche are:
+	1249	i.	**Dianne Marie[8] Laiche, born 07 December 1959 in Lafayette, Lafayette Parish, Louisiana.**
+	1250	ii.	**Douglas David Laiche, born 19 October 1962.**
	1251	iii.	**Donald Laiche, born 21 September 1964. He married Donna Cart 29 April 1995; born 22 June 1968.**

612. Alice Marie[7] Rome (Paul Robert[6], Leona Theresa[5] Robért, (Na-Na), Jean Paul[4], Mathieu[3], Jean[2], Mathieu[1]) was born 08 June 1941 in Donaldsonville,

Ascension Parish, Louisiana. She married **Henry R. Miller, Jr.** 05 September 1959 in St. Charles Borromeo Church, Destrahan, Louisiana. He was born 14 February 1939 in New Orleans, Orleans Parish, Louisiana.

Children of Alice Rome and Henry Miller are:
+   1252   i.   **Vickie Lynn**[8] **Miller, born 19 June 1960 in New Orleans, Orleans Parish, Louisiana.**
     1253   ii.   **Allyson Ann Miller, born 25 August 1961 in New Orleans, Orleans Parish, Louisiana; died 31 July 1962.**
+   1254   iii. **Stephenie Ann Miller, born 04 December 1964 in New Orleans, Orleans Parish, Louisiana.**
+   1255   iv.   **Henry Rezin Miller III, born 13 September 1966 in New Orleans, Orleans Parish, Louisiana.**
+   1256   v.   **Dana Elizabeth Miller, born 25 March 1968 in New Orleans, Orleans Parish, Louisiana.**
+   1257   vi.   **Erin Eileen Miller, born 28 June 1973 in Metairie, Jefferson Parish, Louisiana.**

613. Eileen Mary[7] **Rome** (Paul Robert[6], Leona Theresa[5] Robért, (Na-Na), Jean Paul[4], Mathieu[3], Jean[2], Mathieu[1]) was born 16 February 1944 in New Orleans, Orleans Parish, Louisiana. She married **James Patrick Faucheux, Sr.** 13 July 1963 in St. Charles Borromeo Church, Destrahan, Louisiana. He was born 07 October 1942 in New Orleans, Orleans Parish, Louisiana.

Children of Eileen Rome and James Faucheux are:
+   1258   i.   **Shannon Ann**[8] **Faucheux, born 07 April 1964 in New Orleans, Orleans Parish, Louisiana.**
+   1259   ii.   **James Patrick Faucheux, Jr., born 12 April 1965 in Lutcher, St. James Parish, Louisiana.**
+   1260   iii. **Michelle Ann Faucheux, born 03 December 1966 in Lutcher, St. James Parish, Louisiana.**
+   1261   iv.   **Lisa Marie Faucheux, born 15 May 1973 in Metairie, Jefferson Parish, Louisiana.**

614. John Paul[7] **Rome, Sr.** (Paul Robert[6], Leona Theresa[5] Robért, (Na-Na), Jean Paul[4], Mathieu[3], Jean[2], Mathieu[1]) was born 16 January 1946 in New Orleans, Orleans Parish, Louisiana. He married **Jane Cadow** 30 November 1966 in Kenitra, Morocco. She was born 19 October 1947.

Children of John Rome and Jane Cadow are:
     1262   i.   **Desiree**[8] **Rome, born 28 July 1971. She married Brent Michael Kelley 18 July 1998.**
     1263   ii.   **John Paul Rome,Jr., born 20 January 1975.**
     1264   iii. **Sarah Cardow Rome, born 27 April 1976.**

615. Michael H.[7] **Rome** (Paul Robert[6], Leona Theresa[5] Robért, (Na-Na), Jean Paul[4], Mathieu[3], Jean[2], Mathieu[1]) was born 18 July 1952 in New Orleans, Orleans Parish, Louisiana. He married **Deborah Clouatre** 02 April 1983, daughter of Thomas Clouatre and Lily Marshall.

Children of Michael Rome and Deborah Clouatre are:
- 1265   i.   **Paul Marshall**[8] **Rome, born 14 February 1986.**
- 1266   ii.   **Bryan Rome, born 06 February 1991.**

616. O'Neil Francis[7] **Rome,Jr.** (O'Neil Francis[6], Leona Theresa[5] Robért, (Na-Na), Jean Paul[4], Mathieu[3], Jean[2], Mathieu[1]) was born 27 July 1941 in Baton Rouge, East Baton Rouge Parish, Louisiana. He married **Susan Manley** 06 June 1964 in Baton Rouge, East Baton Rouge Parish, Louisiana. She was born 02 March 1943 in Orleans Parish, New Orleans, Orleans Parish, Louisiana, and died 18 August 2001 in Memphis, Tennessee.

Children of O'Neil Rome and Susan Manley are:
- + 1267   i.   **Ashley Ann**[8] **Rome, born 03 August 1966 in Baton Rouge, East Baton Rouge Parish, Louisiana.**
- + 1268   ii.   **O'Neil Francis Rome,III, born 09 April 1971 in Baton Rouge, East Baton Rouge Parish, Louisiana.**
- 1269   iii.   **Robért Steven Rome, born 28 September 1975 in Orleans Parish, New Orleans, Orleans Parish, Louisiana.**

617. Elizabeth Day[7] **Rome** (O'Neil Francis[6], Leona Theresa[5] Robért, (Na-Na), Jean Paul[4], Mathieu[3], Jean[2], Mathieu[1]) was born 27 November 1943 in Donaldsonville, Ascension Parish, Louisiana. She married **James Rogers Thomas** 03 May 1975 in Tripoli, Libya. He was born 18 July 1927 in Orangeburg, South Carolina.

Children of Elizabeth Rome and James Thomas are:
- 1270   i.   **Jesse Rucker**[8] **Thomas, born 29 October 1976 in Baton Rouge, East Baton Rouge Parish, Louisiana.**
- 1271   ii.   **James Rome Thomas, born 16 May 1978 in Tripoli, Libya.**
- 1272   iii.   **Jennifer Elizabeth Thomas, born 15 October 1980 in County Surrey, England.**

619. Robert Courtland[7] **Blanchard, Jr.** (Lillian Theresa[6] Rome, Leona Theresa[5] Robért, (Na-Na), Jean Paul[4], Mathieu[3], Jean[2], Mathieu[1]) was born 28 December 1941 in Donaldsonville, Ascension Parish, Louisiana. He married **Evelyn Marie Bourgeois** 11 January 1969 in Holy Rosary Catholic Church, St.

Amant, Ascension Parish, Louisiana, daughter of Orile Bourgeois and Bessie Gautreaux. She was born 30 January 1940.

Children of Robert Blanchard and Evelyn Bourgeois are:
+ 1273   i.   **Courtney Marie[8] Blanchard, born 08 February 1971 in Ft. McClelland, Alabama.**
   1274   ii.   **Christine Theresa Blanchard, born 07 June 1974 in Ft. Riley, Kansas. She married Raymond Anthony Fryoux, Jr. 16 June 2001 in Baton Rouge, East Baton Rouge Parish, Louisiana; born 24 June 1974.**

620. Lillian Theresa[7] Blanchard (Lillian Theresa[6] Rome, Leona Theresa[5] Robért, (Na-Na), Jean Paul[4], Mathieu[3], Jean[2], Mathieu[1]) was born 20 July 1944 in Donaldsonville, Ascension Parish, Louisiana. She married **Armand J. LeBlanc** 08 June 1963 in Donaldsonville, Ascension Parish, Louisiana, son of Hansen LeBlanc and Hazel Ramirez. He was born 29 November 1942.

Children of Lillian Blanchard and Armand LeBlanc are:
+ 1275   i.   **Troy Michael[8] LeBlanc, born 26 May 1964 in Donaldsonville, Ascension Parish, Louisiana.**
+ 1276   ii.   **Nicole Monique LeBlanc, born 21 April 1967 in Dallas, Texas.**
+ 1277   iii.   **Michelle Annette LeBlanc, born 02 August 1972 in Atlanta, Georgia.**

621. Madeline Marie[7] Blanchard (Lillian Theresa[6] Rome, Leona Theresa[5] Robért, (Na-Na), Jean Paul[4], Mathieu[3], Jean[2], Mathieu[1]) was born 31 March 1947 in Donaldsonville, Ascension Parish, Louisiana. She married **Everett Paul Gauthier, Jr.** 12 April 1969 in Donaldsonville, Ascension Parish, Louisiana, son of Everett Gauthier and Margaret Burton. He was born 07 April 1946.

Children of Madeline Blanchard and Everett Gauthier are:
+ 1278   i.   **Everett Paul[8] Gauthier, III (Rett), born 17 August 1974 in Baton Rouge, East Baton Rouge Parish, Louisiana.**
   1279   ii.   **Philippe Rene Gauthier, born 02 February 1981 in Baton Rouge, East Baton Rouge Parish, Louisiana.**
   1280   iii.   **Lindsey Marie Gauthier, born 08 November 1987 in Baton Rouge, East Baton Rouge Parish, Louisiana.**

622. Kathy[7] Rome (Ike Antoine[6], Leona Theresa[5] Robért, (Na-Na), Jean Paul[4], Mathieu[3], Jean[2], Mathieu[1]) was born 25 May 1942 in Donaldsonville, Ascension Parish, Louisiana. She married **Lee Madere** 06 February 1967 in Baton Rouge, East Baton Rouge Parish, Louisiana, son of Fernand Madere and Marie Froisy. He was born 19 July 1933.

Children of Kathy Rome and Lee Madere are:

1281   i.   **Julie[8] Madere, born 04 November 1961. She married John Best 23 May 1987.**

1282   ii.   **Mitzie Madere, born 01 April 1970.**

1283   iii.   **Denise Madere, born 12 March 1973.**

624. Cynthia[7] Rome (Charles David[6], Leona Theresa[5] Robért, (Na-Na), Jean Paul[4], Mathieu[3], Jean[2], Mathieu[1]) was born 30 January 1944. She met **(1) Bruno Joseph Egros, Jr. (Divorced)** 28 September 1963 in Ascension Catholic Church, Donaldsonville, Louisiana. She married **(2) Larry E. Ishee** 17 December 1977. He was born 25 March 1943.

Children of Cynthia Rome and Bruno Egros are:

1284   i.   **Jamie Allison[8] Egros, born 08 January 1965. She married Gregory Hughes 10 March 1984.**

1285   ii.   **Bruno Joseph Egros, III, born 15 April 1967.**

625. Carolyn[7] Rome (Charles David[6], Leona Theresa[5] Robért, (Na-Na), Jean Paul[4], Mathieu[3], Jean[2], Mathieu[1]) was born 30 August 1949. She married **(1) MItchell H. Goodspeed** 28 April 1968. He was born 04 October 1947. She married **(2) Blaine Roberts** May 1982.

Children of Carolyn Rome and MItchell Goodspeed are:

\+   1286   i.   **Rome Angette[8] Goodspeed, born 15 August 1971.**

\+   1287   ii.   **Janette Michelle Goodspeed, born 09 August 1974.**

1288   iii.   **Kevin Charles Goodspeed, born 19 January 1977.**

1289   iv.   **Rani Marie Goodspeed, born 11 July 1980.**

626. Christopher Paul[7] Rome (Donald Joseph[6], Leona Theresa[5] Robért, (Na-Na), Jean Paul[4], Mathieu[3], Jean[2], Mathieu[1]) was born 26 November 1959 in Lake Charles, Calcasieu Parish, Louisiana. He married **Kim Angela Rhodes** 04 January 1986 in Houma, Terrebonne Parish, Louisiana. She was born 07 October 1963 in Houma,Terrebonne Parish, Louisiana.

Children of Christopher Rome and Kim Rhodes are:

1290   i.   **Alexander Paul[8] Rome, born 16 February 1992 in Metairie, Jefferson Parish, Louisiana.**

1291   ii.   **Victoria Rhodes Rome, born 02 February 1996 in Metairie, Jefferson Parish, Louisiana.**

1292   iii.   **Adele Marie Rome, born 22 September 1999 in New Orleans. Orleans Parish, Louisiana.**

627. Teresa Ann[7] Rome (Donald Joseph[6], Leona Theresa[5] Robért, (Na-Na), Jean Paul[4], Mathieu[3], Jean[2], Mathieu[1]) was born 30 December 1960 in Lake Charles, Calcasieu Parish, Louisiana. She married **Michael William MacKensie** 05 November 1982 in Las Vagas, Nevada, son of Louis Lee MacKensie. He was born 28 November 1946 in Rayne, Acadia Parish, Louisiana.

Children of Teresa Rome and Michael MacKensie are:

1293	i.	**Sean Rome[8] MacKensie, born 30 August 1985 in New Orleans, Orleans Parish, Louisiana.**
1294	ii.	**Ian Rome MacKensie, born 25 September 1989 in Metairie, Jefferson Parish, Louisiana.**
1295	iii.	**Ryan Rome MacKensie, born 26 August 1991 in Metairie, Jefferson Parish, Louisiana.**

628. Joy Elizabeth[7] Rome (Donald Joseph[6], Leona Theresa[5] Robért, (Na-Na), Jean Paul[4], Mathieu[3], Jean[2], Mathieu[1]) was born 08 July 1962 in Lake Charles, Calcasieu Parish, Louisiana. She married **Doyle George Veneralla** 17 November 1979 in St. Rose, St. Charles Parish, Louisiana.

Child of Joy Rome and Doyle Veneralla is:

1296	i.	**Avrien Joseph[8] Venerella, born 13 June 1980 in Metairie, Jefferson Parish, Louisiana.**

631. James Joseph[7] Robért, Jr. Dr. (James Joseph[6], Raoul Matthew[5], Jean Paul[4], Mathieu[3], Jean[2], Mathieu[1]) was born 02 January 1941 in Union, St. James Parish, Louisiana. He married **Sydney Lee Franchebois** 12 June 1965, daughter of John Francebois and Jeanette Guidry. She was born 27 February 1943 in Church Point, Acadia Parish, Louisiana.

Children of James Robért and Sydney Franchebois are:

+	1297	i.	**Courtney Leah[8] Robért, born 15 March 1967 in Wurzburg, Germany.**
+	1298	ii.	**Deverelle Marie Robért, born 01 March 1970 in Opelousas, St. Landry Parish, Louisiana.**
+	1299	iii.	**James Joseph Robért III, born 24 October 1974 in Opelousas, St. Landry Parish, Louisiana.**
	1300	iv.	**Sarah Elizabeth Robért, born 07 July 1980 in Opelousas, St. Landry Parish, Louisiana. She married Steven Michael Miller 09 June 2007 in St. Landry Catholic Church; born 27 September 1977.**

632. Raoul William[7] Robért, Sr. (James Joseph[6], Raoul Matthew[5], Jean Paul[4], Mathieu[3], Jean[2], Mathieu[1]) was born 24 August 1942 in

Donaldsonville, Ascension Parish, Louisiana. He married **Jonalyn Cruickshank** 15 October 1966 in Liberal, Texas, daughter of John Cruickshank and Virginia Whaley. She was born 17 October 1947 in Amarillo, Texas.

Children of Raoul Robért and Jonalyn Cruickshank are:
- 1301   i.   **Raoul William[8] Robért,Jr., born 06 June 1974 in East Baton Rouge Parish, Baton Rouge, La..**
- + 1302   ii.   **Jon Tucker Robért, born 24 March 1977 in East Baton Rouge Parish, Baton Rouge, La..**
- 1303   iii.   **Leah Paige Robért, born 20 December 1980 in East Baton Rouge Parish, Baton Rouge, La..**

633. Mary Bobbye[7] Robért (James Joseph[6], Raoul Matthew[5], Jean Paul[4], Mathieu[3], Jean[2], Mathieu[1]) was born 14 December 1943 in New Roads, Pointe Coupee Parish, Louisiana. She married **Richard Pollock Meaux** 10 July 1976 in Opelousas, St. Landry Parish, Louisiana, son of Gabriel Meaux and Berta Pollock. He was born 17 March 1935 in Alexandria, Rapides Parish, Louisiana.

Children of Mary Robért and Richard Meaux are:
- 1304   i.   **David Clerfé[8] Meaux, born 29 July 1977 in Chlarleston, South Carolina.**
- 1305   ii.   **Jeanne Marie Meaux, born 10 April 1979 in Charleston, South Carolina.**

638. Joseph Scott[7] Mumphrey (Amalie Marie[6] Robért, (Toot), Raoul Matthew[5], Jean Paul[4], Mathieu[3], Jean[2], Mathieu[1]) was born 19 December 1951. He married **Suzanne Angelique LeDoux** 23 June 1973, daughter of Richard LeDoux and Bertha Manuel.

Child of Joseph Mumphrey and Suzanne LeDoux is:
- 1306   i.   **Anrhony Scott[8] Mumphrey, born 25 February 1975.**

639. Robbie Anne[7] Mumphrey (Amalie Marie[6] Robért, (Toot), Raoul Matthew[5], Jean Paul[4], Mathieu[3], Jean[2], Mathieu[1]) was born 08 October 1953. She married **Leza Delano Savoy, Jr.** 18 June 1971, son of Leza Savoy and Emily Sylvester.

Child of Robbie Mumphrey and Leza Savoy is:
- 1307   i.   **Tina Lynn[8] Savoy, born 12 July 1974.**

644. Robin Andrea[7] Robért (Hulin Joseph[6], Remy Paul[5], Jean Paul[4], Mathieu[3], Jean[2], Mathieu[1]) was born 06 March 1954 in New Orleans, Orleans

Parish, Louisiana. She married **Edmond Ker Birdsong** 27 December 1975 in Academy of Sacred Heart Chapel, New Orleans, Louisiana, son of Frank Birdsong and Sarah Jane. He was born 10 April 1950 in New Orleans, Orleans Parish, Louisiana.

Children of Robin Robért and Edmond Birdsong are:
- 1308   i.   **Samuel Ker[8] Birdsong, born 14 June 1979 in New Orleans, Orleans Parish, Louisiana.**
- 1309   ii.   **Amy Elizabeth Birdsong, born 07 April 1981 in New Orleans, Orleans Parish, Louisiana.**
- 1310   iii.   **Joseph Allen Birdsong, born 20 January 1983 in New Orleans, Orleans Parish, Louisiana.**
- 1311   iv.   **John Taylor Birdsong, born 12 December 1998 in Covington, St. Tammany Parish, Louisiana.**

645. David Bernard[7] Robért (Hulin Joseph[6], Remy Paul[5], Jean Paul[4], Mathieu[3], Jean[2], Mathieu[1]) was born 08 April 1955 in New Orleans, Orleans Parish, Louisiana. He married **Jo Lynn Root** 28 November 1983 in Enterprise, Alabama. She was born 21 January 1960 in Wilberton, Oklahoma.

Children of David Robért and Jo Lynn Root are:
- 1312   i.   **Joanna Danielle[8] Robért, born 11 November 1984 in Ozark, Alabama. She married Christopher William Ridgway 20 May 2005; born 21 February 1971 in Van Ives, California.**
- 1313   ii.   **Mordecai Robért, born 27 June 1986 in Newton, Alabama.**
- 1314   iii.   **Micah Aaron Robért, born 30 December 1987 in New Orleans, Orleans Parish, Louisiana.**
- 1315   iv.   **Jan Rachelle Robért, born 19 March 1990 in Mountain Home, Arkansas.**
- 1316   v.   **Margaret Elizabeth Robért, born 11 January 1992 in Mountain Home, Arkansas.**

646. Nancy Claire[7] Robért (Hulin Joseph[6], Remy Paul[5], Jean Paul[4], Mathieu[3], Jean[2], Mathieu[1]) was born 12 March 1956 in New Orleans, Orleans Parish, Louisiana. She married **Robert Cok DeVries** 10 September 1988 in Little Chapel on the Boardwalk, Wrightsville Beach, North Carolina. He was born 11 November 1953 in Holland, Michigan.

Children of Nancy Robért and Robert DeVries are:
- 1317   i.   **Jeffrey Ross[8] DeVries, born 23 March 1990 in Wilmington, North Carolina.**
- 1318   ii.   **Jason Robert DeVries, born 02 January 1992 in Raleigh, North Carolina.**

650. Nolan Jacques[7] Robért (Hulin Joseph[6], Remy Paul[5], Jean Paul[4], Mathieu[3], Jean[2], Mathieu[1]) was born 07 March 1966 in Hammond,Tangipahoa Parish, Louisiana. He married **Kim Marie McGrath** 22 December 2001 in Sierra Vista, Arizona. She was born 12 January 1970 in Danbury, Ct..

Children of Nolan Robért and Kim McGrath are:
1319	i.	**Kaitlin Kelsey McGrath[8] Robért, born 06 January 1998 in Sierra Vista, Arizona.**
1320	ii.	**Luke McGrath Robért, born 12 April 2005 in Sierra Vista, Arizona.**

651. Remy Pierre[7] Robért (Hulin Joseph[6], Remy Paul[5], Jean Paul[4], Mathieu[3], Jean[2], Mathieu[1]) was born 08 September 1967 in Hammond, Tangipahoa Parish, Louisiana. He married **Jessica Lynn Johns** 07 August 1993 in Port Gamble, Washington. She was born 09 July 1970 in Silver Springs, Maryland.

Children of Remy Robért and Jessica Johns are:
1321	i.	**Renee Ellemarie[8] Robért, born 26 October 1998 in Charlston, South Carolina.**
1322	ii.	**Alyiah Cassandra Robért, born 25 December 2002 in Bramerton, Washington.**

652. Cecil Paul[7] Robért, Jr. (Cecil Paul[6], Remy Paul[5], Jean Paul[4], Mathieu[3], Jean[2], Mathieu[1]) was born 13 August 1954 in Donaldsonville, Ascension Parish, Louisiana. He married **Jaime Terése Robért** 27 January 1984 in St. Anthony Chapel, Darrow, Louisiana, daughter of Carl Robért and George Ann Waguespack. She was born 10 November 1958 in Gonzales, Ascension Parish, Louisiana.

Children of Cecil Robért and Jaime Robért are:
1323	i.	**Bobbye Leigh[8] Robért, born 29 January 1988 in Baton Rouge, East Baton Rouge Parish, Louisiana.**
1324	ii.	**Michael Paul Robért, born 10 October 1989 in Baton Rouge, East Baton Rouge Parish, Louisiana.**
1325	iii.	**Scot Austin Robért, born 12 February 1992 in Baton Rouge, East Baton Rouge Parish, Louisiana.**

655. Waldon Charles[7] Robért (Cecil Paul[6], Remy Paul[5], Jean Paul[4], Mathieu[3], Jean[2], Mathieu[1]) was born 30 December 1961 in Donaldsonville, Ascension Parish, Louisiana. He married **Dawn Marie Savoy** 01 February 1986 in Baton Rouge, East Baton Rouge Parish, Louisiana, daughter of Nolan Savoy and Vicki DeVeer. She was born 23 December 1963.

Children of Waldon Robért and Dawn Savoy are:
- 1326   i.   **Taylor Ashleigh[8] Robért, born 17 September 1987 in Baton Rouge, East Baton Rouge Parish, Louisiana.**
- 1327   ii.   **Jordan Elizabeth Robért, born 31 July 1989 in Baton Rouge, East Baton Rouge Parish, Louisiana.**
- 1328   iii.   **Madison Alminte Robért, born 19 September 1995 in Baton Rouge, East Baton Rouge Parish, Louisiana.**

656. Penny Elizabeth[7] Robért (Cecil Paul[6], Remy Paul[5], Jean Paul[4], Mathieu[3], Jean[2], Mathieu[1]) was born 25 March 1963 in Donaldsonville, Ascension Parish, Louisiana. She married **Edgar Anthony Saucier, III** 17 December 1982 in St. Theresa Catholic Church, Gonzales, Louisiana, son of Edgar Saucier and Dianne Hammel. He was born 19 August 1961 in New Orleans, Orleans Parish, Louisiana.

Children of Penny Robért and Edgar Saucier are:
- 1329   i.   **Lauren Day[8] Saucier, born 24 April 1989 in Baton Rouge, East Baton Rouge Parish, Louisiana.**
- 1330   ii.   **Steven Paul Saucier, born 22 August 1996 in Baton Rouge, East Baton Rouge Parish, Louisiana.**

658. Natalie Marie[7] Robért (Cecil Paul[6], Remy Paul[5], Jean Paul[4], Mathieu[3], Jean[2], Mathieu[1]) was born 09 November 1967 in Donaldsonville, Ascension Parish, Louisiana. She married **(1) Gregory Paul Stelly** 21 November 1991 in Baton Rouge, East Baton Rouge Parish, Louisiana, son of Floyd Stelly and Gloria Laiche. He was born 20 September 1963 in Orleans Parish, New Orleans, Orleans Parish, Louisiana, and died 14 July 2003 in Gonzales, Ascension Parish, Louisiana. She married **(2) Christopher Thomas Trevino, MD, PHD** 02 March 2007 in Houmas House, Burnside, Ascension Parish, Louisiana, son of Richard Trevino and Esther Pena de la Chaumiere. He was born 25 June 1964.

Children of Natalie Robért and Gregory Stelly are:
- 1331   i.   **Cecily Claire[8] Stelly, born 22 May 1995 in Baton Rouge, East Baton Rouge Parish, Louisiana.**
- 1332   ii.   **Easton Robert Stelly, born 30 December 1998 in Baton Rouge, East Baton Rouge Parish, Louisiana.**

659. Alan Joseph[7] Robért (Glenn Jacque[6], Remy Paul[5], Jean Paul[4], Mathieu[3], Jean[2], Mathieu[1]) was born 03 November 1950 in Ascension Parish, Donaldsonville, Louisiana. He married **Theresa Marie Aucoin** 25 August 1978 in Iberville Parish, White Castle, Louisiana, daughter of Lee Aucoin and Jazenette Boudreaux. She was born 28 July 1954 in Iberville Parish, White Castle, Louisiana.

Children of Alan Robért and Theresa Aucoin are:
- **1333**   i.   **Alana Rene[8] Robért, born 23 May 1984 in Baton Rouge, East Baton Rouge Parish, Louisiana.**
- **1334**   ii.   **Kyle Joseph Robért, born 25 December 1987 in Baton Rouge, East Baton Rouge Parish, Louisiana.**
- **1335**   iii.   **Austin Robért, born 31 January 1995.**

660. Glenna Marie[7] Robért (Glenn Jacque[6], Remy Paul[5], Jean Paul[4], Mathieu[3], Jean[2], Mathieu[1]) was born 28 June 1954 in Ascension Parish, Donaldsonville, Louisiana. She married **Eric Hampton Harlan** 28 May 1978 in Ascension Parish, Donaldsonville, Louisiana, son of Leo Harlan and Gwen Huval. He was born 18 October 1954 in Calcasieu Parish, Lake Charles, Louisiana.

Children of Glenna Robért and Eric Harlan are:
- **1336**   i.   **Robért Scott[8] Harlan, born 29 December 1981 in Calcasieu Parish, Lake Charles, Louisiana.**
- **1337**   ii.   **Stephen Joseph Harlan, born 12 August 1984 in Calcasieu Parish, Lake Charles, Louisiana.**

663. Robert Lynn[7] Simoneaux (Mary Lois[6] Robért, Remy Paul[5], Jean Paul[4], Mathieu[3], Jean[2], Mathieu[1]) was born 23 August 1949 in Ascension Parish, Donaldsonville, Louisiana. He married **Carolyn Marie Robertson** 19 July 1969, daughter of William Robinson and Edna Brhan. She was born 23 November 1951.

Children of Robert Simoneaux and Carolyn Robertson are:
- **1338**   i.   **Rachel Anne[8] Simoneaux, born 12 March 1971.**
- **1339**   ii.   **Randi Lauren Simoneaux, born 23 August 1973.**

664. Bruce James[7] Simoneaux (Mary Lois[6] Robért, Remy Paul[5], Jean Paul[4], Mathieu[3], Jean[2], Mathieu[1]) was born 26 February 1951 in Ascension Parish, Donaldsonville, Louisiana. He married **Lynn Granberry** 25 August 1973 in Baton Rouge, East Baton Rouge Parish, Louisiana, daughter of George Granberry and Rosemary McCablein. She was born 03 November 1951 in Baton Rouge, East Baton Rouge Parish, Louisiana.

Children of Bruce Simoneaux and Lynn Granberry are:
- **1340**   i.   **Remy Robert[8] Simoneaux, born 16 January 1978 in Houston, Texas.**
- **1341**   ii.   **Regan Landry Simoneaux, born 06 July 1979 in Houston, Texas.**
- **1342**   iii.   **Landry Lois Simoneaux, born 09 November 1985 in Houston, Texas.**

665. Jill Elaine[7] Simoneaux (Mary Lois[6] Robért, Remy Paul[5], Jean Paul[4], Mathieu[3], Jean[2], Mathieu[1]) was born 07 September 1954 in Baton Rouge, East Baton Rouge Parish, Louisiana. She married **Stephen Mark Dawson** 19 November 1978 in Ascension Parish, Gonzales, Louisiana, son of Harry Dawson and Mary Burnham. He was born 28 November 1953.

Child of Jill Simoneaux and Stephen Dawson is:
   1343   i.   **Katherine Nicole[8] Dawson, born 09 December 1985.**

667. Guy Remy[7] Simoneaux (Mary Lois[6] Robért, Remy Paul[5], Jean Paul[4], Mathieu[3], Jean[2], Mathieu[1]) was born 13 January 1958 in Baton Rouge, East Baton Rouge Parish, Louisiana. He married **Cindy Duhe** 18 July 1981 in Ascension Parish, Gonzales, Louisiana, daughter of Gary Duhe and Peggy Trabeau. She was born 16 May 1959 in Palm Beach, California.

Children of Guy Simoneaux and Cindy Duhe are:
   1344   i.   **Kellie Marie[8] Simoneaux, born 04 September 1984.**
   1345   ii.   **Kayla Anne Simoneaux, born 09 March 1987.**

669. Shelly Lauren[7] Robért (Shelby Lawrence[6], Remy Paul[5], Jean Paul[4], Mathieu[3], Jean[2], Mathieu[1]) was born 17 January 1961 in Baton Rouge, East Baton Rouge Parish, Louisiana. She married **Nate McElwee**.

Children of Shelly Robért and Nate McElwee are:
   1346   i.   **Mary Adelaide[8] McElwee, born 13 August 1993.**
   1347   ii.   **Nathan O'Berry, Jr., born 15 December 1994.**
   1348 iii.   **John Brigham (Briggs) McElwee, born 19 March 2001.**

670. Todd Justin[7] Robért (Shelby Lawrence[6], Remy Paul[5], Jean Paul[4], Mathieu[3], Jean[2], Mathieu[1]) was born 13 August 1962 in Baton Rouge, East Baton Rouge Parish, Louisiana. He married **Melissa Ann Guillot** 24 March 1990 in Ascension Catholic Church, Donaldsonville, Louisiana.

Children of Todd Robért and Melissa Guillot are:
   1349   i.   **Todd Justin[8] Robért II, born 09 August 1993.**
   1350   ii.   **Caroline Joan Robért, born 05 October 1995.**

671. Boyd Houston Joseph[7] Robért (Shelby Lawrence[6], Remy Paul[5], Jean Paul[4], Mathieu[3], Jean[2], Mathieu[1]) was born 24 September 1963 in Baton Rouge, East Baton Rouge Parish, Louisiana. He married **Jackie**.

Children of Boyd Robért and Jackie are:

    1351   i.   **John Houston[8] Robért, born 27 November 1996.**
    1352   ii.   **Hayden Rivers Robért, born 28 December 2000.**

672. Barry Steele[7] Robért (Shelby Lawrence[6], Remy Paul[5], Jean Paul[4], Mathieu[3], Jean[2], Mathieu[1]) was born 24 September 1963 in Baton Rouge, East Baton Rouge Parish, Louisiana. He married **Stephanie Lynn Richard** 29 October 1993 in St. Jules Catholic Church, Belle Rose, Louisiana.

Children of Barry Robért and Stephanie Richard are:

    1353   i.   **Victoria Hayes[8] Robért, born 27 September 1994.**
    1354   ii.   **Hayden Steele Robért, born 18 March 1996.**
    1355 iii.   **Remy Paul Robért, born 12 May 1999.**
    1356   iv.   **Brooks Martin Robért, born 18 October 2001.**

676. Juliette Anne[7] Robért (Matthew Joseph[6], Octave Pierre[5], Jean Paul[4], Mathieu[3], Jean[2], Mathieu[1]) was born 13 March 1959 in Montgomery, Alabama. She married **(1) Richard Epstein**. He was born 17 December 1956 in Denver, Colorado. She married **(2) Timothy Earl Shea** 18 August 1984, son of Joseph Shae and Brenda Belston. He was born 06 March 1959 in Wurzburg, Germany.

Children of Juliette Robért and Timothy Shea are:

    1357   i.   **Brett Myer[8] Epstein, born 29 January 1985 in San Diego, California.**
    1358   ii.   **Adam Albert Epstein, born 02 September 1987 in San Diego, California.**
    1359 iii.   **Christopher Earl Shea, born 28 January 1988 in Thornton, Colorado.**
    1360   iv.   **Dana Marie Shea, born 14 November 1989 in Aurora, Colorado.**
    1361   v.   **Timothy Joseph Shea, born 05 August 1993 in Denver, Colorado.**

677. Charles Herbert[7] Robért (Matthew Joseph[6], Octave Pierre[5], Jean Paul[4], Mathieu[3], Jean[2], Mathieu[1]) was born 27 July 1960 in Montgomery, Alabama. He married **Chantal Marthe Boulanger** 24 April 1998 in Paris, France, daughter of Pierre Boulanger and Solange Francais. She was born 30 July 1960 in Vosges, France.

Children of Charles Robért and Chantal Boulanger are:

    1362   i.   **Henry Balthazar[8] Robért, born 05 November 2000 in Paris, France.**
    1363   ii.   **Louis Matthew Robért, born 15 February 2004 in Paris, France.**

678. Marcie Ann[7] Robért (Robert Francis[6], Octave Pierre[5], Jean Paul[4], Mathieu[3], Jean[2], Mathieu[1]) was born 23 August 1960 in Baton Rouge, East Baton Rouge Parish, Louisiana. She married **Greg Serio** 11 May 1984 in Gonzales, Ascension Parish, Louisiana, son of Eugene Serio and Anne Bondi. He was born 09 September 1958 in New Roads, Point Coupee Parish, Louisiana.

Children of Marcie Robért and Greg Serio are:

1364	i.	**Erin Michelle[8] Serio, born 11 May 1985 in Baton Rouge, East Baton Rouge Parish, Louisiana.**
1365	ii.	**Brian Gregory Serio, born 12 May 1988 in Baton Rouge, East Baton Rouge Parish, Louisiana.**
1366	iii.	**Hayden Scott Serio, born 04 December 1990 in Baton Rouge, East Baton Rouge Parish, Louisiana.**

679. Donna Marie[7] Robért (Robert Francis[6], Octave Pierre[5], Jean Paul[4], Mathieu[3], Jean[2], Mathieu[1]) was born 26 March 1962 in Baton Rouge, East Baton Rouge Parish, Louisiana. She married **Charles Mitchel O'Brien** 20 April 1990 in Darrow, Ascension Parish, Louisiana, son of Julius O'Brien and Canetti Whittington. He was born 26 November 1960 in Centerville, Mississippi.

Child of Donna Robért and Charles O'Brien is:

| 1367 | i. | **Chancee Marie[8] O'Brien, born 15 February 1998 in Baton Rouge, East Baton Rouge Parish, Louisiana.** |

680. Gregory Michael[7] Robért (Robert Francis[6], Octave Pierre[5], Jean Paul[4], Mathieu[3], Jean[2], Mathieu[1]) was born 18 June 1963 in Baton Rouge, East Baton Rouge Parish, Louisiana. He married **Bridget Bearb** 12 February 1988 in Darrow, Ascension Parish, Louisiana, daughter of Osten Bearb and Myrtle Jumonville. She was born 14 July 1968 in Lutcher, St. James Parish, Louisiana.

Children of Gregory Robért and Bridget Bearb are:

1368	i.	**Heather[8] Robért, born 12 September 1989 in La Place, St.John the Baptist Parish, Louisiana ; died 12 September 1989 in La Place, St.John the Baptist Parish, Louisiana .**
1369	ii.	**Kayla Robért, born 12 September 1989 in La Place, St. John the Baptist Parish, Louisiana; died 12 September 1989 in La Place, St. John the Baptist Parish, Louisiana.**
1370	iii.	**Kody Paul Robért, born 27 August 1990 in La Place, St.John the Baptist Parish, Louisiana .**
1371	iv.	**Austin Wayne Robért, born 02 June 1994 in Baton Rouge, East Baton Rouge Parish, Louisiana.**

681. Gary Jerome[7] Robért (Robert Francis[6], Octave Pierre[5], Jean Paul[4],

Mathieu[3], Jean[2], Mathieu[1]) was born 20 May 1965 in Baton Rouge, East Baton Rouge Parish, Louisiana. He married **Renae Flint** 29 August 1986 in Gonzales, Ascension Parish, Louisiana, daughter of Samuel Flint and Mary McKinstrey. She was born 16 April 1966.

Children of Gary Robért and Renae Flint are:

1372	i.	**Shellie Marie[8] Robért, born 27 October 1988 in Baton Rouge, East Baton Rouge Parish, Louisiana.**
1373	ii.	**Jason Lance Robért, born 09 June 1992 in Baton Rouge, East Baton Rouge Parish, Louisiana.**
1374	iii.	**Lance Allen Robért, born 03 September 1990 in Baton Rouge, East Baton Rouge Parish, Louisiana; died 28 September 1990 in Baton Rouge, East Baton Rouge Parish, Louisiana.**

682. Anthony Luke[7] Robért (Robert Francis[6], Octave Pierre[5], Jean Paul[4], Mathieu[3], Jean[2], Mathieu[1]) was born 15 February 1970 in Baton Rouge, East Baton Rouge Parish, Louisiana. He married **Paige Kling** 20 April 1996 in Sorrento, Ascension Parish, Louisiana, daughter of John Kling and Myrtle Brignac. She was born 13 December 1970 in Baton Rouge, East Baton Rouge Parish, Louisiana.

Children of Anthony Robért and Paige Kling are:

1375	i.	**Emily Maria[8] Robért, born 07 October 1997 in Baton Rouge, East Baton Rouge Parish, Louisiana.**
1376	ii.	**Jessie Luke Robért, born 29 September 1999 in Baton Rouge, East Baton Rouge Parish, Louisiana.**

683. Marie Ouida[7] Robért (Paul Gerard[6], Octave Pierre[5], Jean Paul[4], Mathieu[3], Jean[2], Mathieu[1]) was born 25 June 1960 in Lafayette, Lafayette Parish, Louisiana. She married **James Philip Hebert** 12 March 1988 in St. Pius X Catholic Church, Lafayette, Lafayette Parish, Louisiana, son of Alex Hebert and Neva Lee. He was born 29 October 1959 in New Orleans, Orleans Parish, Louisiana.

Children of Marie Robért and James Hebert are:

1377	i.	**Alexander Paul[8] Hebert, born 06 January 1991 in Lafayette, Lafayette Parish, Louisiana.**
1378	ii.	**Celeste Marie Hebert, born 24 May 1994 in Lafayette, Lafayette Parish, Louisiana.**
1379	iii.	**Emilie Marie Hebert, born 28 November 1998 in Lafayette, Lafayette Parish, Louisiana.**

684. John Marius[7] Robért, Jr. (John Marius[6], Octave Pierre[5], Jean Paul[4],

Mathieu[3], Jean[2], Mathieu[1]) was born 31 August 1961 in Baton Rouge, East Baton Rouge Parish, Louisiana. He married **Rachel Lyn Duplessis** 30 December 1994 in St. John Evangelist Church, Prairieville, Ascension Parish, Louisiana, daughter of Burton Duplessis and Florence Daigle. She was born 02 February 1969 in Baton Rouge, East Baton Rouge Parish, Louisiana.

Children of John Robért and Rachel Duplessis are:

1380	i.	**Savannah Marie[8] Robért, born 27 November 1995 in Baton Rouge, East Baton Rouge Parish, Louisiana.**
1381	ii.	**Sarah Michelle Robért, born 20 July 1997 in Baton Rouge, East Baton Rouge Parish, Louisiana.**
1382	iii.	**Andrew Michael Robért, born 03 April 1999 in Baton Rouge, East Baton Rouge Parish, Louisiana.**
1383	iv.	**Nicholas Matthew Robért, born 30 August 2001 in Baton Rouge, East Baton Rouge Parish, Louisiana.**
1384	v.	**John Burton Robért, born 25 May 2004 in Baton Rouge, East Baton Rouge Parish, Louisiana.**

685. Dana Elizabeth[7] Robért (John Marius[6], Octave Pierre[5], Jean Paul[4], Mathieu[3], Jean[2], Mathieu[1]) was born 19 February 1963 in Baton Rouge, East Baton Rouge Parish, Louisiana. She married **Lyndell Wayne Keller, (Divorced)** 16 March 1984 in St. Tammany Parish, Louisiana, son of Eloy Keller and Betty Marlowe. He was born 25 September 1951 in Metairie, Jefferson Parish, Louisiana.

Children of Dana Robért and Lyndell Keller are:

1385	i.	**Katie Elizabeth[8] Keller, born 28 May 1984 in Covington, St. Tammany Parish, Louisiana. She married Brandon Scott Troxclair 31 December 2006 in Burnside, Ascension Parish, Louisiana; born 02 December 1982 in Baton Rouge, East Baton Rouge Parish, Louisiana.**
1386	ii.	**Lyndell Wayne Keller, Jr., born 04 November 1985 in Covington, St. Tammany Parish, Louisiana. He married Sarah Marie George 07 October 2006 in Baton Rouge, East Baton Rouge Parish, Louisiana; born 12 December 1985 in Tampa, Hillsborough County, Florida.**
1387	iii.	**Kyle Christian Keller, born 21 November 1987 in Independence,Tangipahoa Parish, Louisiana.**
1388	iv.	**Ashley Allyn Keller, born 20 September 1991 in Covington, St. Tammany Parish, Louisiana.**
1389	v.	**Naomi Grace Keller, born 05 June 1996 in Baton Rouge, East Baton Rouge Parish, Louisiana.**

686. Christopher James[7] Robért, Sr. (John Marius[6], Octave Pierre[5],

Jean Paul[4], Mathieu[3], Jean[2], Mathieu[1]) was born 21 September 1964 in Baton Rouge, East Baton Rouge Parish, Louisiana. He married **Paula Ann Bourque** 01 February 1991 in St. Theresa Catholic Church, Gonzales, Ascension Parish, Louisiana, daughter of Victor Bourque and Diana Braud. She was born 11 February 1969 in Baton Rouge, East Baton Rouge Parish, Louisiana.

Children of Christopher Robért and Paula Bourque are:

1390   i. **Angelle Marie[8] Robért, born 27 February 1992 in Baton Rouge, East Baton Rouge Parish, Louisiana.**

1391   ii. **Danielle Jenee Robért, born 27 February 1992 in Baton Rouge, East Baton Rouge Parish, Louisiana.**

1392   iii. **Christopher James Robért, Jr., born 14 February 1994 in Baton Rouge, East Baton Rouge Parish, Louisiana.**

1393   iv. **Gabrielle Leigh Robért, born 11 July 2001 in Baton Rouge, East Baton Rouge Parish, Louisiana.**

688. Rebecca Ann[7] Robért (John Marius[6], Octave Pierre[5], Jean Paul[4], Mathieu[3], Jean[2], Mathieu[1]) was born 21 August 1971 in Baton Rouge, East Baton Rouge Parish, Louisiana. She married **Gary Wayne Lee, Jr.** 30 July 1994 in St. John the Evangelist Church, Prairieville, Ascension Parish, Louisiana, son of Gary Lee and Phyllis Loupe. He was born 23 January 1972 in Natchitoches, Natchitoches Parish, Louisiana.

Children of Rebecca Robért and Gary Lee are:

1394   i. **Byan Andrew[8] Lee, born 04 November 1995 in Farmington, San Juan County, New Mexico.**

1395   ii. **Madeline Ruth Lee, born 13 January 1998 in Farmington, San Juan County, New Mexico.**

1396   iii. **David Michael Lee, born 04 February 2000 in Shenandoah, Montgomery County, Texas.**

1397   iv. **Katherine Grace Lee, born 12 May 2004 in Shenandoah, Montgomery County, Texas.**

689. Jennifer Marie[7] Robért (John Marius[6], Octave Pierre[5], Jean Paul[4], Mathieu[3], Jean[2], Mathieu[1]) was born 22 April 1974 in Baton Rouge, East Baton Rouge Parish, Louisiana. She married **James Shawn Usher** 14 August 1999 in Our Lady of Mercy Catholic Church, Baton Rouge, Louisiana, son of James Usher and Brenda Lafleur. He was born 04 February 1969 in California.

Children of Jennifer Robért and James Usher are:

1398   i. **James Robert[8] Usher, born 17 June 2002 in Baton Rouge, East Baton Rouge Parish, Louisiana.**

1399   ii. **Mary Claire Usher, born 17 June 2002 in Baton Rouge, East Baton Rouge Parish, Louisiana.**

1400	iii.	Elizabeth Marie Usher, born 01 March 2004 in Baton Rouge, East Baton Rouge Parish, Louisiana.
1401	iv.	Aimee Noel Usher, born 28 August 2007 in Baton Rouge, East Baton Rouge Parish, Louisiana.

690. Matthew Paul[7] Robért (John Marius[6], Octave Pierre[5], Jean Paul[4], Mathieu[3], Jean[2], Mathieu[1]) was born 24 May 1977 in Baton Rouge, East Baton Rouge Parish, Louisiana. He married **Nicole Marie Mayer** 05 September 2003 in St. Mark Catholic Church, Gonzales, Louisiana, daughter of Rickie Mayer and Tammy Elisar. She was born 27 October 1979 in Baton Rouge, East Baton Rouge Parish, Louisiana.

Child of Matthew Robért and Nicole Mayer is:

1402	i.	Anne Marie[8] Robért, born 26 October 2005 in Baton Rouge, East Baton Rouge Parish, Louisiana.

692. Sharon Elizabeth[7] McCauley (Carolyn Teresa[6] Robért, (Ceyon), Octave Pierre[5], Jean Paul[4], Mathieu[3], Jean[2], Mathieu[1]) was born 12 June 1960 in Shreveport, Caddo Parish, Louisiana. She married **Stephen Mark Morrow** 31 October 1997 in Big Lake, Cameron Parish, Louisiana, son of Robert Morrow and Ruth Wilbert. He was born 24 July 1952 in Arnaudville, St. Martin Parish, Louisiana.

Child of Sharon McCauley and Stephen Morrow is:

1403	i.	Sean Michael[8] Morrow, born 01 October 1998 in Lafayette, Lafayette Parish, Louisiana.

693. Bryan Edward[7] McCauley (Carolyn Teresa[6] Robért, (Ceyon), Octave Pierre[5], Jean Paul[4], Mathieu[3], Jean[2], Mathieu[1]) was born 25 December 1961 in Ville Platte, Evangeline Parish, Louisiana. He married **Natalie Pellerin** 15 November 1986 in Lake Charles, Calcasieu Parish, Louisiana, daughter of James Pellerin and Mona Champagne. She was born 27 October 1964 in Lake Charles, Calcasieu Parish, Louisiana.

Children of Bryan McCauley and Natalie Pellerin are:

1404	i.	Tyler Burton[8] McCauley, born 05 January 1988 in Lake Charles, Calcasieu Parish, Louisiana.
1405	ii.	Lauren Faye McCauley, born 17 May 1989 in Baton Rouge, East Baton Rouge Parish, Louisiana.
1406	iii.	Sarah Katherine McCauley, born 12 August 1995 in Baton Rouge, East Baton Rouge Parish, Louisiana.
1407	iv.	Abigail Teresa McCauley, born 06 January 2001 in Allen, Texas.

697. Brent David[7] Landry (Genevieve Martha[6] Robért, Octave Pierre[5], Jean Paul[4], Mathieu[3], Jean[2], Mathieu[1]) was born 16 November 1967 in Baton Rouge, East Baton Rouge Parish, Louisiana. He married **(1) Melissa Tullier Wilhoite**. He married **(2) Kristen M. Laiche** 12 January 1996 in St. Thomas Catholic Church, Baton Rouge, East Baton Rouge Parish, Louisiana, daughter of Allen Laiche and Janice Andre. She was born 19 December 1973 in Baton Rouge, East Baton Rouge Parish, Louisiana.

Child of Brent Landry and Melissa Wilhoite is:
- 1408   i.   **Jacques Auguste[8] Landry, born 18 April 1990 in Baton Rouge, East Baton Rouge Parish, Louisiana.**

Children of Brent Landry and Kristen Laiche are:
- 1409   i.   **Matthew Thomas[8] Landry, born 26 January 2000 in Baton Rouge, East Baton Rouge Parish, Louisiana; died 09 March 2000 in Baton Rouge, East Baton Rouge Parish, Louisiana.**
- 1410   ii.   **Garrison David Landry, born 06 December 2001 in Baton Rouge, East Baton Rouge Parish, Louisiana.**
- 1411   iii.   **Margaret Ruth Landry, born 17 December 2003 in Baton Rouge, East Baton Rouge Parish, Louisiana.**
- 1412   iv.   **John David Landry, born 24 April 2006 in Baton Rouge, East Baton Rouge Parish, Louisiana.**

698. Pierre Auguste[7] Landry (Genevieve Martha[6] Robért, Octave Pierre[5], Jean Paul[4], Mathieu[3], Jean[2], Mathieu[1]) was born 22 April 1969 in Baton Rouge, East Baton Rouge Parish, Louisiana. He married **Holly Carbo** 17 April 1998 in Ascension Catholic Church, Donaldsonville, Louisiana, daughter of Gerald Carbo and Nedra Blanchard. She was born 07 January 1972 in Donaldsonville, Ascension Parish, Louisiana.

Children of Pierre Landry and Holly Carbo are:
- 1413   i.   **Joseph Auguste[8] Landry, born 24 April 1997 in Baton Rouge, East Baton Rouge Parish, Louisiana.**
- 1414   ii.   **Elaine Michelle Landry, born 03 September 1999 in Baton Rouge, East Baton Rouge Parish, Louisiana.**

699. Jeanne Marie[7] Landry (Genevieve Martha[6] Robért, Octave Pierre[5], Jean Paul[4], Mathieu[3], Jean[2], Mathieu[1]) was born 15 September 1972 in Baton Rouge, East Baton Rouge Parish, Louisiana. She married **Chad Michael Wright** 07 November 1997 in Ascension Catholic Church, Donaldsonville, Louisiana, son of Roy Wright and Sharon Roberts. He was born 02 December 1970 in Baton Rouge, East Baton Rouge Parish, Louisiana.

Children of Jeanne Landry and Chad Wright are:

    1415   i.   **Chase Michael[8] Wright**, born 16 December 1998 in Baton Rouge, East Baton Rouge Parish, Louisiana.

    1416   ii.   **Allie Marie Wright**, born 13 July 2001 in Baton Rouge, East Baton Rouge Parish, Louisiana.

    1417   iii.   **Amy Lee Wright**, born 09 January 2006 in Baton Rouge, East Baton Rouge Parish, Louisiana.

700. Dean Gregory[7] Hebert (Marie Noelle[6] Robért, Octave Pierre[5], Jean Paul[4], Mathieu[3], Jean[2], Mathieu[1]) was born 21 December 1967 in Baton Rouge, East Baton Rouge Parish, Louisiana. He married **Scarlet Bennett** 28 September 1996 in Lake Charles, Calcasieu Parish, Louisiana, daughter of Donald Bennett and Antonia Cormier. She was born 04 November 1972 in Lake Charles, Calcasieu Parish, Louisiana.

Children of Dean Hebert and Scarlet Bennett are:

    1418   i.   **Austin Gregory[8] Hebert**, born 07 July 1995 in Lake Charles, Calcasieu Parish, Louisiana.

    1419   ii.   **David Ryan Hebert**, born 29 April 1999 in Austin, Texas.

    1420   iii.   **Matthew Joseph Hebert**, born 21 September 2004 in Baton Rouge, East Baton Rouge Parish, Louisiana.

702. Cliff Michael[7] Hebert (Marie Noelle[6] Robért, Octave Pierre[5], Jean Paul[4], Mathieu[3], Jean[2], Mathieu[1]) was born 15 September 1971 in Baton Rouge, East Baton Rouge Parish, Louisiana. He married **Stacy Landry** 16 September 1994 in Baton Rouge, East Baton Rouge Parish, Louisiana, daughter of Gregory Landry and Cynthia Trivette. She was born 03 October 1970 in Baton Rouge, East Baton Rouge Parish, Louisiana.

Children of Cliff Hebert and Stacy Landry are:

    1421   i.   **Cameron Michael[8] Hebert**, born 23 January 1995 in Baton Rouge, East Baton Rouge Parish, Louisiana.

    1422   ii.   **Sarah Alexandra Hebert**, born 18 February 1997 in Baton Rouge, East Baton Rouge Parish, Louisiana.

    1423   iii.   **Colin Gregory Hebert**, born 17 February 1999 in Baton Rouge, East Baton Rouge Parish, Louisiana.

    1424   iv.   **Catherine Marie Hebert**, born 21 August 2001 in Baton Rouge, East Baton Rouge Parish, Louisiana.

703. Jean-Paul Josef[7] Robért, Sr. (Peter Octave[6], Octave Pierre[5], Jean Paul[4], Mathieu[3], Jean[2], Mathieu[1]) was born 13 December 1968 in Huntsville, Alabama. He married **Melissa Ann Daughdrill** 21 June 1996 in Baton Rouge,

East Baton Rouge Parish, Louisiana, daughter of Curtis Daughdrill and Deborah Zimlich. She was born 09 September 1968 in Atlanta, Georgia.

Children of Jean-Paul Robért and Melissa Daughdrill are:

1425	i.	Jean-Paul Josef[8] Robért, Jr., born 20 August 2001 in Baton Rouge, East Baton Rouge Parish, Louisiana.
1426	ii.	Samantha Grace Robért, born 10 April 2003 in Baton Rouge, East Baton Rouge Parish, Louisiana.
1427	iii.	Matthew Ross Robért, born 01 April 2005 in Baton Rouge, East Baton Rouge Parish, Louisiana.
1428	iv.	Curtis Joseph Robért, born 08 December 2006 in Baton Rouge, East Baton Rouge Parish, Louisiana.

705. Dana Shea[7] Dardin, (adopted) (Peter Octave[6] Robért, Octave Pierre[5], Jean Paul[4], Mathieu[3], Jean[2], Mathieu[1]) was born 30 November 1974 in Tallahassee, Florida. She married **Tim McConnell** 05 February 1999 in Huntsville, Alabama, son of Terry McConnell and Judie Vince. He was born 23 January 1973 in Grosse Point, Michigan.

Children of Dana Dardin and Tim McConnell are:

| 1429 | i. | Logan Matthew[8] McConnell, born 01 July 2000 in Huntsville, Alabama. |
| 1430 | ii. | Mollie Catherine McConnell, born 26 June 2002 in Huntsville, Alabama. |

706. Sarah Elizabeth[7] Robért (Peter Octave[6], Octave Pierre[5], Jean Paul[4], Mathieu[3], Jean[2], Mathieu[1]) was born 16 January 1980 in Huntsville, Alabama. She married **Christopher Michael Salvail** 31 May 2003 in Huntsville, Alabama, son of Patrick Salvail and Pamela Davoren. He was born 21 December 1979 in Memphis, Tennessee.

Children of Sarah Robért and Christopher Salvail are:

| 1431 | i. | Luke Michael[8] Salvail, born 29 May 2005 in Huntsville, Alabama. |
| 1432 | ii. | Lanie Elizabeth Salvail, born 04 January 2007 in Huntsville, Alabama. |

710. Renée Geralyn[7] Robért (Carl James[6], Rene Benoit[5], Jean Paul[4], Mathieu[3], Jean[2], Mathieu[1]) was born 24 March 1954 in Gonzales, Ascension Parish, Louisiana. She married **Barry Anthony Cannon** 06 July 1973 in St. Theresa of Avila Catholic Church, Gonzales, Louisiana, son of Ray Cannon and Doris Savoy. He was born 07 October 1953 in Gonzales, Ascension Parish, Louisiana.

Children of Renée Robért and Barry Cannon are:
+   **1433**   i.   **Wendi Renée[8] Cannon, born 02 December 1973 in Baton Rouge, East Baton Rouge Parish, Louisiana.**
+   **1434**   ii.   **Tara Terése Cannon, born 19 April 1977 in Baton Rouge, East Baton Rouge Parish, Louisiana.**

   711. Mitzi Marie[7] Robért (Carl James[6], Rene Benoit[5], Jean Paul[4], Mathieu[3], Jean[2], Mathieu[1]) was born 21 May 1955 in Gonzales, Ascension Parish, Louisiana. She married **(1) William Charles Little, (Divorced)** 06 July 1973 in St. Theresa of Avila Catholic Church, Gonzales, Louisiana. She married **(2) Dudley Joseph Mire, Jr.** 20 April 1979 in St. Mark Catholic Church, Gonzales, Louisiana, son of Dudley Mire and Shirley Bourgeois. He was born 26 July 1955 in Gonzales, Ascension Parish, Louisiana.

Children of Mitzi Robért and Dudley Mire are:
   1435   i.   **Terése Marie[8] Mire, born 16 January 1981 in Baton Rouge, East Baton Rouge Parish, Louisiana.**
   1436   ii.   **Dudley Joseph Mire III, born 16 January 1981 in Baton Rouge, East Baton Rouge Parish, Louisiana.**
   1437   iii.   **Hubble Robert Mire, born 20 May 1982 in Baton Rouge, East Baton Rouge Parish, Louisiana.**
   1438   iv.   **Derrick Paul Mire, born 28 July 1983 in Baton Rouge, East Baton Rouge Parish, Louisiana.**

   712. Mona Ann[7] Robért (Carl James[6], Rene Benoit[5], Jean Paul[4], Mathieu[3], Jean[2], Mathieu[1]) was born 07 November 1956 in Gonzales, Ascension Parish, Louisiana. She married **Sloan Lloyd Young** 11 July 1980 in St. Theresa of Avila Catholic Church, Gonzales, Louisiana, son of Samuel Young and Bonnie Bryant. He was born 29 February 1956 in San Benito, Texas.

Children of Mona Robért and Sloan Young are:
   1439   i.   **Lance Michael[8] Young, born 06 March 1982 in Baton Rouge, East Baton Rouge Parish, Louisiana.**
   1440   ii.   **Rae Michelle Young, born 07 January 1985 in Baton Rouge, East Baton Rouge Parish, Louisiana.**
   1441   iii.   **Chet David Young, born 08 July 1986 in Baton Rouge, East Baton Rouge Parish, Louisiana.**

   713. Jaime Terése[7] Robért (Carl James[6], Rene Benoit[5], Jean Paul[4], Mathieu[3], Jean[2], Mathieu[1]) was born 10 November 1958 in Gonzales, Ascension Parish, Louisiana. She married **Cecil Paul Robért, Jr.** 27 January 1984 in St. Anthony Chapel, Darrow, Louisiana, son of Cecil Robért and Betty LeBlanc. He was born 13 August 1954 in Donaldsonville, Ascension Parish, Louisiana.

146

Children are listed above under (652) Cecil Paul Robért, Jr..

714. Danny Gerard[7] Robért (Carl James[6], Rene Benoit[5], Jean Paul[4], Mathieu[3], Jean[2], Mathieu[1]) was born 14 February 1962 in Baton Rouge, East Baton Rouge Parish, Louisiana. He married **Gay Ann Braud** 15 May 1987 in St. Theresa of Avila Catholic Church, Gonzales, Louisiana, daughter of Gayle Braud and Audrey Pradat. She was born 03 January 1962 in New Orleans, Orleans Parish, Louisiana.

Children of Danny Robért and Gay Braud are:

1442	i.	**Cori Danielle[8] Robért, born 05 July 1990 in Baton Rouge, East Baton Rouge Parish, Louisiana.**
1443	ii.	**Randi Michelle Robért, born 19 May 1993 in Baton Rouge, East Baton Rouge Parish, Louisiana.**
1444	iii.	**Ryan Gerald Robért, born 16 May 1996 in Baton Rouge, East Baton Rouge Parish, Louisiana.**

715. Suzanne Marie[7] Robért (Carl James[6], Rene Benoit[5], Jean Paul[4], Mathieu[3], Jean[2], Mathieu[1]) was born 16 June 1964 in Baton Rouge, East Baton Rouge Parish, Louisiana. She married **Jody Don Elisar** 04 May 1984 in St. Theresa of Avila Catholic Church, Gonzales, Louisiana, son of Donald Elisar and Laurie Gautreau. He was born 13 October 1963 in Baton Rouge, East Baton Rouge Parish, Louisiana.

Children of Suzanne Robért and Jody Elisar are:

1445	i.	**Brandon Scot[8] Elisar, born 23 January 1987 in Baton Rouge, East Baton Rouge Parish, Louisiana.**
1446	ii.	**Britney Nicole Elisar, born 15 March 1989 in Baton Rouge, East Baton Rouge Parish, Louisiana.**
1447	iii.	**Kristi Danielle Elisar, born 15 February 1991 in Baton Rouge, East Baton Rouge Parish, Louisiana.**

718. Roland James[7] Robért III (Roland James[6], Roland Jacques[5], Jean Paul[4], Mathieu[3], Jean[2], Mathieu[1]) was born 23 October 1961 in Baton Rouge, East Baton Rouge Parish, Louisiana. He married **Anthea Guagliardo** 08 February 1986 in Hammond, Tangipahoa Parish, Louisiana, daughter of Frank Guagliardo and Fay Tycer. She was born 17 January 1967 in Hammond, Tangipahoa Parish, Louisiana.

Children of Roland Robért and Anthea Guagliardo are:

| 1448 | i. | **Katie Ann[8] Robért, born 31 December 1986 in Baton Rouge, East Baton Rouge Parish, Louisiana.** |

| 1449 | ii. | Roland James Robért IV, born 02 December 1988 in Hammond, Tangipahoa Parish, Louisiana. |
| 1450 | iii. | Tycer Francis Robért, born 09 May 1994 in Baton Rouge, East Baton Rouge Parish, Louisiana. |

719. Michael Joseph[7] Robért, Sr. (Roland James[6], Roland Jacques[5], Jean Paul[4], Mathieu[3], Jean[2], Mathieu[1]) was born 25 September 1962 in Baton Rouge, East Baton Rouge Parish, Louisiana. He married **Caroll Amond** 14 February 1987 in Covington, St. Tammany Parish, Louisiana, daughter of Alexander Amond and Carroll. She was born 14 April 1965 in New Orleans, Orleans Parish, Louisiana.

Children of Michael Robért and Caroll Amond are:

1451	i.	Meagan Alexandra[8] Robért, born 09 February 1991 in New Orleans, Orleans Parish, Louisiana.
1452	ii.	Michael Joseph Robért, Jr., born 14 May 1992 in New Orleans, Orleans Parish, Louisiana.
1453	iii.	Austin Nicholas Robért, born 21 April 1995 in New Orleans, Orleans Parish, Louisiana.
1454	iv.	Alexander James Robért, born 28 May 1999 in New Orleans, Orleans Parish, Louisiana.

720. Adam Paul[7] Robért, Sr. (Roland James[6], Roland Jacques[5], Jean Paul[4], Mathieu[3], Jean[2], Mathieu[1]) was born 02 January 1964 in Baton Rouge, East Baton Rouge Parish, Louisiana. He married **Jody Dominguez** 18 January 1986 in Hammond, Tangipahoa Parish, Louisiana, daughter of Duddly Dominguez and Shirley Brown. She was born 04 December 1966 in New Orleans, Orleans Parish, Louisiana.

Children of Adam Robért and Jody Dominguez are:

| 1455 | i. | Kimberlie Jane[8] Robért, born 31 August 1988 in Hammond, Tangipahoa Parish, Louisiana. |
| 1456 | ii. | Adam Paul Robért, Jr., born 12 August 1996 in Hammond, Tangipahoa Parish, Louisiana. |

721. Thomas Jude[7] Robért (Roland James[6], Roland Jacques[5], Jean Paul[4], Mathieu[3], Jean[2], Mathieu[1]) was born 29 January 1966 in Baton Rouge, East Baton Rouge Parish, Louisiana. He married **Kelli Williams** 30 June 1990 in Covington, St. Tammany Parish, Louisiana, daughter of Rawlin Williams and Audrey Farret. She was born 11 August 1969 in Bogalusa, Washington Parish, Louisiana.

Children of Thomas Robért and Kelli Williams are:

1457	i.	Madison Marguerite[8] Robért, born 21 April 1995 in New Orleans, Orleans Parish, Louisiana.
1458	ii.	Reagan Katherine Robért, born 18 August 1997 in New Orleans, Orleans Parish, Louisiana.
1459	iii.	Kennedy Lane Robért, born 11 September 2000 in New Orleans, Orleans Parish, Louisiana.

722. Larry Denis[7] Robért, Sr. (Roland James[6], Roland Jacques[5], Jean Paul[4], Mathieu[3], Jean[2], Mathieu[1]) was born 14 November 1968. He married **Debbie Beall** 30 December 1989 in Baton Rouge, East Baton Rouge Parish, Louisiana, daughter of Robert Beall and Gloria Stafford. She was born 21 November 1967 in Hammond, Tangipahoa Parish, Louisiana.

Children of Larry Robért and Debbie Beall are:

1460	i.	Larry Denis[8] Robért, Jr., born 05 January 1993 in Hammond, Tangipahoa Parish, Louisiana.
1461	ii.	Sarah Elizabeth Robért, born 20 March 1996 in Baton Rouge, East Baton Rouge Parish, Louisiana.
1462	iii.	Gracie Lynn Robért, born 08 September 2003 in Hammond, Tangipahoa Parish, Louisiana.

725. Kandis Ann[7] Robért (Gayle Patrick[6], Roland Jacques[5], Jean Paul[4], Mathieu[3], Jean[2], Mathieu[1]) was born 26 September 1962 in Baton Rouge, East Baton Rouge Parish, Louisiana. She married **Vance David Venable** 31 May 1986 in Burnside, Ascension Parish, Louisiana (Blessed in St. Theresa Church in 1998), son of John Venable and Catherine Gautreaux. He was born 14 May 1964 in Baton Rouge, East Baton Rouge Parish, Louisiana.

Children of Kandis Robért and Vance Venable are:

1463	i.	Felicia Marie[8] Venable, born 10 March 1991 in Baton Rouge, East Baton Rouge Parish, Louisiana.
1464	ii.	Sarah Kate Venable, born 11 January 1994 in Baton Rouge, East Baton Rouge Parish, Louisiana.
1465	iii.	Emily Ann Venable, born 13 September 1998 in Baton Rouge, East Baton Rouge Parish, Louisiana.

726. Gina Monique[7] Robért (Gayle Patrick[6], Roland Jacques[5], Jean Paul[4], Mathieu[3], Jean[2], Mathieu[1]) was born 22 October 1964 in Baton Rouge, East Baton Rouge Parish, Louisiana. She married **Alvin Paul Medere III** 02 November 1984 in St. Theresa Catholic Church, Gonzales, Ascension Parish, Louisiana, son of Alvin Medere and Juanita Coriell. He was born 19 February 1963 in Donaldsonville, Ascension Parish, Louisiana.

Children of Gina Robért and Alvin Medere are:

1466   i.   **Chelsie Lynn[8] Medere, (Adopted 16 April 1992), born 08 January 1992 in Baton Rouge, East Baton Rouge Parish, Louisiana.**

1467   ii.   **Brennon Doh Medere, (Kun Woo Doh, adopted), born 28 November 2003 in Aidong City, South Korea.**

733. Woodson[7] Harvey III (Val Ann[6] Robért, Roland Jacques[5], Jean Paul[4], Mathieu[3], Jean[2], Mathieu[1]) was born 20 March 1963 in Baton Rouge, East Baton Rouge Parish, Louisiana. He married **Stacie Charmaine Soileau** 12 January 1985 in Pine Prairie, Evangeline Parish, Louisiana. She was born 19 September 1966.

Children of Woodson Harvey and Stacie Soileau are:

1468   i.   **Morgan Elizabeth[8] Harvey, born 20 November 1994 in Ville Platte,Evangeline Parish, Louisiana.**

1469   ii.   **Meghan Elizabeth Harvey, born 23 July 1997 in Ville Platte,Evangeline Parish, Louisiana.**

1470   iii.   **Macey Elise Harvey, born 14 July 1999 in Ville Platte,Evangeline Parish, Louisiana.**

734. Robert Doyle[7] Harvey (Val Ann[6] Robért, Roland Jacques[5], Jean Paul[4], Mathieu[3], Jean[2], Mathieu[1]) was born 25 February 1964 in Baton Rouge, East Baton Rouge Parish, Louisiana. He married **(1) Leisa Gay Blood** 1985 in Bunkie, Avoyelles Parish, Louisiana. She was born 21 December 1969 in Lecompte, Rapides Parish, Louisiana. He married **(2) Lilly Dawn Parish** 10 September 1994.

Children of Robert Harvey and Leisa Blood are:

1471   i.   **Courtney Ann[8] Harvey, born 10 October 1985 in Lafayette, Lafayette Parish, Louisiana. She married Joey Wilde 19 September 2005 in Lafayette, Lafayette Parish, Loiuisiana.**

1472   ii.   **Monique Antonia Harvey, born 01 March 1986 in Lafayette, Lafayette Parish, Louisiana.**

1473   iii.   **Caberial Alexandria Harvey, born 13 November 1990 in Alexandria, Rapides Parish, Louisiana.**

1474   iv.   **Brittney Nichole Harvey, born 11 September 1992 in Baton Rouge, East Baton Rouge Parish, Louisiana.**

735. Wynn Traylor[7] Harvey (Val Ann[6] Robért, Roland Jacques[5], Jean Paul[4], Mathieu[3], Jean[2], Mathieu[1]) was born 18 July 1966 in Houston, Texas. He married **Toni Coates** in St. Landry, Evangeline Parish, Louisiana. She was born 14 March 1965 in Alexandria, Rapides Parish, Louisiana.

150

Children of Wynn Harvey and Toni Coates are:
- 1475   i.   **Wynn Traylor[8] Harvey II**, born 12 July 1992 in Alexandria, Rapides Parish, Louisiana.
- 1476   ii.   **Lainey Cait Harvey**, born 21 March 1995 in Alexandria, Rapides Parish, Louisiana.

736. Valerie Ann[7] Harvey (Val Ann[6] Robért, Roland Jacques[5], Jean Paul[4], Mathieu[3], Jean[2], Mathieu[1]) was born 16 September 1968 in Opelousas, St. Landry Parish, Louisiana. She married **Stephen Mitchell Toups** 09 May 1992 in Baton Rouge, East Baton Rouge Parish, Louisiana. He was born 21 February 1966 in Baton Rouge, East Baton Rouge Parish, Louisiana.

Children of Valerie Harvey and Stephen Toups are:
- 1477   i.   **Stephanie Michele[8] Toups**, born 22 August 1994 in Baton Rouge, East Baton Rouge Parish, Louisiana.
- 1478   ii.   **Shelby McCall Toups**, born 12 April 1997 in Baton Rouge, East Baton Rouge Parish, Louisiana.
- 1479   iii.   **Roland Michael Toups II**, born 28 February 2002 in Baton Rouge, East Baton Rouge Parish, Louisiana.

737. George Brian[7] Harvey (Val Ann[6] Robért, Roland Jacques[5], Jean Paul[4], Mathieu[3], Jean[2], Mathieu[1]) was born 17 August 1970 in Opelousas, St. Landry Parish, Louisiana. He married **Shelly Annette McMaster** 08 August 1992 in Vidor, Texas. She was born 06 August 1973 in Houston, Texas.

Children of George Harvey and Shelly McMaster are:
- 1480   i.   **Bryan Taylor[8] Harvey**, born 13 January 1994 in Baton Rouge, East Baton Rouge Parish, Louisiana.
- 1481   ii.   **Jesseca Lee Ann Harvey**, born 30 September 1996 in LaPlace, St. John the Baptist Parish, Louisiana.
- 1482   iii.   **Lauren Rene Harvey**, born 02 February 1999 in Hammond, Tangipahoa Parish, Louisiana.
- 1483   iv.   **Lynsey Nicole Harvey**, born 02 February 1999 in Hammond, Tangipahoa Parish, Louisiana.
- 1484   v.   **Benjamin Gayle Harvey**, born 06 December 2001 in Hammond, Tangipahoa Parish, Louisiana.
- 1485   vi.   **Kathryn Olivia Harvey**, born 29 September 2004 in Hammond, Tangipahoa Parish, Louisiana.

743. Michelle Christy[7] Robért (Donald Christopher[6], Roland Jacques[5], Jean Paul[4], Mathieu[3], Jean[2], Mathieu[1]) was born 21 November 1969 in Baton Rouge, East Baton Rouge Parish, Louisiana. She married **Brian Savoy** 13 August 1993 in Gonzales, Ascension Parish, Louisiana. He was born 16 June

1966 in Baton Rouge, East Baton Rouge Parish, Louisiana.

Children of Michelle Robért and Brian Savoy are:

 1486   i.   **Laura Ashley[8] Savoy, (Adopted), born 20 May 1988 in San Diego, California.**
 1487   ii. **Brady Michael Savoy, born 25 June 1996 in Baton Rouge, East Baton Rouge Parish, Louisiana.**
 1488   iii. **Seth Brian Savoy, born 30 September 1999 in Baton Rouge, East Baton Rouge Parish, Louisiana.**

744. Amanda Clare[7] Robért (Donald Christopher[6], Roland Jacques[5], Jean Paul[4], Mathieu[3], Jean[2], Mathieu[1]) was born 09 February 1980 in Baton Rouge, East Baton Rouge Parish, Louisiana. She married **Ryan A. Kirby** 29 August 2003 in Gonzales, Ascension Parish, Louisiana, son of Leroy Kirby and Mary Settle. He was born 11 April 1980 in Shreveport, Caddo Parish, Louisiana.

Child of Amanda Robért and Ryan Kirby is:

 1489   i.   **Aidan Cole[8] Kirby, born 15 August 2005 in Shreveport, Caddo Parish, Louisiana.**

Generation No. 7

759. Ralph Joseph[8] Robért (Lawrence[7], Louis Luke[6], Rosemond[5], Jean Baptiste[4], Jean Louis[3], Jean[2], Mathieu[1]) was born 08 December 1942 in Ama, St. Charles Parish, Louisiana, and died 12 October 2007 in Luling, St. Charles Parish, Louisiana. He married **Living Zeringue**, daughter of Frank Zeringue and Marie Dugas.

Children of Ralph Robért and Living Zeringue are:

 1490   i.   **Living[9] Robért. He married Living Babineaux.**
 1491   ii. **Living Robért.**

818. Sharon Ann[8] Waguespack (Larry Pierre[7], Octave Pierre[6], Marie Octavie[5] Robért, ***, Jean Frumence[4], Mathieu[3], Jean[2], Mathieu[1]) was born 16 March 1950 in Burnside, Ascension Parish, Louisiana. She married **Gayle Boudreaux** 19 July 1969. He was born 16 February 1949.

Children of Sharon Waguespack and Gayle Boudreaux are:

 1492   i.   **Michael Shane[9] Boudreaux, born 04 August 1970.**
 1493   ii. **Bret Patrick Boudreaux, born 24 December 1975.**

819. Rebecca Marie[8] Waguespack (Larry Pierre[7], Octave Pierre[6],

Marie Octavie^5 Robért, ***, Jean Frumence^4, Mathieu^3, Jean^2, Mathieu^1) was born 28 September 1951 in Burnside, Ascension Parish, Louisiana. She married **William Bernard Delaune** 07 August 1971 in St. Mary Catholic Church, Union, Louisiana. He was born 25 March 1948.

Children of Rebecca Waguespack and William Delaune are:

    1494   i.   **Clint Michael^9 Delaune, born 24 January 1974.**
    1495   ii.   **Colby Bernard Delaune, born 17 June 1976.**
    1496   iii.   **Cale Murphey Delaune, born 12 November 1980.**

820. Amy Marie^8 Waguespack (Larry Pierre^7, Octave Pierre^6, Marie Octavie^5 Robért, ***, Jean Frumence^4, Mathieu^3, Jean^2, Mathieu^1) was born 29 August 1953 in Burnside, Ascension Parish, Louisiana. She married **Darryl Paul Andermann** 22 February 1974 in St. Mary Catholic Church, Union, Louisiana. He was born 04 March 1952.

Children of Amy Waguespack and Darryl Andermann are:

    1497   i.   **Trish Michael^9 Andermann, born 15 May 1975.**
    1498   ii.   **Randi Lynn Andermann, born 01 September 1977.**
    1499   iii.   **Allison Renee Andermann, born 10 January 1982; died 10 December 1983.**
    1500   iv.   **Hunter Paul Andermann, born 07 October 1984.**

821. Susan Mary^8 Waguespack (Larry Pierre^7, Octave Pierre^6, Marie Octavie^5 Robért, ***, Jean Frumence^4, Mathieu^3, Jean^2, Mathieu^1) was born 21 December 1954 in Burnside, Ascension Parish, Louisiana. She married **Eugene Lawrence Reider, Sr.** 30 June 1972 in St. Mary Catholic Church, Union, Louisiana. He was born 04 October 1951.

Children of Susan Waguespack and Eugene Reider are:

    1501   i.   **Shawna Lynn^9 Reider, born 14 January 1973.**
    1502   ii.   **Eugene Lawrence Reider, Jr., born 03 March 1975.**
    1503   iii.   **Tasha Elizabeth Reider, born 30 October 1979.**

822. Ryan Joseph^8 Waguespack (Larry Pierre^7, Octave Pierre^6, Marie Octavie^5 Robért, ***, Jean Frumence^4, Mathieu^3, Jean^2, Mathieu^1) was born 10 January 1956 in Burnside, Ascension Parish, Louisiana. He married **Darlene Boudreaux** Unknown. She was born 13 November 1955.

Children of Ryan Waguespack and Darlene Boudreaux are:

    1504   i.   Casey Lynn^9 Waguespack, born 26 September 1982.
    1505   ii.   **Shane Joseph Waguespack, born 02 July 1986.**

823. Nanette Marie[8] Waguespack (Larry Pierre[7], Octave Pierre[6], Marie Octavie[5] Robért, ***, Jean Frumence[4], Mathieu[3], Jean[2], Mathieu[1]) was born 26 February 1957 in Burnside, Ascension Parish, Louisiana. She married **(1) Damien Dale Haydel** 06 January 1972 in St. Mary Catholic Church, Union, Louisiana. He was born 04 February 1952. She married **(2) Timmy Prejean** 14 February 1985.

Children of Nanette Waguespack and Damien Haydel are:
  1506   i.   **Sandy Lee[9] Haydel, born 01 July 1972.**
  1507   ii.   **Faith Elizabeth Haydel, born 08 September 1976.**

824. Larry P.[8] Waguespack, Jr. (Larry Pierre[7], Octave Pierre[6], Marie Octavie[5] Robért, ***, Jean Frumence[4], Mathieu[3], Jean[2], Mathieu[1]) was born 03 November 1958 in St. James Parish, Lutcher, Louisiana. He married **Renée Ann Zeringue** 24 August 1979 in St. Joseph Catholic Church, Paulina, Louisiana, daughter of Norman Zeringue and Ethel Deroche. She was born 24 November 1958 in St. James Parish, Lutcher, Louisiana.

Children of Larry Waguespack and Renée Zeringue are:
  1508   i.   **Kassie Leigh[9] Waguespack, born 17 January 1983 in Baton Rouge, East Baton Rouge Parish, Louisiana.**
  1509   ii.   **Amanda Lynn Waguespack, born 04 May 1987 in Baton Rouge, East Baton Rouge Parish, Louisiana.**

826. Chad Anthony[8] Waguespack (Larry Pierre[7], Octave Pierre[6], Marie Octavie[5] Robért, ***, Jean Frumence[4], Mathieu[3], Jean[2], Mathieu[1]) was born 28 June 1961 in Burnside, Ascension Parish, Louisiana. He married **Carol Stephens** 03 June 1982. She was born Unknown.

Children of Chad Waguespack and Carol Stephens are:
  1510   i.   **Melissa Stephens[9] Waguespack, born 09 April 1980.**
  1511   ii.   **Brad A. Waguespack, born 16 November 1986.**

831. Cynthia Ann[8] Keller (Barbara Rita[7] Waguespack, Octave Pierre[6], Marie Octavie[5] Robért, ***, Jean Frumence[4], Mathieu[3], Jean[2], Mathieu[1]) was born 14 November 1954. She married **Leonard Paul Roussel** 01 February 1975 in St. Michael Catholic Church, Convent, Louisiana. He was born 04 September 1951.

Children of Cynthia Keller and Leonard Roussel are:
  1512   i.   **Chad[9] Roussel, born 07 October 1976.**
  1513   ii.   **Jamie Lynne Roussel, born 28 July 1980.**

154

1514   iii. **Stacey Lynn Roussel, born 25 September 1984.**

832. Timothy Joseph[8] Keller (Barbara Rita[7] Waguespack, Octave Pierre[6], Marie Octavie[5] Robért, ***, Jean Frumence[4], Mathieu[3], Jean[2], Mathieu[1]) was born 02 October 1956. He married **Billie Kliebert** 11 August 1978 in St. Joseph Catholic Church, Paulina, Louisiana. She was born 10 May 1959.

Child of Timothy Keller and Billie Kliebert is:
    1515   i. **Candace Ann[9] Keller, born 16 March 1982.**

833. Patrick James[8] Keller (Barbara Rita[7] Waguespack, Octave Pierre[6], Marie Octavie[5] Robért, ***, Jean Frumence[4], Mathieu[3], Jean[2], Mathieu[1]) was born 18 September 1957. He married **Bobbie Lynn Kliebert** 09 August 1980 in St. Joseph Catholic Church, Paulina, Louisiana. She was born 10 May 1959.

Children of Patrick Keller and Bobbie Kliebert are:
    1516   i. **Jeremy Michael[9] Keller, born 20 January 1982.**
    1517   ii. **Aaron Patrick Keller, born 10 October 1983.**
    1518   iii. **Darren Paul Keller, born 10 October 1983.**

834. Phyllis Ann[8] Keller (Barbara Rita[7] Waguespack, Octave Pierre[6], Marie Octavie[5] Robért, ***, Jean Frumence[4], Mathieu[3], Jean[2], Mathieu[1]) was born 22 January 1960. She married **Dave Paul Lemoine** 13 June 1980 in St. Joseph Catholic Church, Paulina, Louisiana. He was born 28 December 1958.

Children of Phyllis Keller and Dave Lemoine are:
    1519   i. **Tiffany Anne[9] Lemoine, born 16 August 1981.**
    1520   ii. **Dana Lynn Lemoine, born 18 February 1983.**
    1521   iii. **Lacey Michelle Lemoine, born 02 March 1988; died 29 March 1988 in Woman's Hospital, Baton Rouge, Louisiana.**

835. Blain Anthony[8] Keller (Barbara Rita[7] Waguespack, Octave Pierre[6], Marie Octavie[5] Robért, ***, Jean Frumence[4], Mathieu[3], Jean[2], Mathieu[1]) was born 16 February 1962. He married **Pam Louque** 11 September 1981 in Sacred Heart Catholic Church, Grammercy, Louisiana. She was born 17 August 1964.

Children of Blain Keller and Pam Louque are:
    1522   i. **Tara Marie[9] Keller, born 04 July 1980.**
    1523   ii. **David Paul Keller, born 29 April 1985.**

836. Jennifer Ann[8] Keller (Barbara Rita[7] Waguespack, Octave Pierre[6],

Marie Octavie[5] Robért, ***, Jean Frumence[4], Mathieu[3], Jean[2], Mathieu[1]) was born 12 November 1964. She married **Bobby Paul McClung** 08 February 1985. He was born 16 August 1962.

Child of Jennifer Keller and Bobby McClung is:
   1524   i.   **Heather Elizabeth[9] McClung, born 13 March 1987.**

838. Wendy Ann[8] Sotile (Genevieve[7] Waguespack, Octave Pierre[6], Marie Octavie[5] Robért, ***, Jean Frumence[4], Mathieu[3], Jean[2], Mathieu[1]) was born 12 February 1958 in Donaldsonville, Ascension Parish, Louisiana. She married **Leo Camille Poirrier** 16 June 1978 in Ascension Catholic Church, Donaldsonville, Louisiana. He was born 07 July 1955.

Children of Wendy Sotile and Leo Poirrier are:
   1525   i.   **Alison Leigh[9] Poirrier, born 07 April 1980 in Baton Rouge, East Baton Rouge Parish, Louisiana.**
   1526   ii.   **Ashley Lynn Poirrier, born 03 November 1982 in Baton Rouge, East Baton Rouge Parish, Louisiana.**

841. Monica Lynne[8] Sotile (Genevieve[7] Waguespack, Octave Pierre[6], Marie Octavie[5] Robért, ***, Jean Frumence[4], Mathieu[3], Jean[2], Mathieu[1]) was born 09 May 1966 in Donaldsonville, Ascension Parish, Louisiana. She married **Patrick Arcement** 25 July 1986 in Ascension Catholic Church, Donaldsonville, Louisiana. He was born Unknown.

Child of Monica Sotile and Patrick Arcement is:
   1527   i.   **Patrick Vincent[9] Arcement, born 09 January 1987.**

844. Robin Marie[8] Guillot (Jacqueline Marie[7] Waguespack, Octave Pierre[6], Marie Octavie[5] Robért, ***, Jean Frumence[4], Mathieu[3], Jean[2], Mathieu[1]) was born 10 September 1962. She married **David Kent Richard** 11 February 1984. He was born 27 January 1955.

Child of Robin Guillot and David Richard is:
   1528   i.   **Alex Michael[9] Richard, born 17 March 1987 in Baton Rouge, East Baton Rouge Parish, Louisiana.**

847. Julie Marie[8] Guillot (Jacqueline Marie[7] Waguespack, Octave Pierre[6], Marie Octavie[5] Robért, ***, Jean Frumence[4], Mathieu[3], Jean[2], Mathieu[1]) was born 21 February 1967 in Baton Rouge, East Baton Rouge Parish, Louisiana. She married **Chad Joseph Bourgoyne** 18 September 1987 in St. Patrick Catholic

Church, Baton Rouge, Louisiana. He was born 22 March 1967.

Child of Julie Guillot and Chad Bourgoyne is:
> 1529   i.   **Casey Lynne[9] Bourgoyne, born 26 September 1988 in Baton Rouge, East Baton Rouge Parish, Louisiana.**

882. Nelda Ann[8] Waguespack (Edgar Joseph[7], Edgar Joseph[6], Marie Octavie[5] Robért, ***, Jean Frumence[4], Mathieu[3], Jean[2], Mathieu[1]) was born 30 September 1951 in Donaldsonville, Ascension Parish, Louisiana. She married **Albert Joseph Banker, Jr. (Buck)** 05 June 1971 in St. Mary Catholic Church, Union, Louisiana. He was born 03 March 1951.

Children of Nelda Waguespack and Albert Banker are:
> 1530   i.   **Jeffry Wade[9] Banker, born 06 November 1972.**
> 1531   ii.   **Brad David Banker, born 12 November 1976.**

883. Judy Marie[8] Waguespack (Edgar Joseph[7], Edgar Joseph[6], Marie Octavie[5] Robért, ***, Jean Frumence[4], Mathieu[3], Jean[2], Mathieu[1]) was born 16 February 1953 in Donaldsonville, Ascension Parish, Louisiana. She married **Gary Joseph Braud** 12 October 1973 in St. Mary Catholic Church, Union, Louisiana. He was born 04 November 1949.

Children of Judy Waguespack and Gary Braud are:
> 1532   i.   **Connie Theresa[9] Braud, born 09 April 1974.**
> 1533   ii.   **Clint Anthony Braud, born 31 May 1979.**

885. Arlene Lucy[8] Waguespack (Edgar Joseph[7], Edgar Joseph[6], Marie Octavie[5] Robért, ***, Jean Frumence[4], Mathieu[3], Jean[2], Mathieu[1]) was born 23 February 1955 in Burnside, Ascension Parish , Louisiana. She married **(1) Tommy Vincent Bihm**. He was born 27 January 1952. She married **(2) James Edward Braud, Jr** 06 July 1975. He was born 09 May 1953.

Children of Arlene Waguespack and James Braud are:
> 1534   i.   **Ryan Douglas[9] Braud, born 01 October 1977.**
> 1535   ii.   **Jamie Lynn Braud, born 22 October 1978.**
> 1536   iii. **Genie Marie Braud, born 09 November 1980.**

886. Marvin Peter[8] Waguespack (Edgar Joseph[7], Edgar Joseph[6], Marie Octavie[5] Robért, ***, Jean Frumence[4], Mathieu[3], Jean[2], Mathieu[1]) was born 18 July 1956. He married **(1) Rachel Anne Lambert** 05 May 1977 in Holy Rosary Catholic Church, St. Amant, Louisiana. She was born 01 October 1958. He married **(2) Marie Lori Thomasee** 27 April 1984. She was born 22 September 1962.

Child of Marvin Waguespack and Rachel Lambert is:
    1537   i.   **Daniel Joseph^9 Waguespack.**

Child of Marvin Waguespack and Marie Thomasee is:
    1538   i.   **Kade Austin^9 Waguespack, born 06 April 1991.**

887. Jason Paul^8 Waguespack (Edgar Joseph^7, Edgar Joseph^6, Marie Octavie^5 Robért, ***, Jean Frumence^4, Mathieu^3, Jean^2, Mathieu^1) was born 18 September 1957 in Lutcher, St. James Parish, Louisiana. He married **Effie Josephine Roussel** 17 November 1979. She was born 18 August 1958.

Children of Jason Waguespack and Effie Roussel are:
    1539   i.   **Amy Marie^9 Waguespack, born 10 November 1981.**
    1540   ii.   **Randy Paul Waguespack, born 09 January 1985.**
    1541   iii.   **Ricky Lee Waguespack, born 18 December 1986.**

888. Jessie Jude^8 Waguespack (Edgar Joseph^7, Edgar Joseph^6, Marie Octavie^5 Robért, ***, Jean Frumence^4, Mathieu^3, Jean^2, Mathieu^1) was born 29 September 1959 in Lutcher, St. James Parish, Louisiana. He married **Sherry Boltin** 02 May 1980 in Sacred Heart Catholic Church, Gramercy, Louisiana. She was born 31 July 1960.

Children of Jessie Waguespack and Sherry Boltin are:
    1542   i.   **Brian Patrick^9 Waguespack, born 27 November 1981.**
    1543   ii.   **Monique Waguespack, born 26 April 1983.**
    1544   iii.   **Tony Jude Waguespack, born 09 April 1985.**

889. Elise Rita^8 Waguespack (Edgar Joseph^7, Edgar Joseph^6, Marie Octavie^5 Robért, ***, Jean Frumence^4, Mathieu^3, Jean^2, Mathieu^1) was born 07 November 1961 in Lutcher, Louisiana. She married **Brian David Hinrichs** 08 April 1989 in St. Michael Catholic Church, Convent, Louisiana. He was born 02 December 1958.

Child of Elise Waguespack and Brian Hinrichs is:
    1545   i.   **Emily Marie^9 Hinrichs, born 08 June 1994.**

890. Donny J.^{8} Troxclair (Sherman Joseph^7, Josepha Marie^6 Zeringue,

Jeanne Clelie[5] Robért, Septime Louis[4], Mathieu[3], Jean[2], Mathieu[1]) was born 24 August 1958 in Lutcher, St. James Parish, Louisiana. He married **Laura Braud** 30 July 1982 in Norco, St. Charles Parish, Louisiana, daughter of Ivy Braud and Winona Lear. She was born 10 August 1960 in New Orleans, Orleans Parish, Louisiana.

Children of Donny Troxclair and Laura Braud are:

    1546   i.   **Justin[9] Troxclair, born 05 April 1986 in LaPlace, St.John the Baptist Parish, Louisiana ?.**

    1547   ii.   **Brad Troxclair, born 30 May 1988 in LaPlace, St. John the Baptist Parish, Louisiana.**

912. Catherine[8] Waguespack (Stanford John[7], Wallis Jean[6], Marie Octavie[5] Robért, ***, Jean Frumence[4], Mathieu[3], Jean[2], Mathieu[1]) was born 08 October 1948 in Donaldsonville, Ascension Parish, Louisiana. She married **Roy Thomas Boudreaux** 06 June 1970 in St. Mary Catholic Church, Union, Louisiana. He was born 01 January 1942.

Children of Catherine Waguespack and Roy Boudreaux are:

    1548   i.   **Troy Jude[9] Boudreaux, born 18 October 1971.**

    1549   ii.   **Jaime Ann Boudreaux, born 15 July 1973.**

    1550   iii.   **Dawn Michelle Boudreaux, born 02 March 1980.**

    1551   iv.   **Brad Thomas Boudreaux, born 19 September 1983.**

913. Kevin John[8] Waguespack (Stanford John[7], Wallis Jean[6], Marie Octavie[5] Robért, ***, Jean Frumence[4], Mathieu[3], Jean[2], Mathieu[1]) was born 21 December 1949 in Donaldsonville, Ascension Parish, Louisiana. He married **Debra Ann Liddell** 17 July 1971 in Ascension Parish, Baker, Louisiana. She was born 27 October 1951.

Children of Kevin Waguespack and Debra Liddell are:

    1552   i.   **Keith John[9] Waguespack, born 09 January 1976.**

    1553   ii.   **Daren Michael Waguespack, born 04 July 1977.**

916. Marjorie Mary[8] Waguespack (Stanford John[7], Wallis Jean[6], Marie Octavie[5] Robért, ***, Jean Frumence[4], Mathieu[3], Jean[2], Mathieu[1]) was born 17 August 1961 in Lutcher, Louisiana. She married **Clay Cranfield** 17 September 1983 in St. Mary Catholic Church, Union, Louisiana. He was born 06 January 1960.

Children of Marjorie Waguespack and Clay Cranfield are:

    1554   i.   **Callen Micah[9] Cranfield, born 24 January 1985.**

1555   ii.   Eileen Mara Cranfield, born 06 August 1988 in Baton Rouge, East Baton Rouge Parish, Louisiana.

936. Gene Gerald[8] LeBlanc (Elgie Mae[7] Waguespack, Edgar Joseph[6], Marie Octavie[5] Robért, ***, Jean Frumence[4], Mathieu[3], Jean[2], Mathieu[1]) was born 27 February 1951 in Donaldsonville, Ascension Parish, Louisiana. He married **Jo Ann Castagnos** 17 November 1972. She was born 16 September 1951.

Children of Gene LeBlanc and Jo Ann Castagnos are:
    1556   i.   **Cliff Michael[9] LeBlanc, born 08 October 1976 in Baton Rouge, East Baton Rouge Parish, Louisiana.**
    1557   ii.   **Brett Mathieu LeBlanc, born 06 August 1980 in Baton Rouge, East Baton Rouge Parish, Louisiana.**
    1558   iii. **Cody Paul LeBlanc, born 15 February 1982 in Baton Rouge, East Baton Rouge Parish, Louisiana.**

937. Glyn Edward[8] LeBlanc (Elgie Mae[7] Waguespack, Edgar Joseph[6], Marie Octavie[5] Robért, ***, Jean Frumence[4], Mathieu[3], Jean[2], Mathieu[1]) was born 03 May 1955 in Donaldsonville, Ascension Parish, Louisiana. He married **Sharon Moss** 23 December 1984 in Shreveport, Louisiana. She was born 23 December.

Children of Glyn LeBlanc and Sharon Moss are:
    1559   i.   **Elise Hope[9] LeBlanc, born 07 October 1985 in Baton Rouge, East Baton Rouge Parish, Louisiana.**
    1560   ii.   **Emily Grace LeBlanc, born 24 March 1988 in Baton Rouge, East Baton Rouge Parish, Louisiana.**

938. Gerilyn Marie[8] LeBlanc (Elgie Mae[7] Waguespack, Edgar Joseph[6], Marie Octavie[5] Robért, ***, Jean Frumence[4], Mathieu[3], Jean[2], Mathieu[1]) was born 17 November 1956 in Donaldsonville, Ascension Parish, Louisiana. She married **Charles Joseph Schexnayder** 17 March 1978 in St. Francis Assissi Catholic Church, Smoke Bend, Louisiana. He was born 02 October 1951.

Child of Gerilyn LeBlanc and Charles Schexnayder is:
    1561   i.   **Kalli Anne[9] Schexnayder, born 27 February 1983 in Jefferson Parish, Matairie, Louisiana.**

939. Kerilyn Mary[8] LeBlanc (Elgie Mae[7] Waguespack, Edgar Joseph[6], Marie Octavie[5] Robért, ***, Jean Frumence[4], Mathieu[3], Jean[2], Mathieu[1]) was born 17 November 1956 in Donaldsonville, Ascension Parish, Louisiana. She married **Curtis Joseph Hebert** Unknown. He was born 29 May 1948.

Child of Kerilyn LeBlanc and Curtis Hebert is:

1562   i.   **Kaycee Lynn[9] Hebert, born 19 November 1981 in Jefferson Parish, Matairie, Louisiana.**

945. Lois Margaret[8] Baudouin (Lois Marie[7] Caillet, Denise Marie[6] Waguespack, Marie Octavie[5] Robért, ***, Jean Frumence[4], Mathieu[3], Jean[2], Mathieu[1]) was born 27 September 1943 in Orleans Parish, New Orleans, Orleans Parish, Louisiana. She married **David Nolan Bishop** 16 November 1963. He was born 14 January 1940.

Children of Lois Baudouin and David Bishop are:

1563   i.   **Julie Frances[9] Bishop, born 14 September 1966.**
1564   ii. **Anne Marie Bishop, born 30 April 1969.**

946. Catherine Mary[8] Baudouin (Lois Marie[7] Caillet, Denise Marie[6] Waguespack, Marie Octavie[5] Robért, ***, Jean Frumence[4], Mathieu[3], Jean[2], Mathieu[1]) was born 07 October 1948. She married **Gerard Edward Burrage** 03 September 1971 in St. Mary Magdalene, Church, Metairie, Louisiana. He was born 21 August 1944.

Children of Catherine Baudouin and Gerard Burrage are:

1565   i.   **Ryan Gerard[9] Burrage, born 23 September 1974.**
1566   ii. **Lindsay Catherine Burrage, born 10 July 1978.**

947. Irby T.[8] Baudouin (Lois Marie[7] Caillet, Denise Marie[6] Waguespack, Marie Octavie[5] Robért, ***, Jean Frumence[4], Mathieu[3], Jean[2], Mathieu[1]) was born 18 January 1953 in Orleans Parish, New Orleans, Orleans Parish, Louisiana. He married **Rena McAhee** 24 September 1976. She was born 24 July 1954.

Child of Irby Baudouin and Rena McAhee is:

1567   i.   **Claire Louise[9] Baudouin, born 10 July 1978.**

955. Patricia Maria[8] Baudouin (Helene[7] Caillet, Denise Marie[6] Waguespack, Marie Octavie[5] Robért, ***, Jean Frumence[4], Mathieu[3], Jean[2], Mathieu[1]) was born 25 September 1949. She married **Joseph Frank Catanzaro** 02 August 1969. He was born 26 December 1946.

Children of Patricia Baudouin and Joseph Catanzaro are:

1568   i.   **Amanda Elaine[9] Catanzaro, born 25 August 1971 in Baton Rouge, East Baton Rouge Parish, Louisiana.**
1569   ii. **Douglas Paul Catanzaro, born 13 August 1975 in Baton Rouge,**

956. Gregory Thomas[8] Baudouin (Helene[7] Caillet, Denise Marie[6] Waguespack, Marie Octavie[5] Robért, ***, Jean Frumence[4], Mathieu[3], Jean[2], Mathieu[1]) was born 25 May 1954. He married **Karen Ann Washer** 05 April 1975. She was born 03 November 1954.

Children of Gregory Baudouin and Karen Washer are:

   1570   i.   **Jennifer Rebecca[9] Baudouin, born 05 August 1979 in East Baton Rouge Parish, Baton Rouge, La..**

   1571   ii.   **Amie Marie Baudouin, born 11 March 1982 in East Baton Rouge Parish, Baton Rouge, La..**

957. Georgia Helene[8] Baudouin (Helene[7] Caillet, Denise Marie[6] Waguespack, Marie Octavie[5] Robért, ***, Jean Frumence[4], Mathieu[3], Jean[2], Mathieu[1]) was born 07 February 1958. She married **Randy Keith Fleniken** 27 January 1978. He was born 17 January 1957.

Child of Georgia Baudouin and Randy Fleniken is:

   1572   i.   **Dawn Michelle[9] Fleniken, born 19 August 1980 in Baton Rouge, East Baton Rouge Parish, Louisiana.**

958. Walter Edgar[8] Millet, III (Hazel Theresa[7] Caillet, Denise Marie[6] Waguespack, Marie Octavie[5] Robért, ***, Jean Frumence[4], Mathieu[3], Jean[2], Mathieu[1]) was born 01 January 1950 in New Orleans, Orleans Parish, Louisiana. He married **Susan Marguerite Doub** 22 June 1974. She was born 11 June 1952 in Bogalousa, Louisiana.

Children of Walter Millet and Susan Doub are:

   1573   i.   **Marguerite Therese[9] Millet, born 29 March 1976 in Jefferson Parish, Marrero, Louisiana.**

   1574   ii.   **Camille Millet, born 13 September 1979 in Jefferson Parish, Matairie, Louisiana.**

959. Emily Clair[8] Millet (Hazel Theresa[7] Caillet, Denise Marie[6] Waguespack, Marie Octavie[5] Robért, ***, Jean Frumence[4], Mathieu[3], Jean[2], Mathieu[1]) was born 26 March 1952 in New Orleans, Orleans Parish, Louisiana. She married **Bryan Gene Beauchamp** 04 August 1973. He was born 21 November 1950 in New Orleans, Orleans Parish, Louisiana.

Children of Emily Millet and Bryan Beauchamp are:

1575 i. Amanda Claire[9] Beauchamp, born 14 September 1976 in Matairie, Louisiana.

1576 ii. Heather Jean Beauchamp, born 14 June 1978 in Matairie, Louisiana.

960. Philip Alan[8] Millet (Hazel Theresa[7] Caillet, Denise Marie[6] Waguespack, Marie Octavie[5] Robért, ***, Jean Frumence[4], Mathieu[3], Jean[2], Mathieu[1]) was born 03 February 1953 in New Orleans, Orleans Parish, Louisiana. He married **Althea Ann Fitch** 03 November 1973. She was born 11 November 1953 in Pineville, Louisiana.

Child of Philip Millet and Althea Fitch is:

1577 i. Summer Helen[9] Millet, born 17 June 1980 in Hammond, Louisiana.

962. Theresa Agnes[8] Millet (Hazel Theresa[7] Caillet, Denise Marie[6] Waguespack, Marie Octavie[5] Robért, ***, Jean Frumence[4], Mathieu[3], Jean[2], Mathieu[1]) was born 30 May 1955 in New Orleans, Orleans Parish, Louisiana. She married **Vernon Paul Meyer** 02 December 1977. He was born 08 March 1955 in Shreveport, Louisiana.

Child of Theresa Millet and Vernon Meyer is:

1578 i. Melissa Renée[9] Meyer, born 20 October 1982 in Houston, Texas.

963. Lester James[8] Millet (Hazel Theresa[7] Caillet, Denise Marie[6] Waguespack, Marie Octavie[5] Robért, ***, Jean Frumence[4], Mathieu[3], Jean[2], Mathieu[1]) was born 02 April 1957 in New Orleans, Orleans Parish, Louisiana. He married **Patricia LaBranche** 18 May 1979. She was born 04 April 1950.

Child of Lester Millet and Patricia LaBranche is:

1579 i. Christi Nicole[9] Millet, born 31 December 1980 in Pascagoula, Mississippi.

964. Martha Louise[8] Millet (Hazel Theresa[7] Caillet, Denise Marie[6] Waguespack, Marie Octavie[5] Robért, ***, Jean Frumence[4], Mathieu[3], Jean[2], Mathieu[1]) was born 30 December 1958 in New Orleans, Orleans Parish, Louisiana. She married **Rickie Anthony St. Pierre**. He was born 01 February 1956.

Children of Martha Millet and Rickie St. Pierre are:

1580 i. Shana Lynne[9] St. Pierre, born 06 November 1978 in Metairie, Louisiana.

1581   ii.   Jessica Claire St. Pierre, born 19 January 1981 in Metairie, Louisiana.

984. Wallis J.^{8} Waguespack, III (Wallis J.^{7}, Wallis Jean^6, Marie Octavie^5 Robért, ***, Jean Frumence^4, Mathieu^3, Jean^2, Mathieu^1) was born 18 July 1947. He married **Chrystal Reeves** Unknown. She was born 05 January 1950.

Children of Wallis Waguespack and Chrystal Reeves are:
1582   i.   **John Wallis^9 Waguespack**, born 01 July 1968.
1583   ii.   **Thomas Christopher Waguespack**, born 01 July 1968.

985. Westley Paul^8 Waguespack, Sr. (Stanley Paul^7, Wallis Jean^6, Marie Octavie^5 Robért, ***, Jean Frumence^4, Mathieu^3, Jean^2, Mathieu^1) was born 15 January 1953. He married **(1) Debra Gant** Abt. 1973. She was born Abt. 1954. He married **(2) Pamela Davison** 26 March 1976. She was born 16 June 1953.

Child of Westley Waguespack and Debra Gant is:
1584   i.   **Westley Paul^9 Waguespack, Jr.**, born 11 March 1974.

Children of Westley Waguespack and Pamela Davison are:
1585   i.   **Nicole Lenore^9 Waguespack**, born 22 July 1982.
1586   ii.   **Brett Charles Waguespack**, born 11 March 1985.
1587   iii. **Brandon Michael Waguespack**, born 29 November 1986 in Kansas City, Jackson County, Missouri; died 07 April 1988 in Kansas City, Jackson County, Missouri.

990. Tanya Ann^8 Waguespack (Seymour Raymond^7, Wallis Jean^6, Marie Octavie^5 Robért, ***, Jean Frumence^4, Mathieu^3, Jean^2, Mathieu^1) was born 23 October 1954. She married **Morris Michael Mitchell** 15 February 1974. He was born 01 December 1954.

Children of Tanya Waguespack and Morris Mitchell are:
1588   i.   **Daniel Raymond^9 Mitchell**, born 22 June 1976.
1589   ii.   **Corey Mathiew Mitchell**, born 14 February 1980.
1590   iii. **Keith Anthony Mitchell**, born 21 June 1982.

991. Karen Ann^8 Waguespack (Seymour Raymond^7, Wallis Jean^6, Marie Octavie^5 Robért, ***, Jean Frumence^4, Mathieu^3, Jean^2, Mathieu^1) was born 29 December 1955. She married **Michael Joseph Minvielle** 30 January 1976 in St. Mary Catholic Church, Union, Louisiana. He was born 22 August 1953.

Children of Karen Waguespack and Michael Minvielle are:

1591   i.   **Melissa Lynn[9] Minvielle, born 01 September 1977.**
1592   ii. **Gerard Michael Minvielle, born 09 January 1980.**
1593   iii. **Cindy Ann Minvielle, born 10 April 1984.**

992. Michelle Marie[8] Waguespack (Seymour Raymond[7], Wallis Jean[6], Marie Octavie[5] Robért, ***, Jean Frumence[4], Mathieu[3], Jean[2], Mathieu[1]) was born 19 April 1957. She married **James Ray Smiley, Jr.** 25 July 1975 in St. Anthony Chapel, Darrow, Louisiana. He was born 08 November 1956.

Children of Michelle Waguespack and James Smiley are:

1594   i.   **Margo Michele[9] Smiley, born 31 August 1976.**
1595   ii. **Meridith Ann Smiley, born 11 August 1979.**
1596   iii. **James Ray Smiley, III, born 20 May 1982.**
1597   iv. **Jason Paul Smiley, born 23 January 1984.**

993. Alice Marie[8] Waguespack (Seymour Raymond[7], Wallis Jean[6], Marie Octavie[5] Robért, ***, Jean Frumence[4], Mathieu[3], Jean[2], Mathieu[1]) was born 29 November 1959. She married **Lee Jude Waggenspack** 29 April 1981 in St. Mary Catholic Church, Union, Louisiana, son of James Waggenspack and Mary Melancon. He was born 03 March 1958 in Baton Rouge, East Baton Rouge Parish, Louisiana.

Children are listed above under (576) Lee Jude Waggenspack.

995. Kurt Dominic[8] Waguespack (Seymour Raymond[7], Wallis Jean[6], Marie Octavie[5] Robért, ***, Jean Frumence[4], Mathieu[3], Jean[2], Mathieu[1]) was born 01 September 1963. He married **Amy Marie Schexnayder** 14 June 1985. She was born 14 September 1964.

Child of Kurt Waguespack and Amy Schexnayder is:

1598   i.   **Brooke Nicole[9] Waguespack, born 12 June 1987 in Baton Rouge, East Baton Rouge Parish, Louisiana.**

997. Christine Anne[8] Dornier (Lenora Theresa[7] Waguespack, Wallis Jean[6], Marie Octavie[5] Robért, ***, Jean Frumence[4], Mathieu[3], Jean[2], Mathieu[1]) was born 15 September 1949. She married **(1) Lonnie Hutson** 24 May 1969. He was born 15 June 1949. She married **(2) Kelsey Malone House** 04 September 1983. He was born 25 September 1944.

Child of Christine Dornier and Kelsey House is:

1599   i.   Cody Malone[9] House, born 12 October 1985.

998. Lynette Marie[8] **Schexnaydre** (Berthile Joseph[7], Berthile Joseph[6], Henry Joseph[5], Marie Antoinette[4] Robért, Mathieu[3], Jean[2], Mathieu[1]) was born 24 June 1949 in Ascension Parish, Burnside, Louisiana, and died 26 January 2006 in Orleans Parish, New Orleans, Orleans Parish, Louisiana. She married **Ross Guerard Allen, Jr.** 06 December 1974 in Ascension Parish Catholic Church, Donaldsonville, Louisiana. He was born 08 November 1947 in Orleans Parish, New Orleans, Orleans Parish, Louisiana.

Child of Lynette Schexnaydre and Ross Allen is:
   1600   i.   **Nicholas**[9] **Allen, born 05 November 1978 in Orleans Parish, New Orleans, Orleans Parish, Louisiana.**

999. Craig Joseph[8] **Schexnaydre** (Berthile Joseph[7], Berthile Joseph[6], Henry Joseph[5], Marie Antoinette[4] Robért, Mathieu[3], Jean[2], Mathieu[1]) was born 28 July 1951. He married **Debra Ann Foster** 11 January 1975. She was born 28 August 1952.

Children of Craig Schexnaydre and Debra Foster are:
   1601   i.   **Jody Lynne**[9] **Schexnaydre, born 11 December 1978.**
   1602   ii.   **Ryan Joseph Schexnaydre, born 10 March 1984.**

1000. Myles Michael[8] **Schexnaydre** (Berthile Joseph[7], Berthile Joseph[6], Henry Joseph[5], Marie Antoinette[4] Robért, Mathieu[3], Jean[2], Mathieu[1]) was born 02 December 1954. He married **Nevil Ann Waguespack** 14 May 1976 in St. Mary Catholic Church, Union, Louisiana, daughter of Gerald Waguespack and Marian Troxclair. She was born 10 January 1957 in Gonzales, Ascension Parish, Louisiana.

Children of Myles Schexnaydre and Nevil Waguespack are:
   1603   i.   **Alan Joseph**[9] **Schexnaydre, born 31 July 1977 in Baton Rouge, East Baton Rouge Parish, Louisiana. He married Kacie Lynn Andrews; born in Baton Rouge, East Baton Rouge Parish, Louisiana.**
   1604   ii.   **Andrew Schexnaydre, born 16 October 1982 in Baton Rouge, East Baton Rouge Parish, Louisiana.**

1001. Kim Marie[8] **Schexnaydre** (Berthile Joseph[7], Berthile Joseph[6], Henry Joseph[5], Marie Antoinette[4] Robért, Mathieu[3], Jean[2], Mathieu[1]) was born 15 May 1957. She married **(2) Edmond William Templet** 07 September 1978. He was born 19 October 1958.

Child of Kim Marie Schexnaydre is:
    1605   i. **Kim Marie[9] Schexnaydre, born 10 December 1976; died 10 December 1976.**

Children of Kim Schexnaydre and Edmond Templet are:
    1606   i. **Eric Paul[9] Templet, born 20 April 1979.**
    1607   ii. **Jana Marie Templet, born 09 November 1982.**

1002. Jeffery Joseph[8] Schexnaydre (Berthile Joseph[7], Berthile Joseph[6], Henry Joseph[5], Marie Antoinette[4] Robért, Mathieu[3], Jean[2], Mathieu[1]) was born 18 July 1958. He married **Susie Saurage** 19 October 1984. She was born 12 December 1961.

Child of Jeffery Schexnaydre and Susie Saurage is:
    1608   i. **Alicia Marie[9] Schexnaydre, born 30 March 1985.**

1004. John Joseph[8] Canatella, Jr. (Mercedes Ann[7] Waguespack, Wallis Jean[6], Marie Octavie[5] Robért, ***, Jean Frumence[4], Mathieu[3], Jean[2], Mathieu[1]) was born 10 November 1953. He married **Lynn Janice Witt** 24 November 1969. She was born 08 November 1954.

Children of John Canatella and Lynn Witt are:
    1609   i. **John Joseph[9] Canatella, born 28 January 1970.**
    1610   ii. **Ryan Joseph Canatella, born 25 July 1978.**

1005. Todd James[8] Canatella (Mercedes Ann[7] Waguespack, Wallis Jean[6], Marie Octavie[5] Robért, ***, Jean Frumence[4], Mathieu[3], Jean[2], Mathieu[1]) was born 06 September 1955. He married **Vivian Theresa Manguna** 04 October 1973 in Our Lady of Divine Province. She was born 28 November 1954.

Children of Todd Canatella and Vivian Manguna are:
    1611   i. **Todd James[9] Canatella, Jr., born 31 March 1974.**
    1612   ii. **Nikole Maree Canatella, born 07 June 1979.**

1006. Cheryl Ann[8] Canatella (Mercedes Ann[7] Waguespack, Wallis Jean[6], Marie Octavie[5] Robért, ***, Jean Frumence[4], Mathieu[3], Jean[2], Mathieu[1]) was born 26 November 1957. She married John Anthony Pennino 20 September 1974 He was born 23 October 1951.

Children of Cheryl Canatella and John Pennino are:

1613   i.   **Angela Ann[9] Pennino, born 15 May 1975.**

1614   ii.   **Melissa Ann Pennino, born 05 July 1978.**

1615   iii.   **John Anthony Pennino, Jr., born 05 October 1981.**

1007. Kenneth[8] Haydel (Jessie Joseph[7], Elda Augustine[6] Waguespack, Marie Octavie[5] Robért, ***, Jean Frumence[4], Mathieu[3], Jean[2], Mathieu[1]) was born 21 July 1951 in New Orleans, Orleans Parish, Louisiana. He married **Anne Elizabeth Guillot** 06 June 1975 in St. Joan of Arc, Laplace, Louisiana. She was born 07 February 1953 in Orange, Texas.

Children of Kenneth Haydel and Anne Guillot are:

1616   i.   **Ashley Anne[9] Haydel, born 09 January 1980 in Jefferson Parish, Metairie, Louisiana.**

1617   ii.   **Kenneth James Haydel, Jr., born 26 December 1981 in Jefferson Parish, Metairie.**

1013. Gerald Jude[8] Waguespack (Gerald Marie[7], George Nicholas[6], Marie Octavie[5] Robért, ***, Jean Frumence[4], Mathieu[3], Jean[2], Mathieu[1]) was born 17 July 1954 in Gonzales, Ascension Parish, Louisiana. He married **Anita Louise Chauvin** 30 May 1975 in St. Mary Catholic Church, Union, Louisiana, daughter of Philip Chauvin and Tilda Chauvin. She was born 25 September 1956 in Lutcher, St. James Parish, Louisiana.

Children of Gerald Waguespack and Anita Chauvin are:

+   1618   i.   **Philip Brent[9] Waguespack, born 10 July 1977 in Baton Rouge, East Baton Rouge Parish, Louisiana.**

+   1619   ii.   **Aaron Marie Waguespack, born 24 June 1979 in Baton Rouge, East Baton Rouge Parish, Louisiana.**

     1620   iii.   **Gerri Lynn Waguespack, born 05 December 1981 in Baton Rouge, East Baton Rouge Parish, Louisiana. She married Timothy Allen Bowler 05 May 2006 in St. Mary Catholic Church, Union, Louisiana; born 17 April 1980.**

1014. Georgene Marie[8] Waguespack (Gerald Marie[7], George Nicholas[6], Marie Octavie[5] Robért, ***, Jean Frumence[4], Mathieu[3], Jean[2], Mathieu[1]) was born 10 December 1955. She married **Louis Joseph Latino, Jr.** 27 February 1976. He was born 07 April 1951.

Children of Georgene Waguespack and Louis Latino are:

+   1621   i.   **Jessica Marie[9] Latino, born 17 January 1978 in Baton Rouge, East Baton Rouge Parish, Louisiana.**

1622   ii.   Matthew Louis Latino, born 21 April 1982 in Baton Rouge, East
                Baton Rouge Parish, Louisiana.

1015. Nevil Ann[8] Waguespack (Gerald Marie[7], George Nicholas[6], Marie Octavie[5] Robért, ***, Jean Frumence[4], Mathieu[3], Jean[2], Mathieu[1]) was born 10 January 1957 in Gonzales, Ascension Parish, Louisiana. She married **Myles Michael Schexnaydre** 14 May 1976 in St. Mary Catholic Church, Union, Louisiana, son of Berthile Schexnaydre and Ola Mae Waguespack. He was born 02 December 1954.

Children are listed above under (1000) Myles Michael Schexnaydre.

1016. Paula Ann[8] Waguespack (Gerald Marie[7], George Nicholas[6], Marie Octavie[5] Robért, ***, Jean Frumence[4], Mathieu[3], Jean[2], Mathieu[1]) was born 29 July 1958. She married **Randy Bourgeois, Sr.** 10 May 1978 in Union, St. James Parish, Louisiana. He was born 08 June 1953.

Children of Paula Waguespack and Randy Bourgeois are:
    1623   i.   **Randy[9] Bourgeois, Jr., born 16 September 1978 in Baton Rouge, East Baton Rouge Parish, Louisiana. He married Christen Gautreau; born September 1982.**
    1624   ii. **Jeanette Marie Bourgeois, born May 1983 in Baton Rouge, East Baton Rouge Parish, Louisiana. She married Brian Thomas Schexnaydre; born 11 October 1983.**

1017. Roberta Therese[8] Waguespack (Gerald Marie[7], George Nicholas[6], Marie Octavie[5] Robért, ***, Jean Frumence[4], Mathieu[3], Jean[2], Mathieu[1]) was born 08 October 1960. She married **(1) Jeffrey Paul LeBlanc, Sr. (Divorced)** 02 October 1981 in St. Mary Catholic Chapel, Union, Louisiana. He was born 21 November 1960. She married **(2) Daniel David Robichaux** 04 March 1989 in Gonzales, Ascension Parish, Louisiana. He was born 17 February 1956.

Children of Roberta Waguespack and Jeffrey LeBlanc are:
    1625   i.   **Jeffrey Paul[9] LeBlanc, Jr., born 12 December 1982 in Baton Rouge, East Baton Rouge Parish, Louisiana.**
    1626   ii. **Jay Gerald LeBlanc, born 21 March 1986 in Baton Rouge, East Baton Rouge Parish, Louisiana.**

Children of Roberta Waguespack and Daniel Robichaux are:
+   1627   i.   **Jeffrey Paul[9] Robichaux, (Adopted), born 12 December 1982 in Baton Rouge, East Baton Rouge Parish, Louisiana.**
    1628   ii. **Jay Gerald Robichaux, (Adopted), born 21 March 1986 in Baton Rouge, East Baton Rouge Parish, Louisiana.**

1629   iii.   Danielle Marie Robichaux, born 04 December 1992 in Houma, Terrebonne Parish, Louisiana.

1020. Adrian Charles[8] **Waguespack** (Richard[7], George Nicholas[6], Marie Octavie[5] Robért, ***, Jean Frumence[4], Mathieu[3], Jean[2], Mathieu[1]) was born 16 February 1952 in Gonzales, Ascension Parish, Louisiana. He married **Rhonda Gayle Simoneaux, (Divorced)** 12 April 1986 in Gonzales, Ascension Parish, Louisiana, daughter of F.S. Simoneaux and Betty DeArmond. She was born 10 February 1955 in Baton Rouge, East Baton Rouge Parish, Louisiana.

Child of Adrian Waguespack and Rhonda Simoneaux is:
    1630   i.   **Adrian Jade**[9] **Waguespack, born 24 September 1986 in Baton Rouge, East Baton Rouge Parish, Louisiana.**

1021. Michael Curtis[8] **Waguespack** (Richard[7], George Nicholas[6], Marie Octavie[5] Robért, ***, Jean Frumence[4], Mathieu[3], Jean[2], Mathieu[1]) was born 30 June 1953 in Gonzales, Ascension Parish, Louisiana. He married **Vicki Lynn Goodman** 14 April 1972 in St. Theresa Catholic Church, Gonzales, Ascension Parish, Louisiana, daughter of Ivory Goodman and Audrey Clouatre. She was born 07 January 1955 in Gonzales, Ascension Parish, Louisiana.

Children of Michael Waguespack and Vicki Goodman are:
+   **1631**   i.   **Tobie Mikael**[9] **Waguespack, born 12 October 1973 in Baton Rouge, East Baton Rouge Parish, Louisiana.**
+   **1632**   ii.   **Joanie Lynn Waguespack, born 11 June 1976 in Baton Rouge, East Baton Rouge Parish, Louisiana.**
    1633   iii.   **Mandie Lee Waguespack, born 16 September 1980 in Baton Rouge, East Baton Rouge Parish, Louisiana.**
    1634   iv.   **Tyler Michael Waguespack, born 19 December 1990 in Baton Rouge, East Baton Rouge Parish, Louisiana.**

1022. Rhonda Faye[8] **Waguespack** (Richard[7], George Nicholas[6], Marie Octavie[5] Robért, ***, Jean Frumence[4], Mathieu[3], Jean[2], Mathieu[1]) was born 02 November 1954 in Gonzales, Ascension Parish, Louisiana. She married **(1) Joseph Mark Bourque** 24 May 1974 in St. Theresa Catholic Church, Gonzales, Ascension Parish, Louisiana, son of Cleveland Bourque and Rita Lanoux. He was born 19 July 1954. She married **(2) John Martin Gaughan** 23 April 1994, son of Francis Gaughan and Rose MacFarland. He was born 11 February 1948.

Children of Rhonda Waguespack and Joseph Bourque are:
+   **1635**   i.   **George Nicholas (Gee)**[9] **Bourque, born 12 October 1978 in West Monroe, Ouachita Parish, Louisiana.**
    1636   ii.   **Cody Michael Bourque, born 11 June 1980 in Baton Rouge, East**

Baton Rouge Parish, Louisiana.

1023. Bonnie Ann[8] Waguespack (Richard[7], George Nicholas[6], Marie Octavie[5] Robért, ***, Jean Frumence[4], Mathieu[3], Jean[2], Mathieu[1]) was born 30 July 1957 in Gonzales, Ascension Parish, Louisiana. She married **Randy Gerard Simpson** 09 September 1977 in St. Theresa Catholic Church, Gonzales, Ascension Parish, Louisiana, son of Elvin Simpson and Beverly Major. He was born 29 September 1955 in Baton Rouge, East Baton Rouge Parish, Louisiana.

Children of Bonnie Waguespack and Randy Simpson are:
- 1637   i.   **Cade[9] Simpson, born 10 September 1980 in Baton Rouge, East Baton Rouge Parish, Louisiana.**
- 1638   ii. **Quinn David Simpson, born 16 December 1982 in Baton Rouge, East Baton Rouge Parish, Louisiana. He married Ashlee Danielle Pourciau in First Baptist Church, Gonzales, Ascension Parish, Louisiana.**
- 1639   iii. **Korey Dean Simpson, born 12 February 1986 in Baton Rouge, East Baton Rouge Parish, Louisiana.**

1024. George Keith[8] Waguespack (Richard[7], George Nicholas[6], Marie Octavie[5] Robért, ***, Jean Frumence[4], Mathieu[3], Jean[2], Mathieu[1]) was born 20 March 1961 in Lutcher, St. James Parish, Louisiana. He married **Elaine C. McNabb** 17 August 1991 in Baton Rouge, East Baton Rouge Parish, Louisiana. She was born 27 March 1960.

Children of George Waguespack and Elaine McNabb are:
- 1640   i.   **George Nicholas[9] Waguespack, born 05 September 1993.**
- 1641   ii. **Emily Claire Waguespack, born 14 September 1995.**

1025. Kelli Jean[8] Waguespack (Richard[7], George Nicholas[6], Marie Octavie[5] Robért, ***, Jean Frumence[4], Mathieu[3], Jean[2], Mathieu[1]) was born 02 November 1970 in Baton Rouge, East Baton Rouge Parish, Louisiana. She married **Cody Wayne Johns, (Divorced Feb. 2006)** 20 September 1997 in St. Theresa Catholic Church, Gonzales, Ascension Parish, Louisiana, son of Kindell Johns and Debra Castete. He was born 12 May 1973 in Jonesville, Catahoula Parish, Louisiana.

Children of Kelli Waguespack and Cody Johns are:
- 1642   i.   **Brody Paul[9] Johns, born 10 July 1998 in Baton Rouge, East Baton Rouge Parish, Louisiana.**
- 1643   ii. **Parker Wayne Johns, born 06 November 2001 in Baton Rouge, East Baton Rouge Parish, Louisiana.**

1026. Edward Arthur[8] Michel (Thelma Marie[7] Brou, Delia Philomene[6] Waguespack, Marie Octavie[5] Robért, ***, Jean Frumence[4], Mathieu[3], Jean[2], Mathieu[1]) was born 04 May 1948 in Donaldsonville, Ascension Parish, Louisiana. He married **Mary Clair Dardenne** 23 December 1972 in St. George Catholic Church, Baton Rouge, Louisiana. She was born 02 April 1949.

Children of Edward Michel and Mary Dardenne are:

1644	i.	**Ashley Elizabeth[9] Michel, born 20 January 1977 in Baton Rouge, East Baton Rouge Parish, Louisiana.**
1645	ii.	**Katie Allison Michel, born 08 November 1979 in Baton Rouge, East Baton Rouge Parish, Louisiana.**
1646	iii.	**Jennifer Clair Michel, born 27 January 1983 in Baton Rouge, East Baton Rouge Parish, Louisiana.**

1028. Donna Marie[8] Blanchard (Doris Therése[7] Brou, Delia Philomene[6] Waguespack, Marie Octavie[5] Robért, ***, Jean Frumence[4], Mathieu[3], Jean[2], Mathieu[1]) was born 18 June 1954 in Donaldsonville, Ascension Parish, Louisiana, and died Unknown in Belle Rose, Louisiana. She married **David Michael Landry** 18 June 1976 in St. Jules Catholic Church, Belle Rose, Louisiana. He was born 05 October 1954.

Children of Donna Blanchard and David Landry are:

1647	i.	**Jessica Leigh[9] Landry, born 02 January 1978 in Thibodaux, Lafourche Parish, Louisiana.**
1648	ii.	**Travis John Landry, born 18 January 1983 in Thibodaux, Lafourche Parish, Louisiana.**

1029. Constance Anne[8] Blanchard (Doris Therése[7] Brou, Delia Philomene[6] Waguespack, Marie Octavie[5] Robért, ***, Jean Frumence[4], Mathieu[3], Jean[2], Mathieu[1]) was born 11 July 1955 in Donaldsonville, Ascension Parish, Louisiana. She married **(1) Joseph Blanchard, III** 18 July 1975 in St. Jules Catholic Church, Belle Rose, Louisiana. He was born 17 July 1954. She married **(2) Steve Strapola** 15 June 1990 in New Orleans, Orleans Parish, Louisiana. He was born Unknown.

Children of Constance Blanchard and Joseph Blanchard are:

1649	i.	**Aimee Lynn[9] Blanchard, born 07 December 1976 in Thibodaux, Lafourche Parish, Louisiana.**
1650	ii.	**Laurie Elizabeth Blanchard, born 05 February 1979 in Thibodaux, Lafourche Parish, Louisiana.**
1651	iii.	**Rebecca Anne Blanchard, born 31 May 1981 in Thibodaux, Lafourche Parish, Louisiana.**

1030. Julie Therese[8] Blanchard (Doris Therése[7] Brou, Delia Philomene[6] Waguespack, Marie Octavie[5] Robért, ***, Jean Frumence[4], Mathieu[3], Jean[2], Mathieu[1]) was born 08 February 1957 in Donaldsonville, Ascension Parish, Louisiana, and died Unknown in Assumption Parish, Napoleonville. Louisiana. She married **Donald Neal Acosta** 24 October 1980 in St. Jules Catholic Church, Belle Rose, Louisiana. He was born 25 May 1957 in Donaldsonville, Ascension Parish, Louisiana.

Children of Julie Blanchard and Donald Acosta are:

> 1652   i.   **Joseph Jerome[9] Acosta, born 17 March 1982 in Thibodaux, Lafourche Parish, Louisiana.**
>
> 1653   ii.   **Sarah Elizabeth Acosta, born 17 November 1984 in Thibodaux, Lafourche Parish, Louisiana.**

1031. Lauren Claire[8] Blanchard (Doris Therése[7] Brou, Delia Philomene[6] Waguespack, Marie Octavie[5] Robért, ***, Jean Frumence[4], Mathieu[3], Jean[2], Mathieu[1]) was born 12 February 1960 in Donaldsonville, Ascension Parish, Louisiana, and died Unknown in Houma, Louisiana. She married **Michael Gerard Johnson, Sr.** 18 December 1978 in St. Jules Catholic Church, Belle Rose, Louisiana. He was born 12 December 1958.

Children of Lauren Blanchard and Michael Johnson are:

> 1654   i.   **Michael Gerard[9] Johnson, Jr., born 13 July 1979 in Thibodaux, Lafourche Parish, Louisiana.**
>
> 1655   ii.   **Jason Emile Johnson, born 07 April 1982 in Thibodaux, Lafourche Parish, Louisiana.**
>
> 1656   iii.   **Christina Marie Velma Johnson, born 14 May 1985 in Thibodaux, Lafourche Parish, Louisiana.**

1032. Marvin Clay[8] Blanchard (Doris Therése[7] Brou, Delia Philomene[6] Waguespack, Marie Octavie[5] Robért, ***, Jean Frumence[4], Mathieu[3], Jean[2], Mathieu[1]) was born 13 September 1961 in Donaldsonville, Ascension Parish, Louisiana, and died Unknown in Assumption Parish, Napoleonville. Louisiana. He married **Lisa Usey** 24 July 1981 in Ascension Catholic Church, Donaldsonville, Louisiana. She was born 05 May 1962 in Donaldsonville, Ascension Parish, Louisiana.

Children of Marvin Blanchard and Lisa Usey are:

> 1657   i.   **Jennifer Marie[9] Blanchard, born 17 December 1982 in Baton Rouge, East Baton Rouge Parish, Louisiana.**
>
> 1658   ii.   **Clay Michael Blanchard, born 27 July 1986 in McComb, Mississippi.**

1034. Joseph Charles[8] Danos (Joyce Ann[7] Brou, Delia Philomene[6] Waguespack, Marie Octavie[5] Robért, ***, Jean Frumence[4], Mathieu[3], Jean[2], Mathieu[1]) was born 10 June 1958 in Raceland, Lafourche Parish, Louisiana. He married **Sheri Duplechin** 19 August 1983 in St. Joseph Catholic Church, Thibodaux, Louisiana. She was born 10 June 1958 in New Orleans, Orleans Parish, Louisiana.

Child of Joseph Danos and Sheri Duplechin is:
    1659   i.   **Leigh Ann[9] Danos, born 12 July 1984 in Thibodaux, Lafourche Parish, Louisiana.**

1047. Dawn Marie[8] Waguespack (Leroy Joseph[7], Frumence Hubert[6], Marie Octavie[5] Robért, ***, Jean Frumence[4], Mathieu[3], Jean[2], Mathieu[1]) was born 07 April 1961 in Lutcher, Louisiana. She married **Paul J. Tucker** 04 November 1982 in Morgan City, Louisiana. He was born 05 August 1960 in Laurel, Mississippi.

Child of Dawn Waguespack and Paul Tucker is:
    1660   i.   **Nathalie Lynn[9] Tucker, born 06 May 1983 in Baton Rouge, East Baton Rouge Parish, Louisiana.**

1049. Vickie Ann[8] Waguespack (Clyde Paul[7], Frumence Hubert[6], Marie Octavie[5] Robért, ***, Jean Frumence[4], Mathieu[3], Jean[2], Mathieu[1]) was born 12 April 1959 in Lutcher, Louisiana. She married **Billy Brown, Sr.** 25 September 1976 in Gonzales, Ascension Parish, Louisiana. He was born 29 April 1957.

Children of Vickie Waguespack and Billy Brown are:
    1661   i.   **Billy[9] Brown, Jr., born 20 January 1977 in Lutcher, Louisiana.**
    1662   ii.   **Lucas Paul Brown, born 29 April 1979 in Lutcher, Louisiana.**
    1663   iii. **Adam Michael Brown, born 01 July 1987 in Lutcher, Louisiana.**

1050. Trudi Marie[8] Waguespack (Clyde Paul[7], Frumence Hubert[6], Marie Octavie[5] Robért, ***, Jean Frumence[4], Mathieu[3], Jean[2], Mathieu[1]) was born 14 December 1959 in Lutcher, Louisiana. She married **Simon Guidry,(Benny)** 06 March 1982 in St. Theresa Catholic Church, Gonzales, Louisiana. He was born Unknown.

Child of Trudi Waguespack and Simon Guidry is:
    1664   i.   **Ashley Simone[9] Guidry, born 22 November 1982 in Baton Rouge, East Baton Rouge Parish, Louisiana.**

1051. Monica Ann[8] Waguespack (Clyde Paul[7], Frumence Hubert[6], Marie Octavie[5] Robért, ***, Jean Frumence[4], Mathieu[3], Jean[2], Mathieu[1]) was born 29 August 1962 in Lutcher, Louisiana. She married **Gussie J. Bourgeois** 27 February 1979. He was born 04 March 1960 in Gonzales, Ascension Parish, Louisiana.

Child of Monica Waguespack and Gussie Bourgeois is:
  1665   i. **Lance Joseph[9] Bourgeois, born 17 August 1979 in Lutcher, Louisiana.**

1054. Kerry Ann[8] Waguespack (Kerry Gerard[7], Frumence Hubert[6], Marie Octavie[5] Robért, ***, Jean Frumence[4], Mathieu[3], Jean[2], Mathieu[1]) was born 07 February 1963. She married **Richard Rossi, Jr.** Unknown.

Children of Kerry Waguespack and Richard Rossi are:
  1666   i. **Michele Leigh[9] Rossi, born 12 July 1981.**
  1667   ii. **Jena Renee Rossi, born 20 April 1983.**

1062. Stacy Louise[8] Lanoux (Cathy Marie[7] Waguespack, Clarence Anthony[6], Marie Octavie[5] Robért, ***, Jean Frumence[4], Mathieu[3], Jean[2], Mathieu[1]) was born 05 September 1965 in Baton Rouge, East Baton Rouge Parish, Louisiana. She married **Doug Joseph Melancon** 10 January 1987 in St. Theresa Catholic Church, Gonzales, Louisiana. He was born Unknown.

Child of Stacy Lanoux and Doug Melancon is:
  1668   i. **Ross John[9] Melancon, born 01 February 1989 in Baton Rouge, East Baton Rouge Parish, Louisiana.**

1066. Wade Anthony[8] Harelson (Brenda Ann[7] Waguespack, Clarence Anthony[6], Marie Octavie[5] Robért, ***, Jean Frumence[4], Mathieu[3], Jean[2], Mathieu[1]) was born 21 October 1962. He married **Catherine Hebert** Unknown in Our Lady of Prompt Succor Church, White Castle, Louisiana.

Children of Wade Harelson and Catherine Hebert are:
  1669   i. **Jennifer Lynne[9] Harelson, born 26 March 1987 in Baton Rouge, East Baton Rouge Parish, Louisiana.**
  1670   ii. **Jonathan Hebert Harelson, born 26 March 1987 in Baton Rouge, East Baton Rouge Parish, Louisiana.**
  1671   iii. **Jacob Charles Harelson, born 10 October 1988 in Baton Rouge, East Baton Rouge Parish, Louisiana**

1079. Shandra Anne^8 Part (Phyllis Anne^7 Robért, Lester^6, Wallace Jean^5, Jean Frumence^4, Mathieu^3, Jean^2, Mathieu^1) was born 23 March 1971 in Panama City, Florida. She married **Larry Brown, (Divorced)**.

Children of Shandra Part and Larry Brown are:
    1672   i.   **Lauren^9 Brown.**
    1673   ii.   **Logan Brown.**

1094. Kent Alan^8 Schexnaydre (Vernon^7, Berthile Joseph^6, Henry Joseph^5, Marie Antoinette^4 Robért, Mathieu^3, Jean^2, Mathieu^1) was born 21 May 1953 in Baton Rouge, East Baton Rouge Parish, Louisiana. He married **Donna Laiche** 14 February 1975. She was born Abt. 1955.

Child of Kent Schexnaydre and Donna Laiche is:
    1674   i.   **Wade M.^{9} Schexnaydre, born Abt. 1977.**

1172. Lisa Marie^8 Savoie (Sybil Stanilaus^7 Milano, Maude Marie^6 Robért, Joseph Olide^5, Jean Paul^4, Mathieu^3, Jean^2, Mathieu^1) was born 22 September 1956 in New Orleans, Orleans Parish, Louisiana. She married **O'Neil Joseph Parenton,Jr.** 18 August 1979 in Ascension Catholic Church, Donaldsonville, Louisiana, son of O'Neil Parenton and Peggy Mcdermott. He was born 27 July.

Children of Lisa Savoie and O'Neil Parenton are:
    1675   i.   **O'Neil Joseph^9 Parenton, III, born 12 December 1981 in New Orleans, Orleans Parish, Louisiana.**
    1676   ii.   **Jenna Leigh Parenton, born 17 February 1985 in Baton Rouge, East Baton Rouge Parish, Louisiana.**
    1677   iii.   **Brian Gerald Parenton, born 12 June 1987 in Baton Rouge, East Baton Rouge Parish, Louisiana.**

1173. Jon Anthony^8 Savoie,Jr (Sybil Stanilaus^7 Milano, Maude Marie^6 Robért, Joseph Olide^5, Jean Paul^4, Mathieu^3, Jean^2, Mathieu^1) was born 05 July 1958 in New Orleans, Orleans Parish, Louisiana. He married **Carol Marie Songy** 07 August 1981 in St. Phillip Catholic Church, Vacherie, Louisiana, daughter of Russell Songy and Rosa Gravois. She was born 15 April.

Children of Jon Savoie and Carol Songy are:
    1678   i.   **Sarah Elizabeth^9 Savoie, born 10 June 1983 in Metairie, Jefferson Parish, Louisiana.**
    1679   ii.   **Leslie Ann Savoie, born 02 September 1985 in Metairie, Jefferson Parish, Louisiana.**
    1680   iii.   **Michelle Marie Savoie, born 22 January 1987 in Metairie, Jefferson**

Parish, Louisiana.

1681   iv.   Caroline Elizabeth Savoie, born 08 August 1995 in Baton Rouge, East Baton Rouge Parish, Louisiana.

1174. Daniel Nicholas[8] Savoie (Sybil Stanilaus[7] Milano, Maude Marie[6] Robért, Joseph Olide[5], Jean Paul[4], Mathieu[3], Jean[2], Mathieu[1]) was born 04 April 1960 in New Orleans, Orleans Parish, Louisiana. He married **Cheryl Lynn Salaun** 06 August 1988 in St. Dominic Catholic Church, New Orleans, Louisiana, daughter of James Salaun and Kathleen Virostra.

Children of Daniel Savoie and Cheryl Salaun are:

1682   i.   **Blake D.[9] Savoie, born 14 August 1990 in Baton Rouge, East Baton Rouge Parish, Louisiana.**

1683   ii.   **Nicholas J. Savoie, born 04 December 1992 in Baton Rouge, East Baton Rouge Parish, Louisiana.**

1684   iii.   **Kelsey Nicole Savoie, born 19 August 1995 in Baton Rouge, East Baton Rouge Parish, Louisiana.**

1175. Michelle Ann[8] Savoie (Sybil Stanilaus[7] Milano, Maude Marie[6] Robért, Joseph Olide[5], Jean Paul[4], Mathieu[3], Jean[2], Mathieu[1]) was born 27 June 1961 in New Orleans, Orleans Parish, Louisiana. She married **Paul Hillman** 23 April 1988 in Ascension Catholic Church, Donaldsonville, Louisiana, son of J. Hillman and Joyce Craft. He was born Unknown.

Children of Michelle Savoie and Paul Hillman are:

1685   i.   **Brittany Michelle[9] Hillman, born 14 November 1989 in Baton Rouge, East Baton Rouge Parish, Louisiana.**

1686   ii.   **Kaitlyn Elizabeth Hillman, born 31 May 1992 in Baton Rouge, East Baton Rouge Parish, Louisiana.**

1687   iii.   **Joshua Paul Hillman, born 14 November 1995 in Baton Rouge, East Baton Rouge Parish, Louisiana.**

1176. Stephanie Jo[8] Savoie (Sybil Stanilaus[7] Milano, Maude Marie[6] Robért, Joseph Olide[5], Jean Paul[4], Mathieu[3], Jean[2], Mathieu[1]) was born 30 October 1962 in New Orleans, Orleans Parish, Louisiana. She married **(1) William Ransom Pipes** in Ascension Catholic Church, Donaldsonville, Louisiana, son of Richard Pipes and Jo Ransom. She married **(2) Ronald Kent Babb** 28 August 2005 in New Orleans, Orleans Parish, Louisiana.

Children of Stephanie Savoie and William Pipes are:

1688   i.   **Ransom Paul[9] Pipes, born 30 January 1990 in Baton Rouge, East Baton Rouge Parish, Louisiana.**

1689   ii.   **Jon Hayes Pipes, born 21 June 1993 in Baton Rouge, East Baton**

Rouge Parish, Louisiana.
1690   iii. **Victoria Anne Pipes, born 10 April 1996 in Baton Rouge, East Baton Rouge Parish, Louisiana.**

1177. Pamela Joan[8] Savoie (Sybil Stanilaus[7] Milano, Maude Marie[6] Robért, Joseph Olide[5], Jean Paul[4], Mathieu[3], Jean[2], Mathieu[1]) was born 29 April 1964 in New Orleans, Orleans Parish, Louisiana. She married **Darren S. Landry** 22 September 1990 in Ascension Catholic Church, Donaldsonville, Louisiana.

Children of Pamela Savoie and Darren Landry are:
1691   i. **Hunter Thomas[9] Landry, born 24 August 1995 in Baton Rouge, East Baton Rouge Parish, Louisiana.**
1692   ii. **Bailey Christopher Landry, born 09 January 1998 in Baton Rouge, East Baton Rouge Parish, Louisiana.**
1693   iii. **Riley Landry, born 06 November 2001 in Baton Rouge, East Baton Rouge Parish, Louisiana.**

1178. Mona Marie[8] Milano (Paul Anthony[7], Maude Marie[6] Robért, Joseph Olide[5], Jean Paul[4], Mathieu[3], Jean[2], Mathieu[1]) was born 27 September 1961 in Paincourtville, Assumption Parish, Louisiana. She married **Ronnie Joseph Rodrigue, Sr.** 29 January 1982. He was born 18 October 1957 in Paincourtville, Assumption Parish, Louisiana.

Children of Mona Milano and Ronnie Rodrigue are:
1694   i. **Meredith Michelle[9] Rodrigue, born 20 October 1983 in Baton Rouge, East Baton Rouge Parish, Louisiana.**
1695   ii. **Melissa Marie Rodrigue, born 23 September 1985 in Baton Rouge, East Baton Rouge Parish, Louisiana.**
1696   iii. **Ronnie Joseph Rodrigue, Jr, born 16 July 1987 in Baton Rouge, East Baton Rouge Parish, Louisiana.**
1697   iv. **Ryan Joseph Rodrigue, born 19 February 1993 in Baton Rouge, East Baton Rouge Parish, Louisiana.**

1180. Rae Anne[8] Milano (Paul Anthony[7], Maude Marie[6] Robért, Joseph Olide[5], Jean Paul[4], Mathieu[3], Jean[2], Mathieu[1]) was born 10 September 1967 in Donaldsonville, Ascension Parish, Louisiana. She married **(Divorced) Unnamed**.

Child of Rae Milano and (Divorced) Unnamed is:
1698   i. **Brennan[9] Milano, born 27 February 1997 in Baton Rouge, East Baton Rouge Parish, Louisiana.**

1181. Nicholas Wilbert[8] Milano (Paul Anthony[7], Maude Marie[6] Robért,

Joseph Olide[5], Jean Paul[4], Mathieu[3], Jean[2], Mathieu[1]) was born 08 September 1971 in Baton Rouge, East Baton Rouge Parish, Louisiana. He married **Dana Duplessis**.

Children of Nicholas Milano and Dana Duplessis are:

    1699   i.   **Nicholas[9] Milano, born 04 July 1999 in Baton Rouge, East Baton Rouge Parish, Louisiana.**

    1700   ii.   **Lexi Milano, born 10 October 2001 in Baton Rouge, East Baton Rouge Parish, Louisiana.**

1182. Melissa Lee[8] Thiac (Janice Ann[7] Milano, Maude Marie[6] Robért, Joseph Olide[5], Jean Paul[4], Mathieu[3], Jean[2], Mathieu[1]) was born 27 May 1957 in Frankfurt, Germany. She married **Allen Thomas Noel** 20 January 1979 in Thibodaux, Lafourche Parish, Louisiana, son of L. Noel and Nevil Gonzales. He was born 23 November 1955 in Donaldsonville, Ascension Parish, Louisiana.

Children of Melissa Thiac and Allen Noel are:

+   1701   i.   **Matthew Thomas[9] Noel, born 06 July 1980 in Thibodaux, Lafourche Parish, Louisiana.**

    1702   ii.   **Brandon Michael Noel, born 23 March 1983 in Thibodaux, Lafourche Parish, Louisiana. He married Megan Alger 05 May 2006 in Baton Rouge, East Baton Rouge Parish, Louisiana.**

1183. Cindy Marie[8] Thiac (Janice Ann[7] Milano, Maude Marie[6] Robért, Joseph Olide[5], Jean Paul[4], Mathieu[3], Jean[2], Mathieu[1]) was born 19 November 1958 in Thibodaux, Lafourche Parish, Louisiana. She married **Nicholas K. Edrington III** 14 June 1980 in Thibodaux, Lafourche Parish, Louisiana, son of Nicholas Edrington and Virgie Naquin.

Children of Cindy Thiac and Nicholas Edrington are:

+   1703   i.   **Nicholas K.[9] Edrington IV, born 21 December 1981 in Thibodaux, Lafourche Parish, Louisiana.**

    1704   ii.   **Amy Elizabeth Edrington, born 27 July 1983 in Thibodaux, Lafourche Parish, Louisiana.**

1184. Peggy Jo[8] Thiac (Janice Ann[7] Milano, Maude Marie[6] Robért, Joseph Olide[5], Jean Paul[4], Mathieu[3], Jean[2], Mathieu[1]) was born 15 March 1960 in Thibodaux, Lafourche Parish, Louisiana. She married **Paul Joseph Toups** 21 February 1981 in Thibodaux, Lafourche Parish, Louisiana.

Children of Peggy Thiac and Paul Toups are:

    1705   i.   **Lauren Elizabeth[9] Toups, born 13 November 1983 in Thibodaux, Lafourche Parish, Louisiana.**

| 1706 | ii. | Erin Alyce Toups, born 01 May 1986 in Thibodaux, Lafourche Parish, Louisiana. |
| 1707 | iii. | Kristen Nicole Toups, born 17 August 1988 in Thibodaux, Lafourche Parish, Louisiana. |

1186. Mary Beth[8] Thiac (Janice Ann[7] Milano, Maude Marie[6] Robért, Joseph Olide[5], Jean Paul[4], Mathieu[3], Jean[2], Mathieu[1]) was born 23 November 1963 in Thibodaux, Lafourche Parish, Louisiana. She married **Craig Zeringue** 27 November 1982 in Thibodaux, Lafourche Parish, Louisiana.

Children of Mary Thiac and Craig Zeringue are:

1708	i.	Lance Michael[9] Zeringue, born 11 July 1986 in Webster, Texas.
1709	ii.	Sarah Elizabeth Zeringue, born 07 June 1989 in Friendswood, Texas.
1710	iii.	Emily Michelle Zeringue, born 07 October 1993 in Friendswood, Texas.

1187. Timothy Paul[8] Thiac (Janice Ann[7] Milano, Maude Marie[6] Robért, Joseph Olide[5], Jean Paul[4], Mathieu[3], Jean[2], Mathieu[1]) was born 12 May 1965 in Thibodaux, Lafourche Parish, Louisiana. He married **Sarah Sternfels** 30 March 1985 in Thibodaux, Lafourche Parish, Louisiana, daughter of Ronald Sternfels and Gretchen Kern.

Children of Timothy Thiac and Sarah Sternfels are:

| 1711 | i. | Corey Michael[9] Thiac, born 18 August 1985 in Thibodaux, Lafourche Parish, Louisiana. |
| 1712 | ii. | Timothy Paul Thiac, born 28 March 1990 in New Orleans, Orleans Parish, Louisiana. |

1188. Jamie Lynne[8] Anderson (Myrna Marie[7] Milano, Maude Marie[6] Robért, Joseph Olide[5], Jean Paul[4], Mathieu[3], Jean[2], Mathieu[1]) was born 07 January 1962 in Paincourtville, Assumption Parish, Louisiana. She married **Lewis (Bud) Barlow** 08 October 1982 in Thibodaux, Lafourche Parish, Louisiana, son of Roger Barlow and Electa Gomez. He was born 23 September 1957 in White Castle, Iberville Parish, Louisiana.

Children of Jamie Anderson and Lewis Barlow are:

1713	i.	Megan Elizabeth[9] Barlow, born 27 April 1983 in Baton Rouge, East Baton Rouge Parish, Louisiana.
1714	ii.	Addie Lynne Barlow, born 04 October 1984 in Thibodaux, Lafourche Parish, Louisiana.
1715	iii.	Kyle Roger Barlow, born 29 January 1988 in Lake Charles, Calcasieu Parish, Louisiana.

1189. Frederic (Fritz)[8] Anderson (Myrna Marie[7] Milano, Maude Marie[6] Robért, Joseph Olide[5], Jean Paul[4], Mathieu[3], Jean[2], Mathieu[1]) was born 05 September 1964 in Paincourtville, Assumption Parish, Louisiana. He met **Celeste Knoblock**. She was born in Thibodaux, Lafourche Parish, Louisiana.

Child of Frederic Anderson and Celeste Knoblock is:

   1716   i. **Jake[9] Anderson, born 07 May 1992 in Thibodaux, Lafourche Parish, Louisiana.**

1190. David Jerome[8] Anderson (Myrna Marie[7] Milano, Maude Marie[6] Robért, Joseph Olide[5], Jean Paul[4], Mathieu[3], Jean[2], Mathieu[1]) was born 11 June 1967 in Donaldsonville, Ascension Parish, Louisiana. He married **Jenny Carpenter** 22 March 1991 in Guam, daughter of Dallas Morton and Christine Carpenter. She was born 29 November 1969 in Jacksonville, North Carolina.

Children of David Anderson and Jenny Carpenter are:

   1717   i. **Stephen Douglas[9] Anderson, born 26 September 1991 in Guam.**
   1718   ii. **Sean Phillip Anderson, born 02 October 1997 in Tallahassee, Florida.**

1192. Jessica Therese[8] Anderson (Myrna Marie[7] Milano, Maude Marie[6] Robért, Joseph Olide[5], Jean Paul[4], Mathieu[3], Jean[2], Mathieu[1]) was born 08 August 1980 in Baton Rouge, East Baton Rouge Parish, Louisiana. She married **George Halliburton Ware III** 30 May 2001 in Jamaica, son of George Ware and Sandra Smith. He was born 06 February 1970 in Germany.

Children of Jessica Anderson and George Ware are:

   1719   i. **Chandler Halliburton[9] Ware, born 30 August 2001 in Lake Charles, Calcasieu Parish, Louisiana.**
   1720   ii. **Grayson Paul Ware, born 03 July 2006 in Lake Charles, Calcasieu Parish, Louisiana.**

1198. Daria Ann[8] Babin (Fay Marie[7] Robért, Joseph Nemours[6], Joseph Olide[5], Jean Paul[4], Mathieu[3], Jean[2], Mathieu[1]) was born 23 October 1962 in Baton Rouge, East Baton Rouge Parish, Louisiana, and died 13 September 2004 in Baton Rouge, East Baton Rouge Parish, Louisiana. She married **Brett Patrick Babin** 19 November 1982 in St. Theresa Catholic Church, Gonzales, Louisiana, son of William Babin and Lura Villier. He was born 31 December 1961 in Gonzales, Ascension Parish, Louisiana.

Children of Daria Babin and Brett Babin are:

1721   i.   **Brooke Nichole[9] Babin, born 24 July 1987 in Baton Rouge, East Baton Rouge Parish, Louisiana.**

1722   ii.   **Patrick Joseph Babin, born 26 June 1991 in Baton Rouge, East Baton Rouge Parish, Louisiana.**

1199. Blaise Anthony[8] Babin (Fay Marie[7] Robért, Joseph Nemours[6], Joseph Olide[5], Jean Paul[4], Mathieu[3], Jean[2], Mathieu[1]) was born 04 June 1964 in Baton Rouge, East Baton Rouge Parish, Louisiana. He married **Reine Ann Legendre** 04 June 1988 in Holy Ghost Catholic Church, Hammond, Louisiana, daughter of Eugene Legendre and Audrey Abate. She was born 06 January 1965 in New Orleans, Orleans Parish, Louisiana.

Children of Blaise Babin and Reine Legendre are:

1723   i.   **Zachary Chase[9] Babin, born 14 September 1989 in Baton Rouge, East Baton Rouge Parish, Louisiana.**

1724   ii.   **Lincoln Alexander Babin, born 27 January 1991 in Baton Rouge, East Baton Rouge Parish, Louisiana.**

1725   iii.   **Ethan Talbot Babin, born 12 December 1991 in Baton Rouge, East Baton Rouge Parish, Louisiana.**

1726   iv.   **Anne-Claire Babin, born 20 December 2001 in Baton Rouge, East Baton Rouge Parish, Louisiana.**

1200. Steven Paul[8] Babin (Fay Marie[7] Robért, Joseph Nemours[6], Joseph Olide[5], Jean Paul[4], Mathieu[3], Jean[2], Mathieu[1]) was born 07 October 1969 in Baton Rouge, East Baton Rouge Parish, Louisiana. He married **Lisa Lené Longanecker** 26 June 1992 in St. Anne Catholic Church, Sorrento, Ascension Parish, Louisiana, daughter of Wilson Longanecker and Nita Pertuis. She was born 06 April 1969 in Baton Rouge, East Baton Rouge Parish, Louisiana.

Children of Steven Babin and Lisa Longanecker are:

1727   i.   **Brynn Alise[9] Babin, born 03 October 1995 in Baton Rouge, East Baton Rouge Parish, Louisiana.**

1728   ii.   **Reed Joseph Babin, born 23 June 2000 in Baton Rouge, East Baton Rouge Parish, Louisiana.**

1201. Kari Marie[8] Sheets (Frances Elizabeth[7] Robért, Joseph Nemours[6], Joseph Olide[5], Jean Paul[4], Mathieu[3], Jean[2], Mathieu[1]) was born 11 November 1963 in Gonzales, Ascension Parish, Louisiana. She married **Mark Hillman** 03 March 1984.

Child of Kari Sheets and Mark Hillman is:

1729   i.   **Christopher Ryan[9] Hillman, born 03 May 1986 in East Baton Rouge**

Parish, Baton Rouge, Louisiana.

1207. Russell Joseph[8] Robért (Joseph Reginald[7], Joseph Nemours[6], Joseph Olide[5], Jean Paul[4], Mathieu[3], Jean[2], Mathieu[1]) was born 28 March 1980 in Baton Rouge, East Baton Rouge Parish, Louisiana. He married **Brittni Nicole Gautreau** 13 August 2004. She was born 12 June 1981.

Child of Russell Robért and Brittni Gautreau is:
  1730   i. **Addison Grace[9] Robért, born 09 March 2007.**

1211. Brian Paul[8] Robért (Terry Jude[7], Joseph Nemours[6], Joseph Olide[5], Jean Paul[4], Mathieu[3], Jean[2], Mathieu[1]) was born 21 November 1974 in Gonzales, Ascension Parish, Louisiana. He married **Nancy Olivia Branscum** 24 July 1999 in Zoar Baptist Church, Baton Rouge, East Baton Rouge Parish, Louisiana.

Child of Brian Robért and Nancy Branscum is:
  1731   i. **Ava Nichole[9] Robért, born 06 February 2006 in Houston, Harris County, Texas.**

1222. Denise Ann[8] Babin (Stanley Joseph[7], Adele Ann[6] Robért, Joseph Olide[5], Jean Paul[4], Mathieu[3], Jean[2], Mathieu[1]) was born 24 February 1966 in Marrero, Jefferson Parish, Louisiana.

Child of Denise Ann Babin is:
  1732   i. **Michael Scott[9] Babin, born 18 February 1982 in New Orleans, Orleans Parish, Louisiana.**

1232. Suzette Estelle[8] Rome (Robert Louis[7], Louis Joseph[6], Leona Theresa[5] Robért, (Na-Na), Jean Paul[4], Mathieu[3], Jean[2], Mathieu[1]) was born 05 September 1968 in Baton Rouge, East Baton Rouge Parish, Louisiana. She married **George Douglas Say** 27 March 1993 in Our Lady of Mercy Catholic Church, Baton Rouge, Louisiana, son of Robert Say and Frances Whitney. He was born 25 September 1967 in Baton Rouge, East Baton Rouge Parish, Louisiana.

Children of Suzette Rome and George Say are:
  1733   i.   **Alexander Douglas[9] Say, born 23 August 1995 in Shreveport, Caddo Parish, Louisiana.**
  1734   ii. **Parker Robert Say, born 22 August 1996 in Baton Rouge, East Baton Rouge Parish, Louisiana.**
  1735   iii. **Whitney Estelle Say, born 25 June 1998 in Baton Rouge, East Baton Rouge Parish, Louisiana.**
  1736   iv. **Harrison George Say, born 24 May 2001 in Baton Rouge, East**

1233. Byron Robert[8] Rome (Robert Louis[7], Louis Joseph[6], Leona Theresa[5] Robért, (Na-Na), Jean Paul[4], Mathieu[3], Jean[2], Mathieu[1]) was born 04 September 1970 in Baton Rouge, East Baton Rouge Parish, Louisiana. He married **Marci Reneé Madatic** 18 December 1998 in Baton Rouge, East Baton Rouge Parish, Louisiana, daughter of John Madatic and Elaine Erskine. She was born 11 January 1971 in Fredricksburg, Virginia.

Children of Byron Rome and Marci Madatic are:
1737	i.	**Carter Byron[9] Rome, born 08 August 2000 in Baton Rouge, East Baton Rouge Parish, Louisiana.**
1738	ii.	**John Benton Rome, born 10 June 2002 in Baton Rouge, East Baton Rouge Parish, Louisiana.**
1739	iii.	**Adeline Estelle Rome, born 08 March 2006 in Baton Rouge, East Baton Rouge Parish, Louisiana.**

1234. Carey Louis[8] Rome (Robert Louis[7], Louis Joseph[6], Leona Theresa[5] Robért, (Na-Na), Jean Paul[4], Mathieu[3], Jean[2], Mathieu[1]) was born 08 March 1972 in Baton Rouge, East Baton Rouge Parish, Louisiana. He married **Jana Reneé Luce** 06 May 2000 in Memphis, Tennessee, daughter of John Luce and Linda Theus. She was born 11 October 1974 in Lubbock, Texas.

Children of Carey Rome and Jana Luce are:
1740	i.	**Olivia Frances[9] Rome, born 27 August 2004 in Birmingham, Alabama.**
1741	ii.	**Hillary Louis Rome, born 31 January 2006 in Birmingham, Alabama.**

1235. Gregg Lawrence[8] Rome (Robert Louis[7], Louis Joseph[6], Leona Theresa[5] Robért, (Na-Na), Jean Paul[4], Mathieu[3], Jean[2], Mathieu[1]) was born 09 February 1975 in Baton Rouge, East Baton Rouge Parish, Louisiana. He married **Amy Elizabeth Blue, (Divorced 2007)** 17 May 2002 in Baton Rouge, East Baton Rouge Parish, Louisiana, daughter of Kenneth Blue and Dixie Williams. She was born 10 January 1977 in Baton Rouge, East Baton Rouge Parish, Louisiana.

Child of Gregg Rome and Amy Blue is:
1742	i.	**Burgin Elizabeth[9] Rome, born 29 February 2004 in Baton Rouge, East Baton Rouge Parish, Louisiana.**

1236. Michelle Margaret[8] Rome (Ronald Richard[7], Louis Joseph[6], Leona Theresa[5] Robért, (Na-Na), Jean Paul[4], Mathieu[3], Jean[2], Mathieu[1]) was born 13

March 1967 in Baton Rouge, East Baton Rouge Parish, Louisiana. She married **Robert Michael Kallam** 03 August 1991 in Our Lady of Mercy Catholic Church, Baton Rouge, Louisiana, son of Charles Kallam and Velma Langlinais. He was born 05 June 1965 in Lafayette, Lafayette Parish, Louisiana.

Children of Michelle Rome and Robert Kallam are:

1743	i.	**Barrett Michael[9] Kallam, born 18 August 1995 in Baton Rouge, East Baton Rouge Parish, Louisiana.**
1744	ii.	**Caroline Annabel Kallam, born 07 February 1998 in Lafayette, Lafayette Parish, Louisiana.**
1745	iii.	**Benjamin Robert Kallam, born 24 May 1999 in Lafayette, Lafayette Parish, Louisiana.**
1746	iv.	**William Rome Kallam, born 04 April 2001 in Lafayette, Lafayette Parish, Louisiana.**

1237. Aimee Cecile[8] Rome (Ronald Richard[7], Louis Joseph[6], Leona Theresa[5] Robért, (Na-Na), Jean Paul[4], Mathieu[3], Jean[2], Mathieu[1]) was born 02 December 1968 in Baton Rouge, East Baton Rouge Parish, Louisiana. She married **Steven Cassius Aaron** 21 March 1998 in St. Aloysuis Catholic Church, Baton Rouge, East Baton Rouge Parish, Louisiana, son of Joseph Aaron and Helen Trahan. He was born 03 January 1962 in Crowley, Acadia Parish, Louisiana.

Children of Aimee Rome and Steven Aaron are:

1747	i.	**Lindsey Cecile[9] Aaron, born 29 December 2000 in Salt Lake City, Salt Lake County, Utah.**
1748	ii.	**Faye Elizabeth Aaron, born 27 January 2003 in Lafayette, Lafayette Parish, Louisiana.**

1238. Paul Taggart[8] Barber, Jr. (Judith Anne[7] Rome, Louis Joseph[6], Leona Theresa[5] Robért, (Na-Na), Jean Paul[4], Mathieu[3], Jean[2], Mathieu[1]) was born 05 May 1961 in Baton Rouge, East Baton Rouge Parish, Louisiana. He married **Marcelena Baretta** 06 October 1989 in University Baptist Church. She was born 12 June 1961 in Houston, Texas.

Children of Paul Barber and Marcelena Baretta are:

1749	i.	**Michael Paul[9] Barber, born 12 April 1990 in Baton Rouge, East Baton Rouge Parish, Louisiana.**
1750	ii.	**Robert Louis Barber, born 12 November 1991 in Baton Rouge, East Baton Rouge Parish, Louisiana.**
1751	iii.	**Landon Mitchell Barber, born 06 April 1996 in Baton Rouge, East Baton Rouge Parish, Louisiana.**

1239. Madalyn Monique[8] **Barber** (Judith Anne[7] Rome, Louis Joseph[6], Leona Theresa[5] Robért, (Na-Na), Jean Paul[4], Mathieu[3], Jean[2], Mathieu[1]) was born 08 February 1963 in Baton Rouge, East Baton Rouge Parish, Louisiana. She married **Barry Lee Moore II** 30 May 1989 in St. Aloysuis Church, Baton Rouge, Louisiana, son of Barry Moore and Carolyn Clay. He was born 13 January 1958 in Baton Rouge, East Baton Rouge Parish, Louisiana.

Children of Madalyn Barber and Barry Moore are:
- 1752   i.   **Mathew Barber**[9] **Moore, born 18 June 1993 in Baton Rouge, East Baton Rouge Parish, Louisiana.**
- 1753   ii.   **William Barber Moore, born 20 March 1996 in Baton Rouge, East Baton Rouge Parish, Louisiana.**

1242. Patrick Hillard[8] **Barber** (Judith Anne[7] Rome, Louis Joseph[6], Leona Theresa[5] Robért, (Na-Na), Jean Paul[4], Mathieu[3], Jean[2], Mathieu[1]) was born 27 September 1971 in Baton Rouge, East Baton Rouge Parish, Louisiana. He married **Kellie Lynn Maris** 23 June 2001.

Children of Patrick Barber and Kellie Maris are:
- 1754   i.   **Ava Beran**[9] **Barber, born 23 November 2001 in Nashville, Tennessee.**
- 1755   ii.   **Martha Isabel Barber, born 18 June 2004 in Jackson, Tennessee.**

1244. Steven Louis[8] **Sockrider** (Eleanor Loretta[7] Rome, Louis Joseph[6], Leona Theresa[5] Robért, (Na-Na), Jean Paul[4], Mathieu[3], Jean[2], Mathieu[1]) was born 09 April 1963 in Baton Rouge, East Baton Rouge Parish, Louisiana. He married **Kimberly Georgia Hacker** 27 May 1995 in First United Methodist Church, Fort Lauderdale, Florida, daughter of Merritt Hacker and Helena. She was born 27 November 1968 in New York.

Children of Steven Sockrider and Kimberly Hacker are:
- 1756   i.   **Austin Louis**[9] **Sockrider, born 26 April 1999 in Boca Raton, Florida.**
- 1757   ii.   **Kyle Merritt Sockrider, born 17 April 2001 in Boca Raton, Florida.**

1245. Gary Wayne[8] **Sockrider** (Eleanor Loretta[7] Rome, Louis Joseph[6], Leona Theresa[5] Robért, (Na-Na), Jean Paul[4], Mathieu[3], Jean[2], Mathieu[1]) was born 08 October 1965 in Shreveport, Caddo Parish, Louisiana. He married **Lori Kathleen Johnson** 26 May 2001 in Boulder, Boulder County, Colorado, daughter of Don Johnson and Claudia Cone. She was born 08 July 1965 in Dallas, Texas.

Children of Gary Sockrider and Lori Johnson are:

1758	i.	Aidan Christopher[9] Sockrider, born 14 October 2003 in Boulder, Boulder County, Colorado.
1759	ii.	Eleanor Monique Sockrider, born 05 May 2006 in Boulder, Boulder County, Colorado.

1246. Christopher Sean[8] Sockrider (Eleanor Loretta[7] Rome, Louis Joseph[6], Leona Theresa[5] Robért, (Na-Na), Jean Paul[4], Mathieu[3], Jean[2], Mathieu[1]) was born 25 October 1970 in Shreveport, Caddo Parish, Louisiana. He married **Stephanie Ann Walker** 24 July 1993 in Holy Trinity Catholic Church, Shreveport, Louisiana, daughter of Cynthia Brightwell Walker. She was born 14 May 1971 in Shreveport, Caddo Parish, Louisiana.

Children of Christopher Sockrider and Stephanie Walker are:

1760	i.	Benjamin Finley[9] Sockrider, born 30 December 1999 in Shreveport, Caddo Parish, Louisiana.
1761	ii.	Walker Alan Sockrider, born 29 May 2003 in Shreveport, Caddo Parish, Louisiana.
1762	iii.	Grant Christopher Sockrider, born 12 November 2004 in Shreveport, Caddo Parish, Louisiana.
1763	iv.	James Henry Sockrider, born 14 May 2007 in Shreveport, Caddo Parish, Louisiana.

1249. Dianne Marie[8] Laiche (Suzanne P.[7] Rome, Paul Robert[6], Leona Theresa[5] Robért, (Na-Na), Jean Paul[4], Mathieu[3], Jean[2], Mathieu[1]) was born 07 December 1959 in Lafayette, Lafayette Parish, Louisiana. She married **Jeffrey Anthony Chrisman** 18 May 1985. He was born 18 May 1958.

Children of Dianne Laiche and Jeffrey Chrisman are:

1764	i.	Jillian Elizabeth[9] Chrisman, born 01 April 1988.
1765	ii.	Jeffery Steven Chrisman, born 11 August 1990.
1766	iii.	Nikki Allison Chrisman, born 24 June 1996.

1250. Douglas David[8] Laiche (Suzanne P.[7] Rome, Paul Robert[6], Leona Theresa[5] Robért, (Na-Na), Jean Paul[4], Mathieu[3], Jean[2], Mathieu[1]) was born 19 October 1962. He married **Kirsten Anderson** 13 May 1994. She was born 22 April 1962.

Children of Douglas Laiche and Kirsten Anderson are:

1767	i.	Sam Monette[9] Blum, born 25 September 1982.
1768	ii.	Kaysie Christine Nordby Anderson Blum, born 14 April 1987.
1769	iii.	Douglas David Laiche, Jr., born 12 October 1995.

1252. Vickie Lynn[8] Miller (Alice Marie[7] Rome, Paul Robert[6], Leona Theresa[5] Robért, (Na-Na), Jean Paul[4], Mathieu[3], Jean[2], Mathieu[1]) was born 19 June 1960 in New Orleans, Orleans Parish, Louisiana. She married **Galen Anthony Tramonte** 06 October 1978 in St. Charles Borromeo Church, Destrahan, Louisiana. He was born 25 July 1958 in Luling, St. Charles Parish, Louisiana.

Children of Vickie Miller and Galen Tramonte are:

    1770   i.   **Lauren Elizabeth[9] Tramonte, born 10 May 1979 in Metairie, Jefferson Parish, Louisiana. She married Brian Joseph Toups 20 November 2004 in St. Charles Borromeo Church, Destrahan, Louisiana; born 20 September 1978 in Metairie, Jefferson Parish, Louisiana.**

    1771   ii.   **Gaylynn Ann Tramonte, born 06 January 1982 in Metairie, Jefferson Parish, Louisiana.**

+   1772   iii.   **Nicole Maria Tramonte, born 01 March 1984 in Metairie, Jefferson Parish, Louisiana.**

1254. Stephenie Ann[8] Miller (Alice Marie[7] Rome, Paul Robert[6], Leona Theresa[5] Robért, (Na-Na), Jean Paul[4], Mathieu[3], Jean[2], Mathieu[1]) was born 04 December 1964 in New Orleans, Orleans Parish, Louisiana. She married **Thomas Paul Becnel** 02 May 1986 in St. Charles Borromeo Church, Destrahan, Louisiana. He was born 23 December 1964 in Lutcher, St. James Parish, Louisiana.

Children of Stephenie Miller and Thomas Becnel are:

    1773   i.   **Kayla Christine[9] Becnel, born 01 December 1988 in Metairie, Jefferson Parish, Louisiana.**

    1774   ii.   **Chelsea Michelle Becnel, born 26 July 1991 in Metairie, Jefferson Parish, Louisiana.**

    1775   iii.   **Gabrielle Nicole Becnel, born 08 March 1993 in Metairie, Jefferson Parish, Louisiana.**

    1776   iv.   **Zachary Thomas Becnel, born 26 March 1999 in Metairie, Jefferson Parish, Louisiana.**

1255. Henry Rezin[8] Miller III (Alice Marie[7] Rome, Paul Robert[6], Leona Theresa[5] Robért, (Na-Na), Jean Paul[4], Mathieu[3], Jean[2], Mathieu[1]) was born 13 September 1966 in New Orleans, Orleans Parish, Louisiana. He married **Melissa Gerianne Felder** 01 September 1989 in Sacred Heart of Jesus, Norco, St. Charles Parish, Louisiana. She was born 29 June 1966 in New Orleans, Orleans Parish, Louisiana.

Children of Henry Miller and Melissa Felder are:

    1777   i.   **Alexis Victoria[9] Miller, born 02 May 1995 in Coral Springs, Florida.**

    1778   ii.   **Brittany Nicole Miller, born 16 October 1997 in Tampa, Florida.**

    1779   iii.   **Haley Renee Miller, born 01 June 2001 in Coral Springs, Florida.**

1780   iv.   Ally Noel Miller, born 15 December 2003 in The Woodlands, Texas.

1256. Dana Elizabeth[8] Miller (Alice Marie[7] Rome, Paul Robert[6], Leona Theresa[5] Robért, (Na-Na), Jean Paul[4], Mathieu[3], Jean[2], Mathieu[1]) was born 25 March 1968 in New Orleans, Orleans Parish, Louisiana. She married **Joseph Matthew Herbert** 20 November 1993 in St. Charles Borromeo Church, Destrahan, Louisiana. He was born 12 April 1968 in Lakewood, New Jersey.

Children of Dana Miller and Joseph Herbert are:
1781   i.   **Alexander Joseph[9] Herbert, born 13 August 1995 in New Orleans, Orleans Parish, Louisiana.**
1782   ii.   **Madison Claire Herbert, born 05 February 1998 in New Orleans, Orleans Parish, Louisiana.**
1783   iii. **Nicholas Henry Miller, born 19 November 1999 in New Orleans, Orleans Parish, Louisiana.**

1257. Erin Eileen[8] Miller (Alice Marie[7] Rome, Paul Robert[6], Leona Theresa[5] Robért, (Na-Na), Jean Paul[4], Mathieu[3], Jean[2], Mathieu[1]) was born 28 June 1973 in Metairie, Jefferson Parish, Louisiana. She married **Bryan Craig Green** 08 February 1997 in St. Charles Borromeo Church, Destrahan, Louisiana. He was born 17 October 1973 in Metairie, Jefferson Parish, Louisiana.

Children of Erin Miller and Bryan Green are:
1784   i.   **Matthew William[9] Green, born 22 November 1999 in Little Rock, Arkansas.**
1785   ii.   **Megan Allyson Green, born 28 January 2002 in Pensacola, Florida.**
1786   iii. **Molly Elizabeth Green, born 28 February 2006 in Greenville, South Carolina.**

1258. Shannon Ann[8] Faucheux (Eileen Mary[7] Rome, Paul Robert[6], Leona Theresa[5] Robért, (Na-Na), Jean Paul[4], Mathieu[3], Jean[2], Mathieu[1]) was born 07 April 1964 in New Orleans, Orleans Parish, Louisiana. She married **John Michael Jordan** 21 December 1990 in Ascension of our Lord Church, LaPlace, St. John the Baptist Parish, Louisiana. He was born 05 May 1957 in Jackson, Mississippi.

Children of Shannon Faucheux and John Jordan are:
1787   i.   **Andrew Levine[9] Jordan, born 10 June 1996 in Metairie, Jefferson Parish, Louisiana.**
1788   ii.   **Amanda Claire Jordan, born 10 June 1996 in Metairie, Jefferson Parish, Louisiana.**

1259. James Patrick[8] Faucheux, Jr. (Eileen Mary[7] Rome, Paul Robert[6],

Leona Theresa[5] Robért, (Na-Na), Jean Paul[4], Mathieu[3], Jean[2], Mathieu[1]) was born 12 April 1965 in Lutcher, St. James Parish, Louisiana. He married **(1) Cherie Ann McDougal** 26 December 1986 in St. Michaels Church, Chalmette, St. Bernard Parish, Louisiana. She was born 02 September 1967 in Chalmette, St. Bernard Parish, Louisiana. He married **(2) Samantha Vondel George** 10 November 2001 in Baton Rouge, East Baton Rouge Parish, Louisiana. She was born 26 December 1970 in Baton Rouge, East Baton Rouge Parish, Louisiana.

Child of James Faucheux and Cherie McDougal is:
  1789   i.   **James Patrick[9] Faucheux III, born 23 June 1987 in New Orleans, Orleans Parish, Louisiana.**

Children of James Faucheux and Samantha George are:
  1790   i.   **Dorian Jeremiah[9] Faucheux, born 15 September 2005 in Baton Rouge, East Baton Rouge Parish, Louisiana.**
  1791   ii.   **Datren Quintel Robertson,(stepson), born 14 December 1990 in Baton Rouge, East Baton Rouge Parish, Louisiana.**

1260. Michelle Ann[8] Faucheux (Eileen Mary[7] Rome, Paul Robert[6], Leona Theresa[5] Robért, (Na-Na), Jean Paul[4], Mathieu[3], Jean[2], Mathieu[1]) was born 03 December 1966 in Lutcher, St. James Parish, Louisiana. She married **Peter Timothy Montz** 18 February 1989 in St. Joan of Arc Church, LaPlace, St. John the Baptist Parish, Louisiana. He was born 27 November 1964 in New Orleans, Orleans Parish, Louisiana.

Children of Michelle Faucheux and Peter Montz are:
  1792   i.   **Erika Elizabeth[9] Montz, born 01 November 1990 in LaPlace, St. John the Baptist Parish, Louisiana.**
  1793   ii.   **Rachael Reneé Montz, born 17 June 1992 in LaPlace, St. John the Baptist Parish, Louisiana.**

1261. Lisa Marie[8] Faucheux (Eileen Mary[7] Rome, Paul Robert[6], Leona Theresa[5] Robért, (Na-Na), Jean Paul[4], Mathieu[3], Jean[2], Mathieu[1]) was born 15 May 1973 in Metairie, Jefferson Parish, Louisiana. She married **Andrew Joseph Pregeant** 27 September 1997 in St. Joan of Arc Church, LaPlace, St. John the Baptist Parish, Louisiana. He was born 11 July 1973 in Metairie, Jefferson Parish, Louisiana.

Children of Lisa Faucheux and Andrew Pregeant are:
  1794   i.   **Cade Andrew[9] Pregeant, born 12 September 2003 in LaPlace, St. John the Baptist Parish, Louisiana.**
  1795   ii.   **Bryce Raymond Pregeant, born 09 September 2005 in LaPlace, St.**

1267. Ashley Ann[8] Rome (O'Neil Francis[7], O'Neil Francis[6], Leona Theresa[5] Robért, (Na-Na), Jean Paul[4], Mathieu[3], Jean[2], Mathieu[1]) was born 03 August 1966 in Baton Rouge, East Baton Rouge Parish, Louisiana. She married **Douglas Burbank** 27 June 1992 in Houston, Texas.

Children of Ashley Rome and Douglas Burbank are:
  1796   i.   **Elaine Nicole[9] Burbank, born 07 May 1995.**
  1797   ii.   **Robért Douglas Burbank, born 20 March 1998.**

1268. O'Neil Francis[8] Rome,III (O'Neil Francis[7], O'Neil Francis[6], Leona Theresa[5] Robért, (Na-Na), Jean Paul[4], Mathieu[3], Jean[2], Mathieu[1]) was born 09 April 1971 in Baton Rouge, East Baton Rouge Parish, Louisiana. He married **Leah Himelright** 01 February 1997 in Memphis Texas.

Child of O'Neil Rome and Leah Himelright is:
  1798   i.   **Mia Juliana[9] Rome, born 01 May 1997.**

1273. Courtney Marie[8] Blanchard (Robert Courtland[7], Lillian Theresa[6] Rome, Leona Theresa[5] Robért, (Na-Na), Jean Paul[4], Mathieu[3], Jean[2], Mathieu[1]) was born 08 February 1971 in Ft. McClelland, Alabama. She married **René Hebert** 11 June 2005 in Lafayette, Lafayette Parish, Loiuisiana. He was born 22 June 1975.

Children of Courtney Blanchard and René Hebert are:
  1799   i.   **Kaitlyn Renée[9] Hebert, born 11 April 2006 in Lafayette, Lafayette Parish, Louisiana.**
  1800   ii.   **Rachel Marie Hebert, born 18 September 2007 in Lafayette, Lafayette Parish, Louisiana.**
  1801   iii.   **Michelle Theresa Hebert, born 18 September 2007 in Lafayette, Lafayette Parish, Louisiana.**

1275. Troy Michael[8] LeBlanc (Lillian Theresa[7] Blanchard, Lillian Theresa[6] Rome, Leona Theresa[5] Robért, (Na-Na), Jean Paul[4], Mathieu[3], Jean[2], Mathieu[1]) was born 26 May 1964 in Donaldsonville, Ascension Parish, Louisiana. He married **Angela Catherine Brown** 17 June 1989. She was born 17 March 1966 in Mississippi.

Children of Troy LeBlanc and Angela Brown are:
  1802   i.   **Melanie Marie[9] LeBlanc, born 02 September 1993.**

1803 ii. **Alexandre Renée LeBlanc, born 10 July 1995.**
1804 iii. **Michael Joseph LeBlanc, born 19 November 1997.**

1276. Nicole Monique[8] LeBlanc (Lillian Theresa[7] Blanchard, Lillian Theresa[6] Rome, Leona Theresa[5] Robért, (Na-Na), Jean Paul[4], Mathieu[3], Jean[2], Mathieu[1]) was born 21 April 1967 in Dallas, Texas. She married **James David Rafferty** 10 February 1996 in Woodstock, Illinois. He was born 12 February 1965.

Child of Nicole LeBlanc and James Rafferty is:
1805 i. **Courtland James[9] Rafferty, born 25 April 2006 in Illinois.**

1277. Michelle Annette[8] LeBlanc (Lillian Theresa[7] Blanchard, Lillian Theresa[6] Rome, Leona Theresa[5] Robért, (Na-Na), Jean Paul[4], Mathieu[3], Jean[2], Mathieu[1]) was born 02 August 1972 in Atlanta, Georgia. She married **Keith Torrey**. He was born 09 September 1971.

Children of Michelle LeBlanc and Keith Torrey are:
1806 i. **Austin Reily[9] Torrey, born 25 December 2002 in Wisconsin.**
1807 ii. **Peyton James Torrey, born 22 December 2004 in Wisconsin.**

1278. Everett Paul[8] Gauthier, III (Rett) (Madeline Marie[7] Blanchard, Lillian Theresa[6] Rome, Leona Theresa[5] Robért, (Na-Na), Jean Paul[4], Mathieu[3], Jean[2], Mathieu[1]) was born 17 August 1974 in Baton Rouge, East Baton Rouge Parish, Louisiana. He married **(1) Margaret Hayes**. He married **(2) Nathalie Clarac** 09 August 2002. She was born 15 December 1972.

Child of Everett Gauthier and Margaret Hayes is:
1808 i. **Samuel Everett[9] Gauthier, born 14 September 1994 in Baton Rouge, East Baton Rouge Parish, Louisiana.**

Child of Everett Gauthier and Nathalie Clarac is:
1809 i. **Cedric Alexandre[9] Gauthier, born 10 June 2004 in Dayton, Ohio.**

1286. Rome Angette[8] Goodspeed (Carolyn[7] Rome, Charles David[6], Leona Theresa[5] Robért, (Na-Na), Jean Paul[4], Mathieu[3], Jean[2], Mathieu[1]) was born 15 August 1971. She married **Lee Oliver** 02 March 1991.

Children of Rome Goodspeed and Lee Oliver are:
1810 i. **Branden Lee[9] Oliver, born 07 January 1993.**
1811 ii. **Alex Charles Oliver, born 11 May 1994.**

1287. Janette Michelle⁸ Goodspeed (Carolyn⁷ Rome, Charles David⁶, Leona Theresa⁵ Robért, (Na-Na), Jean Paul⁴, Mathieu³, Jean², Mathieu¹) was born 09 August 1974. She married **Ryan Hovey** 30 December 1994.

Children of Janette Goodspeed and Ryan Hovey are:
| 1812 | i. | **Haley Marie⁹ Hovey, born 30 May 1995.** |
| 1813 | ii. | **Carley Ann Hovey, born 27 February 1997.** |

1297. Courtney Leah⁸ Robért (James Joseph⁷, James Joseph⁶, Raoul Matthew⁵, Jean Paul⁴, Mathieu³, Jean², Mathieu¹) was born 15 March 1967 in Wurzburg, Germany. She married **(2) John Stacy Armand, (Divorced)** 1984 in St. Landry Catholic Church, Opelousas, St. Landry Parish, Louisiana. He was born 28 April 1962. She married **(3) John Lester Moreau, (Divorced)** 04 December 1992 in Civil Wedding: by Judge Kenneth Boagni. He was born 13 October 1967. She married **(4) David Earl Tillson** 15 March 2002 in Academy of The Sacred Heart. He was born 28 July 1955.

Child of Courtney Leah Robért is:
| 1814 | i. | **Joy Helaine⁹ Smith, born 29 May 1982 in Opelousas, St. Landry Parish, Louisiana.** |

Child of Courtney Robért and John Armand is:
| + | 1815 | i. | **Allison Celeste⁹ Armand, born 11 August 1984 in Opelousas, St. Landry Parish, Louisiana.** |

Children of Courtney Robért and John Moreau are:
| 1816 | i. | **Hannah Elizabeth⁹ Moreau, born 22 February 1994 in Opelousas, St. Landry Parish, Louisiana.** |
| 1817 | ii. | **Connor Robert Moreau, born 04 June 1996 in Opelousas, St. Landry Parish, Louisiana.** |

Children of Courtney Robért and David Tillson are:
| 1818 | i. | **Catherine Elaine⁹ Tillson, (Stepchild), born 04 February 1986.** |
| 1819 | ii. | **Cullen Alexander Tillson, (Stepchild), born 08 October 1993.** |

1298. Deverelle Marie⁸ Robért (James Joseph⁷, James Joseph⁶, Raoul Matthew⁵, Jean Paul⁴, Mathieu³, Jean², Mathieu¹) was born 01 March 1970 in Opelousas, St. Landry Parish, Louisiana. She married **Theobert George Venable, Sr.** 05 June 1993 in St. Landry Catholic Church, Opelousas, St. Landry Parish, Louisiana. He was born 11 April 1969.

Children of Deverelle Robért and Theobert Venable are:

1820   i.   **Theobert George[9] Venable, Jr., born 06 November 1995 in Lafayette, Lafayette Parish, Louisiana.**

1821   ii.   **Ann-Elyse Venable, born 29 July 2005 in Opelousas, St. Landry Parish, Louisiana.**

1299.   James Joseph[8] Robért III (James Joseph[7], James Joseph[6], Raoul Matthew[5], Jean Paul[4], Mathieu[3], Jean[2], Mathieu[1]) was born 24 October 1974 in Opelousas, St. Landry Parish, Louisiana. He married **Kara Ruth Kerley, (Divorced)** 06 May 2003 in Austin, Texas. She was born 01 October 1973.

Child of James Robért and Kara Kerley is:

1822   i.   **Tatum Quinn[9] Robért, born 06 January 2006 in Scottsdale, Arizona.**

1302.   Jon Tucker[8] Robért (Raoul William[7], James Joseph[6], Raoul Matthew[5], Jean Paul[4], Mathieu[3], Jean[2], Mathieu[1]) was born 24 March 1977 in East Baton Rouge Parish, Baton Rouge, La.. He married **Shelby Karns** 31 July 2004 in Playa Del Carmec, Mexico, daughter of Barry Karns and Julie Doff. She was born 02 December 1977 in Baton Rouge, East Baton Rouge Parish, Louisiana.

Children of Jon Robért and Shelby Karns are:

1823   i.   **Noah Miles[9] Robért, born 23 March 2006 in Baton Rouge, East Baton Rouge Parish, Louisiana.**

1824   ii.   **Josephine Lauren Robért, born 31 May 2007 in Baton Rouge, East Baton Rouge Parish, Louisiana.**

1433.   Wendi Renée[8] Cannon (Renée Geralyn[7] Robért, Carl James[6], Rene Benoit[5], Jean Paul[4], Mathieu[3], Jean[2], Mathieu[1]) was born 02 December 1973 in Baton Rouge, East Baton Rouge Parish, Louisiana. She married **Davey Decoteau** 11 January 2002 in St. Mark Catholic Church, Gonzales, Louisiana, son of Elsey Decoteau and Renée St. John. He was born 14 June 1972 in Baton Rouge, East Baton Rouge Parish, Louisiana.

Children of Wendi Cannon and Davey Decoteau are:

1825   i.   **Braize Renée[9] Decoteau, born 03 February 2005 in Baton Rouge, East Baton Rouge Parish, Louisiana.**

1826   ii.   **Dason Joseph Decoteau, born 01 September 2006 in Baton Rouge, East Baton Rouge Parish, Louisiana.**

1434.   Tara Terése[8] Cannon (Renée Geralyn[7] Robért, Carl James[6], Rene

Benoit[5], Jean Paul[4], Mathieu[3], Jean[2], Mathieu[1]) was born 19 April 1977 in Baton Rouge, East Baton Rouge Parish, Louisiana. She married **Cody Michael Trabeau** 23 July 1999 in St. Mark Catholic Church, Gonzales, Louisiana, son of Wilbert Trabeau and Lana LeBlanc. He was born 13 July 1976 in Baton Rouge, East Baton Rouge Parish, Louisiana.

Children of Tara Cannon and Cody Trabeau are:

    1827   i.   **Brody Michael[9] Trabeau, born 31 July 2002 in Baton Rouge, East Baton Rouge Parish, Louisiana.**

    1828   ii.   **Braxon James Trabeau, born 18 February 2006 in Baton Rouge, East Baton Rouge Parish, Louisiana.**

Generation No. 8

1618. Philip Brent[9] Waguespack (Gerald Jude[8], Gerald Marie[7], George Nicholas[6], Marie Octavie[5] Robért, ***, Jean Frumence[4], Mathieu[3], Jean[2], Mathieu[1]) was born 10 July 1977 in Baton Rouge, East Baton Rouge Parish, Louisiana. He married **Jacey Lynn Simpson** 08 August 2003 in St. Theresa Catholic Church, Gonzales, Ascension Parish, Louisiana, daughter of Elvin Simpson and Gay Gautreau. She was born 27 June 1979.

Child of Philip Waguespack and Jacey Simpson is:

    1829   i.   **Corin Marie[10] Waguespack, born 22 August 2006 in Baton Rouge, East Baton Rouge Parish, Louisiana.**

1619. Aaron Marie[9] Waguespack (Gerald Jude[8], Gerald Marie[7], George Nicholas[6], Marie Octavie[5] Robért, ***, Jean Frumence[4], Mathieu[3], Jean[2], Mathieu[1]) was born 24 June 1979 in Baton Rouge, East Baton Rouge Parish, Louisiana. She married **Brian Matthew Bateman** 06 June 2003 in St. Mary Catholic Church, Union, Louisiana, son of Edmond Bateman and Joycelyn Duvernay. He was born 10 May 1979.

Child of Aaron Waguespack and Brian Bateman is:

    1830   i.   **Brady Edmond[10] Bateman, born 08 April 2007 in Baton Rouge, East Baton Rouge Parish, Louisiana.**

1621. Jessica Marie[9] Latino (Georgene Marie[8] Waguespack, Gerald Marie[7], George Nicholas[6], Marie Octavie[5] Robért, ***, Jean Frumence[4], Mathieu[3], Jean[2], Mathieu[1]) was born 17 January 1978 in Baton Rouge, East Baton Rouge Parish, Louisiana. She married **Dwayne A. Thomassee** 26 May 2001 in Gonzales, Ascension Parish, Louisiana. He was born 28 August 1974.

Children of Jessica Latino and Dwayne Thomassee are:

    1831   i.   **Madelyn M.[10] Thomassee, born 28 October 2002 in Lafayette, Lafayette Parish, Louisiana.**

    1832   ii.   **Tatum L. Thomassee, born 18 June 2004 in Lafayette, Lafayette Parish, Louisiana.**

1627. Jeffrey Paul[9] Robichaux, (Adopted) (Roberta Therese[8] Waguespack, Gerald Marie[7], George Nicholas[6], Marie Octavie[5] Robért, ***, Jean Frumence[4], Mathieu[3], Jean[2], Mathieu[1]) was born 12 December 1982 in Baton Rouge, East Baton Rouge Parish, Louisiana. He married **Ashley Wallace** in Gonzales, Ascension Parish, Louisiana.

Child of Jeffrey Robichaux and Ashley Wallace is:

    1833   i.   **Aidan Paul[10] Robichaux, born 10 February 2007.**

1631. Tobie Mikael[9] Waguespack (Michael Curtis[8], Richard[7], George Nicholas[6], Marie Octavie[5] Robért, ***, Jean Frumence[4], Mathieu[3], Jean[2], Mathieu[1]) was born 12 October 1973 in Baton Rouge, East Baton Rouge Parish, Louisiana. She married **Devon P. Decoteau** 16 April 1999 in St. Theresa Catholic Church, Gonzales, Ascension Parish, Louisiana, son of Wayne Decoteau and Cynthia Decoteau.

Children of Tobie Waguespack and Devon Decoteau are:

    1834   i.   **Seline Victoria[10] Decoteau, born 05 September 2002 in Baton Rouge, East Baton Rouge Parish, Louisiana.**

    1835   ii.   **Michael Wayne Decoteau, born 01 November 2005 in Baton Rouge, East Baton Rouge Parish, Louisiana.**

1632. Joanie Lynn[9] Waguespack (Michael Curtis[8], Richard[7], George Nicholas[6], Marie Octavie[5] Robért, ***, Jean Frumence[4], Mathieu[3], Jean[2], Mathieu[1]) was born 11 June 1976 in Baton Rouge, East Baton Rouge Parish, Louisiana. She married **Blake Joseph Prejean** 06 August 1999 in St. Theresa Catholic Church, Gonzales, Ascension Parish, Louisiana. He was born 02 June 1977 in Baton Rouge, East Baton Rouge Parish, Louisiana.

Children of Joanie Waguespack and Blake Prejean are:

    1836   i.   **Hallie Malayne[10] Prejean, born 10 May 2003 in Baton Rouge, East Baton Rouge Parish, Louisiana.**

    1837   ii.   **Ramsie Lynn Prejean, born 29 September 2006 in Baton Rouge, East Baton Rouge Parish, Louisiana.**

1635. George Nicholas (Gee)[9] Bourque (Rhonda Faye[8] Waguespack,

Richard[7], George Nicholas[6], Marie Octavie[5] Robért, ***, Jean Frumence[4], Mathieu[3], Jean[2], Mathieu[1]) was born 12 October 1978 in West Monroe, Ouachita Parish, Louisiana. He married **Jaime Yvonne Granier**, daughter of Brent Granier and Nancy Lambert. She was born 30 April 1979 in Denham Springs, Livingston Parish, Louisiana.

Child of George Bourque and Jaime Granier is:

    1838   i. **Josie Nicole Granier[10] Bourque, born 03 October 2006 in Baton Rouge, East Baton Rouge Parish, Louisiana.**

1701. Matthew Thomas[9] Noel (Melissa Lee[8] Thiac, Janice Ann[7] Milano, Maude Marie[6] Robért, Joseph Olide[5], Jean Paul[4], Mathieu[3], Jean[2], Mathieu[1]) was born 06 July 1980 in Thibodaux, Lafourche Parish, Louisiana. He married **Amanda Schexnayder** 08 October 2004 in LaPlace, St. John the Baptist Parish, Louisiana.

Child of Matthew Noel and Amanda Schexnayder is:

    1839   i. **Ethan Thomas[10] Noel, born 13 January 2007 in Baton Rouge, East Baton Rouge Parish, Louisiana.**

1703. Nicholas K.[9] Edrington IV (Cindy Marie[8] Thiac, Janice Ann[7] Milano, Maude Marie[6] Robért, Joseph Olide[5], Jean Paul[4], Mathieu[3], Jean[2], Mathieu[1]) was born 21 December 1981 in Thibodaux, Lafourche Parish, Louisiana. He married **Mary Wegner** 19 August 2002 in Moreno Valley, California.

Children of Nicholas Edrington and Mary Wegner are:

    1840   i. **Cali Ann[10] Edrington, born 12 November 2005 in Thibodaux, Lafourche Parish, Louisiana.**
    1841   ii. **Katelyn Elizabeth Edrington, born 12 November 2005 in Thibodaux, Lafourche Parish, Louisiana.**

1772. Nicole Maria[9] Tramonte (Vickie Lynn[8] Miller, Alice Marie[7] Rome, Paul Robert[6], Leona Theresa[5] Robért, (Na-Na), Jean Paul[4], Mathieu[3], Jean[2], Mathieu[1]) was born 01 March 1984 in Metairie, Jefferson Parish, Louisiana. She married **Kevin Dawkins Moore** 26 March 2005 in Baton Rouge, East Baton Rouge Parish, Louisiana. He was born 23 May 1976 in Baton Rouge, East Baton Rouge Parish, Louisiana.

Children of Nicole Tramonte and Kevin Moore are:

    1842   i. **Anna Katherine[10] Moore, born 11 September 2003 in New Orleans, Orleans Parish, Louisiana.**
    1843   ii. **Tyler Joseph Moore, born 15 September 2006 in New Orleans,**

Orleans Parish, Louisiana.

1815. Allison Celeste[9] **Armand** (Courtney Leah[8] Robért, James Joseph[7], James Joseph[6], Raoul Matthew[5], Jean Paul[4], Mathieu[3], Jean[2], Mathieu[1]) was born 11 August 1984 in Opelousas, St. Landry Parish, Louisiana. She married **Juston Paul Stelly** 30 October 2004 in Our Lady of Mercy, Opelousas, St. Landry Parish, Louisiana. He was born 10 November 1983.

Child of Allison Armand and Juston Stelly is:
 1844   i.   **Dawson Armand**[10] **Stelly, born 26 April 2006 in Opelousas, St. Landry Parish, Louisiana.**

Endnotes

1. Glenn R. Conrad, *Abstract of Civil Records of St. Charles Parish.*
2. St. Charles Parish Records 1771-1900, Marriage Records.
3. St. John the Baptist Parish Marriages.
4. *Archdiocese of New Orleans Sacramental Records.*
5. St. Charles Borromeo Catholic Church, Destrehan, Louisiana.
6. *Archdiocese of New Orleans Sacramental Records.*
7. St. Charles Parish Records 1771-1900, Marriage Records.
8. *Archdiocese of New Orleans Sacramental Records.*
9. St. John the Baptist Parish Marriages.
10. *Archdiocese of New Orleans Sacramental Records.*
11. *Louisiana State Death Index.*
12. St. Charles Parish Records 1771-1900, Marriage Records.
13. *Archdiocese of New Orleans Sacramental Records.*
14. *Lafourche Parish, Marriages 1820-1900.*
15. *Archdiocese of New Orleans Sacramental Records.*
16. *St. John the Baptist Parish Civil Records.*
17. *Abstract of Civil Records of St. John the Baptist Parish.*
18. *Archdiocese of New Orleans Sacramental Records.*
19. St. Charles Parish Records 1771-1900, Marriage Records.
20. Nicholas Russell Murray, *St. John the Baptist Parish Marriage Records.*
21. *Lafourche Parish, Marriages 1820-1900.*
22. Nicholas Russell Murray, *St. John the Baptist Parish Marriage Records.*
23. *Archdiocese of New Orleans Sacramental Records.*
24. Nicholas Russell Murray, *St. John the Baptist Parish Marriage Records.*
25. *Archdiocese of New Orleans Sacramental Records.*
26. *Lafourche Parish, Marriages 1820-1900.*
27. *Diocese of Baton Rouge Catholic Church Records.*
28. *St. James Parish Marriage Book.*
29. *Archdiocese of New Orleans Sacramental Records.*
30. *St. James Parish Marriage Book.*
31. *Archdiocese of New Orleans Sacramental Records.*

32. Nicholas Russell Murray, *St. John the Baptist Parish Marriage Records.*
33. *St. John the Baptist Parish Civil Records.*
34. Nicholas Russell Murray, *St. John the Baptist Parish Marriage Records.*
35. *Archdiocese of New Orleans Sacramental Records.*
36. Nicholas Russell Murray, *St. John the Baptist Parish Marriage Records*, SJB 5-290.
37. Nicholas Russell Murray, *St. John the Baptist Parish Marriage Records.*
38. *Social Security Death Index.*
39. *Diocese of Baton Rouge Catholic Church Records.*
40. *St. Phillip Catholic Church Records, Vacherie, Louisisna.*
41. *Diocese of Baton Rouge Catholic Church Records.*
42. Nicholas Russell Murray, *St. John the Baptist Parish Marriage Records.*
43. *Diocese of Baton Rouge Catholic Church Records.*
44. St. Charles Parish Records 1771-1900, Marriage Records.
45. *Diocese of Baton Rouge Catholic Church Records.*
46. The Robért Family Book II By Ruth Robért
47. Ruth Robert, *Robert Family Book II.*
48. Nicholas Russell Murray, *St. John the Baptist Parish Marriage Records.*
49. *Archdiocese of New Orleans Sacramental Records.*
50. Nicholas Russell Murray, *St. John the Baptist Parish Marriage Records.*
51. *Archdiocese of New Orleans Sacramental Records.*
52. *Diocese of Baton Rouge Catholic Church Records.*
53. *Archdiocese of New Orleans Sacramental Records.*
54. *Diocese of Baton Rouge Catholic Church Records.*
55. *Archdiocese of New Orleans Sacramental Records.*
56. St. James Cemetary
57. *Archdiocese of New Orleans Sacramental Records.*
58. St. James Parish Records.
59. *Archdiocese of New Orleans Sacramental Records.*

Kinship of Jean Robért, *-***

Name	Relationship with Jean Robért	Civil	Canon
Aaron, Faye Elizabeth	5th great-granddaughter	VII	7
Aaron, Lindsey Cecile	5th great-granddaughter	VII	7
Aaron, Steven Cassius	Husband of the 4th great-granddaughter		
Abadie, Francois Andre	Husband of the half grandniece		
Abadie, Marguerite Julitte	Wife of the 2nd great-grandnephew		
Abadie, Marie Celina	Half great-grandniece	V	4
Abadie, Marie Louise	Half great-grandniece	V	4
Abadie, Richard	Husband of the great-granddaughter		
Ablicki, Leopold Michael	Husband of the 3rd great-granddaughter		
Ackerman, Marie Barbe	Grandmother of the wife		
Acosta, Dolores Grace, (To-Lou)	Wife of the 3rd great-grandson		
Acosta, Donald Neal	Husband of the 4th great-granddaughter		
Acosta, Joseph Jerome	5th great-grandson	VII	7
Acosta, Sam	Husband of the 3rd great-granddaughter		
Acosta, Sarah Elizabeth	5th great-granddaughter	VII	7
Agosta, Adrian Anthony	4th great-grandson	VI	6
Agosta, Andrew Rene	4th great-grandson	VI	6
Agosta, Lucie Janelle	4th great-granddaughter	VI	6
Ahlander, Laura Lynne	Partner of the 3rd great-grandson		
Aiken, James Randall	Husband of the 4th great-granddaughter		
Alger, Megan	Wife of the 5th great-grandson		
Allen, Charles Henry	Husband of the 4th great-granddaughter		
Allen, Nicholas	5th great-grandson	VII	7
Allen, Ross Guerard, Jr.	Husband of the 4th great-granddaughter		
Altazin, Kenneth Wayne	Husband of the 4th great-granddaughter		
Amond, Caroll	Wife of the 3rd great-grandson		
Anderman, Carla	Wife of the 3rd great-grandson		
Andermann, Allison Renee	5th great-granddaughter	VII	7
Andermann, Darryl Paul	Husband of the 4th great-granddaughter		
Andermann, Hunter Paul	5th great-grandson	VII	7
Andermann, Paulette Ann	Wife of the 3rd great-grandnephew		
Andermann, Randi Lynn	5th great-granddaughter	VII	7
Andermann, Trish Michael	5th great-granddaughter	VII	7
Anderson, David Jerome	4th great-grandson	VI	6
Anderson, Frederic (Fritz)	4th great-grandson	VI	6
Anderson, Frederic John	Husband of the 3rd great-granddaughter		
Anderson, Jake	5th great-grandson	VII	7
Anderson, Jamie Lynne	4th great-granddaughter	VI	6
Anderson, Jason Paul	4th great-grandson	VI	6
Anderson, Jessica Therese	4th great-granddaughter	VI	6
Anderson, Kirsten	Wife of the 4th great-grandson		
Anderson, Mary Jane	Wife of the 4th great-grandson		
Anderson, Sean Phillip	5th great-grandson	VII	7
Anderson, Stephen Douglas	5th great-grandson	VII	7
Andrews, Kacie Lynn	Wife of the 5th great-grandson		
Arcement	Husband of the great-grandniece		
Arcement, Patrick	Husband of the 4th great-granddaughter		
Arcement, Patrick Vincent	5th great-grandson	VII	7
Arcenaux, Jeanne	Wife of the 2nd great-grandnephew		
Arceneaux, Isabelle	Daughter-in-law		
Arceneaux, Marilyn Marie	Wife of the 3rd great-grandson		
Arceneaux, Melissa Ann	Wife of the 4th great-grandson		
Armand, Allison Celeste	5th great-granddaughter	VII	7
Armand, John Stacy, (Divorced)	Ex-husband of the 4th great-granddaughter		
Aubert, Laurent	Husband of the 2nd great-granddaughter		

Kinship of Jean Robért, *-***

Name	Relationship with Jean Robért	Civil	Canon
Aucoin, James Paul, Jr.	Husband of the 3rd great-granddaughter		
Aucoin, Kimberly Lynn	4th great-granddaughter	VI	6
Aucoin, Theresa Marie	Wife of the 3rd great-grandson		
Augusta	Wife of the 2nd great-grandnephew		
Authement, Philomene Odilia	Wife of the great-grandnephew		
Autin, Marie Amazelie	Wife of the great-grandson		
Averett, Margie Clara	Wife of the 2nd great-grandson		
Aymond, Warren Joseph	Husband of the 4th great-granddaughter		
Babb, Ronald Kent	Husband of the 4th great-granddaughter		
Babin, Amedee, Sr.	Husband of the grandniece		
Babin, Anne-Claire	5th great-granddaughter	VII	7
Babin, Ashlie Ann	4th great-granddaughter	VI	6
Babin, Barbara Elizabeth	3rd great-granddaughter	V	5
Babin, Blaise Anthony	4th great-grandson	VI	6
Babin, Blake Anthony	4th great-grandson	VI	6
Babin, Bret	Husband of the 3rd great-grandniece		
Babin, Brett Patrick	Husband of the 4th great-granddaughter		
Babin, Brooke Nichole	5th great-granddaughter	VII	7
Babin, Brynn Alise	5th great-granddaughter	VII	7
Babin, Casey Jude	4th great-granddaughter	VI	6
Babin, Catherine Jane	Wife of the 3rd great-grandson		
Babin, Daria Ann	4th great-granddaughter	VI	6
Babin, Denise Ann	4th great-granddaughter	VI	6
Babin, Ethan Talbot	5th great-grandson	VII	7
Babin, Jet	Wife of the 3rd great-grandnephew		
Babin, Kenneth Anthony	3rd great-grandson	V	5
Babin, Kenneth Anthony, Jr.	4th great-grandson	VI	6
Babin, Leslie Ann	3rd great-granddaughter	V	5
Babin, Lincoln Alexander	5th great-grandson	VII	7
Babin, Lynne Mary	3rd great-granddaughter	V	5
Babin, Michael Scott	5th great-grandson	VII	7
Babin, Patrick Joseph	5th great-grandson	VII	7
Babin, Ralph John	Husband of the 3rd great-granddaughter		
Babin, Reed Joseph	5th great-grandson	VII	7
Babin, Stanley Joseph	3rd great-grandson	V	5
Babin, Stanley Robert	Husband of the 2nd great-granddaughter		
Babin, Steven Paul	4th great-grandson	VI	6
Babin, Wade Joseph	4th great-grandson	VI	6
Babin, Zachary Chase	5th great-grandson	VII	7
Babineaux, Living	Wife of the 5th great-grandson		
Bachman, Margarethe	Great-grandmother of the wife		
Bailey, Harry	Husband of the 3rd great-grandniece		
Ballmer, Dallas James	Husband of the 4th great-granddaughter		
Banker, Albert Joseph, Jr. (Buck)	Husband of the 4th great-granddaughter		
Banker, Brad David	5th great-grandson	VII	7
Banker, Jeffry Wade	5th great-grandson	VII	7
Barber, Anna Michael, (infant)	4th great-granddaughter	VI	6
Barber, Ava Beran	5th great-granddaughter	VII	7
Barber, Landon Mitchell	5th great-grandson	VII	7
Barber, Madalyn Monique	4th great-granddaughter	VI	6
Barber, Martha Isabel	5th great-granddaughter	VII	7
Barber, Michael Paul	5th great-grandson	VII	7
Barber, Patrick Hillard	4th great-grandson	VI	6
Barber, Paul Taggart	Husband of the 3rd great-granddaughter		
Barber, Paul Taggart, Jr.	4th great-grandson	VI	6

*Kinship of Jean Robért, *-****

Name	Relationship with Jean Robért	Civil	Canon
Barber, Robert Louis	5th great-grandson	VII	7
Barber, Stephen Michael,(infant)	4th great-grandson	VI	6
Baretta, Marcelena	Wife of the 4th great-grandson		
Barlow, Addie Lynne	5th great-granddaughter	VII	7
Barlow, Kyle Roger	5th great-grandson	VII	7
Barlow, Lewis (Bud)	Husband of the 4th great-granddaughter		
Barlow, Megan Elizabeth	5th great-granddaughter	VII	7
Barlow, Stacy Ann	Wife of the 4th great-grandson		
Barrsis, Marie	Wife of the grandnephew		
Bateman, Brady Edmond	6th great-grandson	VIII	8
Bateman, Brian Matthew	Husband of the 5th great-granddaughter		
Baudouin, Amie Marie	5th great-granddaughter	VII	7
Baudouin, Catherine Mary	4th great-granddaughter	VI	6
Baudouin, Claire Louise	5th great-granddaughter	VII	7
Baudouin, Donald Michael, Jr	4th great-grandson	VI	6
Baudouin, Donald Michael, Sr.	Husband of the 3rd great-granddaughter		
Baudouin, Gary Michael	4th great-grandson	VI	6
Baudouin, Georgia Helene	4th great-granddaughter	VI	6
Baudouin, Gregory Thomas	4th great-grandson	VI	6
Baudouin, Irby T.	4th great-grandson	VI	6
Baudouin, Irby Telesphore, Jr.	Husband of the 3rd great-granddaughter		
Baudouin, Jane Frances	4th great-granddaughter	VI	6
Baudouin, Jennifer Rebecca	5th great-granddaughter	VII	7
Baudouin, Lois Margaret	4th great-granddaughter	VI	6
Baudouin, Patricia Maria	4th great-granddaughter	VI	6
Beall, Debbie	Wife of the 3rd great-grandson		
Bearb, Bridget	Wife of the 3rd great-grandson		
Beauchamp, Amanda Claire	5th great-granddaughter	VII	7
Beauchamp, Bryan Gene	Husband of the 4th great-granddaughter		
Beauchamp, Heather Jean	5th great-granddaughter	VII	7
Becnel, Bernard Benjamine, Sr.	Husband of the 3rd great-granddaughter		
Becnel, Chelsea Michelle	5th great-granddaughter	VII	7
Becnel, Claire Cecilia	Wife of the 4th great-grandson		
Becnel, Gabrielle Nicole	5th great-granddaughter	VII	7
Becnel, Kayla Christine	5th great-granddaughter	VII	7
Becnel, Marlene Marie	3rd great-granddaughter	V	5
Becnel, Matthew,(infant)	3rd great-grandson	V	5
Becnel, Michael,(infant)	3rd great-grandson	V	5
Becnel, Randy Joseph,(infant)	3rd great-grandson	V	5
Becnel, Ronny John	3rd great-grandson	V	5
Becnel, Thomas Paul	Husband of the 4th great-granddaughter		
Becnel, Verney E.,Jr.	3rd great-grandson	V	5
Becnel, Verney Etienne	Husband of the 2nd great-granddaughter		
Becnel, Wade Benedict	3rd great-grandson	V	5
Becnel, Zachary Thomas	5th great-grandson	VII	7
Belflower, Russell Lee	Husband of the 3rd great-grandniece		
Bellish, Annie, (Dinah)	Wife of the 2nd great-grandson		
Belsome, Adelaide	Wife of the grandson		
Belsome, André, Jr.	Half 2nd cousin of the wife		
Belsome, John Henry	Half 2nd cousin of the wife		
Belsome, Marie Marguerite	Half 2nd cousin of the wife		
Belsome, Melanie <Melazie>	Daughter-in-law		
Bennett, Rebecca	Wife of the 3rd great-grandson		
Bennett, Scarlet	Wife of the 3rd great-grandson		
Benson, Jean Anna	Wife of the 3rd great-grandson		

*Kinship of Jean Robért, *-****

Name	Relationship with Jean Robért	Civil	Canon
Bercegeay, Marie Edna	Wife of the 3rd great-grandson		
Bergeron, Alice	Wife of the 3rd great-grandson		
Bergeron, Brandi Jude	4th great-granddaughter	VI	6
Bergeron, Brett Elizabeth	4th great-granddaughter	VI	6
Bergeron, Elmo, Jr.	Husband of the 3rd great-granddaughter		
Berthelot, Helena Ann	Wife of the 4th great-grandson		
Bertrand, Alex J.	Great-grandnephew	V	4
Bertrand, Aléxis	Brother-in-law		
Bertrand, Charles A.	Grandnephew	IV	3
Bertrand, Jean Baptiste, Jr.	Son-in-law		
Bertrand, Leandre	Husband of the grandniece		
Bertrand, Louis	Grandnephew	IV	3
Bertrand, Louise	Niece	III	2
Bertrand, Louise Anna	Grandniece	IV	3
Bertrand, Marie Amelie	Grandniece	IV	3
Bertrand, Marie Delphine	Niece	III	2
Bertrand, Octavie F.	Grandniece	IV	3
Bertrand, Pierre Louis	Nephew	III	2
Bertrand, Pierre Louis II	Grandnephew	IV	3
Bertrand, Theodore	Great-grandnephew	V	4
Bertrand, Theogene	Great-grandnephew	V	4
Bertrand, Thomas Leo	Grandnephew	IV	3
Best, John	Husband of the 4th great-granddaughter		
Betty	Wife of the 2nd great-grandnephew		
Bienvenu, Alden	Husband of the 3rd great-granddaughter		
Bihm, Tommy Vincent	Husband of the 4th great-granddaughter		
Binder, Joseph Victor	Husband of the 4th great-granddaughter		
Birdsall, Susane Bercell	Wife of the grandnephew		
Birdsong, Amy Elizabeth	4th great-granddaughter	VI	6
Birdsong, Edmond Ker	Husband of the 3rd great-granddaughter		
Birdsong, John Taylor	4th great-grandson	VI	6
Birdsong, Joseph Allen	4th great-grandson	VI	6
Birdsong, Samuel Ker	4th great-grandson	VI	6
Bishop, Anne Marie	5th great-granddaughter	VII	7
Bishop, David Nolan	Husband of the 4th great-granddaughter		
Bishop, Julie Frances	5th great-granddaughter	VII	7
Blackwell, Randy	Husband of the 4th great-granddaughter		
Blades, Glenda Ann	Wife of the 3rd great-grandson		
Blanchard, Aimee Lynn	5th great-granddaughter	VII	7
Blanchard, Cathy J.	Wife of the 4th great-grandson		
Blanchard, Christine Theresa	4th great-granddaughter	VI	6
Blanchard, Clay Michael	5th great-grandson	VII	7
Blanchard, Constance Anne	4th great-granddaughter	VI	6
Blanchard, Courtney Marie	4th great-granddaughter	VI	6
Blanchard, Donna Marie	4th great-granddaughter	VI	6
Blanchard, Jennifer Marie	5th great-granddaughter	VII	7
Blanchard, Joseph, III	Husband of the 4th great-granddaughter		
Blanchard, Julie Therese	4th great-granddaughter	VI	6
Blanchard, Lauren Claire	4th great-granddaughter	VI	6
Blanchard, Laurie Elizabeth	5th great-granddaughter	VII	7
Blanchard, Lillian Theresa	3rd great-granddaughter	V	5
Blanchard, Living	Husband of the 4th great-granddaughter		
Blanchard, Madeline Marie	3rd great-granddaughter	V	5
Blanchard, Marvin Clay	4th great-grandson	VI	6
Blanchard, Raymond Francois	Husband of the 3rd great-granddaughter		

Kinship of Jean Robért, *-***

Name	Relationship with Jean Robért	Civil	Canon
Blanchard, Rebecca Anne	5th great-granddaughter	VII	7
Blanchard, Robert Courtland, Jr.	3rd great-grandson	V	5
Blanchard, Robert Courtland, Sr.	Husband of the 2nd great-granddaughter		
Blood, Leisa Gay	Wife of the 3rd great-grandson		
Blue, Amy Elizabeth, (Divorced 2007)	Ex-wife of the 4th great-grandson		
Blum, Kaysie Christine Nordby Anderson	5th great-granddaughter	VII	7
Blum, Sam Monette	5th great-grandson	VII	7
Boltin, Sherry	Wife of the 4th great-grandson		
Bonvillian, Jo Ann	Wife of the 4th great-grandson		
Borne, Betty	Wife of the 4th great-grandson		
Borne, Marie Louise, < Borise>	Wife of the great-grandson		
Borne, Shirlie	Wife of the 3rd great-grandson		
Bouchereau, Lori	Wife of the 3rd great-grandnephew		
Boudreaux, Brad Thomas	5th great-grandson	VII	7
Boudreaux, Bret Patrick	5th great-grandson	VII	7
Boudreaux, Daisy	Wife of the 2nd great-grandson		
Boudreaux, Darlene	Wife of the 4th great-grandson		
Boudreaux, Dawn Michelle	5th great-granddaughter	VII	7
Boudreaux, Gayle	Husband of the 4th great-granddaughter		
Boudreaux, Jaime Ann	5th great-granddaughter	VII	7
Boudreaux, Melvin	4th great-grandson	VI	6
Boudreaux, Michael Shane	5th great-grandson	VII	7
Boudreaux, Newell Roy	Husband of the 3rd great-granddaughter		
Boudreaux, Rob	Husband of the 4th great-granddaughter		
Boudreaux, Roy Thomas	Husband of the 4th great-granddaughter		
Boudreaux, Tilda	4th great-granddaughter	VI	6
Boudreaux, Troy Jude	5th great-grandson	VII	7
Boulanger, Chantal Marthe	Wife of the 3rd great-grandson		
Bourg, Bambi Ann	4th great-granddaughter	VI	6
Bourg, Bertile Joseph	4th great-grandson	VI	6
Bourg, Brad Paul	4th great-grandson	VI	6
Bourg, Brennan Michael	4th great-grandson	VI	6
Bourg, Claude, Jr.	Husband of the 3rd great-granddaughter		
Bourgeois, Andrew, Sr.	Husband of the 3rd great-granddaughter		
Bourgeois, Barbara	Wife of the 3rd great-grandson		
Bourgeois, Bertha	Wife of the 2nd great-grandson		
Bourgeois, Bryan Patrick	4th great-grandson	VI	6
Bourgeois, Charley Joseph	Husband of the 3rd great-granddaughter		
Bourgeois, Evelyn Marie	Wife of the 3rd great-grandson		
Bourgeois, Gussie J.	Husband of the 4th great-granddaughter		
Bourgeois, Irma	Wife of the grandnephew		
Bourgeois, Jeanette Marie	5th great-granddaughter	VII	7
Bourgeois, Julienne	Wife of the grandson		
Bourgeois, Lance Joseph	5th great-grandson	VII	7
Bourgeois, Marie Adele	Wife of the nephew		
Bourgeois, Marie Celine	Wife of the great-grandnephew		
Bourgeois, Mary Alice	Wife of the grandnephew		
Bourgeois, Mathew Charles	4th great-grandson	VI	6
Bourgeois, Michelle Renee	4th great-granddaughter	VI	6
Bourgeois, Randy, Jr.	5th great-grandson	VII	7
Bourgeois, Randy, Sr.	Husband of the 4th great-granddaughter		
Bourgeois, Thelma	Wife of the great-grandnephew		
Bourgoyne, Casey Lynne	5th great-granddaughter	VII	7
Bourgoyne, Chad Joseph	Husband of the 4th great-granddaughter		
Bourque, Cody Michael	5th great-grandson	VII	7

Kinship of Jean Robért, *-***

Name	Relationship with Jean Robért	Civil	Canon
Bourque, George Nicholas (Gee)	5th great-grandson	VII	7
Bourque, Joseph Mark	Husband of the 4th great-granddaughter		
Bourque, Josie Nicole Granier	6th great-granddaughter	VIII	8
Bourque, Paula Ann	Wife of the 3rd great-grandson		
Bourque, Russell	Husband of the 4th great-granddaughter		
Bourque, Shirly Ann	Wife of the 3rd great-grandson		
Boustany, Michele Elaine	Wife of the 3rd great-grandson		
Bouy, Euphrasie Froiselee, (Tante Pay-Pay), ***	Wife of the grandson		
Bowler, Timothy Allen	Husband of the 5th great-granddaughter		
Brady, Carole Claire	Wife of the 3rd great-grandson		
Branscum, Nancy Olivia	Wife of the 4th great-grandson		
Brantley, Romney	Wife of the 4th great-grandson		
Braud, Clint Anthony	5th great-grandson	VII	7
Braud, Connie Theresa	5th great-granddaughter	VII	7
Braud, Gary Joseph	Husband of the 4th great-granddaughter		
Braud, Gay Ann	Wife of the 3rd great-grandson		
Braud, Genie Marie	5th great-granddaughter	VII	7
Braud, James Edward, Jr	Husband of the 4th great-granddaughter		
Braud, Jamie Lynn	5th great-granddaughter	VII	7
Braud, Laura	Wife of the 4th great-grandson		
Braud, Rosalind Rita	Wife of the 3rd great-grandson		
Braud, Ryan Douglas	5th great-grandson	VII	7
Braud, Steffi	Wife of the 4th great-grandson		
Breard, Wendy Rose	Wife of the 4th great-grandson		
Breaux, Janice Mary	Wife of the 4th great-grandson		
Breaux, Toussaint Edouard Florent	Husband of the great-granddaughter		
Brewerton, Elizabeth Ruth	Wife of the great-grandson		
Brien, James Joseph, Jr.	Husband of the 4th great-granddaughter		
Brignac, Betty Anne	Wife of the 3rd great-grandson		
Brignac, Rena	Wife of the half 3rd great-grandnephew		
Brou, Adele Philomene	Great-grandniece	V	4
Brou, Alan John	4th great-grandson	VI	6
Brou, Albertine, (Tante Bat)	Wife of the great-grandson		
Brou, André Augustine, Jr. (Mickey)	3rd great-grandson	V	5
Brou, André Augustine, Sr. (Cap)	2nd great-grandson	IV	4
Brou, Anna Nell	2nd great-grandniece	VI	5
Brou, Antoine Otto	2nd great-grandson	IV	4
Brou, Antoine Paul	2nd great-grandson	IV	4
Brou, Audrey M.	3rd great-granddaughter	V	5
Brou, Beulah Cecile	2nd great-grandniece	VI	5
Brou, Carol Mae	2nd great-grandniece	VI	5
Brou, Cheryl Ann	4th great-granddaughter	VI	6
Brou, Clement Anthony	2nd great-grandnephew	VI	5
Brou, Clement Antoine	Husband of the great-grandniece		
Brou, Clemil Joseph	2nd great-grandnephew	VI	5
Brou, Dale John	3rd great-grandson	V	5
Brou, Dana Michelle	4th great-granddaughter	VI	6
Brou, David Paul	4th great-grandson	VI	6
Brou, Deborah Lin	4th great-granddaughter	VI	6
Brou, Delta Mary	2nd great-granddaughter	IV	4
Brou, Denise Marie	4th great-granddaughter	VI	6
Brou, Donald James	4th great-grandson	VI	6
Brou, Doris Thérése	3rd great-granddaughter	V	5
Brou, Edith Marie	2nd great-granddaughter	IV	4
Brou, Elaine Gail	4th great-granddaughter	VI	6

*Kinship of Jean Robért, *-****

Name	Relationship with Jean Robért	Civil	Canon
Brou, Euphrosine	Wife of the great-grandson		
Brou, Faustin Mammes	Husband of the grandniece		
Brou, Glenn Stephen	4th great-grandson	VI	6
Brou, Goldie Marie, (Giggle)	3rd great-granddaughter	V	5
Brou, Gordon William	4th great-grandson	VI	6
Brou, Grace Mary	3rd great-granddaughter	V	5
Brou, Gregory Michael	4th great-grandson	VI	6
Brou, Harold James	3rd great-grandson	V	5
Brou, Honore Augustin, (Tee Parrain)	Husband of the great-granddaughter		
Brou, Horace Joseph	2nd great-grandson	IV	4
Brou, Hubert Joseph, Fr.	3rd great-grandson	V	5
Brou, Irene Marie, (Shoot)	Great-grandniece	V	4
Brou, Ivy Ann	2nd great-grandniece	VI	5
Brou, James Joseph	4th great-grandson	VI	6
Brou, Jeanne Florence	Wife of the 3rd great-grandson		
Brou, Jeffrey John	4th great-grandson	VI	6
Brou, Jennifer Leigh	4th great-granddaughter	VI	6
Brou, Joan Mae	3rd great-granddaughter	V	5
Brou, John Robért	4th great-grandson	VI	6
Brou, Joseph Clemil	3rd great-grandson	V	5
Brou, Joseph Octave	2nd great-grandnephew	VI	5
Brou, Joyce Ann	3rd great-granddaughter	V	5
Brou, Julie Claire	4th great-granddaughter	VI	6
Brou, Karen Ann	4th great-granddaughter	VI	6
Brou, Kenneth Paul	3rd great-grandson	V	5
Brou, Laura Marie	4th great-granddaughter	VI	6
Brou, Lena	2nd great-grandniece	VI	5
Brou, Leone M.	2nd great-grandniece	VI	5
Brou, Leslie Marie	4th great-granddaughter	VI	6
Brou, Linda Marie	4th great-granddaughter	VI	6
Brou, Lucille	2nd great-granddaughter	IV	4
Brou, Lynn Anthony	3rd great-grandson	V	5
Brou, Marcel Jean	Great-grandnephew	V	4
Brou, Marcelle Theresa	3rd great-granddaughter	V	5
Brou, Margaret Ann	3rd great-granddaughter	V	5
Brou, Marie Elvie	2nd great-granddaughter	IV	4
Brou, Marie Noel	4th great-granddaughter	VI	6
Brou, Marie Therése	3rd great-granddaughter	V	5
Brou, Marie Octavie, *	Wife of the grandson		
Brou, Marjorie Rita, (Sr. Margaret)	3rd great-granddaughter	V	5
Brou, Marvin Anthony	3rd great-grandson	V	5
Brou, Mazie Mae	2nd great-grandniece	VI	5
Brou, Michelle Margaret	4th great-granddaughter	VI	6
Brou, Mildred Rita	2nd great-grandniece	VI	5
Brou, Octave Joseph	Great-grandnephew	V	4
Brou, Paul Charles	3rd great-grandson	V	5
Brou, Paula Jane	4th great-granddaughter	VI	6
Brou, Rene Francois, Sr.	Husband of the great-granddaughter		
Brou, Rene Francois, Jr.	2nd great-grandson	IV	4
Brou, Renée Claire	4th great-granddaughter	VI	6
Brou, Rita Philomene	2nd great-granddaughter	IV	4
Brou, Robert Joseph	2nd great-grandson	IV	4
Brou, Ronald Paul, Jr.	4th great-grandson	VI	6
Brou, Ronald Paul, Sr.	3rd great-grandson	V	5
Brou, Rowena Theresa	3rd great-granddaughter	V	5

Kinship of Jean Robért, *-***

Name	Relationship with Jean Robért	Civil	Canon
Brou, Sharon Elizabeth	4th great-granddaughter	VI	6
Brou, Sybil	4th great-granddaughter	VI	6
Brou, Thelma Marie	3rd great-granddaughter	V	5
Brou, Therése Arthemese Goldie	2nd great-granddaughter	IV	4
Brou, Warren Jude, Jr.	4th great-grandson	VI	6
Brou, Warren Jude, Sr.	3rd great-grandson	V	5
Broussard, David Gregg	Husband of the 3rd great-granddaughter		
Brown, Adam Michael	5th great-grandson	VII	7
Brown, Angela Catherine	Wife of the 4th great-grandson		
Brown, Billy, Jr.	5th great-grandson	VII	7
Brown, Billy, Sr.	Husband of the 4th great-granddaughter		
Brown, Larry, (Divorced)	Ex-husband of the 4th great-granddaughter		
Brown, Lauren	5th great-granddaughter	VII	7
Brown, Logan	5th great-grandson	VII	7
Brown, Lucas Paul	5th great-grandson	VII	7
Brown, Phyllis Ellen	Wife of the 3rd great-grandson		
Bruno, Paul	Husband of the 4th great-granddaughter		
Brusle, Antoine	Husband of the grandmother		
Burbank, Douglas	Husband of the 4th great-granddaughter		
Burbank, Elaine Nicole	5th great-granddaughter	VII	7
Burbank, Robért Douglas	5th great-grandson	VII	7
Burch, Charlene Ann	Wife of the 3rd great-grandson		
Burrage, Gerard Edward	Husband of the 4th great-granddaughter		
Burrage, Lindsay Catherine	5th great-granddaughter	VII	7
Burrage, Ryan Gerard	5th great-grandson	VII	7
Buss, Jennifer	Wife of the 3rd great-grandson		
Cadow, Jane	Wife of the 3rd great-grandson		
Caillet, Charles Joseph	4th great-grandson	VI	6
Caillet, Cyril Anthony, Jr.	3rd great-grandson	V	5
Caillet, Cyril Antoine, Sr.	Husband of the 2nd great-granddaughter		
Caillet, David Anthony	4th great-grandson	VI	6
Caillet, Edward Anthony	4th great-grandson	VI	6
Caillet, Edward Gerard	4th great-grandson	VI	6
Caillet, Florence Elizabeth	3rd great-granddaughter	V	5
Caillet, Frances Ellen	4th great-granddaughter	VI	6
Caillet, Hazel Theresa	3rd great-granddaughter	V	5
Caillet, Helen Denise	4th great-granddaughter	VI	6
Caillet, Helene	3rd great-granddaughter	V	5
Caillet, Irma	Wife of the 2nd great-grandson		
Caillet, Leola Sophie	3rd great-granddaughter	V	5
Caillet, Lois Marie	3rd great-granddaughter	V	5
Caillet, Lowell Paul	4th great-grandson	VI	6
Caillet, Mary Claire	4th great-granddaughter	VI	6
Caillet, Mary Joan	4th great-granddaughter	VI	6
Caillet, Muriel Ann	3rd great-granddaughter	V	5
Caillet, Odell Francis	3rd great-grandson	V	5
Caillet, Paul Christian	4th great-grandson	VI	6
Caillet, Paul Victor, (P.V.)	3rd great-grandson	V	5
Caillet, Paula Ruth	4th great-granddaughter	VI	6
Caillet, Peggy Jo	4th great-granddaughter	VI	6
Caillet, Shirley Mae	3rd great-granddaughter	V	5
Callegan, Earlene	Wife of the 2nd great-grandson		
Canatella, Cheryl Ann	4th great-granddaughter	VI	6
Canatella, John Joseph	Husband of the 3rd great-granddaughter		
Canatella, John Joseph	5th great-grandson	VII	7

Kinship of Jean Robért, *-***

Name	Relationship with Jean Robért	Civil	Canon
Canatella, John Joseph, Jr.	4th great-grandson	VI	6
Canatella, Kathleen Rose	Wife of the 4th great-grandson		
Canatella, Nikole Maree	5th great-granddaughter	VII	7
Canatella, Ryan Joseph	5th great-grandson	VII	7
Canatella, Todd James	4th great-grandson	VI	6
Canatella, Todd James, Jr.	5th great-grandson	VII	7
Candies, Davlynn Ann	Wife of the 4th great-grandson		
Cangelosia, Thechla Rita	Wife of the 3rd great-grandson		
Cannon, Barry Anthony	Husband of the 3rd great-granddaughter		
Cannon, Tara Terése	4th great-granddaughter	VI	6
Cannon, Wendi Renée	4th great-granddaughter	VI	6
Cantrell, Joseph Gregory	Husband of the 3rd great-grandniece		
Capello, Marjorie	Wife of the 2nd great-grandson		
Carbo, Gladys	Wife of the half 3rd great-grandnephew		
Carbo, Holly	Wife of the 3rd great-grandson		
Carithers, Russell D.	Husband of the 4th great-granddaughter		
Caro, Arthur	Husband of the grandniece		
Carpenter, Jenny	Wife of the 4th great-grandson		
Cart, Donna	Wife of the 4th great-grandson		
Casagrande, Ashley Nicole	4th great-granddaughter	VI	6
Casagrande, Jeffrey Joseph	4th great-grandson	VI	6
Casagrande, Joseph Edward, Jr.	Husband of the 3rd great-granddaughter		
Cascio, Karen Elizabeth	Wife of the 3rd great-grandson		
Castagnos, Jo Ann	Wife of the 4th great-grandson		
Catanzaro, Amanda Elaine	5th great-granddaughter	VII	7
Catanzaro, Douglas Paul	5th great-grandson	VII	7
Catanzaro, Joseph Frank	Husband of the 4th great-granddaughter		
Cavalier, Joe	Husband of the 4th great-granddaughter		
Cazenave, Roy	Husband of the half 2nd great-grandniece		
Cedotal, Keith Michael	Husband of the 4th great-granddaughter		
Chabaud, Alvin J.	Husband of the 2nd great-granddaughter		
Chachere, Jean	Husband of the 4th great-granddaughter		
Chalier, Marie Aimee,<Chaleur>	Wife of the grandson		
Champagne, Adelaide	Wife of the half 1st cousin		
Champagne, Auguste	Wife of the great-grandson		
Champagne, Dianne, (Dee)	4th great-granddaughter	VI	6
Champagne, Eugene Oscar	Nephew of the wife		
Champagne, Eugene, Jr.	Husband of the grandniece		
Champagne, Eugene, Sr.	Grandnephew of the wife		
Champagne, Irving P.	Husband of the 3rd great-granddaughter		
Champagne, Jean Baptiste III	Nephew of the wife		
Champagne, Joseph Florestan	Grandnephew of the wife		
Champagne, Joseph Florestan	Husband of the grandniece		
Champagne, Joseph Iba	Husband of the great-grandniece		
Champagne, Larry, (Specks)	4th great-grandson	VI	6
Champagne, Marie Celestine	2nd great-grandniece of the wife		
Champagne, Marie Orphise	2nd great-grandniece	VI	5
Champagne, Paul	4th great-grandson	VI	6
Champagne, Paula Ann	4th great-granddaughter	VI	6
Champagne, Theresa	Wife of the great-grandnephew		
Champaigne, Honorine	Wife of the 2nd great-grandson		
Charmaine	Wife of the 3rd great-grandson		
Chastain, Sonny	Husband of the 3rd great-grandniece		
Chauvin, Albert Francois	Husband of the 2nd great-grandniece		
Chauvin, Alcide	Husband of the grandniece		

*Kinship of Jean Robért, *-****

Name	Relationship with Jean Robért	Civil	Canon
Chauvin, Anita Louise	Wife of the 4th great-grandson		
Chauvin, Donald Julian	2nd great-grandnephew	VI	5
Chauvin, Gerald	Great-grandnephew	V	4
Chauvin, Heloise Marie	2nd great-grandniece	VI	5
Chauvin, Hypolite	Husband of the grandniece		
Chauvin, Ida Marie	2nd great-grandniece	VI	5
Chauvin, Julie	3rd great-grandniece	VII	6
Chauvin, Mae Merancia	3rd great-grandniece	VII	6
Chauvin, Marie Marceline	3rd great-grandniece	VII	6
Chauvin, Rene Jean	Great-grandnephew	V	4
Chauvin, Simon	3rd great-grandnephew	VII	6
Chauvin, Vlyna Blanche	3rd great-grandniece	VII	6
Chrisman, Jeffery Steven	5th great-grandson	VII	7
Chrisman, Jeffrey Anthony	Husband of the 4th great-granddaughter		
Chrisman, Jillian Elizabeth	5th great-granddaughter	VII	7
Chrisman, Nikki Allison	5th great-granddaughter	VII	7
Cicero, Betty Carole	Wife of the 2nd great-grandson		
Cieutat, Gertrude	Wife of the 2nd great-grandson		
Cire, Elise Agnes	Wife of the 2nd great-grandson		
Cire, Odette	Wife of the 2nd great-grandson		
Cire, Rose Elizabeth	Wife of the 2nd great-grandson		
Clarac, Nathalie	Wife of the 4th great-grandson		
Clouatre, Deborah	Wife of the 3rd great-grandson		
Coates, Toni	Wife of the 3rd great-grandson		
Coignet, Jean Baptiste	Husband of the niece		
Cointment, Gladys Lucille, (Dee-Dee)	Wife of the great-grandson		
Collins, Brennan Robért	Half 4th great-grandnephew	VIII	7
Collins, James J., Jr.	Husband of the half 3rd great-grandniece		
Collins, James Joseph	Half 4th great-grandnephew	VIII	7
Collins, Michael Waldon	Half 4th great-grandnephew	VIII	7
Comeaux, Hazel	Wife of the great-grandson		
Comeaux, Preston	Husband of the 2nd great-granddaughter		
Compagna, Stephen Joseph	Husband of the 4th great-granddaughter		
Conner, Connie Marie, (Divorced)	Wife of the 4th great-grandson		
Cormier, Joyce Marie	Wife of the 4th great-grandson		
Courville, Betty	Wife of the 4th great-grandson		
Cox, Barth Louis	4th great-grandson	VI	6
Cox, George Louis, Jr.	Husband of the 3rd great-granddaughter		
Cox, Janeen Anne	4th great-granddaughter	VI	6
Cox, Jedd Joseph	4th great-grandson	VI	6
Cox, Penny Marie	4th great-granddaughter	VI	6
Cox, Thad Jude	4th great-grandson	VI	6
Cranfield, Callen Micah	5th great-grandson	VII	7
Cranfield, Clay	Husband of the 4th great-granddaughter		
Cranfield, Eileen Mara	5th great-granddaughter	VII	7
Crews, Cheryl Ann	Wife of the 4th great-grandson		
Cruickshank, Jonalyn	Wife of the 3rd great-grandson		
Dagebert, Marie	Great-grandmother	III	3
Daigle, Carmen Marie	Wife of the 3rd great-grandson		
Daigle, Chrystal	4th great-granddaughter	VI	6
Daigle, Dana	4th great-granddaughter	VI	6
Daigle, Roy	Husband of the 3rd great-granddaughter		
Daigle, Terri	4th great-granddaughter	VI	6
Danos, Herbert Joseph	Husband of the 3rd great-granddaughter		
Danos, Jacqueline Marie	4th great-granddaughter	VI	6

Kinship of Jean Robért, *-***

Name	Relationship with Jean Robért	Civil	Canon
Danos, Jane Marie	4th great-granddaughter	VI	6
Danos, Jerome Paul	4th great-grandson	VI	6
Danos, John Herbert	4th great-grandson	VI	6
Danos, Joseph Charles	4th great-grandson	VI	6
Danos, Joy Noella	4th great-granddaughter	VI	6
Danos, Leigh Ann	5th great-granddaughter	VII	7
Dardard, Augustine	Husband of the great-granddaughter		
Dardenne, Mary Clair	Wife of the 4th great-grandson		
Dardin, Dana Shea, (adopted)	3rd great-granddaughter	V	5
Dardin, Victor Edward, (adopted)	3rd great-grandson	V	5
Daughdrill, Melissa Ann	Wife of the 3rd great-grandson		
Davison, Pamela	Wife of the 4th great-grandson		
Dawson, Katherine Nicole	4th great-granddaughter	VI	6
Dawson, Stephen Mark	Husband of the 3rd great-granddaughter		
Decareaux, Edna Marie	Wife of the 2nd great-grandson		
Decareaux, Marie	Wife of the 2nd great-grandnephew		
Decareaux, Ruth	Wife of the 2nd great-grandson		
Decarreau, Fernand	Husband of the 2nd great-granddaughter		
Decoteau, Braize Renée	5th great-granddaughter	VII	7
Decoteau, Dason Joseph	5th great-grandson	VII	7
Decoteau, Davey	Husband of the 4th great-granddaughter		
Decoteau, Devon P.	Husband of the 5th great-granddaughter		
Decoteau, Michael Wayne	6th great-grandson	VIII	8
Decoteau, Seline Victoria	6th great-granddaughter	VIII	8
Degruise, Josephine Verlouan	Wife of the grandnephew		
Degruise, Victorin	Husband of the great-grandniece		
Delatte, Debbie	Wife of the 3rd great-grandnephew		
Delaune, Cale Murphey	5th great-grandson	VII	7
Delaune, Cedric Jude	Husband of the 4th great-granddaughter		
Delaune, Clint Michael	5th great-grandson	VII	7
Delaune, Colby Bernard	5th great-grandson	VII	7
Delaune, Cynthia Ann	Wife of the 4th great-grandson		
Delaune, James Rene	Husband of the 3rd great-grandniece		
Delaune, Warner	Husband of the 3rd great-grandniece		
Delaune, William Bernard	Husband of the 4th great-granddaughter		
Deroche, Ethel	Wife of the 2nd great-grandnephew		
DeVries, Jason Robert	4th great-grandson	VI	6
DeVries, Jeffrey Ross	4th great-grandson	VI	6
DeVries, Robert Cok	Husband of the 3rd great-granddaughter		
Diez, Michael David	Husband of the 4th great-granddaughter		
DiGiovanni, Kori Jude	4th great-granddaughter	VI	6
DiGiovanni, Pat Joseph	Husband of the 3rd great-granddaughter		
DiGiovanni, Pat Joseph, Jr.	4th great-grandson	VI	6
Dirks, Charles L.	Husband of the 3rd great-granddaughter		
Dixon, Lyle	Husband of the 4th great-granddaughter		
Doiron, Todd Christopher	Husband of the 4th great-granddaughter		
Dominguez, Jody	Wife of the 3rd great-grandson		
Donlin, Michelle Juliana	Wife of the 3rd great-grandson		
Doran, Mary Myrthee	Wife of the 2nd great-grandson		
Dore, Christine	Wife of the uncle		
Dornier, Christine Anne	4th great-granddaughter	VI	6
Dornier, Joseph Garland	Husband of the 3rd great-granddaughter		
Dornier, Paula A.	Wife of the 4th great-grandson		
Doub, Susan Marguerite	Wife of the 4th great-grandson		
DuBois, H. Paul	Husband of the 3rd great-granddaughter		

Kinship of Jean Robért, *-***

Name	Relationship with Jean Robért	Civil	Canon
Dubois, Meché Ann	4th great-granddaughter	VI	6
Dubois, Terry Gail	Husband of the 3rd great-granddaughter		
Dubois, Todd	4th great-grandson	VI	6
Ducote, Beryl Jane	Wife of the 2nd great-grandson		
Dugas, Annabel Mary	Wife of the 2nd great-grandson		
Dugas, Loretta Cecile	Wife of the 2nd great-grandson		
Dugas, Marie	Wife of the 2nd great-grandson		
Duhan, J.D., Jr.	Husband of the 3rd great-grandniece		
Duhe, Cindy	Wife of the 3rd great-grandson		
Dunham, Melba L.	Wife of the 2nd great-grandson		
Dupeire, Earnest	Husband of the 2nd great-granddaughter		
Duplechin, Sheri	Wife of the 4th great-grandson		
Duplessis, Dana	Ex-wife of the 4th great-grandson		
Duplessis, Rachel Lyn	Wife of the 3rd great-grandson		
Dupre, Emile	Husband of the 4th great-granddaughter		
Dupre', Verna Louise	Wife of the 3rd great-grandson		
Dupuis	Brother-in-law		
Dupuis, Rose Emma	Niece	III	2
Durapau, Living	Wife of the 3rd great-grandson		
Ebey, Betty	Wife of the 3rd great-grandnephew		
Eckert, Donna Lynn	Wife of the 4th great-grandson		
Edelmaire, Andre, Jr.	Half 1st cousin of the wife		
Edelmaire, Andre, Sr.	Half uncle of the wife		
Edelmaire, Jean Adam	Grandfather of the wife		
Edelmaire, Marie Magdelaine, * ** ***	Mother-in-law		
Edelmayer, Johann Adam	Half granduncle of the wife		
Edelmayer, Marianne	Half 1st cousin once removed of the wife		
Edelmeier, Marie Christine	Half 1st cousin once removed of the wife		
Edelmeyer, Johann H. J.	Great-grandfather of the wife		
Edrington, Amy Elizabeth	5th great-granddaughter	VII	7
Edrington, Cali Ann	6th great-granddaughter	VIII	8
Edrington, Katelyn Elizabeth	6th great-granddaughter	VIII	8
Edrington, Nicholas K. III	Husband of the 4th great-granddaughter		
Edrington, Nicholas K. IV	5th great-grandson	VII	7
Egros, Bruno Joseph, Jr. (Divorced)	Ex-husband of the 3rd great-granddaughter		
Egros, Bruno Joseph, III	4th great-grandson	VI	6
Egros, Jamie Allison	4th great-granddaughter	VI	6
Eliassen, Elinor Margaret	Wife of the 3rd great-grandson		
Elisar, Brandon Scot	4th great-grandson	VI	6
Elisar, Britney Nicole	4th great-granddaughter	VI	6
Elisar, Jody Don	Husband of the 3rd great-granddaughter		
Elisar, Kristi Danielle	4th great-granddaughter	VI	6
Epstein, Adam Albert	4th great-grandson	VI	6
Epstein, Brett Myer	4th great-grandson	VI	6
Epstein, Richard	Husband of the 3rd great-granddaughter		
Esneault, Cora	Wife of the great-grandnephew		
Fahrig, Gwendolyn Bernice	Wife of the 3rd great-grandson		
Falcon, Andra Constance	3rd great-grandniece	VII	6
Falcon, Andrew Joseph	Husband of the 2nd great-grandniece		
Falcon, Drew Thomas	3rd great-grandnephew	VII	6
Falcon, Joseph Nelson	3rd great-grandnephew	VII	6
Falcon, Julie Ann	3rd great-grandniece	VII	6
Falcon, Paul Brou	3rd great-grandnephew	VII	6
Falcon, Simone Marie	3rd great-grandniece	VII	6
Falgoust, Antoinette	Wife of the 3rd great-grandson		

*Kinship of Jean Robért, *-****

Name	Relationship with Jean Robért	Civil	Canon
algoust, Elia	Wife of the 2nd great-grandson		
algoust, Louise Augustine	Wife of the great-grandnephew		
algoust, Sylvia	Wife of the 3rd great-grandnephew		
andel, Mary Elizabeth, (Nookie)	Wife of the 3rd great-grandson		
arris, John Joseph	Husband of the 3rd great-granddaughter		
aucheux, Anatole Joseph	Husband of the 3rd great-granddaughter		
aucheux, Andre	Half nephew	III	2
aucheux, Andre	Half grandnephew	IV	3
aucheux, Anita	Half 2nd great-grandniece	VI	5
aucheux, Arsene	Half grandniece	IV	3
aucheux, Arthemise	Wife of the nephew		
aucheux, Arthemise Marie	Half niece	III	2
aucheux, Benoit Alphonse Alfred	Half nephew	III	2
aucheux, Delia Felonise	Wife of the grandson		
aucheux, Dorian Jeremiah	5th great-grandson	VII	7
aucheux, Emile (Conoon)	Husband of the 3rd great-granddaughter		
aucheux, Eugene	Half grandnephew	IV	3
aucheux, Eugenie	Half grandniece	IV	3
aucheux, Eveline Anne	Half great-grandniece	V	4
aucheux, Felonise	Wife of the half nephew		
aucheux, Fergus	Half great-grandnephew	V	4
aucheux, Francois	Half nephew	III	2
aucheux, Francoise Arsene	Half niece	III	2
aucheux, Genevieve Esteve	Half niece	III	2
aucheux, Hortense Agatha	Wife of the grandnephew		
aucheux, James Patrick III	5th great-grandson	VII	7
aucheux, James Patrick, Jr.	4th great-grandson	VI	6
aucheux, James Patrick, Sr.	Husband of the 3rd great-granddaughter		
aucheux, Jean Christain	Half grandnephew	IV	3
aucheux, Jean Ezra	Half great-grandnephew	V	4
aucheux, Jean M.	Half 2nd great-grandnephew	VI	5
aucheux, Joseph Severin	Half grandnephew	IV	3
aucheux, Julie	Daughter-in-law		
aucheux, Leone	Wife of the 2nd great-grandson		
aucheux, Lisa Marie	4th great-granddaughter	VI	6
aucheux, Living	Half 2nd great-grandniece	VI	5
aucheux, Louis Francoise	Husband of the half aunt		
aucheux, Louis III	Half nephew	III	2
aucheux, Ma. Fergus	Half grandnephew	IV	3
aucheux, Marie	Half 1st cousin once removed	V	3
aucheux, Marie Celina	Half grandniece	IV	3
aucheux, Marie Felicie	Half 2nd great-grandniece	VI	5
aucheux, Marie Mathilda	Half great-grandniece	V	4
aucheux, Melanie Alminte	Half 2nd great-grandniece	VI	5
aucheux, Michelle Ann	4th great-granddaughter	VI	6
aucheux, Myrtille Antoinette	Half niece	III	2
aucheux, Norbert	Half nephew	III	2
aucheux, Pierre	Half 1st cousin	IV	2
aucheux, Pierre Amedee	Half nephew	III	2
aucheux, Pierre Louis, Jr. (Touchet)	Half brother-in-law		
aucheux, Rosa	Wife of the 2nd great-grandson		
aucheux, Seraphin	Half grandnephew	IV	3
aucheux, Shannon Ann	4th great-granddaughter	VI	6
aucheux, Theresie	Wife of the half nephew		
aucheux, Thildroud	Half grandnephew	IV	3

*Kinship of Jean Robért, *-****

Name	Relationship with Jean Robért	Civil	Canon
Faucheux, Ursin	Half grandnephew	IV	3
Faucheux, Ursin	Half great-grandnephew	V	4
Faucheux, Victor Louis	Half great-grandnephew	V	4
Favre, Living	Husband of the 4th great-granddaughter		
Felder, Melissa Gerianne	Wife of the 4th great-grandson		
Fell, John Steven	Husband of the 4th great-granddaughter		
Fitch, Althea Ann	Wife of the 4th great-grandson		
Fitzgerald, Adrian Ellis	Husband of the 4th great-granddaughter		
Fleniken, Dawn Michelle	5th great-granddaughter	VII	7
Fleniken, Randy Keith	Husband of the 4th great-granddaughter		
Flint, Renae	Ex-wife of the 3rd great-grandson		
Flood, Gerald Francis, (Jerry)	Husband of the 4th great-granddaughter		
Foerster, Brenda Lynn	Wife of the 4th great-grandson		
Folse, Agnes Zoe	Wife of the grandnephew		
Folse, Amelie	Wife of the grandnephew		
Folse, Antoine Royley	Husband of the 3rd great-granddaughter		
Folse, Bernard Marcellus	Husband of the niece		
Folse, Catherine Adele	Grandniece	IV	3
Folse, Edward (Edouard)	Husband of the niece		
Folse, Eugene, Jr.	Grandnephew	IV	3
Folse, Eugene, Sr.	Husband of the niece		
Folse, Eugenie	Great-grandniece	V	4
Folse, Euphrosine	Grandniece	IV	3
Folse, Felicite Azema, **	Wife of the nephew		
Folse, Felix	Husband of the grandniece		
Folse, Francois	Great-grandnephew	V	4
Folse, Hector Joseph	Husband of the great-granddaughter		
Folse, Hermine	Wife of the great-grandson		
Folse, Jean Norbert	Husband of the grandniece		
Folse, Joseph	Great-grandnephew	V	4
Folse, Joseph	Husband of the great-grandniece		
Folse, Julienne Zulema	Grandniece	IV	3
Folse, Marcellus Benoit	Husband of the grandniece		
Folse, Marguerite Ophelia	Grandniece	IV	3
Folse, Marie Almaise	Grandniece	IV	3
Folse, Marie Annette	Great-grandniece	V	4
Folse, Marie Euphamie	Wife of the half great-grandnephew		
Folse, Marie Hermine	Great-grandniece	V	4
Folse, Mathilde	Great-grandniece	V	4
Folse, Norbert	Great-grandnephew	V	4
Folse, Octave	Grandnephew	IV	3
Folse, Oleus Pierre	2nd great-grandnephew	VI	5
Folse, Palmyre	Grandniece	IV	3
Ford, Charles Joseph	4th great-grandson	VI	6
Ford, Joseph Patrick	Husband of the 3rd great-granddaughter		
Ford, Living	4th great-grandson	VI	6
Ford, Living	4th great-granddaughter	VI	6
Ford, Martha Bridgitte	Wife of the 3rd great-grandson		
Fortier, Nita	Wife of the 2nd great-grandnephew		
Fortner, William D.	Husband of the 3rd great-granddaughter		
Foss, Toue	Wife of the 4th great-grandson		
Foster, Debra Ann	Wife of the 4th great-grandson		
Foster, Frankie	Wife of the 3rd great-grandson		
Fournet, Anne Elizabeth	Wife of the 4th great-grandson		
Fournier, Helen Mae	Wife of the 3rd great-grandson		

Kinship of Jean Robért, *-***

Name	Relationship with Jean Robért	Civil	Canon
Foxworth, Emmet Allen	4th great-grandson	VI	6
Foxworth, Emmett Allen, Sr.	Husband of the 3rd great-granddaughter		
Foxworth, Steven Glen	4th great-grandson	VI	6
Foxworth, Tammy Ann	4th great-granddaughter	VI	6
Franchebois, Sydney Lee	Wife of the 3rd great-grandson		
Frederic, Patrick Jude	Husband of the 3rd great-granddaughter		
Frederick, Angelique Alice	Wife of the half great-grandnephew		
Freeze, Hugh Alphonso	Husband of the 4th great-granddaughter		
Fremin, Dale Joseph, Jr.	Husband of the 4th great-granddaughter		
Friloux, Dennis J.	Husband of the 3rd great-granddaughter		
Friloux, Edgar Joseph	Husband of the 3rd great-granddaughter		
Friloux, George J.	Husband of the great-granddaughter		
Friloux, Lucia	Wife of the great-grandson		
Friloux, Winfield Joseph	4th great-grandson	VI	6
Fryoux, Raymond Anthony, Jr.	Husband of the 4th great-granddaughter		
Fuselier, Gerald Anthony	Husband of the 3rd great-granddaughter		
Gabor, Virginia	Wife of the 2nd great-grandnephew		
Gadel, Ann Marie	Wife of the 3rd great-grandson		
Gallagher, Kristy	Wife of the 4th great-grandson		
Gant, Debra	Wife of the 4th great-grandson		
Gaspard, Lee Roy F.	Husband of the half 3rd great-grandniece		
Gaubert, Eunice	Wife of the 3rd great-grandson		
Gaudet, Charles Francois	Husband of the grandniece		
Gaudet, Charles Myrtile	Husband of the grandniece		
Gaudet, Hortense Aimee	Wife of the grandnephew		
Gaughan, John Martin	Husband of the 4th great-granddaughter		
Gauthier, Cedric Alexandre	5th great-granddaughter	VII	7
Gauthier, Everett Paul, Jr.	Husband of the 3rd great-granddaughter		
Gauthier, Everett Paul, III (Rett)	4th great-grandson	VI	6
Gauthier, Lindsey Marie	4th great-granddaughter	VI	6
Gauthier, Philippe Rene	4th great-grandson	VI	6
Gauthier, Samuel Everett	5th great-grandson	VII	7
Gautreau, Brittni Nicole	Wife of the 4th great-grandson		
Gautreau, Christen	Wife of the 5th great-grandson		
Gautreau, Mildred	Wife of the 2nd great-grandson		
Gautreau, Myrtle Marie	Wife of the 3rd great-grandson		
Gautreaux, Craig	Husband of the 4th great-granddaughter		
George, Samantha Vondel	Wife of the 4th great-grandson		
George, Sarah Marie	Wife of the 4th great-grandson		
Glynn, Laura Nell	Wife of the 3rd great-grandson		
Gomez, Carolyn	Wife of the 3rd great-grandson		
Gonzales, Jane	Wife of the 3rd great-grandson		
Gonzales, John	Husband of the 3rd great-granddaughter		
Gonzales, Signa M., (Patsy)	Wife of the 2nd great-grandson		
Gonzales, Warren H.	Husband of the 2nd great-granddaughter		
Goodman, Vicki Lynn	Wife of the 4th great-grandson		
Goodspeed, Janette Michelle	4th great-granddaughter	VI	6
Goodspeed, Kevin Charles	4th great-grandson	VI	6
Goodspeed, Mitchell H.	Husband of the 3rd great-granddaughter		
Goodspeed, Rani Marie	4th great-granddaughter	VI	6
Goodspeed, Rome Angette	4th great-granddaughter	VI	6
Granberry, Lynn	Wife of the 3rd great-grandson		
Granier, Anna Apolonia	Wife of the great-grandson		
Granier, Jaime Yvonne	Wife of the 5th great-grandson		
Granier, Marie Azelie	Wife of the great-grandson		

*Kinship of Jean Robért, *-****

Name	Relationship with Jean Robért	Civil	Canon
Granier, Marie Elodie	Wife of the great-grandson		
Granier, Marie Felicite	Wife of the great-grandson		
Gravois, Noland	4th great-grandnephew of the wife		
Green, Bryan Craig	Husband of the 4th great-granddaughter		
Green, Matthew William	5th great-grandson	VII	7
Green, Megan Allyson	5th great-granddaughter	VII	7
Green, Molly Elizabeth	5th great-granddaughter	VII	7
Guagliardo, Anthea	Wife of the 3rd great-grandson		
Guercio, Brenda Theresa	4th great-granddaughter	VI	6
Guercio, Camella Catherine	4th great-granddaughter	VI	6
Guercio, Josephine	Wife of the 3rd great-grandson		
Guercio, Luke H.	4th great-grandson	VI	6
Guercio, Maria	4th great-granddaughter	VI	6
Guercio, Marian Theresa	4th great-granddaughter	VI	6
Guercio, Marilyn Ann	4th great-granddaughter	VI	6
Guercio, Russell Joseph	4th great-grandson	VI	6
Guercio, Sam J., Sr. (Blue)	Husband of the 3rd great-granddaughter		
Guercio, Sam Joseph, Jr.	4th great-grandson	VI	6
Guidry, Ashley Simone	5th great-granddaughter	VII	7
Guidry, Emma	Wife of the 3rd great-grandson		
Guidry, Hope Ann	Wife of the 4th great-grandson		
Guidry, Simon,(Benny)	Husband of the 4th great-granddaughter		
Guillory, Ogden Luke	Husband of the half 3rd great-grandniece		
Guillot, Aline	Wife of the grandson		
Guillot, Anne Elizabeth	Wife of the 4th great-grandson		
Guillot, Bryan Joseph, Jr.	4th great-grandson	VI	6
Guillot, Bryan Joseph,Sr.	Husband of the 3rd great-granddaughter		
Guillot, Diane Marie	4th great-granddaughter	VI	6
Guillot, Julie Marie	4th great-granddaughter	VI	6
Guillot, Keith Joseph	4th great-grandson	VI	6
Guillot, Marie Louise	Great-grandmother	III	3
Guillot, Melissa Ann	Wife of the 3rd great-grandson		
Guillot, Michael Joseph, (infant)	4th great-grandson	VI	6
Guillot, Michelle Marie	4th great-granddaughter	VI	6
Guillot, Robin Marie	4th great-granddaughter	VI	6
Guillotte, Pauline Ophelia	Wife of the grandnephew		
Guistiniano, Anthony Jude	4th great-grandson	VI	6
Guistiniano, Blaine Nicholas	4th great-grandson	VI	6
Guistiniano, Erin Theresa	4th great-granddaughter	VI	6
Guistiniano, Joseph Paul	Husband of the 3rd great-granddaughter		
Guistiniano, Joseph Paul,Jr.	4th great-grandson	VI	6
Guistiniano, Robin Jude	4th great-granddaughter	VI	6
Guistiniano, Todd Gerald	4th great-grandson	VI	6
Hacker, Kimberly Georgia	Wife of the 4th great-grandson		
Hanson, Belvas Lynn	Wife of the 4th great-grandson		
Harelson, Donald Ray	Husband of the 3rd great-granddaughter		
Harelson, Gary Paul	4th great-grandson	VI	6
Harelson, Glen Thomas	4th great-grandson	VI	6
Harelson, Jacob Charles	5th great-grandson	VII	7
Harelson, Jennifer Lynne	5th great-granddaughter	VII	7
Harelson, Jody Robért	4th great-grandson	VI	6
Harelson, Jonathan Hebert	5th great-grandson	VII	7
Harelson, Wade Anthony	4th great-grandson	VI	6
Hargrave, Mildred	Wife of the 4th great-grandson		
Harlan, Eric Hampton	Husband of the 3rd great-granddaughter		

Kinship of Jean Robért, *-***

Name	Relationship with Jean Robért	Civil	Canon
Harlan, Robért Scott	4th great-grandson	VI	6
Harlan, Stephen Joseph	4th great-grandson	VI	6
Harp, Lettie	Wife of the 3rd great-grandson		
Harper, Jody	Wife of the 2nd great-grandnephew		
Harvey, Benjamin Gayle	4th great-grandson	VI	6
Harvey, Brittney Nichole	4th great-granddaughter	VI	6
Harvey, Bryan Taylor	4th great-grandson	VI	6
Harvey, Caberial Alexandria	4th great-granddaughter	VI	6
Harvey, Courtney Ann	4th great-granddaughter	VI	6
Harvey, George Brian	3rd great-grandson	V	5
Harvey, Jesseca Lee Ann	4th great-granddaughter	VI	6
Harvey, Kathryn Olivia	4th great-granddaughter	VI	6
Harvey, Lainey Cait	4th great-grandson	VI	6
Harvey, Lauren Rene	4th great-granddaughter	VI	6
Harvey, Lynsey Nicole	4th great-granddaughter	VI	6
Harvey, Macey Elise	4th great-granddaughter	VI	6
Harvey, Meghan Elizabeth	4th great-granddaughter	VI	6
Harvey, Monique Antonia	4th great-granddaughter	VI	6
Harvey, Morgan Elizabeth	4th great-granddaughter	VI	6
Harvey, Robert Doyle	3rd great-grandson	V	5
Harvey, Valerie Ann	3rd great-granddaughter	V	5
Harvey, Woodson III	3rd great-grandson	V	5
Harvey, Woodson, Jr.	Husband of the 2nd great-granddaughter		
Harvey, Wynn Traylor	3rd great-grandson	V	5
Harvey, Wynn Traylor II	4th great-grandson	VI	6
Haydel, Achille	Husband of the grandniece		
Haydel, Antoine Ernest	3rd great-grandson	V	5
Haydel, Ashley Anne	5th great-granddaughter	VII	7
Haydel, Cesaire Eva	Great-grandniece	V	4
Haydel, Chris, Rev.	4th great-grandson	VI	6
Haydel, Craig David	4th great-grandson	VI	6
Haydel, Damien Dale	Husband of the 4th great-granddaughter		
Haydel, Ernest	Husband of the 2nd great-granddaughter		
Haydel, Faith Elizabeth	5th great-granddaughter	VII	7
Haydel, George J., Sr	Husband of the 3rd great-granddaughter		
Haydel, Jennie Marie	3rd great-granddaughter	V	5
Haydel, Jessie Joseph	3rd great-grandson	V	5
Haydel, Kenneth	4th great-grandson	VI	6
Haydel, Kenneth James, Jr.	5th great-grandson	VII	7
Haydel, Laurance	2nd great-grandniece of the wife		
Haydel, Marie Antonia	Great-grandniece	V	4
Haydel, Marie Azelie	Wife of the grandson		
Haydel, Rita Theresa	3rd great-granddaughter	V	5
Haydel, Sam	Husband of the 2nd great-granddaughter		
Haydel, Sandy Lee	5th great-granddaughter	VII	7
Hayes, Margaret	Wife of the 4th great-grandson		
Hebert, Alexander Paul	4th great-grandson	VI	6
Hebert, Annette Marie	Wife of the great-grandson		
Hebert, Austin Gregory	4th great-grandson	VI	6
Hebert, Brenen	Husband of the 4th great-granddaughter		
Hebert, Cameron Michael	4th great-grandson	VI	6
Hebert, Catherine	Wife of the 4th great-grandson		
Hebert, Catherine Marie	4th great-granddaughter	VI	6
Hebert, Celeste Marie	4th great-granddaughter	VI	6
Hebert, Cleo Joseph, Jr.	Husband of the 2nd great-granddaughter		

*Kinship of Jean Robért, *-****

Name	Relationship with Jean Robért	Civil	Canon
Hebert, Cliff Michael	3rd great-grandson	V	5
Hebert, Colin Gregory	4th great-grandson	VI	6
Hebert, Curtis Joseph	Husband of the 4th great-granddaughter		
Hebert, David Ryan	4th great-grandson	VI	6
Hebert, Dean Gregory	3rd great-grandson	V	5
Hebert, Edna	Wife of the 2nd great-grandnephew		
Hebert, Emilie Marie	4th great-granddaughter	VI	6
Hebert, James Philip	Husband of the 3rd great-granddaughter		
Hebert, Jeffery Paul	3rd great-grandson	V	5
Hebert, Kaitlyn Renée	5th great-granddaughter	VII	7
Hebert, Kaycee Lynn	5th great-granddaughter	VII	7
Hebert, Matthew Joseph	4th great-grandson	VI	6
Hebert, Michelle Theresa	5th great-granddaughter	VII	7
Hebert, Monica Lynn	Wife of the 3rd great-grandson		
Hebert, Rachel Marie	5th great-granddaughter	VII	7
Hebert, René	Husband of the 4th great-granddaughter		
Hebert, Sarah Alexandra	4th great-granddaughter	VI	6
Hedberg, Cathy	Wife of the 4th great-grandson		
Hellouin, Amy	3rd great-granddaughter	V	5
Hellouin, Brent, Sr.	3rd great-grandson	V	5
Hellouin, Carl	3rd great-grandson	V	5
Hellouin, Martin Carville, Dr.	Husband of the 2nd great-granddaughter		
Hellouin, Mitzi	3rd great-granddaughter	V	5
Herbert, Albert Joseph	Great-grandnephew	V	4
Herbert, Alexander Joseph	5th great-grandson	VII	7
Herbert, Amedee Vasseaur	Husband of the grandniece		
Herbert, Erneth	2nd great-grandniece	VI	5
Herbert, Joseph Matthew	Husband of the 4th great-granddaughter		
Herbert, Madison Claire	5th great-granddaughter	VII	7
Herman, Christine	Wife of the 4th great-grandson		
Hernandez, Bruce Joseph	3rd great-grandnephew	VII	6
Hernandez, Gerald Louis	3rd great-grandnephew	VII	6
Hernandez, Robbie Ann	3rd great-grandniece	VII	6
Hernandez, Robért	Husband of the 2nd great-grandniece		
Hernandez, Vallie Lucy	Wife of the great-grandson		
Hidalgo, James Joseph	Husband of the 4th great-granddaughter		
Hill, Beverly Ann	Wife of the 3rd great-grandson		
Hill, Rebecca Ann	Wife of the 4th great-grandson		
Hill, Ronald Austin	Husband of the 4th great-granddaughter		
Hillburn, David	Husband of the 4th great-granddaughter		
Hillman, Brittany Michelle	5th great-granddaughter	VII	7
Hillman, Christopher Ryan	5th great-grandson	VII	7
Hillman, Joshua Paul	5th great-grandson	VII	7
Hillman, Kaitlyn Elizabeth	5th great-granddaughter	VII	7
Hillman, Mark	Husband of the 4th great-granddaughter		
Hillman, Paul	Husband of the 4th great-granddaughter		
Himel, Delmas	Husband of the great-grandniece		
Himelright, Leah	Wife of the 4th great-grandson		
Hinrichs, Brian David	Husband of the 4th great-granddaughter		
Hinrichs, Emily Marie	5th great-granddaughter	VII	7
Hirtzel, Verena R	Great-grandmother of the wife		
Hogan, Thomas	Husband of the great-grandniece		
Holder, Ray E.	Husband of the 2nd great-granddaughter		
Holzenthal, Leo	Husband of the 2nd great-grandniece		
Hoover, Catherine Louisa	Wife of the 2nd great-grandson		

Kinship of Jean Robért, *-***

Name	Relationship with Jean Robért	Civil	Canon
House, Cody Malone	5th great-grandson	VII	7
House, Kelsey Malone	Husband of the 4th great-granddaughter		
Hovey, Carley Ann	5th great-granddaughter	VII	7
Hovey, Haley Marie	5th great-granddaughter	VII	7
Hovey, Ryan	Husband of the 4th great-granddaughter		
Hughes, Gregory	Husband of the 4th great-granddaughter		
Hutson, Lonnie	Husband of the 4th great-granddaughter		
Hymel, A. C.	Husband of the 3rd great-granddaughter		
Hymel, Etienne Camille	Husband of the half great-grandniece		
Hymel, Ferducie	Half 2nd great-grandnephew	VI	5
Hymel, Lawrence Emelien	Husband of the 2nd great-granddaughter		
Hymel, Living	Wife of the half 3rd great-grandnephew		
Hymel, Madeline Marie	3rd great-granddaughter	V	5
Hymel, Marie	Wife of the 2nd great-grandnephew		
Hymel, Melanie	Wife of the half nephew		
Hymel, Odalie	Wife of the 2nd great-grandson		
Hymel, Septime	Half 3rd great-grandnephew	VII	6
Hymel, Zelia	Wife of the great-grandson		
Iglinsky, Blanche Marie	Wife of the 3rd great-grandson		
Ishee, Larry E.	Husband of the 3rd great-granddaughter		
Ivey, Justin Paul	4th great-grandson	VI	6
Ivey, Paul	Husband of the 3rd great-granddaughter		
Jackie	Wife of the 3rd great-grandson		
Jacob, Lynne	Wife of the 3rd great-grandnephew		
Jacobs, Nolan	Husband of the 2nd great-grandniece		
Jane	Wife of the 4th great-grandson		
Janelle	Wife of the 4th great-grandson		
Jarreau, Donnie	Husband of the 3rd great-grandniece		
Jarreau, Penny	Wife of the 4th great-grandson		
Jeanette	Wife of the 3rd great-grandson		
Joffrion, Felix Joseph	Husband of the 4th great-granddaughter		
Johns, Brody Paul	5th great-grandson	VII	7
Johns, Cody Wayne, (Divorced Feb. 2006)	Ex-husband of the 4th great-granddaughter		
Johns, Jessica Lynn	Wife of the 3rd great-grandson		
Johns, Parker Wayne	5th great-grandson	VII	7
Johnson, Christina Marie Velma	5th great-granddaughter	VII	7
Johnson, Jason Emile	5th great-grandson	VII	7
Johnson, Lori Kathleen	Wife of the 4th great-grandson		
Johnson, Michael Gerard, Jr.	5th great-grandson	VII	7
Johnson, Michael Gerard, Sr.	Husband of the 4th great-granddaughter		
Jordan, Amanda Claire	5th great-granddaughter	VII	7
Jordan, Andrew Levine	5th great-grandson	VII	7
Jordan, John Michael	Husband of the 4th great-granddaughter		
Jumonville, Doris	Wife of the 3rd great-grandson		
Jumonville, Marie Louise	Wife of the 3rd great-grandson		
Kahanic, Matthew Alan	Husband of the 3rd great-granddaughter		
Kallam, Barrett Michael	5th great-grandson	VII	7
Kallam, Benjamin Robert	5th great-grandson	VII	7
Kallam, Caroline Annabel	5th great-granddaughter	VII	7
Kallam, Robert Michael	Husband of the 4th great-granddaughter		
Kallam, William Rome	5th great-grandson	VII	7
Karam, George	Husband of the 3rd great-grandniece		
Karns, Shelby	Wife of the 4th great-grandson		
Keller, Aaron Patrick	5th great-grandson	VII	7
Keller, Ashley Allyn	4th great-granddaughter	VI	6

*Kinship of Jean Robért, *-****

Name	Relationship with Jean Robért	Civil	Canon
Keller, Blain Anthony	4th great-grandson	VI	6
Keller, Candace Ann	5th great-granddaughter	VII	7
Keller, Cynthia Ann	4th great-granddaughter	VI	6
Keller, Darren Paul	5th great-grandson	VII	7
Keller, David Paul	4th great-grandson	VI	6
Keller, David Paul	5th great-grandson	VII	7
Keller, Jennifer Ann	4th great-granddaughter	VI	6
Keller, Jeremy Michael	5th great-grandson	VII	7
Keller, Katie Elizabeth	4th great-granddaughter	VI	6
Keller, Kyle Christian	4th great-grandson	VI	6
Keller, Lyndell Wayne, (Divorced)	Ex-husband of the 3rd great-granddaughter		
Keller, Lyndell Wayne, Jr.	4th great-grandson	VI	6
Keller, Milton, Jr.	Husband of the 3rd great-granddaughter		
Keller, Naomi Grace	4th great-granddaughter	VI	6
Keller, Pamela Ann	4th great-granddaughter	VI	6
Keller, Patrick James	4th great-grandson	VI	6
Keller, Phyllis Ann	4th great-granddaughter	VI	6
Keller, Tara Marie	5th great-granddaughter	VII	7
Keller, Timothy Joseph	4th great-grandson	VI	6
Keller, Winceslas	Wife of the half 2nd great-grandnephew		
Kelley, Brent Michael	Husband of the 4th great-granddaughter		
Kenny, Myrtle	Wife of the 3rd great-grandson		
Kerley, Kara Ruth, (Divorced)	Ex-wife of the 4th great-grandson		
Kindler	Husband of the granddaughter		
King, Shane Michael	Husband of the 4th great-granddaughter		
Kinler, Erasie	Daughter-in-law		
Kinler, Estelle	Wife of the great-grandson		
Kinler, Robért Jacque	Husband of the 4th great-granddaughter		
Kirby, Aidan Cole	4th great-granddaughter	VI	6
Kirby, Ryan A.	Husband of the 3rd great-granddaughter		
Kleiber, Theodule Joseph	Husband of the grandniece		
Kliebert, Billie	Wife of the 4th great-grandson		
Kliebert, Bobbie Lynn	Wife of the 4th great-grandson		
Kling, Paige	Wife of the 3rd great-grandson		
Knoblock, Celeste	Friend of the 4th great-grandson		
Knoblock, Ida Genevieve	Wife of the great-grandnephew		
Knoblock, Marguerite Olympe	Wife of the great-grandnephew		
Kracht, Kathleen Elizabeth	Wife of the 4th great-grandson		
Krotz, Thelma M.	Wife of the 3rd great-grandson		
LaBranche, Patricia	Wife of the 4th great-grandson		
LaHaye, Ouida Nell	Wife of the 2nd great-grandson		
Laiche, Dianne Marie	4th great-granddaughter	VI	6
Laiche, Donald	4th great-grandson	VI	6
Laiche, Donna	Wife of the 4th great-grandson		
Laiche, Douglas David	4th great-grandson	VI	6
Laiche, Douglas David, Jr.	5th great-grandson	VII	7
Laiche, Kristen M.	Wife of the 3rd great-grandson		
Laiche, Leon	Husband of the 3rd great-granddaughter		
Lambert, Delphine (Deiphine)	Grandniece	IV	3
Lambert, Geneviéve Uranie	Grandniece	IV	3
Lambert, Howard	Husband of the 3rd great-granddaughter		
Lambert, Howard Joseph, Jr.	4th great-grandson	VI	6
Lambert, Irene	Grandniece	IV	3
Lambert, Josephine Adele	Grandniece	IV	3
Lambert, Louis, Jr.	Husband of the niece		

Kinship of Jean Robért, *-***

Name	Relationship with Jean Robért	Civil	Canon
Lambert, Marie Louise	4th great-granddaughter	VI	6
Lambert, Mark Timothy	4th great-grandson	VI	6
Lambert, Rachel Anne	Wife of the 4th great-grandson		
Lambert, Raymond Paul	4th great-grandson	VI	6
Lambert, Rebecca	Wife of the 3rd great-grandson		
Lamotte, André Marton	Husband of the niece		
Lamotte, Maria	Grandniece	IV	3
Landeche, Tina Marie	Wife of the 4th great-grandson		
Landry, Amy Ruth	3rd great-granddaughter	V	5
Landry, Annette	3rd great-granddaughter	V	5
Landry, Arlene Marie	Wife of the 4th great-grandson		
Landry, Armentine	Wife of the great-grandson		
Landry, Bailey Christopher	5th great-grandson	VII	7
Landry, Brandon Yates	4th great-grandson	VI	6
Landry, Brent David	3rd great-grandson	V	5
Landry, Bridget Lisa	Wife of the 3rd great-grandson		
Landry, Cindy	Wife of the 3rd great-grandnephew		
Landry, Clarence Auguste, (Gus)	Husband of the 2nd great-granddaughter		
Landry, Darren S.	Husband of the 4th great-granddaughter		
Landry, David Michael	Husband of the 4th great-granddaughter		
Landry, Dennis, (Poncho)	Husband of the 3rd great-granddaughter		
Landry, Duane Joseph	3rd great-grandson	V	5
Landry, Elaine Michelle	4th great-granddaughter	VI	6
Landry, Ella Faustene	Wife of the 3rd great-grandson		
Landry, Ethel Marie	Wife of the great-grandson		
Landry, Garrison David	4th great-grandson	VI	6
Landry, Hunter Thomas	5th great-grandson	VII	7
Landry, Jacqueline Ann	Wife of the 3rd great-grandson		
Landry, Jacques Auguste	4th great-grandson	VI	6
Landry, Jeanne Marie	3rd great-granddaughter	V	5
Landry, Jessica Leigh	5th great-granddaughter	VII	7
Landry, John David	4th great-grandson	VI	6
Landry, Joseph Auguste	4th great-grandson	VI	6
Landry, Julia	Wife of the great-grandnephew		
Landry, Karen Patricia	Wife of the 4th great-grandson		
Landry, Lawrence Joseph	Husband of the 2nd great-granddaughter		
Landry, Leah Michelle	4th great-granddaughter	VI	6
Landry, Leona	Wife of the great-grandson		
Landry, Leontine	Wife of the great-grandson		
Landry, Margaret Ruth	4th great-granddaughter	VI	6
Landry, Marguerite Melicere	Wife of the grandnephew		
Landry, Matthew Thomas	4th great-grandson	VI	6
Landry, Patrick Joseph	Husband of the 4th great-granddaughter		
Landry, Pierre Auguste	3rd great-grandson	V	5
Landry, Riley	5th great-grandson	VII	7
Landry, Stacy	Wife of the 3rd great-grandson		
Landry, Stephen Yates	Husband of the 3rd great-granddaughter		
Landry, Travis John	5th great-grandson	VII	7
Lanoux, John Wayne, Jr.	4th great-grandson	VI	6
Lanoux, John Wayne, Sr.	Husband of the 3rd great-granddaughter		
Lanoux, Shelly Marie	4th great-granddaughter	VI	6
Lanoux, Simone	4th great-granddaughter	VI	6
Lanoux, Stacy Louise	4th great-granddaughter	VI	6
LaPlace, Joseph John, Jr.	Husband of the 2nd great-grandniece		
Lasseigne, Gerald J.	Husband of the 3rd great-grandniece		

Kinship of Jean Robért, *-***

Name	Relationship with Jean Robért	Civil	Canon
Latino, Jessica Marie	5th great-granddaughter	VII	7
Latino, Louis Joseph, Jr.	Husband of the 4th great-granddaughter		
Latino, Matthew Louis	5th great-grandson	VII	7
LaTorre, Dorothea Henrietta	Wife of the 2nd great-grandson		
Lauve, Alice Marie	Wife of the 2nd great-grandson		
Lauve, Louis John	Husband of the 2nd great-granddaughter		
Laville, Helene	Wife of the great-grandnephew		
LeBlanc, Alexandre Renée	5th great-granddaughter	VII	7
LeBlanc, Alida Marie	4th great-granddaughter	VI	6
LeBlanc, Allen	Husband of the half 3rd great-grandniece		
LeBlanc, Alminte, (Sis)	Half 3rd great-grandniece	VII	6
LeBlanc, Annie Day	Wife of the 2nd great-grandson		
LeBlanc, Armand J.	Husband of the 3rd great-granddaughter		
LeBlanc, Betty Ann	Half 3rd great-grandniece	VII	6
LeBlanc, Brett Mathieu	5th great-grandson	VII	7
LeBlanc, Charles	Husband of the 4th great-granddaughter		
LeBlanc, Cliff Michael	5th great-grandson	VII	7
LeBlanc, Cody Paul	5th great-grandson	VII	7
LeBlanc, Darren	4th great-grandson	VI	6
LeBlanc, Doris Catherine Anne	Wife of the 3rd great-grandson		
LeBlanc, Dwain Joseph	4th great-grandson	VI	6
LeBlanc, Earnest Joseph	Husband of the 4th great-granddaughter		
LeBlanc, Edward Louis	Husband of the 3rd great-granddaughter		
LeBlanc, Elise Hope	5th great-granddaughter	VII	7
LeBlanc, Elsie	Wife of the 3rd great-grandnephew		
LeBlanc, Emily Grace	5th great-granddaughter	VII	7
LeBlanc, Estelle Marie	Wife of the 3rd great-grandson		
LeBlanc, Frankie	Half 3rd great-grandniece	VII	6
LeBlanc, Gene Gerald	4th great-grandson	VI	6
LeBlanc, Gerilyn Marie	4th great-granddaughter	VI	6
LeBlanc, Glyn Edward	4th great-grandson	VI	6
LeBlanc, Hope Elizabeth	4th great-granddaughter	VI	6
LeBlanc, James B.	Half 4th great-grandnephew	VIII	7
LeBlanc, Janelle	Wife of the 3rd great-grandson		
LeBlanc, Jay Gerald	5th great-grandson	VII	7
LeBlanc, Jeddy Joseph, Jr.	4th great-grandson	VI	6
LeBlanc, Jeddy Joseph, Sr.	Husband of the 3rd great-granddaughter		
LeBlanc, Jeffrey Paul, Jr.	5th great-grandson	VII	7
LeBlanc, Jeffrey Paul, Sr. (Divorced)	Ex-husband of the 4th great-granddaughter		
LeBlanc, Keith Gerard	4th great-grandson	VI	6
LeBlanc, Kenny John	Husband of the 4th great-granddaughter		
LeBlanc, Kerilyn Mary	4th great-granddaughter	VI	6
LeBlanc, Kyle Joseph	4th great-grandson	VI	6
Leblanc, Leland	Husband of the 4th great-granddaughter		
LeBlanc, Leonard Clement, Sr.	Husband of the 2nd great-granddaughter		
LeBlanc, Leonard, Jr.	3rd great-grandson	V	5
LeBlanc, Leonas	3rd great-granddaughter	V	5
LeBlanc, Linda M.	Half 4th great-grandniece	VIII	7
LeBlanc, Linda Marie	Wife of the 2nd great-grandnephew		
LeBlanc, Lori Therese	4th great-granddaughter	VI	6
LeBlanc, Lydia Ann	4th great-granddaughter	VI	6
LeBlanc, Marcia Leigh	4th great-granddaughter	VI	6
LeBlanc, Marie Louise	3rd great-granddaughter	V	5
LeBlanc, Melanie Marie	5th great-granddaughter	VII	7
LeBlanc, Michael Joseph	5th great-grandson	VII	7

*Kinship of Jean Robért, *-****

Name	Relationship with Jean Robért	Civil	Canon
eBlanc, Michael Paul	3rd great-grandson	V	5
eBlanc, Michelle Annette	4th great-granddaughter	VI	6
eBlanc, Nicole Monique	4th great-granddaughter	VI	6
eBlanc, Patsy Ruth	Half 3rd great-grandniece	VII	6
eBlanc, Robert	4th great-grandson	VI	6
eBlanc, Robért J., (Cap)	Half 3rd great-grandnephew	VII	6
eBlanc, Robért J., Jr.	Half 4th great-grandnephew	VIII	7
eBlanc, Rosemary	3rd great-granddaughter	V	5
eBlanc, Ruffin Joseph	Husband of the 3rd great-granddaughter		
eBlanc, Shirley P.	Wife of the half 3rd great-grandnephew		
eBlanc, Susan	4th great-granddaughter	VI	6
eBlanc, Troy Michael	4th great-grandson	VI	6
eBlanc, Vicki Lyn	4th great-granddaughter	VI	6
eBlanc, Waldon Charles, Sr.	Husband of the half 2nd great-grandniece		
eBlanc, Waldon, Jr.	Half 3rd great-grandnephew	VII	6
eBlanc, Wharton Armand	Husband of the 3rd great-granddaughter		
eBlanc, Wharton Armand, Jr.	4th great-grandson	VI	6
eBouef, Emma Dell Marie	Wife of the 2nd great-grandson		
eDoux, Suzanne Angelique	Wife of the 3rd great-grandson		
ee, Byan Andrew	4th great-grandson	VI	6
ee, David Michael	4th great-grandson	VI	6
ee, Gary Wayne, Jr.	Husband of the 3rd great-granddaughter		
ee, Katherine Grace	4th great-granddaughter	VI	6
ee, Madeline Ruth	4th great-granddaughter	VI	6
efort, Kenneth	Husband of the 4th great-granddaughter		
efort, Matilda	Wife of the 2nd great-grandnephew		
egendre, Reine Ann	Wife of the 4th great-grandson		
eglue, Randell Clement	Husband of the 4th great-granddaughter		
ejeune, Sylvestre, (Legendre)	Husband of the great-grandniece		
eloup, Anne	2nd great-grandmother	IV	4
emoine, Dana Lynn	5th great-granddaughter	VII	7
emoine, Dave Paul	Husband of the 4th great-granddaughter		
emoine, Lacey Michelle	5th great-granddaughter	VII	7
emoine, Tiffany Anne	5th great-granddaughter	VII	7
essard, Mercedean Marie	Wife of the 3rd great-grandson		
etulle, Glory Mary	Wife of the 2nd great-grandson		
ewis, Jeffrey Dean	Husband of the 4th great-granddaughter		
iddell, Debra Ann	Wife of the 4th great-grandson		
ittle, William Charles, (Divorced)	Ex-husband of the 3rd great-granddaughter		
onganecker, Lisa Lené	Wife of the 4th great-grandson		
opinto, Tinna	Wife of the 4th great-grandson		
orio, Sadie	Wife of the 2nd great-grandson		
oupe, Seraphine, <Loup>	Wife of the nephew		
ouque, Pam	Wife of the 4th great-grandson		
ouviere, Edmond	Spouse of the 2nd great-granddaughter		
uce, Jana Reneé	Wife of the 4th great-grandson		
uquette, Cynthia	4th great-grandniece of the wife		
MacKensie, Ian Rome	4th great-grandson	VI	6
MacKensie, Michael William	Husband of the 3rd great-granddaughter		
MacKensie, Ryan Rome	4th great-grandson	VI	6
MacKensie. Sean Rome	4th great-grandson	VI	6
Madatic, Marci Reneé	Wife of the 4th great-grandson		
Maddock, Hazel	Wife of the 3rd great-grandson		
Madere, Antoine Sidney, Jr.	4th great-grandson	VI	6
Madere, Antoine Sidney, Sr.	Husband of the 3rd great-granddaughter		

*Kinship of Jean Robért, *-****

Name	Relationship with Jean Robért	Civil	Canon
Madere, Denise	4th great-granddaughter	VI	6
Madere, Joan Ann	4th great-granddaughter	VI	6
Madere, John Williams	Husband of the 3rd great-granddaughter		
Madere, Judith Ann	4th great-granddaughter	VI	6
Madere, Julie	4th great-granddaughter	VI	6
Madere, June Mary	4th great-granddaughter	VI	6
Madere, Lee	Husband of the 3rd great-granddaughter		
Madere, Lynn Terese	4th great-granddaughter	VI	6
Madere, Marlene Ann	4th great-granddaughter	VI	6
Madere, Mary Elizabeth	4th great-granddaughter	VI	6
Madere, Mitzie	4th great-granddaughter	VI	6
Madere, William Joseph	4th great-grandson	VI	6
Maggiore, August John	4th great-grandson	VI	6
Maggiore, Ernest Joseph	4th great-grandson	VI	6
Maggiore, John August	Husband of the 3rd great-granddaughter		
Magill, Paul Pierre	4th great-grandson	VI	6
Magill, Victoria Ann	4th great-granddaughter	VI	6
Magill, William Medford	4th great-grandson	VI	6
Magill., Medford William	Husband of the 3rd great-granddaughter		
Mahler, Denis John	Husband of the 4th great-granddaughter		
Maillard, Eugenie	Wife of the grandson		
Maillard, Genevieve	Half aunt	III	2
Malliard, Jacques	Half uncle	III	2
Malliard, Jacques Pere,(Mayard)	Husband of the grandmother		
Malliard, Louis	Half uncle	III	2
Malliard, Paul	Half uncle	III	2
Manguna, Vivian Theresa	Wife of the 4th great-grandson		
Manley, Susan	Wife of the 3rd great-grandson		
Many, Barry	3rd great-grandnephew	VII	6
Many, Brent	3rd great-grandnephew	VII	6
Many, Donna	3rd great-grandniece	VII	6
Many, J.Timothy	3rd great-grandnephew	VII	6
Many, Karen	3rd great-grandniece	VII	6
Many, Warren J.	Husband of the 2nd great-grandniece		
Marchand, Antoine	2nd great-grandfather	IV	4
Marchand, Catherine	Grandmother	II	2
Marchand, Charles Nicolas	Granduncle	IV	3
Marchand, Helene	Grandaunt	IV	3
Marchand, Nicolas	Great-grandfather	III	3
Margaret	Wife of the 2nd great-grandson		
Margiotta, Marie Mary	Wife of the 3rd great-grandson		
Marino, Rita Lynn	Wife of the 4th great-grandson		
Maris, Kellie Lynn	Wife of the 4th great-grandson		
Marix, Louis Hill	Husband of the 4th great-granddaughter		
Martin, Barbara Ann	Wife of the 3rd great-grandson		
Martin, Brenda Ann	Wife of the 3rd great-grandson		
Martin, Dorothy Lea	Wife of the 3rd great-grandson		
Martine, Agnes Lillian	Wife of the 3rd great-grandson		
Martinez, Marie Ursuline, (Seline)	Wife of the 2nd great-grandson		
Matherne, Andrew Paul	Husband of the 4th great-granddaughter		
Matherne, Craig Michael	Husband of the 4th great-granddaughter		
Matherne, Eugenie Laura	Wife of the grandnephew		
Matherne, Kevin	Husband of the 4th great-granddaughter		
Matranga, Marcia, (Divorced)	Ex-wife of the 2nd great-grandson		
Maurin, Charles Horace, Jr.	Husband of the 3rd great-granddaughter		

*Kinship of Jean Robért, *-****

Name	Relationship with Jean Robért	Civil	Canon
Maurin, Charles, III.	4th great-grandson	VI	6
Maurin, Mary Beatrice	4th great-granddaughter	VI	6
Maurin, Robert Patrick	4th great-grandson	VI	6
Mayer, Nicole Marie	Wife of the 3rd great-grandson		
Mayerhoff, Mary Jean	Wife of the 4th great-grandson		
McAhee, Rena	Wife of the 4th great-grandson		
McCauley, Abigail Teresa	4th great-granddaughter	VI	6
McCauley, Bryan Edward	3rd great-grandson	V	5
McCauley, Carol Burton, M.D.	Husband of the 2nd great-granddaughter		
McCauley, Catherine	3rd great-granddaughter	V	5
McCauley, Lauren Faye	4th great-granddaughter	VI	6
McCauley, Sarah Katherine	4th great-granddaughter	VI	6
McCauley, Sharon Elizabeth	3rd great-granddaughter	V	5
McCauley, Tyler Burton	4th great-grandson	VI	6
McClelland, Mary Elizabeth	4th great-granddaughter	VI	6
McClelland, Michael	4th great-grandson	VI	6
McClelland, Neal	4th great-grandson	VI	6
McClelland, Richard Scott	4th great-grandson	VI	6
McClelland, Robért	Husband of the 3rd great-granddaughter		
McClelland, Robért B.	4th great-grandson	VI	6
McClung, Bobby Paul	Husband of the 4th great-granddaughter		
McClung, Heather Elizabeth	5th great-granddaughter	VII	7
McConnell, Logan Matthew	4th great-grandson	VI	6
McConnell, Mollie Catherine	4th great-granddaughter	VI	6
McConnell, Tim	Husband of the 3rd great-granddaughter		
McDougal, Cherie Ann	Wife of the 4th great-grandson		
McElwee, John Brigham (Briggs)	4th great-grandson	VI	6
McElwee, Mary Adelaide	4th great-granddaughter	VI	6
McElwee, Nate	Husband of the 3rd great-granddaughter		
McGovern, Kelly	Husband of the 4th great-granddaughter		
McGrath, Kim Marie	Wife of the 3rd great-grandson		
McLaughlin, Martha Ann	Wife of the 3rd great-grandson		
McMaster, Shelly Annette	Wife of the 3rd great-grandson		
McNabb, Elaine C.	Wife of the 4th great-grandson		
McNicoll, Carol	Wife of the 4th great-grandson		
Meaux, David Clerfé	4th great-grandson	VI	6
Meaux, Jeanne Marie	4th great-granddaughter	VI	6
Meaux, Richard Pollock	Husband of the 3rd great-granddaughter		
Medere, Alvin Paul III	Husband of the 3rd great-granddaughter		
Medere, Brennon Doh, (Kun Woo Doh, adopted)	4th great-grandson	VI	6
Medere, Chelsie Lynn, (Adopted 16 April 1992)	4th great-granddaughter	VI	6
Medine, Rebecca Geralyn	Wife of the 4th great-grandson		
Melancon, Doug Joseph	Husband of the 4th great-granddaughter		
Melancon, Mary Ann	Wife of the 2nd great-grandson		
Melancon, Myrna Marie	Wife of the 2nd great-grandson		
Melancon, Ross John	5th great-grandson	VII	7
Meliet, Living	Wife of the 4th great-grandson		
Menard, Catherine Marie, *- **- ***	Mother	I	1
Menard, Elizabeth	Aunt	III	2
Menard, Jean Baptiste I	Uncle	III	2
Menard, Jeanne	Half aunt	III	2
Menard, Louis Pierre dit Haver	Grandfather	II	2
Menard, Pierre	Great-grandfather	III	3
Menard, Pierre Barthelemy	Uncle	III	2
Meyer, Melissa Renée	5th great-granddaughter	VII	7

*Kinship of Jean Robért, *-****

Name	Relationship with Jean Robért	Civil	Canon
Meyer, Vernon Paul	Husband of the 4th great-granddaughter		
Michel, Ashley Elizabeth	5th great-granddaughter	VII	7
Michel, Edward Arthur	4th great-grandson	VI	6
Michel, Edward Lawless	Husband of the 3rd great-granddaughter		
Michel, Felicie	Wife of the 3rd great-grandson		
Michel, Jennifer Clair	5th great-granddaughter	VII	7
Michel, Katie Allison	5th great-granddaughter	VII	7
Michel, Louise Marie	Wife of the half 3rd great-grandnephew		
Michel, Stephen Michael	4th great-grandson	VI	6
Migliore, Mary	Wife of the 3rd great-grandson		
Milano, Brennan	5th great-grandson	VII	7
Milano, Jacquline Marie	Wife of the 3rd great-grandson		
Milano, Janice Ann	3rd great-granddaughter	V	5
Milano, Kim Ann	4th great-granddaughter	VI	6
Milano, Lexi	5th great-granddaughter	VII	7
Milano, Mona Marie	4th great-granddaughter	VI	6
Milano, Myrna Marie	3rd great-granddaughter	V	5
Milano, Nicholas	5th great-grandson	VII	7
Milano, Nicholas Dominic	Husband of the 2nd great-granddaughter		
Milano, Nicholas Wilbert	4th great-grandson	VI	6
Milano, Paul Anthony	3rd great-grandson	V	5
Milano, Rae Anne	4th great-granddaughter	VI	6
Milano, Sybil Stanilaus	3rd great-granddaughter	V	5
Miller, Alexis Victoria	5th great-granddaughter	VII	7
Miller, Ally Noel	5th great-grandson	VII	7
Miller, Allyson Ann	4th great-granddaughter	VI	6
Miller, Brian Dale	Husband of the 4th great-granddaughter		
Miller, Brittany Nicole	5th great-granddaughter	VII	7
Miller, Dana Elizabeth	4th great-granddaughter	VI	6
Miller, Erin Eileen	4th great-granddaughter	VI	6
Miller, Haley Renee	5th great-granddaughter	VII	7
Miller, Henry R., Jr.	Husband of the 3rd great-granddaughter		
Miller, Henry Rezin III	4th great-grandson	VI	6
Miller, Kaprice Ann	Wife of the 3rd great-grandson		
Miller, Nicholas Henry	5th great-grandson	VII	7
Miller, Stephenie Ann	4th great-granddaughter	VI	6
Miller, Steven Michael	Husband of the 4th great-granddaughter		
Miller, Vickie Lynn	4th great-granddaughter	VI	6
Millet, Camille	5th great-granddaughter	VII	7
Millet, Christi Nicole	5th great-granddaughter	VII	7
Millet, Emily Clair	4th great-granddaughter	VI	6
Millet, Ivan George	4th great-grandson	VI	6
Millet, Lester James	4th great-grandson	VI	6
Millet, Marguerite Therese	5th great-granddaughter	VII	7
Millet, Martha Louise	4th great-granddaughter	VI	6
Millet, Philip Alan	4th great-grandson	VI	6
Millet, Summer Helen	5th great-granddaughter	VII	7
Millet, Theresa Agnes	4th great-granddaughter	VI	6
Millet, Walter Edgar, Jr.	Husband of the 3rd great-granddaughter		
Millet, Walter Edgar, III	4th great-grandson	VI	6
Millican, Kelly Leann	4th great-granddaughter	VI	6
Mills, Ronald Munro	Husband of the 4th great-granddaughter		
Minvielle, Cindy Ann	5th great-granddaughter	VII	7
Minvielle, Gerard Michael	5th great-grandson	VII	7
Minvielle, Melissa Lynn	5th great-granddaughter	VII	7

*Kinship of Jean Robért, *-****

Name	Relationship with Jean Robért	Civil	Canon
Minvielle, Michael Joseph	Husband of the 4th great-granddaughter		
Mire, Derrick Paul	4th great-grandson	VI	6
Mire, Dudley Joseph III	4th great-grandson	VI	6
Mire, Dudley Joseph, Jr.	Husband of the 3rd great-granddaughter		
Mire, Hubble Robert	4th great-grandson	VI	6
Mire, Randi Ann	Wife of the 2nd great-grandson		
Mire, Seraphin	Husband of the 2nd great-granddaughter		
Mire, Terése Marie	4th great-granddaughter	VI	6
Mistretta, Lena Gloria	Wife of the 2nd great-grandson		
Mistretta, Marie Carmen	Wife of the 2nd great-grandson		
Mitchell, Corey Mathiew	5th great-grandson	VII	7
Mitchell, Daniel Raymond	5th great-grandson	VII	7
Mitchell, Keith Anthony	5th great-grandson	VII	7
Mitchell, Morris Michael	Husband of the 4th great-granddaughter		
Mitchell, Rose Lee	Wife of the 3rd great-grandson		
Modica, Steven	Husband of the 4th great-granddaughter		
Montagnino, Susan	Wife of the 3rd great-grandson		
Montz, Erika Elizabeth	5th great-granddaughter	VII	7
Montz, Peter Timothy	Husband of the 4th great-granddaughter		
Montz, Rachael Reneé	5th great-granddaughter	VII	7
Montz, Zema	Husband of the 2nd great-grandniece		
Moore, Anna Katherine	6th great-granddaughter	VIII	8
Moore, Barry Lee II	Husband of the 4th great-granddaughter		
Moore, Catherine A.	Wife of the 2nd great-grandson		
Moore, George M.	Husband of the great-grandniece		
Moore, Kevin Dawkins	Husband of the 5th great-granddaughter		
Moore, Mathew Barber	5th great-grandson	VII	7
Moore, Tyler Joseph	6th great-grandson	VIII	8
Moore, William Barber	5th great-grandson	VII	7
Moran, Maydel	Wife of the half 5th great-grandnephew		
Moreau, Connor Robert	5th great-grandson	VII	7
Moreau, Hannah Elizabeth	5th great-granddaughter	VII	7
Moreau, John Lester, (Divorced)	Ex-husband of the 4th great-granddaughter		
Morgan, James	Husband of the 4th great-granddaughter		
Morris, Jeanne Marie	Wife of the 2nd great-grandson		
Morrow, Sean Michael	4th great-grandson	VI	6
Morrow, Stephen Mark	Husband of the 3rd great-granddaughter		
Moss, Sharon	Wife of the 4th great-grandson		
Muller, Janet	Wife of the 3rd great-grandson		
Mumphrey, Anrhony Scott	4th great-grandson	VI	6
Mumphrey, Anthony	Husband of the 2nd great-granddaughter		
Mumphrey, Joseph Scott	3rd great-grandson	V	5
Mumphrey, Linda Marie	3rd great-granddaughter	V	5
Mumphrey, Michael Louis	3rd great-grandson	V	5
Mumphrey, Peggy Jane	3rd great-granddaughter	V	5
Mumphrey, Ray Anthony	3rd great-grandson	V	5
Mumphrey, Robbie Anne	3rd great-granddaughter	V	5
Mumphrey, Robért Neil	3rd great-grandson	V	5
Mumphrey, Terri Gerilyn	3rd great-granddaughter	V	5
Murrell, Harold	Husband of the 4th great-granddaughter		
Mury, Odette	Wife of the 3rd great-grandson		
Napoli, Mary Elizabeth	Wife of the 3rd great-grandson		
Naquin, Alice May	Wife of the 2nd great-grandson		
Naquin, Neva	Wife of the 2nd great-grandson		
Nebel, Raymond	Husband of the 4th great-granddaughter		

*Kinship of Jean Robért, *-****

Name	Relationship with Jean Robért	Civil	Canon
Nelson, Trudy	Wife of the 3rd great-grandson		
Nethery, Stephanie Bryant	Wife of the 4th great-grandson		
Ng, Michael	Husband of the 4th great-granddaughter		
Noel, Allen Thomas	Husband of the 4th great-granddaughter		
Noel, Brandon Michael	5th great-grandson	VII	7
Noel, Ethan Thomas	6th great-grandson	VIII	8
Noel, Matthew Thomas	5th great-grandson	VII	7
Noto, Janice Normae	Wife of the 2nd great-grandson		
O'Berry, Nathan, Jr.	4th great-grandson	VI	6
O'Brien, Chancee Marie	4th great-granddaughter	VI	6
O'Brien, Charles Mitchel	Husband of the 3rd great-granddaughter		
Odell, Michael	Husband of the 4th great-granddaughter		
Odom, Joseph Neal	Husband of the 4th great-granddaughter		
Oliver, Alex Charles	5th great-grandson	VII	7
Oliver, Branden Lee	5th great-grandson	VII	7
Oliver, Lee	Husband of the 4th great-granddaughter		
Ollie	Wife of the 2nd great-grandnephew		
Opperman, Sherri Theresa	Wife of the 2nd great-grandson		
Ory, Marie	Wife of the 3rd great-grandson		
Ory, Palmer	Husband of the half grandniece		
Oschwald, Ruby	Wife of the 2nd great-grandson		
Oubre, Cecil J.	Husband of the 3rd great-granddaughter		
Oubre, Irma Marie	Wife of the 2nd great-grandson		
Oubre, Vivian Leah	Wife of the 3rd great-grandson		
Oubre, Wanda	Wife of the 3rd great-grandson		
Ourso, Stella	Wife of the 2nd great-grandson		
Overby, Eilene	Wife of the 2nd great-grandnephew		
Owens, Saundra Frances	Wife of the 2nd great-grandson		
Pailette, Sherry A.	Wife of the 3rd great-grandson		
Palermo, Peter	Husband of the 4th great-granddaughter		
Palmer, Living	Husband of the half 4th great-grandniece		
Parenton, Brian Gerald	5th great-grandson	VII	7
Parenton, Jenna Leigh	5th great-granddaughter	VII	7
Parenton, O'Neil Joseph, III	5th great-grandson	VII	7
Parenton, O'Neil Joseph, Jr.	Husband of the 4th great-granddaughter		
Parish, Lilly Dawn	Wife of the 3rd great-grandson		
Parr, Louis	Husband of the 2nd great-granddaughter		
Parr, Mary Karen	3rd great-granddaughter	V	5
Parsons, Nancy	Wife of the 4th great-grandson		
Part, Jodey Lynne	4th great-granddaughter	VI	6
Part, John	Husband of the 3rd great-granddaughter		
Part, Leslie Therése	4th great-granddaughter	VI	6
Part, Shandra Anne	4th great-granddaughter	VI	6
Payton, Donald Kay	Husband of the 4th great-granddaughter		
Pellerin, Natalie	Wife of the 3rd great-grandson		
Pennino, Angela Ann	5th great-granddaughter	VII	7
Pennino, John Anthony	Husband of the 4th great-granddaughter		
Pennino, John Anthony, Jr.	5th great-grandson	VII	7
Pennino, Melissa Ann	5th great-granddaughter	VII	7
Perque, Colon J.	Husband of the 2nd great-grandniece		
Petermann, Alison	Wife of the 3rd great-grandson		
Peterson, Jules	Husband of the 4th great-granddaughter		
Petit, Odile	Wife of the 3rd great-grandson		
Peytavin, Marie Carmelite	Wife of the 3rd great-grandson		
Pierce, William Allen	Husband of the 4th great-granddaughter		

Kinship of Jean Robért, *-***

Name	Relationship with Jean Robért	Civil	Canon
ipes, Jon Hayes	5th great-grandson	VII	7
ipes, Ransom Paul	5th great-grandson	VII	7
ipes, Victoria Anne	5th great-granddaughter	VII	7
ipes, William Ransom	Husband of the 4th great-granddaughter		
itre, Brenda	Wife of the 4th great-grandson		
izzolato, Anne Marie	4th great-granddaughter	VI	6
izzolato, Elizabeth Diane	4th great-granddaughter	VI	6
izzolato, Monica Christine	4th great-granddaughter	VI	6
izzolato, Paul Joseph	4th great-grandson	VI	6
izzolato, Vincent Paul	Husband of the 3rd great-granddaughter		
lauche, Pam	Wife of the 4th great-grandson		
oche, Adele Frances	4th great-granddaughter	VI	6
oche, Anthony Gayle, Jr.	4th great-grandson	VI	6
oche, Anthony Gayle, Sr. (Dr.)	Husband of the 3rd great-granddaughter		
oche, Claire Elizabeth	4th great-granddaughter	VI	6
oirrier, Alison Leigh	5th great-granddaughter	VII	7
oirrier, Ashley Lynn	5th great-granddaughter	VII	7
oirrier, Leo Camille	Husband of the 4th great-granddaughter		
ollet, Francois	Husband of the half grandniece		
ollet, Marie Palmyre	Wife of the half great-grandnephew		
orta, Lionel Vincent	Husband of the 3rd great-granddaughter		
orta, Randal Jude	4th great-grandson	VI	6
orta, Resa Lynn	4th great-granddaughter	VI	6
orta, Robin Dianne	Wife of the 3rd great-grandnephew		
ourciau, Ashlee Danielle	Wife of the 5th great-grandson		
regeant, Andrew Joseph	Husband of the 4th great-granddaughter		
regeant, Bryce Raymond	5th great-grandson	VII	7
regeant, Cade Andrew	5th great-grandson	VII	7
rejean, Blake Joseph	Husband of the 5th great-granddaughter		
rejean, Hallie Malayne	6th great-granddaughter	VIII	8
rejean, Ramsie Lynn	6th great-granddaughter	VIII	8
rejean, Timmy	Husband of the 4th great-granddaughter		
restenbach, Arthur	3rd great-grandnephew	VII	6
restenbach, William Paul	Husband of the 2nd great-grandniece		
Rafferty, Courtland James	5th great-grandson	VII	7
Rafferty, James David	Husband of the 4th great-granddaughter		
Ragusa, Guy Tony	Husband of the 3rd great-grandniece		
Ramber, Neil	Husband of the 4th great-granddaughter		
Rateau, Celine	Wife of the great-grandnephew		
Rauch, Andrew	4th great-grandson	VI	6
Rauch, Elizabeth Ann	3rd great-granddaughter	V	5
Rauch, Myra Margaret	3rd great-granddaughter	V	5
Rauch, Thomas J. III	3rd great-grandson	V	5
Rauch, Thomas J.,Jr.	Husband of the 2nd great-granddaughter		
Rayne, Edmonde Marie, (Dee)	Wife of the 2nd great-grandson		
Reed, Martin Joseph	Husband of the 4th great-granddaughter		
Reeves, Chrystal	Wife of the 4th great-grandson		
Reider, Eugene Lawrence, Jr.	5th great-grandson	VII	7
Reider, Eugene Lawrence, Sr.	Husband of the 4th great-granddaughter		
Reider, Shawna Lynn	5th great-granddaughter	VII	7
Reider, Tasha Elizabeth	5th great-granddaughter	VII	7
Rhodes, Kim Angela	Wife of the 3rd great-grandson		
Rhodes, Les	Husband of the 4th great-granddaughter		
Rhoton, Lurienne	Wife of the 2nd great-grandson		
Richard, Alex Michael	5th great-grandson	VII	7

Kinship of Jean Robért, *-***

Name	Relationship with Jean Robért	Civil	Canon
Richard, Alton Joseph	Husband of the 3rd great-granddaughter		
Richard, Catheline	Wife of the 3rd great-grandson		
Richard, David Kent	Husband of the 4th great-granddaughter		
Richard, Dawn Elizabeth	4th great-granddaughter	VI	6
Richard, Mark Rory	4th great-grandson	VI	6
Richard, Rhonda Margaret	4th great-granddaughter	VI	6
Richard, Robyn Ann	4th great-granddaughter	VI	6
Richard, Stephanie Lynn	Wife of the 3rd great-grandson		
Ridgdell, Kenneth	Husband of the 4th great-granddaughter		
Ridgway, Christopher William	Husband of the 4th great-granddaughter		
Riley, Terry	Wife of the 4th great-grandson		
Rivet, Ralph, Jr.	Husband of the 3rd great-grandniece		
Robért, Aaron Paul	4th great-grandson	VI	6
Robért, Adalbo	2nd great-grandson	IV	4
Robért, Adam Paul, Jr.	4th great-grandson	VI	6
Robért, Adam Paul, Sr.	3rd great-grandson	V	5
Robért, Addison Grace	5th great-granddaughter	VII	7
Robért, Adel	2nd great-granddaughter	IV	4
Robért, Adele Ann	2nd great-granddaughter	IV	4
Robért, Adele Marie	2nd great-granddaughter	IV	4
Robért, Agnes	3rd great-granddaughter	V	5
Robért, Alan Joseph	3rd great-grandson	V	5
Robért, Alana Rene	4th great-granddaughter	VI	6
Robért, Albin, (Nick)	2nd great-grandson	IV	4
Robért, Alcide	Great-grandson	III	3
Robért, Aleina	2nd great-granddaughter	IV	4
Robért, Alexander James	4th great-grandson	VI	6
Robért, Alfred	Grandson	II	2
Robért, Alfred A.	2nd great-grandson	IV	4
Robért, Alice	4th great-granddaughter	VI	6
Robért, Alida	2nd great-granddaughter	IV	4
Robért, Aline	2nd great-granddaughter	IV	4
Robért, Alphonse	2nd great-grandson	IV	4
Robért, Althea Adolphine	3rd great-granddaughter	V	5
Robért, Alvin Joseph, Sr. (Al)	2nd great-grandson	IV	4
Robért, Alvin Joseph, Jr.	3rd great-grandson	V	5
Robért, Alyiah Cassandra	4th great-granddaughter	VI	6
Robért, Amalie Marie, (Toot)	2nd great-granddaughter	IV	4
Robért, Amanda Clare	3rd great-granddaughter	V	5
Robért, Amedee Jean	Great-grandson	III	3
Robért, Amedee, Jr.	2nd great-grandson	IV	4
Robért, Amedee, Sr.	Great-grandson	III	3
Robért, Amy	4th great-granddaughter	VI	6
Robért, Anaise	3rd great-granddaughter	V	5
Robért, Anastasia	2nd great-granddaughter	IV	4
Robért, Anastasie	Great-granddaughter	III	3
Robért, Anatole	Great-granddaughter	III	3
Robért, Andrew Michael	4th great-grandson	VI	6
Robért, Angelele Monique	4th great-granddaughter	VI	6
Robért, Angelle Marie	4th great-granddaughter	VI	6
Robért, Ann	Wife of the 2nd great-grandnephew		
Robért, Anne Marie	4th great-granddaughter	VI	6
Robért, Anne Marie, (Grand-Fille)	2nd great-granddaughter	IV	4
Robért, Annie	3rd great-granddaughter	V	5
Robért, Anthony Luke	3rd great-grandson	V	5

Kinship of Jean Robért, *-***

Name	Relationship with Jean Robért	Civil	Canon
Robért, Anthony Paul	4th great-grandson	VI	6
Robért, Anthony Wilson	3rd great-grandson	V	5
Robért, Armand	2nd great-grandson	IV	4
Robért, Ashley	4th great-grandson	VI	6
Robért, Ashley Marie	3rd great-granddaughter	V	5
Robért, Austin	4th great-grandson	VI	6
Robért, Austin Nicholas	4th great-grandson	VI	6
Robért, Austin Wayne	4th great-grandson	VI	6
Robért, Ava Nichole	5th great-granddaughter	VII	7
Robért, Barry Steele	3rd great-grandson	V	5
Robért, Beatrice	3rd great-granddaughter	V	5
Robért, Beatrice Marie	3rd great-granddaughter	V	5
Robért, Ben	4th great-grandson	VI	6
Robért, Benoit	Grandson	II	2
Robért, Benoit, (Ben)	2nd great-grandson	IV	4
Robért, Bernard Francis, Jr.	4th great-grandson	VI	6
Robért, Bernard Francis, Sr.	3rd great-grandson	V	5
Robért, Bertha	2nd great-granddaughter	IV	4
Robért, Bertice	2nd great-grandson	IV	4
Robért, Bobbye Leigh	4th great-granddaughter	VI	6
Robért, Boyd Houston Joseph	3rd great-grandson	V	5
Robért, Brian Paul	4th great-grandson	VI	6
Robért, Bridget Marie	3rd great-granddaughter	V	5
Robért, Brittney Leigh	4th great-granddaughter	VI	6
Robért, Brooks Martin	4th great-grandson	VI	6
Robért, Bruce Paul	4th great-grandson	VI	6
Robért, Camille	Daughter	I	1
Robért, Carl	3rd great-grandson	V	5
Robért, Carl James, (Hubble)	2nd great-grandson	IV	4
Robért, Carmen	3rd great-granddaughter	V	5
Robért, Caroline Joan	4th great-granddaughter	VI	6
Robért, Carolyn	3rd great-granddaughter	V	5
Robért, Carolyn Teresa, (Ceyon)	2nd great-granddaughter	IV	4
Robért, Casandra	4th great-granddaughter	VI	6
Robért, Catherine Ann	3rd great-granddaughter	V	5
Robért, Cecil Paul, Jr.	3rd great-grandson	V	5
Robért, Cecil Paul, Sr	2nd great-grandson	IV	4
Robért, Cecile	Great-granddaughter	III	3
Robért, Cecile Marie	2nd great-granddaughter	IV	4
Robért, Chad Patrick	3rd great-grandson	V	5
Robért, Charlene Lucy	4th great-granddaughter	VI	6
Robért, Charles	3rd great-grandson	V	5
Robért, Charles Earl, Jr.	4th great-grandson	VI	6
Robért, Charles Earl, Sr.	3rd great-grandson	V	5
Robért, Charles Herbert	3rd great-grandson	V	5
Robért, Charles Louis, (Tellie)	2nd great-grandson	IV	4
Robért, Cherie Ann	4th great-granddaughter	VI	6
Robért, Cheryl	3rd great-granddaughter	V	5
Robért, Cheryl	4th great-granddaughter	VI	6
Robért, Cheryl Ann	4th great-granddaughter	VI	6
Robért, Christopher James, Jr.	4th great-grandson	VI	6
Robért, Christopher James, Sr.	3rd great-grandson	V	5
Robért, Claire	2nd great-granddaughter	IV	4
Robért, Clara Ann	3rd great-granddaughter	V	5
Robért, Claudia M., (Ba-Low)	2nd great-granddaughter	IV	4

Kinship of Jean Robért, *-***

Name	Relationship with Jean Robért	Civil	Canon
Robért, Clifford	4th great-grandson	VI	6
Robért, Clinton Joseph	3rd great-grandson	V	5
Robért, Clovis Jean	Great-grandson	III	3
Robért, Colby Charles	4th great-grandson	VI	6
Robért, Cori Danielle	4th great-granddaughter	VI	6
Robért, Courtney Blake	3rd great-granddaughter	V	5
Robért, Courtney Leah	4th great-granddaughter	VI	6
Robért, Curtis	3rd great-grandson	V	5
Robért, Curtis Joseph	4th great-grandson	VI	6
Robért, Cyril	2nd great-grandson	IV	4
Robért, Dale Anthony	3rd great-grandson	V	5
Robért, Dale Thomas, Jr.	4th great-grandson	VI	6
Robért, Dale Thomas, Sr.	3rd great-grandson	V	5
Robért, Dana Elizabeth	3rd great-granddaughter	V	5
Robért, Daniel Steven	3rd great-grandson	V	5
Robért, Danielle Jenee	4th great-granddaughter	VI	6
Robért, Danny Gerard	3rd great-grandson	V	5
Robért, David Bernard	3rd great-grandson	V	5
Robért, David Paul	3rd great-grandson	V	5
Robért, David Paul	3rd great-grandson	V	5
Robért, David Raymond	4th great-grandson	VI	6
Robért, David Ryan	4th great-grandson	VI	6
Robért, Delia Marie	Granddaughter	II	2
Robért, Delphine	2nd great-granddaughter	IV	4
Robért, Denise Marie	4th great-granddaughter	VI	6
Robért, Deverelle Marie	4th great-granddaughter	VI	6
Robért, Dewey Joseph	3rd great-grandson	V	5
Robért, Donald Christopher, (Don)	2nd great-grandson	IV	4
Robért, Donna Marie	3rd great-granddaughter	V	5
Robért, Donna Theresa	4th great-granddaughter	VI	6
Robért, Doran J.	3rd great-grandson	V	5
Robért, Dorothy Elizabeth, (Fat)	2nd great-granddaughter	IV	4
Robért, Douglas Joseph	3rd great-grandson	V	5
Robért, Dru Marie	3rd great-granddaughter	V	5
Robért, Dudley	3rd great-grandson	V	5
Robért, Eddie	4th great-grandson	VI	6
Robért, Edgar	2nd great-grandson	IV	4
Robért, Edna Marie	2nd great-granddaughter	IV	4
Robért, Edward	Grandson	II	2
Robért, Effie	3rd great-granddaughter	V	5
Robért, Elma	2nd great-granddaughter	IV	4
Robért, Elmira Marie	Great-granddaughter	III	3
Robért, Elyse J.	2nd great-granddaughter	IV	4
Robért, Emile	Grandson	II	2
Robért, Emily Maria	4th great-granddaughter	VI	6
Robért, Emma Mae	3rd great-granddaughter	V	5
Robért, Eranbert	2nd great-grandson	IV	4
Robért, Erin Ruth	3rd great-granddaughter	V	5
Robért, Ernest	2nd great-grandson	IV	4
Robért, Ernest Francis	3rd great-grandson	V	5
Robért, Ernestine	Granddaughter	II	2
Robért, Estelle	Granddaughter	II	2
Robért, Estelle	Granddaughter	II	2
Robért, Estelle Marie	2nd great-granddaughter	IV	4
Robért, Estelle Sydleie	Great-granddaughter	III	3

Kinship of Jean Robért, *-***

Name	Relationship with Jean Robért	Civil	Canon
Robért, Ethelyne	3rd great-granddaughter	V	5
Robért, Etienne	Grandson	II	2
Robért, Eugene	2nd great-grandson	IV	4
Robért, Eugene Thomas, Jr.	4th great-grandson	VI	6
Robért, Eugene Thomas, Sr.	3rd great-grandson	V	5
Robért, Eujene Joseph	3rd great-grandson	V	5
Robért, Faryl Charles	3rd great-grandson	V	5
Robért, Fay Marie	3rd great-granddaughter	V	5
Robért, Felecien Peter, (Bill)	2nd great-grandson	IV	4
Robért, Felix John, (Benny)	2nd great-grandson	IV	4
Robért, Floremond	Great-grandson	III	3
Robért, Floyd	4th great-grandson	VI	6
Robért, Frances Elizabeth	3rd great-granddaughter	V	5
Robért, Francis Farrel, (infant)	2nd great-grandson	IV	4
Robért, Frumence	2nd great-grandson	IV	4
Robért, Gabrielle Leigh	4th great-granddaughter	VI	6
Robért, Gardon	3rd great-grandson	V	5
Robért, Gary Jerome	3rd great-grandson	V	5
Robért, Gayle Patrick	2nd great-grandson	IV	4
Robért, Gayle Renee	4th great-granddaughter	VI	6
Robért, Genevieve Martha	2nd great-granddaughter	IV	4
Robért, Geneviève Octavie	Sister	II	1
Robért, Genevieve Palmire	Granddaughter	II	2
Robért, George	2nd great-grandson	IV	4
Robért, George Pierre, (Toby)	2nd great-grandson	IV	4
Robért, Georgina F.	Wife of the great-grandson		
Robért, Gerald	4th great-grandson	VI	6
Robért, Gina Monique	3rd great-granddaughter	V	5
Robért, Gladys	2nd great-granddaughter	IV	4
Robért, Glenn Jacque	2nd great-grandson	IV	4
Robért, Glenna Marie	3rd great-granddaughter	V	5
Robért, Grace	3rd great-granddaughter	V	5
Robért, Gracie Lynn	4th great-granddaughter	VI	6
Robért, Gregory Michael	3rd great-grandson	V	5
Robért, Gustave	2nd great-grandson	IV	4
Robért, Guy	4th great-grandson	VI	6
Robért, Gwendalyne	3rd great-granddaughter	V	5
Robért, Gwendolyn Therese	4th great-granddaughter	VI	6
Robért, Harold	3rd great-grandson	V	5
Robért, Harry Clay	3rd great-grandson	V	5
Robért, Harry Paul, Jr.	3rd great-grandson	V	5
Robért, Harry Paul, Sr.	2nd great-grandson	IV	4
Robért, Hayden Rivers	4th great-grandson	VI	6
Robért, Hayden Steele	4th great-grandson	VI	6
Robért, Heather	4th great-granddaughter	VI	6
Robért, Hebert	3rd great-grandson	V	5
Robért, Heloise	Daughter	I	1
Robért, Henry Balthazar	4th great-grandson	VI	6
Robért, Herman Anthony, Jr.	4th great-grandson	VI	6
Robért, Herman Anthony, Sr.	3rd great-grandson	V	5
Robért, Hewitt Patrick, (Jap)	Husband of the 3rd great-granddaughter		
Robert, Hilda	3rd great-granddaughter	V	5
Robert, Horace Joseph	3rd great-grandson	V	5
Robért, Hortense	Great-granddaughter	III	3
Robért, Hubert	Husband of the 3rd great-granddaughter		

Kinship of Jean Robért, *-***

Name	Relationship with Jean Robért	Civil	Canon
Robért, Hubert, Jr.	Grandson	II	2
Robért, Hubert, Sr.	Son	I	1
Robért, Hulin Joseph	2nd great-grandson	IV	4
Robért, Infant	2nd great-granddaughter	IV	4
Robért, Irby Paul	3rd great-grandson	V	5
Robért, Jacques Christopher	3rd great-grandson	V	5
Robért, Jaime Terése	3rd great-granddaughter	V	5
Robért, Jake Vincent	3rd great-grandson	V	5
Robért, James	4th great-grandson	VI	6
Robért, James	3rd great-grandson	V	5
Robért, James Joseph III	4th great-grandson	VI	6
Robért, James Joseph, Jr. Dr.	3rd great-grandson	V	5
Robért, James Joseph, Sr.	2nd great-grandson	IV	4
Robért, James Theotine	2nd great-grandson	IV	4
Robért, Jamie Marie	3rd great-granddaughter	V	5
Robért, Jan Elizabeth	4th great-granddaughter	VI	6
Robért, Jan Rachelle	4th great-granddaughter	VI	6
Robért, Jane Ann Marie	3rd great-granddaughter	V	5
Robért, Janet	4th great-granddaughter	VI	6
Robért, Jason Lance	4th great-grandson	VI	6
Robért, Jean II	Son	I	1
Robért, Jean Louis	Son	I	1
Robért, Jean Baptiste	Grandson	II	2
Robért, Jean Baptiste	Grandson	II	2
Robért, Jean Frumence, ***	Grandson	II	2
Robért, Jean Omér, Jr. (Noon)	2nd great-grandson	IV	4
Robért, Jean Paul, *	Grandson	II	2
Robért, Jean Ursin	Great-grandson	III	3
Robért, Jean Wallace, Jr.	2nd great-grandson	IV	4
Robért, Jean, *-***	Self		0
Robért, Jeanne <unknown>	Wife of the 2nd great-grandson		
Robért, Jeanne Clelie	Great-granddaughter	III	3
Robért, Jean-Paul Josef, Jr.	4th great-granddaughter	VI	6
Robért, Jean-Paul Josef, Sr.	3rd great-grandson	V	5
Robért, Jeffery Michael	4th great-grandson	VI	6
Robért, Jeffery Paul	3rd great-grandson	V	5
Robért, Jeffery Paul	3rd great-grandson	V	5
Robért, Jeffrey Joseph	3rd great-grandson	V	5
Robért, Jennifer Ann	4th great-granddaughter	VI	6
Robért, Jennifer Marie	3rd great-granddaughter	V	5
Robért, Jeremy Paul	4th great-grandson	VI	6
Robért, Jessie Luke	4th great-grandson	VI	6
Robért, Joanna Danielle	4th great-granddaughter	VI	6
Robért, Jody	4th great-grandson	VI	6
Robért, Joe Anne	3rd great-granddaughter	V	5
Robért, Joel Michael	3rd great-grandson	V	5
Robért, John Baptiste	2nd great-grandson	IV	4
Robért, John Burton	4th great-grandson	VI	6
Robért, John Houston	4th great-grandson	VI	6
Robért, John Joseph,(infant)	2nd great-grandson	IV	4
Robért, John Marius, Jr.	3rd great-grandson	V	5
Robért, John Marius, Sr.	2nd great-grandson	IV	4
Robért, John Taylor	3rd great-grandson	V	5
Robért, Jon Tucker	4th great-grandson	VI	6
Robért, Jordan Elizabeth	4th great-granddaughter	VI	6

*Kinship of Jean Robért, *-****

Name	Relationship with Jean Robért	Civil	Canon
Robért, Joseph	3rd great-grandson	V	5
Robért, Joseph Nemours, (Jo Jo)	2nd great-grandson	IV	4
Robért, Joseph Olide, (Do-Doot)	Great-grandson	III	3
Robért, Joseph Reginald, (Reggie)	3rd great-grandson	V	5
Robért, Joseph W.	2nd great-grandson	IV	4
Robért, Josephine Lauren	5th great-granddaughter	VII	7
Robért, Joshua Blake	4th great-grandson	VI	6
Robért, Joyce	3rd great-granddaughter	V	5
Robért, Joyce Ann	2nd great-granddaughter	IV	4
Robért, Juanita	3rd great-granddaughter	V	5
Robért, Julie Eugenie, **	Sister	II	1
Robért, Juliette Anne	3rd great-granddaughter	V	5
Robért, Kaitlin Kelsey McGrath	4th great-granddaughter	VI	6
Robért, Kandis Ann	3rd great-granddaughter	V	5
Robért, Karen Lynn	4th great-granddaughter	VI	6
Robért, Katherine Ann	4th great-granddaughter	VI	6
Robért, Katie Ann	4th great-granddaughter	VI	6
Robért, Kay Ann	4th great-granddaughter	VI	6
Robért, Kayla	4th great-granddaughter	VI	6
Robért, Keeley Paul	3rd great-grandson	V	5
Robért, Keith Brian	3rd great-grandson	V	5
Robért, Keith Michael	4th great-grandson	VI	6
Robért, Kennedy Lane	4th great-grandson	VI	6
Robért, Kevin James	4th great-grandson	VI	6
Robért, Kevin Paul	3rd great-grandson	V	5
Robért, Kimberlie Jane	4th great-granddaughter	VI	6
Robért, Kimberly Ann	4th great-granddaughter	VI	6
Robért, Kirk David	3rd great-grandson	V	5
Robért, Kody Paul	4th great-grandson	VI	6
Robért, Kristy Ann	4th great-granddaughter	VI	6
Robért, Kyle Joseph	4th great-grandson	VI	6
Robért, Lance Allen	4th great-grandson	VI	6
Robért, Lane Anthony	3rd great-grandson	V	5
Robért, Larry Denis, Jr.	4th great-grandson	VI	6
Robért, Larry Denis, Sr.	3rd great-grandson	V	5
Robért, Laura	2nd great-granddaughter	IV	4
Robért, Laura	3rd great-granddaughter	V	5
Robért, Lawrence	Great-grandson	III	3
Robért, Lawrence	3rd great-grandson	V	5
Robért, Leah	3rd great-granddaughter	V	5
Robért, Leah Paige	4th great-granddaughter	VI	6
Robért, Leona	3rd great-granddaughter	V	5
Robért, Leona Theresa, (Na-Na)	Great-granddaughter	III	3
Robért, Leonie	3rd great-granddaughter	V	5
Robért, Leroy	3rd great-grandson	V	5
Robért, Lester	2nd great-grandson	IV	4
Robért, Libby	2nd great-grandson	IV	4
Robért, Lillian Theresa, (Lil)	2nd great-granddaughter	IV	4
Robért, Linda	3rd great-granddaughter	V	5
Robért, Linda Lea	4th great-granddaughter	VI	6
Robért, Linda Raye	3rd great-granddaughter	V	5
Robért, Lionel Joseph	2nd great-grandson	IV	4
Robért, Living	4th great-grandson	VI	6
Robért, Living	4th great-grandson	VI	6
Robért, Living	4th great-grandson	VI	6

*Kinship of Jean Robért, *-****

Name	Relationship with Jean Robért	Civil	Canon
Robért, Living	4th great-granddaughter	VI	6
Robért, Living	5th great-grandson	VII	7
Robért, Living	5th great-granddaughter	VII	7
Robért, Living	4th great-granddaughter	VI	6
Robért, Living	4th great-granddaughter	VI	6
Robért, Lloyd	3rd great-grandson	V	5
Robért, Loretta	4th great-granddaughter	VI	6
Robért, Louis	Grandson	II	2
Robért, Louis Luke	2nd great-grandson	IV	4
Robért, Louis Matthew	4th great-grandson	VI	6
Robért, Louis Wayne	4th great-grandson	VI	6
Robért, Lucien Augustin	3rd great-grandson	V	5
Robért, Luke	3rd great-grandson	V	5
Robért, Luke McGrath	4th great-grandson	VI	6
Robért, Lynn Jude, Jr.	3rd great-grandson	V	5
Robért, Lynn Jude, Sr. (Noon)	2nd great-grandson	IV	4
Robért, Mable	3rd great-granddaughter	V	5
Robért, Mable	2nd great-granddaughter	IV	4
Robért, Madison Alminte	4th great-granddaughter	VI	6
Robért, Madison Marguerite	4th great-granddaughter	VI	6
Robért, Mae Therèse, (Manette)	2nd great-granddaughter	IV	4
Robért, Magda M.	2nd great-granddaughter	IV	4
Robért, Marcia Ann	4th great-granddaughter	VI	6
Robért, Marcie Ann	3rd great-granddaughter	V	5
Robért, Margaret Elizabeth	4th great-granddaughter	VI	6
Robért, Maria Theresa	4th great-granddaughter	VI	6
Robért, Marian Theresa	3rd great-granddaughter	V	5
Robért, Marianne Esteve	Granddaughter	II	2
Robért, Marianne Melanie	Daughter	I	1
Robért, Marie	2nd great-granddaughter	IV	4
Robért, Marie Noelle	2nd great-granddaughter	IV	4
Robért, Marie Ouida	3rd great-granddaughter	V	5
Robért, Marie Antoinette	Granddaughter	II	2
Robért, Marie Evelina	Great-granddaughter	III	3
Robért, Marie Octavie, ***	Great-granddaughter	III	3
Robért, Marie Oneilda	Great-granddaughter	III	3
Robért, Marie Palmyre, (Tee-Nannan)	Great-granddaughter	III	3
Robért, Marie Phelonise	Granddaughter	II	2
Robért, Marie, (neice)	3rd great-granddaughter	V	5
Robért, Marion	3rd great-grandson	V	5
Robért, Mark Eugene	3rd great-grandson	V	5
Robért, Mark Wayne	4th great-grandson	VI	6
Robért, Martha Marie	3rd great-granddaughter	V	5
Robért, Martha Philomene, (Bot)	Great-granddaughter	III	3
Robért, Marti Luther	3rd great-grandson	V	5
Robért, Mary Bobbye	3rd great-granddaughter	V	5
Robért, Mary Catherine	3rd great-granddaughter	V	5
Robért, Mary Elizabeth,(Betty)	2nd great-granddaughter	IV	4
Robért, Mary Lois	2nd great-granddaughter	IV	4
Robért, Mathieu, *- **- ***	Father	I	1
Robért, Mathieu, Jr. (Yen-Yen)	Grandson	II	2
Robért, Mathieu, Sr. *- ***	Son	I	1
Robért, Matthew Joseph	2nd great-grandson	IV	4
Robért, Matthew Lynn	4th great-grandson	VI	6
Robért, Matthew Paul	3rd great-grandson	V	5

Kinship of Jean Robért, *-***

Name	Relationship with Jean Robért	Civil	Canon
Robért, Matthew Ross	4th great-grandson	VI	6
Robért, Maude Marie	2nd great-granddaughter	IV	4
Robért, Maxie, Jr.	3rd great-grandson	V	5
Robért, Maxie, Sr.	2nd great-grandson	IV	4
Robért, Maybelle	4th great-granddaughter	VI	6
Robért, Meagan Alexandra	4th great-granddaughter	VI	6
Robért, Melanie Odile	Granddaughter	II	2
Robért, Micah Aaron	4th great-grandson	VI	6
Robért, Michael Emile, (lived only 16 hours)	3rd great-grandson	V	5
Robért, Michael Joseph	4th great-grandson	VI	6
Robért, Michael Joseph, Jr.	4th great-grandson	VI	6
Robért, Michael Joseph, Sr.	3rd great-grandson	V	5
Robért, Michael Jude	4th great-grandson	VI	6
Robért, Michael Octave	3rd great-grandson	V	5
Robért, Michael Paul	4th great-grandson	VI	6
Robért, Michael Paul	4th great-grandson	VI	6
Robért, Michelle Christy	3rd great-granddaughter	V	5
Robért, Michelle Renee	4th great-granddaughter	VI	6
Robért, Mitzi Marie	3rd great-granddaughter	V	5
Robért, Mona Ann	3rd great-granddaughter	V	5
Robért, Mordecai	4th great-grandson	VI	6
Robért, Morris	2nd great-grandson	IV	4
Robért, Murphy Vincent	3rd great-grandson	V	5
Robért, Myron	4th great-grandson	VI	6
Robért, Myrtile Mathilde Marie	Great-granddaughter	III	3
Robért, Myrtis Agnes	4th great-granddaughter	VI	6
Robért, Nancy Claire	3rd great-granddaughter	V	5
Robért, Natalie Marie	3rd great-granddaughter	V	5
Robért, Nathan Paul	4th great-grandson	VI	6
Robért, Neola Marie	2nd great-granddaughter	IV	4
Robért, Nicholas Matthew	4th great-grandson	VI	6
Robért, Noah Dominique	2nd great-grandson	IV	4
Robért, Noah Miles	5th great-grandson	VII	7
Robért, Noelie	2nd great-granddaughter	IV	4
Robért, Nolan Jacques	3rd great-grandson	V	5
Robért, Norbert	Son	I	1
Robért, Norbert	3rd great-grandson	V	5
Robért, Norbert, Jr.	Grandson	II	2
Robért, Norman Anthony	2nd great-grandson	IV	4
Robért, Octave	2nd great-grandson	IV	4
Robért, Octave Pierre	Great-grandson	III	3
Robért, Odette	2nd great-granddaughter	IV	4
Robért, Odile	2nd great-granddaughter	IV	4
Robért, Odille	Granddaughter	II	2
Robért, Oliver	2nd great-grandson	IV	4
Robért, Oliver Paul, Jr.	3rd great-grandson	V	5
Robért, Oliver Paul, Sr. (Tucker)	2nd great-grandson	IV	4
Robért, Omèr Jean, Sr.	Great-grandson	III	3
Robért, Oneziford	2nd great-granddaughter	IV	4
Robért, Opphonse Ernest	Husband of the 2nd great-granddaughter		
Robért, Optime	Grandson	II	2
Robért, Optime	2nd great-grandson	IV	4
Robért, Palmire	2nd great-granddaughter	IV	4
Robért, Palmire Marie	Granddaughter	II	2
Robért, Pamela Sue	4th great-granddaughter	VI	6

*Kinship of Jean Robért, *-****

Name	Relationship with Jean Robért	Civil	Canon
Robért, Pat	4th great-grandson	VI	6
Robért, Patrick	4th great-grandson	VI	6
Robért, Paul Gerard	2nd great-grandson	IV	4
Robért, Paul,(infant)	2nd great-grandson	IV	4
Robért, Paula Cecile, (Tow-Tow)	Great-granddaughter	III	3
Robért, Pauline	2nd great-granddaughter	IV	4
Robért, Pearl Marguerite	3rd great-granddaughter	V	5
Robért, Penny Elizabeth	3rd great-granddaughter	V	5
Robért, Peter Octave	2nd great-grandson	IV	4
Robért, Philip Stewart	3rd great-grandson	V	5
Robért, Philogene	2nd great-grandson	IV	4
Robért, Phyllis Anne	3rd great-granddaughter	V	5
Robért, Pierre Amedee	Grandson	II	2
Robért, Prudent	2nd great-grandson	IV	4
Robért, Rachel Lynn	4th great-granddaughter	VI	6
Robért, Rachel Maria	3rd great-granddaughter	V	5
Robért, Ralph Joseph	4th great-grandson	VI	6
Robért, Randal James	3rd great-grandson	V	5
Robért, Randall Paul	4th great-grandson	VI	6
Robért, Randi Michelle	4th great-granddaughter	VI	6
Robért, Raoul Matthew	Great-grandson	III	3
Robért, Raoul William, Sr.	3rd great-grandson	V	5
Robért, Raoul William,Jr.	4th great-grandson	VI	6
Robért, Ray	3rd great-grandson	V	5
Robért, Raymond Simon, Jr.	3rd great-grandson	V	5
Robért, Raymond Simon, Sr.	2nd great-grandson	IV	4
Robért, Reagan Katherine	4th great-granddaughter	VI	6
Robért, Rebecca Ann	3rd great-granddaughter	V	5
Robért, Rebecca Elise	4th great-granddaughter	VI	6
Robért, Remy Paul	Great-grandson	III	3
Robért, Remy Paul	4th great-grandson	VI	6
Robért, Remy Pierre	3rd great-grandson	V	5
Robért, Rene Benoit, (Ne-Nall)	Great-grandson	III	3
Robért, Renee Ellemarie	4th great-granddaughter	VI	6
Robért, Renée Geralyn	3rd great-granddaughter	V	5
Robért, Renell Joseph	3rd great-grandson	V	5
Robért, Richard Charles	Husband of the 2nd great-grandniece		
Robért, Rickey John	3rd great-grandson	V	5
Robért, Rivis	3rd great-grandson	V	5
Robért, Robert Francis	2nd great-grandson	IV	4
Robért, Robin Andrea	3rd great-granddaughter	V	5
Robért, Robyn Elizabeth	4th great-granddaughter	VI	6
Robért, Roland	3rd great-grandson	V	5
Robért, Roland Jacques, Sr. (Pan-Am)	Great-grandson	III	3
Robért, Roland James III	3rd great-grandson	V	5
Robért, Roland James IV	4th great-grandson	VI	6
Robért, Roland James,Jr. (Row)	2nd great-grandson	IV	4
Robért, Ronald	3rd great-grandson	V	5
Robért, Rose Marie	3rd great-granddaughter	V	5
Robért, Roselie Marie	3rd great-granddaughter	V	5
Robért, Rosemond	Husband of the great-granddaughter		
Robért, Rosine Philomene	2nd great-granddaughter	IV	4
Robért, Roy Michael	3rd great-grandson	V	5
Robért, Ruby	3rd great-granddaughter	V	5
Robért, Rurick Anthony	2nd great-grandson	IV	4

Kinship of Jean Robért, *-***

Name	Relationship with Jean Robért	Civil	Canon
Robért, Russell Joseph	4th great-grandson	VI	6
Robért, Ryan Gerald	4th great-grandson	VI	6
Robért, Samantha Grace	4th great-granddaughter	VI	6
Robért, Sarah Elizabeth	3rd great-granddaughter	V	5
Robért, Sarah Elizabeth	4th great-granddaughter	VI	6
Robért, Sarah Elizabeth	4th great-granddaughter	VI	6
Robért, Sarah Michelle	4th great-granddaughter	VI	6
Robért, Sardos, (Nonc P-P)	Grandson	II	2
Robért, Savannah Marie	4th great-granddaughter	VI	6
Robért, Scot Austin	4th great-grandson	VI	6
Robért, Septime	Great-grandson	III	3
Robért, Septime Louis, Sr.	Grandson	II	2
Robért, Septime, Jr.	Great-grandson	III	3
Robért, Shelby	3rd great-grandson	V	5
Robért, Shelby Lawrence	2nd great-grandson	IV	4
Robért, Shellie Marie	4th great-granddaughter	VI	6
Robért, Shelly Lauren	3rd great-granddaughter	V	5
Robért, Sheree Michelle	4th great-granddaughter	VI	6
Robért, Shirline	3rd great-grandson	V	5
Robért, Sosthine	Grandson	II	2
Robért, Stella	2nd great-granddaughter	IV	4
Robért, Stephanie	4th great-granddaughter	VI	6
Robért, Stephanie Ann	3rd great-granddaughter	V	5
Robért, Stephen Adam, (Steve)	2nd great-grandson	IV	4
Robért, Susan Marie	4th great-granddaughter	VI	6
Robért, Suzanne Marie	3rd great-granddaughter	V	5
Robért, Tatum Quinn	5th great-grandson	VII	7
Robért, Taylor Ashleigh	4th great-granddaughter	VI	6
Robért, Taylor Morris	3rd great-grandson	V	5
Robért, Terry Jude	3rd great-grandson	V	5
Robért, Theotine	Great-grandson	III	3
Robért, Therése	2nd great-granddaughter	IV	4
Robért, Thomas James	2nd great-grandson	IV	4
Robért, Thomas Jude	3rd great-grandson	V	5
Robért, Todd Justin	3rd great-grandson	V	5
Robért, Todd Justin II	4th great-grandson	VI	6
Robért, Toni Therese	4th great-granddaughter	VI	6
Robért, Tycer Francis	4th great-granddaughter	VI	6
Robért, Udger	Grandson	II	2
Robért, Ursin	Grandson	II	2
Robért, Val Ann	2nd great-granddaughter	IV	4
Robért, Valerie	2nd great-grandson	IV	4
Robért, Vernon	4th great-grandson	VI	6
Robért, Victor	2nd great-grandson	IV	4
Robért, Victoria Hayes	4th great-granddaughter	VI	6
Robért, Vivian Cecilia	3rd great-granddaughter	V	5
Robért, Waldon Charles	3rd great-grandson	V	5
Robért, Wallace Jean, Sr.	Great-grandson	III	3
Robért, Warren F.	4th great-grandson	VI	6
Robért, Wesley David	3rd great-grandson	V	5
Robért, William	2nd great-grandson	IV	4
Robért, Willie	4th great-grandson	VI	6
Robért, Willie A.	3rd great-grandson	V	5
Robért, Willis Louis Mathieu	Great-grandson	III	3
Robért, Winna Marie	2nd great-granddaughter	IV	4

*Kinship of Jean Robért, *-****

Name	Relationship with Jean Robért	Civil	Canon
Roberts, Blaine	Husband of the 3rd great-granddaughter		
Robertson, Carolyn Marie	Wife of the 3rd great-grandson		
Robertson, Datren Quintel,(stepson)	5th great-grandson	VII	7
Robichaux, Aidan Paul	6th great-grandson	VIII	8
Robichaux, Benoit V.	Husband of the 3rd great-granddaughter		
Robichaux, Daniel David	Husband of the 4th great-granddaughter		
Robichaux, Danielle Marie	5th great-granddaughter	VII	7
Robichaux, Enola	Wife of the 3rd great-grandnephew		
Robichaux, Hubert Joseph	Great-grandnephew of the wife		
Robichaux, Jay Gerald, (Adopted)	5th great-grandson	VII	7
Robichaux, Jeffrey Paul, (Adopted)	5th great-grandson	VII	7
Robichaux, Louisiana Marie	Wife of the great-grandnephew		
Robichaux, Margaret Frances	Wife of the 3rd great-grandson		
Rodi, Marie Louise	Wife of the grandnephew		
Rodrigue, Melissa Marie	5th great-granddaughter	VII	7
Rodrigue, Meredith Michelle	5th great-granddaughter	VII	7
Rodrigue, Ronald	Husband of the 4th great-granddaughter		
Rodrigue, Ronnie Joseph, Jr	5th great-grandson	VII	7
Rodrigue, Ronnie Joseph, Sr.	Husband of the 4th great-granddaughter		
Rodrigue, Ryan Joseph	5th great-grandson	VII	7
Roger, André	Husband of the mother		
Roger, Francoise	Half sister	II	1
Rome, Adele Marie	4th great-granddaughter	VI	6
Rome, Adeline Estelle	5th great-granddaughter	VII	7
Rome, Aimee Cecile	4th great-granddaughter	VI	6
Rome, Alexander Paul	4th great-grandson	VI	6
Rome, Alfred Joseph	2nd great-grandnephew	VI	5
Rome, Alice Marie	3rd great-granddaughter	V	5
Rome, Ashley Ann	4th great-granddaughter	VI	6
Rome, Beulah	2nd great-grandniece	VI	5
Rome, Bryan	4th great-grandson	VI	6
Rome, Burgin Elizabeth	5th great-granddaughter	VII	7
Rome, Byron Robert	4th great-grandson	VI	6
Rome, Carey Louis	4th great-grandson	VI	6
Rome, Carolyn	3rd great-granddaughter	V	5
Rome, Carter Byron	5th great-grandson	VII	7
Rome, Charles David, (C.D.)	2nd great-grandson	IV	4
Rome, Christopher Paul	3rd great-grandson	V	5
Rome, Cynthia	3rd great-granddaughter	V	5
Rome, Desiree	4th great-granddaughter	VI	6
Rome, Donald Joseph, (Jug Head)	2nd great-grandson	IV	4
Rome, Donovan	3rd great-grandson	V	5
Rome, Edith Reneè	3rd great-granddaughter	V	5
Rome, Eileen Mary	3rd great-granddaughter	V	5
Rome, Eleanor Loretta	3rd great-granddaughter	V	5
Rome, Eleonore	3rd great-grandniece of the wife		
Rome, Elizabeth Day	3rd great-granddaughter	V	5
Rome, Eunice	2nd great-grandniece	VI	5
Rome, Evelie	3rd great-grandniece of the wife		
Rome, Eveline	2nd great-grandniece	VI	5
Rome, Felicity Ida	Wife of the great-grandnephew		
Rome, Francois Alfred	Husband of the great-grandniece		
Rome, Georgine	Wife of the half 2nd great-grandnephew		
Rome, Geraldine	2nd great-grandniece	VI	5
Rome, Gregg Lawrence	4th great-grandson	VI	6

Kinship of Jean Robért, *-***

Name	Relationship with Jean Robért	Civil	Canon
Rome, Gregory Allen	3rd great-grandson	V	5
Rome, Hilda	2nd great-grandniece	VI	5
Rome, Hillary Louis	5th great-granddaughter	VII	7
Rome, Ike Antoine	2nd great-grandson	IV	4
Rome, Jean Landry	Great-grandnephew of the wife		
Rome, John Augustin, Jr.	3rd great-grandson	V	5
Rome, John Augustin, Sr. (Gus)	2nd great-grandson	IV	4
Rome, John Benton	5th great-grandson	VII	7
Rome, John Paul, Sr.	3rd great-grandson	V	5
Rome, John Paul,Jr.	4th great-grandson	VI	6
Rome, Joseph Louis, Sr. ***	Husband of the great-granddaughter		
Rome, Joy Elizabeth	3rd great-granddaughter	V	5
Rome, Judith Anne	3rd great-granddaughter	V	5
Rome, Kathy	3rd great-granddaughter	V	5
Rome, Leone	2nd great-grandniece	VI	5
Rome, Lillian Theresa	2nd great-granddaughter	IV	4
Rome, Louis Joseph, Jr.	2nd great-grandson	IV	4
Rome, Louis Leon	3rd great-grandnephew of the wife		
Rome, Lucille Marie, (Lucy)	2nd great-granddaughter	IV	4
Rome, Marie Stella	Wife of the half 2nd great-grandnephew		
Rome, Melvin	2nd great-grandnephew	VI	5
Rome, Mia Juliana	5th great-granddaughter	VII	7
Rome, Michael H.	3rd great-grandson	V	5
Rome, Michelle Margaret	4th great-granddaughter	VI	6
Rome, Mildred	2nd great-grandniece	VI	5
Rome, Molda	Wife of the great-grandnephew		
Rome, Nemour	2nd great-grandnephew	VI	5
Rome, Olivia Frances	5th great-granddaughter	VII	7
Rome, O'Neil Francis	2nd great-grandson	IV	4
Rome, O'Neil Francis,Jr.	3rd great-grandson	V	5
Rome, O'Neil Francis,III	4th great-grandson	VI	6
Rome, Paul Marshall	4th great-grandson	VI	6
Rome, Paul Robert	2nd great-grandson	IV	4
Rome, Richard Charles	3rd great-grandson	V	5
Rome, Rita G.	Wife of the half 3rd great-grandnephew		
Rome, Robbie	2nd great-grandnephew	VI	5
Rome, Robert Louis	3rd great-grandson	V	5
Rome, Robért Steven	4th great-grandson	VI	6
Rome, Ronald Richard	3rd great-grandson	V	5
Rome, Sarah Cardow	4th great-granddaughter	VI	6
Rome, Signa Mathieu	3rd great-granddaughter	V	5
Rome, Suzanne P.	3rd great-granddaughter	V	5
Rome, Suzette Estelle	4th great-granddaughter	VI	6
Rome, Teresa Ann	3rd great-granddaughter	V	5
Rome, Victoria Rhodes	4th great-granddaughter	VI	6
Root, Jo Lynn	Wife of the 3rd great-grandson		
Roques, Achille	Husband of the 2nd great-granddaughter		
Rossi, Jena Renee	5th great-granddaughter	VII	7
Rossi, Michele Leigh	5th great-granddaughter	VII	7
Rossi, Richard, Jr.	Husband of the 4th great-granddaughter		
Rousseau, Lee Anna	Wife of the 2nd great-grandson		
Roussel, Chad	5th great-grandson	VII	7
Roussel, Effie Josephine	Wife of the 4th great-grandson		
Roussel, Jamie Lynne	5th great-granddaughter	VII	7
Roussel, Leonard Paul	Husband of the 4th great-granddaughter		

*Kinship of Jean Robért, *-****

Name	Relationship with Jean Robért	Civil	Canon
Roussel, Mona	Wife of the 3rd great-grandson		
Roussel, Stacey Lynn	5th great-granddaughter	VII	7
Rowell, David Francis	Husband of the 4th great-granddaughter		
Roy, Malea Rachel	Wife of the 4th great-grandson		
Ruiz, James	Husband of the 3rd great-grandniece		
Russell, Ima Lorene	Wife of the 4th great-grandson		
Sagona, Judy Elizabeth	Wife of the 4th great-grandson		
Saia, Salvadore	Husband of the 3rd great-grandniece		
Salas, Victor	Husband of the 4th great-granddaughter		
Salaun, Cheryl Lynn	Wife of the 4th great-grandson		
Salvail, Christopher Michael	Husband of the 3rd great-granddaughter		
Salvail, Lanie Elizabeth	4th great-granddaughter	VI	6
Salvail, Luke Michael	4th great-grandson	VI	6
Sanders, Jeannie Arlene	Wife of the 2nd great-grandson		
Sandoz, Tosy	Husband of the 3rd great-granddaughter		
Saucier, Edgar Anthony, III	Husband of the 3rd great-granddaughter		
Saucier, Lauren Day	4th great-granddaughter	VI	6
Saucier, Steven Paul	4th great-grandson	VI	6
Saurage, Susie	Wife of the 4th great-grandson		
Savoie, Blake D.	5th great-grandson	VII	7
Savoie, Caroline Elizabeth	5th great-granddaughter	VII	7
Savoie, Daniel Nicholas	4th great-grandson	VI	6
Savoie, Eunice Norma Marie	Wife of the 4th great-grandson		
Savoie, Jon Anthony	Husband of the 3rd great-granddaughter		
Savoie, Jon Anthony,Jr	4th great-grandson	VI	6
Savoie, Kelsey Nicole	5th great-granddaughter	VII	7
Savoie, Leslie Ann	5th great-granddaughter	VII	7
Savoie, Lisa Marie	4th great-granddaughter	VI	6
Savoie, Michelle Ann	4th great-granddaughter	VI	6
Savoie, Michelle Marie	5th great-granddaughter	VII	7
Savoie, Nicholas J.	5th great-grandson	VII	7
Savoie, Pamela Joan	4th great-granddaughter	VI	6
Savoie, Sarah Elizabeth	5th great-granddaughter	VII	7
Savoie, Stephanie Jo	4th great-granddaughter	VI	6
Savoy, Brady Michael	4th great-grandson	VI	6
Savoy, Brian	Husband of the 3rd great-granddaughter		
Savoy, Dawn Marie	Wife of the 3rd great-grandson		
Savoy, Laura Ashley, (Adopted)	4th great-granddaughter	VI	6
Savoy, Leza Delano, Jr.	Husband of the 3rd great-granddaughter		
Savoy, Seth Brian	4th great-grandson	VI	6
Savoy, Tina Lynn	4th great-granddaughter	VI	6
Say, Alexander Douglas	5th great-grandson	VII	7
Say, George Douglas	Husband of the 4th great-granddaughter		
Say, Harrison George	5th great-grandson	VII	7
Say, Parker Robert	5th great-grandson	VII	7
Say, Whitney Estelle	5th great-granddaughter	VII	7
Scallon, Rita	Wife of the 2nd great-grandnephew		
Schexnayder, Alan Manuel	Half 6th great-grandnephew	X	9
Schexnayder, Albert	Son-in-law		
Schexnayder, Alherry Joseph	Great-grandson	III	3
Schexnayder, Amanda	Wife of the 5th great-grandson		
Schexnayder, Amy Marie	Wife of the 4th great-grandson		
Schexnayder, Antoinette	2nd great-granddaughter	IV	4
Schexnayder, Azelie	2nd great-granddaughter	IV	4
Schexnayder, Cecila	2nd great-granddaughter	IV	4

Kinship of Jean Robért, *-***

Name	Relationship with Jean Robért	Civil	Canon
Schexnayder, Charles Joseph	Husband of the 4th great-granddaughter		
Schexnayder, Claire	4th great-granddaughter	VI	6
Schexnayder, Clara Belle	4th great-granddaughter	VI	6
Schexnayder, Claude	3rd great-grandson	V	5
Schexnayder, Clemence	Wife of the half 1st cousin		
Schexnayder, Edgar Joseph III	Half 5th great-grandnephew	IX	8
Schexnayder, Edgar Joseph, Sr.	Husband of the half 3rd great-grandniece		
Schexnayder, Edgar, Jr.	Half 4th great-grandnephew	VIII	7
Schexnayder, Edwin Joseph	2nd great-grandson	IV	4
Schexnayder, Edwin Joseph, Jr.	3rd great-grandson	V	5
Schexnayder, Elodie	2nd great-granddaughter	IV	4
Schexnayder, Emilien	Husband of the half grandniece		
Schexnayder, Emilien	Grandson	II	2
Schexnayder, Emilien Joseph	Great-grandson	III	3
Schexnayder, Epiphany (Etienne), Sr.	Half 2nd cousin of the wife		
Schexnayder, Epiphany <Tiffany>, Jr.	Son-in-law		
Schexnayder, Ethel	Wife of the 2nd great-grandson		
Schexnayder, Furcy	Great-grandnephew	V	4
Schexnayder, Gary	Half 4th great-grandnephew	VIII	7
Schexnayder, Genevieve	3rd great-granddaughter	V	5
Schexnayder, Gerrard (Jerry)	4th great-grandson	VI	6
Schexnayder, Gilbert	Great-grandson	III	3
Schexnayder, Hubert Joseph	Great-grandson	III	3
Schexnayder, Inette	3rd great-granddaughter	V	5
Schexnayder, Jean Marcellin, (Zoot)	2nd great-grandson	IV	4
Schexnayder, Kalli Anne	5th great-granddaughter	VII	7
Schexnayder, Kelley	4th great-grandson	VI	6
Schexnayder, Kent	4th great-grandson	VI	6
Schexnayder, Kevin Mark	4th great-grandson	VI	6
Schexnayder, Kim	4th great-granddaughter	VI	6
Schexnayder, Louis Bartholomu	Great-grandson	III	3
Schexnayder, Madeline Marie	Half 6th great-grandniece	X	9
Schexnayder, Marcelin	Husband of the grandniece		
Schexnayder, Marcelin Ursin	Great-grandnephew	V	4
Schexnayder, Marcellin	Grandson	II	2
Schexnayder, Marcellin G.	2nd great-grandson	IV	4
Schexnayder, Marcellin O	2nd great-grandson	IV	4
Schexnayder, Marie	Wife of the grandson		
Schexnayder, Marie Beatrice	Wife of the 2nd great-grandson		
Schexnayder, Marie Marcelline	2nd great-granddaughter	IV	4
Schexnayder, Marie Octavie	Wife of the nephew		
Schexnayder, Marie Azelino	Great-granddaughter	III	3
Schexnayder, Marie Donna	3rd great-granddaughter	V	5
Schexnayder, Mary Ann	4th great-granddaughter	VI	6
Schexnayder, Odile	2nd great-granddaughter	IV	4
Schexnayder, Optime Joseph	Great-grandson	III	3
Schexnayder, Orenia	2nd great-granddaughter	IV	4
Schexnayder, Phedlise	Wife of the 2nd great-grandnephew		
Schexnayder, Philomine	Great-grandniece	V	4
Schexnayder, Pierre Roman	2nd great-grandson	IV	4
Schexnayder, Robin	Half 4th great-grandniece	VIII	7
Schexnayder, Rosa T.	2nd great-granddaughter	IV	4
Schexnayder, Rose	4th great-granddaughter	VI	6
Schexnayder, Sidney, Jr.	2nd great-grandson	IV	4
Schexnayder, Simon Joseph	3rd great-grandson	V	5

243

Kinship of Jean Robért, *-***

Name	Relationship with Jean Robért	Civil	Canon
Schexnayder, Susie	Half 4th great-grandniece	VIII	7
Schexnayder, Victor Arnold	3rd great-grandson	V	5
Schexnayder, Victor Joseph,Sr.	2nd great-grandson	IV	4
Schexnayder, Willis	2nd great-grandson	IV	4
Schexnayder, Zoe Suzanna	2nd great-granddaughter	IV	4
Schexnaydre, Ada	2nd great-granddaughter	IV	4
Schexnaydre, Agnes	2nd great-granddaughter	IV	4
Schexnaydre, Alan Joseph	5th great-grandson	VII	7
Schexnaydre, Albert Simon	Great-grandson	III	3
Schexnaydre, Alceé	2nd great-grandson	IV	4
Schexnaydre, Alicia Marie	5th great-granddaughter	VII	7
Schexnaydre, Andrew	5th great-grandson	VII	7
Schexnaydre, Angela Ann	4th great-granddaughter	VI	6
Schexnaydre, Anne	2nd great-granddaughter	IV	4
Schexnaydre, Antonia, (ya-ya)	Great-granddaughter	III	3
Schexnaydre, Bernadette Marie	2nd great-granddaughter	IV	4
Schexnaydre, Bertha M.	2nd great-granddaughter	IV	4
Schexnaydre, Berthile Joseph, Jr. (Bert)	3rd great-grandson	V	5
Schexnaydre, Berthile Joseph, Sr. *	2nd great-grandson	IV	4
Schexnaydre, Bertin, (Boo Boo)	2nd great-grandson	IV	4
Schexnaydre, Bianca	3rd great-granddaughter	V	5
Schexnaydre, Blaine Thaddeus	4th great-grandson	VI	6
Schexnaydre, Boyd Joseph	4th great-grandson	VI	6
Schexnaydre, Brian Thomas	4th great-grandson	VI	6
Schexnaydre, Carmen Ann	4th great-granddaughter	VI	6
Schexnaydre, Cecile Marie	2nd great-granddaughter	IV	4
Schexnaydre, Chris Michael	4th great-grandson	VI	6
Schexnaydre, Clara	2nd great-granddaughter	IV	4
Schexnaydre, Clint Michael	4th great-grandson	VI	6
Schexnaydre, Clyde Thaddeus	3rd great-grandson	V	5
Schexnaydre, Connie Theresa	3rd great-granddaughter	V	5
Schexnaydre, Craig Joseph	4th great-grandson	VI	6
Schexnaydre, Crystal Michelle	4th great-granddaughter	VI	6
Schexnaydre, Dale Anthony	4th great-grandson	VI	6
Schexnaydre, Dayton	3rd great-grandson	V	5
Schexnaydre, Delia	2nd great-granddaughter	IV	4
Schexnaydre, Dennis Thomas	2nd great-grandson	IV	4
Schexnaydre, Diane Marie	4th great-granddaughter	VI	6
Schexnaydre, Dirk P.	4th great-grandson	VI	6
Schexnaydre, Dolores Edith,(Doe-Doe)	3rd great-granddaughter	V	5
Schexnaydre, Earl Joseph	3rd great-grandson	V	5
Schexnaydre, Edith Marie, (Bo-Boot)	3rd great-granddaughter	V	5
Schexnaydre, Effie	2nd great-granddaughter	IV	4
Schexnaydre, Elaine Rita	3rd great-granddaughter	V	5
Schexnaydre, Elise Marie	2nd great-granddaughter	IV	4
Schexnaydre, Ellen Claire	4th great-granddaughter	VI	6
Schexnaydre, Ferducie F.	2nd great-grandson	IV	4
Schexnaydre, Floribert Pierre, *	Husband of the granddaughter		
Schexnaydre, Francois	Husband of the half 2nd great-grandniece		
Schexnaydre, Guy Grancis	4th great-grandson	VI	6
Schexnaydre, Henry Joseph, Sr *	Great-grandson	III	3
Schexnaydre, Henry, Jr.	2nd great-grandson	IV	4
Schexnaydre, Imelda	2nd great-granddaughter	IV	4
Schexnaydre, Ione Theresa	3rd great-granddaughter	V	5
Schexnaydre, Iris Joan	4th great-granddaughter	VI	6

*Kinship of Jean Robért, *-****

Name	Relationship with Jean Robért	Civil	Canon
Schexnaydre, James Maurice	4th great-grandson	VI	6
Schexnaydre, Jay Michael	4th great-grandson	VI	6
Schexnaydre, Jeffery Joseph	4th great-grandson	VI	6
Schexnaydre, Jody Lynne	5th great-granddaughter	VII	7
Schexnaydre, Julian Pierre, Sr. (Zoo)	2nd great-grandson	IV	4
Schexnaydre, Julian Pierre,Jr.	3rd great-grandson	V	5
Schexnaydre, Katheleen	3rd great-granddaughter	V	5
Schexnaydre, Kenneth, (Ke-Ken)	3rd great-grandson	V	5
Schexnaydre, Kent Alan	4th great-grandson	VI	6
Schexnaydre, Kim Marie	4th great-granddaughter	VI	6
Schexnaydre, Kim Marie	5th great-granddaughter	VII	7
Schexnaydre, Kip J.	4th great-grandson	VI	6
Schexnaydre, Lamar	4th great-grandson	VI	6
Schexnaydre, Lance Paul	4th great-grandson	VI	6
Schexnaydre, Larry Joseph	4th great-grandson	VI	6
Schexnaydre, Laurence	2nd great-granddaughter	IV	4
Schexnaydre, Lee, (Bill)	2nd great-grandson	IV	4
Schexnaydre, Lorain	3rd great-granddaughter	V	5
Schexnaydre, Loraine	2nd great-granddaughter	IV	4
Schexnaydre, Lorna Mary	4th great-granddaughter	VI	6
Schexnaydre, Lyle	3rd great-grandson	V	5
Schexnaydre, Lynette Marie	4th great-granddaughter	VI	6
Schexnaydre, Marie	3rd great-granddaughter	V	5
Schexnaydre, Marie Anastasie	Wife of the half great-grandnephew		
Schexnaydre, Marie Louise Clara	Great-granddaughter	III	3
Schexnaydre, Marlene Marie	3rd great-granddaughter	V	5
Schexnaydre, Mathilda Valerie	2nd great-granddaughter	IV	4
Schexnaydre, Myles Michael	4th great-grandson	VI	6
Schexnaydre, Neal Joseph	4th great-grandson	VI	6
Schexnaydre, Nolte Pierre	3rd great-grandson	V	5
Schexnaydre, Oleus, Jr. (Rusty)	3rd great-grandson	V	5
Schexnaydre, Oleus, Sr.	2nd great-grandson	IV	4
Schexnaydre, Olide	2nd great-grandson	IV	4
Schexnaydre, Oliva	2nd great-grandson	IV	4
Schexnaydre, Olympe,(may-yea)	Great-granddaughter	III	3
Schexnaydre, Rita	2nd great-granddaughter	IV	4
Schexnaydre, Roberta Ann	3rd great-granddaughter	V	5
Schexnaydre, Ryan Joseph	5th great-grandson	VII	7
Schexnaydre, Sidney, Sr.	Great-grandson	III	3
Schexnaydre, Stacey Marie	4th great-granddaughter	VI	6
Schexnaydre, Tab Andrew	4th great-grandson	VI	6
Schexnaydre, Terri Lynne	4th great-granddaughter	VI	6
Schexnaydre, Timothy	3rd great-grandson	V	5
Schexnaydre, Troy Michael	4th great-grandson	VI	6
Schexnaydre, Verna Agnes	4th great-granddaughter	VI	6
Schexnaydre, Vernon, (Coon)	3rd great-grandson	V	5
Schexnaydre, Wade M.	5th great-grandson	VII	7
Schexnaydre, Wilfred J., Jr.	2nd great-grandson	IV	4
Schexnaydre, Wilfred Joseph	Great-grandson	III	3
Schoff, David	Husband of the 2nd great-grandniece		
Schwietzer, Wilmer B.	Husband of the 2nd great-grandniece		
Serio, Brian Gregory	4th great-grandson	VI	6
Serio, Erin Michelle	4th great-granddaughter	VI	6
Serio, Greg	Husband of the 3rd great-granddaughter		
Serio, Hayden Scott	4th great-grandson	VI	6

*Kinship of Jean Robért, *-****

Name	Relationship with Jean Robért	Civil	Canon
Seymour, Constance Lorraine	Wife of the 2nd great-grandson		
Shaddinger, Scott	Husband of the 4th great-granddaughter		
Shaffer, Eric Stanley	Husband of the 4th great-granddaughter		
Shaheen, George Joseph, Jr.	Husband of the 4th great-granddaughter		
Shea, Christopher Earl	4th great-grandson	VI	6
Shea, Dana Marie	4th great-granddaughter	VI	6
Shea, Timothy Earl	Husband of the 3rd great-granddaughter		
Shea, Timothy Joseph	4th great-grandson	VI	6
Sheets, Anne Marie	4th great-granddaughter	VI	6
Sheets, Damian Michael	4th great-grandson	VI	6
Sheets, J. Ferrel	Husband of the 3rd great-granddaughter		
Sheets, Kari Marie	4th great-granddaughter	VI	6
Sheets, Robin Michelle	4th great-granddaughter	VI	6
Sheets, Sandy Theresa	4th great-granddaughter	VI	6
Shepherd, Torrie Juanita	Wife of the 4th great-grandson		
Sherrwood, Joan Karen, (Divorced)	Ex-wife of the 3rd great-grandson		
Shows, Edmond Wade	Husband of the 4th great-granddaughter		
Shows, Priscilla Lane	Wife of the 2nd great-grandson		
Shrider, Laurie	Wife of the 3rd great-grandson		
Siegel, Living	Husband of the half 3rd great-grandniece		
Simon, Amelie <Emelie>	Wife of the nephew		
Simon, Earl S.	Half 3rd great-grandnephew	VII	6
Simon, Joseph Thomas	Husband of the half 2nd great-grandniece		
Simon, Joseph Thomas	Husband of the half 2nd great-grandniece		
Simon, Marie Erasie	Wife of the 2nd great-grandson		
Simon, Mary Alice	Wife of the 3rd great-grandson		
Simon, Prudent	Husband of the 2nd great-granddaughter		
Simon, Virginia Marie	Wife of the half 2nd great-grandnephew		
Simoneaux, Brian Alvin	3rd great-grandson	V	5
Simoneaux, Bruce James	3rd great-grandson	V	5
Simoneaux, Cindy Olive	Wife of the 3rd great-grandson		
Simoneaux, Guy Remy	3rd great-grandson	V	5
Simoneaux, Jill Elaine	3rd great-granddaughter	V	5
Simoneaux, Kayla Anne	4th great-granddaughter	VI	6
Simoneaux, Kellie Marie	4th great-granddaughter	VI	6
Simoneaux, Landry Lois	4th great-granddaughter	VI	6
Simoneaux, Mervin J.	Husband of the 2nd great-granddaughter		
Simoneaux, Rachel Anne	4th great-granddaughter	VI	6
Simoneaux, Randi Lauren	4th great-granddaughter	VI	6
Simoneaux, Regan Landry	4th great-granddaughter	VI	6
Simoneaux, Remy Robert	4th great-grandson	VI	6
Simoneaux, Rhonda Gayle, (Divorced)	Ex-wife of the 4th great-grandson		
Simoneaux, Robert Lynn	3rd great-grandson	V	5
Simoneaux, Wade Michael	3rd great-grandson	V	5
Simpson, Cade	5th great-grandson	VII	7
Simpson, Jacey Lynn	Wife of the 5th great-grandson		
Simpson, Korey Dean	5th great-grandson	VII	7
Simpson, Quinn David	5th great-grandson	VII	7
Simpson, Randy Gerard	Husband of the 4th great-granddaughter		
Smiley, James Ray, Jr.	Husband of the 4th great-granddaughter		
Smiley, James Ray, III	5th great-grandson	VII	7
Smiley, Jason Paul	5th great-grandson	VII	7
Smiley, Kenny	Husband of the 3rd great-grandniece		
Smiley, Margo Michele	5th great-granddaughter	VII	7
Smiley, Meridith Ann	5th great-granddaughter	VII	7

Kinship of Jean Robért, *-***

Name	Relationship with Jean Robért	Civil	Canon
Smith, Adrian R.	4th great-grandson	VI	6
Smith, Donald Russel	Husband of the 3rd great-granddaughter		
Smith, Gretchen Kay	4th great-granddaughter	VI	6
Smith, Joy Caryl	Wife of the 4th great-grandson		
Smith, Joy Helaine	5th great-granddaughter	VII	7
Smith, Lauren Marie	4th great-granddaughter	VI	6
Smith, Patricia	Wife of the 3rd great-grandson		
Smith, Russel Cortez	Husband of the 4th great-granddaughter		
Smith, Sue T.	Wife of the 4th great-grandson		
Sockrider, Aidan Christopher	5th great-grandson	VII	7
Sockrider, Austin Louis	5th great-grandson	VII	7
Sockrider, Benjamin Finley	5th great-grandson	VII	7
Sockrider, Christopher Sean	4th great-grandson	VI	6
Sockrider, Eleanor Monique	5th great-granddaughter	VII	7
Sockrider, Gary Wayne	4th great-grandson	VI	6
Sockrider, Grant Christopher	5th great-grandson	VII	7
Sockrider, Herman Finley, Jr.	Husband of the 3rd great-granddaughter		
Sockrider, James Henry	5th great-grandson	VII	7
Sockrider, Keith Brian	4th great-grandson	VI	6
Sockrider, Kyle Merritt	5th great-grandson	VII	7
Sockrider, Steven Louis	4th great-grandson	VI	6
Sockrider, Walker Alan	5th great-grandson	VII	7
Soignet, Elmo Andrew	Husband of the 3rd great-granddaughter		
Soignet, Robin Marie	4th great-granddaughter	VI	6
Soignet., Elmo	4th great-grandson	VI	6
Soileau, Stacie Charmaine	Wife of the 3rd great-grandson		
Solomon, David Joseph	Husband of the 3rd great-granddaughter		
Songy, Carol Marie	Wife of the 4th great-grandson		
Songy, Jeanne	Wife of the 3rd great-grandson		
Sotile, Lisa Marie	4th great-granddaughter	VI	6
Sotile, Monica Lynne	4th great-granddaughter	VI	6
Sotile, Vincent Joseph, (Beazy)	Husband of the 3rd great-granddaughter		
Sotile, Vincent Joseph, Jr.	4th great-grandson	VI	6
Sotile, Wendy Ann	4th great-granddaughter	VI	6
Spears, William	Husband of the 4th great-granddaughter		
Spitzfaden, Newton Joseph	Husband of the 2nd great-granddaughter		
St. Pierre, Jessica Claire	5th great-granddaughter	VII	7
St. Pierre, Rickie Anthony	Husband of the 4th great-granddaughter		
St. Pierre, Shana Lynne	5th great-granddaughter	VII	7
Stansbury, Mary	Wife of the 2nd great-grandnephew		
Stelly, Cecily Claire	4th great-granddaughter	VI	6
Stelly, Dawson Armand	6th great-grandson	VIII	8
Stelly, Easton Robert	4th great-grandson	VI	6
Stelly, Gregory Paul	Husband of the 3rd great-granddaughter		
Stelly, Juston Paul	Husband of the 5th great-granddaughter		
Stephens, Barbera	Wife of the 3rd great-grandson		
Stephens, Carol	Wife of the 4th great-grandson		
Stephens, Joseph Thomas	Husband of the 4th great-granddaughter		
Stephens, Sue	Wife of the 3rd great-grandson		
Sternfels, Sarah	Wife of the 4th great-grandson		
Stevens, Blake Edwards	4th great-grandson	VI	6
Stevens, Greg Patrick	4th great-grandson	VI	6
Stevens, Mark Alvin	4th great-grandson	VI	6
Stevens, Murray Edward	Husband of the 3rd great-granddaughter		
Stevens, Patrice Marie	4th great-granddaughter	VI	6

*Kinship of Jean Robért, *-****

Name	Relationship with Jean Robért	Civil	Canon
Stewart, Elizabeth Adele	Wife of the 2nd great-grandson		
Stewart, Janet Marie	Wife of the 3rd great-grandnephew		
Stewart, Kim	Wife of the 4th great-grandson		
Strapola, Steve	Husband of the 4th great-granddaughter		
Swanson, Gregory Joseph	Husband of the 4th great-granddaughter		
Sylvester, Thomas	Husband of the 4th great-granddaughter		
Tabor, James Martin	Husband of the 4th great-granddaughter		
Talbot, Douglas Ellis	Husband of the 4th great-granddaughter		
Tamplain, Thomas W.	Husband of the 2nd great-granddaughter		
Tannehill, Ester	Wife of the 4th great-grandson		
Tassin, Fred Joseph	Husband of the 4th great-granddaughter		
Tassin, Marie Elina	Wife of the half grandnephew		
Taylor, Adam Waggenspack	4th great-grandson	VI	6
Taylor, Brad Keith	4th great-grandson	VI	6
Taylor, Danny Keith	Husband of the 3rd great-granddaughter		
Taylor, Jason David	Husband of the 4th great-granddaughter		
Taylor, Mark Daniel	4th great-grandson	VI	6
Taylor, Mary Jewell	Wife of the 2nd great-grandson		
Templet, Edmond William	Husband of the 4th great-granddaughter		
Templet, Eric Paul	5th great-grandson	VII	7
Templet, Jana Marie	5th great-granddaughter	VII	7
Templet, Kevin Gerard	3rd great-grandnephew	VII	6
Templet, Odon Jean	Husband of the 2nd great-grandniece		
Templet, Timothy Albert	3rd great-grandnephew	VII	6
Terwilliger, Gary	Husband of the 3rd great-granddaughter		
Terwilliger, Martin Wall	4th great-grandson	VI	6
Theriot, Deborah	Wife of the 4th great-grandson		
Thiac, Byron Joseph	Husband of the 3rd great-granddaughter		
Thiac, Cindy Marie	4th great-granddaughter	VI	6
Thiac, Corey Michael	5th great-grandson	VII	7
Thiac, Julie Lynn	4th great-granddaughter	VI	6
Thiac, Mary Beth	4th great-granddaughter	VI	6
Thiac, Melissa Lee	4th great-granddaughter	VI	6
Thiac, Peggy Jo	4th great-granddaughter	VI	6
Thiac, Timothy Paul	4th great-grandson	VI	6
Thiac, Timothy Paul	5th great-grandson	VII	7
Thibeau, Duane Armond	Husband of the 4th great-granddaughter		
Thibodaux, Adele Marie	Grandniece	IV	3
Thibodaux, Eveline Marie	Grandniece	IV	3
Thibodaux, Genevieve Irma	Grandniece	IV	3
Thibodaux, Pierre	Husband of the niece		
Thibodaux, Zeolide Marie	Grandniece	IV	3
Thibodeaux, Pierre	Husband of the grandniece		
Thielke, David James	Husband of the 4th great-granddaughter		
Thomas, James Rogers	Husband of the 3rd great-granddaughter		
Thomas, James Rome	4th great-grandson	VI	6
Thomas, Jennifer Elizabeth	4th great-grandson	VI	6
Thomas, Jesse Rucker	4th great-grandson	VI	6
Thomasee, Marie Lori	Wife of the 4th great-grandson		
Thomassee, Dwayne A.	Husband of the 5th great-granddaughter		
Thomassee, Madelyn M.	6th great-granddaughter	VIII	8
Thomassee, Tatum L.	6th great-granddaughter	VIII	8
Thompson, Rosemary	Wife of the 4th great-grandson		
Tillson, Catherine Elaine, (Stepchild)	5th great-granddaughter	VII	7
Tillson, Cullen Alexander, (Stepchild)	5th great-grandson	VII	7

Kinship of Jean Robért, *-***

Name	Relationship with Jean Robért	Civil	Canon
Tillson, David Earl	Husband of the 4th great-granddaughter		
Toledano, Amanda Leocadie	Daughter-in-law		
Tonseth, Edward Scott	Husband of the 4th great-granddaughter		
Torres, Claire Marie	Wife of the 2nd great-grandson		
Torres, Marie Francesca (Frances)	Wife of the 2nd great-grandson		
Torrey, Austin Reily	5th great-grandson	VII	7
Torrey, Keith	Husband of the 4th great-granddaughter		
Torrey, Peyton James	5th great-grandson	VII	7
Toups, Brian Joseph	Husband of the 5th great-granddaughter		
Toups, Eleanor	Daughter-in-law		
Toups, Erin Alyce	5th great-granddaughter	VII	7
Toups, Joseph	Husband of the grandniece		
Toups, Joseph Ambrose	Husband of the grandniece		
Toups, Kristen Nicole	5th great-granddaughter	VII	7
Toups, Lauren Elizabeth	5th great-granddaughter	VII	7
Toups, Paul Joseph	Husband of the 4th great-granddaughter		
Toups, Roland Michael II	4th great-grandson	VI	6
Toups, Shelby McCall	4th great-grandson	VI	6
Toups, Stephanie Michele	4th great-granddaughter	VI	6
Toups, Stephen Mitchell	Husband of the 3rd great-granddaughter		
Townes, Terry Lynn	Wife of the 3rd great-grandson		
Trabeau, Braxon James	5th great-grandson	VII	7
Trabeau, Brody Michael	5th great-grandson	VII	7
Trabeau, Cody Michael	Husband of the 4th great-granddaughter		
Tramonte, Galen Anthony	Husband of the 4th great-granddaughter		
Tramonte, Gaylynn Ann	5th great-granddaughter	VII	7
Tramonte, Lauren Elizabeth	5th great-granddaughter	VII	7
Tramonte, Nicole Maria	5th great-granddaughter	VII	7
Tregre, Eva Marie	Wife of the 2nd great-grandnephew		
Tregre, Noelle	Wife of the half great-grandnephew		
Tregre, Teresa	Wife of the half 2nd great-grandnephew		
Trevino, Christopher Thomas, MD, PHD	Husband of the 3rd great-granddaughter		
Trosclair, Marie	Wife of the half grandnephew		
Troxclair, Adlice Marie	3rd great-granddaughter	V	5
Troxclair, Alma Rita	Half 3rd great-grandniece	VII	6
Troxclair, Anatole Sylvestre	Half 2nd great-grandniece	VI	5
Troxclair, Angele Marie	Half 2nd great-grandniece	VI	5
Troxclair, Aurelie Silvie	Half 2nd great-grandniece	VI	5
Troxclair, Bessie	3rd great-granddaughter	V	5
Troxclair, Brad	5th great-grandson	VII	7
Troxclair, Brandon Scott	Husband of the 4th great-granddaughter		
Troxclair, Catherine Alice	Wife of the 3rd great-grandson		
Troxclair, Davis P., (Slack)	3rd great-grandson	V	5
Troxclair, Delores Marie	2nd great-grandniece	VI	5
Troxclair, Donny J.	4th great-grandson	VI	6
Troxclair, Dunkin Joseph	Half 3rd great-grandnephew	VII	6
Troxclair, Earlene Marie	2nd great-grandniece	VI	5
Troxclair, Emilien Paul	Half 2nd great-grandnephew	VI	5
Troxclair, Ethel A.	Half 3rd great-grandniece	VII	6
Troxclair, Expire Nicholas	Husband of the half grandniece		
Troxclair, Felix F.	Half 2nd great-grandnephew	VI	5
Troxclair, Germaine M.	Wife of the half 3rd great-grandnephew		
Troxclair, Hettie	Half 3rd great-grandniece	VII	6
Troxclair, Irma Marie	Half 2nd great-grandniece	VI	5
Troxclair, Joseph Aubert	Half 2nd great-grandnephew	VI	5

Kinship of Jean Robért, *-***

Name	Relationship with Jean Robért	Civil	Canon
Troxclair, Joseph Emile, Jr.	Half 3rd great-grandnephew	VII	6
Troxclair, Joseph Emile, Sr.	Half 2nd great-grandnephew	VI	5
Troxclair, Joseph H.	Half 2nd great-grandnephew	VI	5
Troxclair, Joseph Oliver	Half 2nd great-grandnephew	VI	5
Troxclair, Joseph Oliver, Jr.	2nd great-grandnephew	VI	5
Troxclair, Josephine	Wife of the half grandnephew		
Troxclair, Justin	5th great-grandson	VII	7
Troxclair, Lea Marie	Half 3rd great-grandniece	VII	6
Troxclair, Leo	2nd great-grandnephew	VI	5
Troxclair, Leona	3rd great-grandniece of the wife		
Troxclair, Leonard M. II	Half 3rd great-grandnephew	VII	6
Troxclair, Leone	Wife of the half grandnephew		
Troxclair, Lillie E.	Half 3rd great-grandniece	VII	6
Troxclair, Mable Lucy	Half 3rd great-grandniece	VII	6
Troxclair, Mammie Marie	Half 3rd great-grandniece	VII	6
Troxclair, Marcel	Husband of the 2nd great-granddaughter		
Troxclair, Mariam	3rd great-granddaughter	V	5
Troxclair, Marian, (Sis)	Half 3rd great-grandniece	VII	6
Troxclair, Marie Amelia	Half 2nd great-grandniece	VI	5
Troxclair, Marie Bernadette	Wife of the great-grandson		
Troxclair, Marie Clorinne	Half 2nd great-grandniece	VI	5
Troxclair, Marie Genevieve	Half 2nd great-grandniece	VI	5
Troxclair, Marie Myrtle	Half 2nd great-grandniece	VI	5
Troxclair, Mary E.	Wife of the 2nd great-grandnephew		
Troxclair, Mary G.	Half 2nd great-grandniece	VI	5
Troxclair, Mathilde	Wife of the half grandnephew		
Troxclair, Maurice Leonard	Half 2nd great-grandnephew	VI	5
Troxclair, Melanie	Wife of the half grandnephew		
Troxclair, Narcisse Joseph	Half 2nd great-grandnephew	VI	5
Troxclair, Nicholas F.	Half 2nd great-grandnephew	VI	5
Troxclair, Nicholas L.	Half 2nd great-grandnephew	VI	5
Troxclair, Noel N.	Half 3rd great-grandnephew	VII	6
Troxclair, Noel Nicholas	Half great-grandnephew	V	4
Troxclair, Octavie Marie	Half 2nd great-grandniece	VI	5
Troxclair, Odette M.	Half 2nd great-grandniece	VI	5
Troxclair, Paul	Half 3rd great-grandnephew	VII	6
Troxclair, Roland Andre	Half 3rd great-grandnephew	VII	6
Troxclair, Sherman Joseph	3rd great-grandson	V	5
Troxclair, Sidney E.	Half 2nd great-grandnephew	VI	5
Troxclair, Simon	Half 2nd great-grandnephew	VI	5
Troxclair, Stanley Etienne	Half 3rd great-grandnephew	VII	6
Troxclair, Stelma	Half 3rd great-grandniece	VII	6
Troxclair, Suzanne Felicie	Wife of the half grandnephew		
Troxclair, Urbin Joseph	Half great-grandnephew	V	4
Troxclair, Warren	Half 3rd great-grandnephew	VII	6
Troxclair, Winnie Rita	2nd great-grandniece	VI	5
Troxclair, Zelia Rosalie	Half 2nd great-grandniece	VI	5
Troxler, Marie	Wife of the half grandnephew		
Tucker, Nathalie Lynn	5th great-granddaughter	VII	7
Tucker, Paul J.	Husband of the 4th great-granddaughter		
Unknown	Wife of the grandnephew		
Unnamed, (Divorced)	Ex-husband of the 4th great-granddaughter		
Usey, Lisa	Wife of the 4th great-grandson		
Usher, Aimee Noel	4th great-granddaughter	VI	6
Usher, Elizabeth Marie	4th great-granddaughter	VI	6

Kinship of Jean Robért, *-***

Name	Relationship with Jean Robért	Civil	Canon
Usher, James Robert	4th great-grandson	VI	6
Usher, James Shawn	Husband of the 3rd great-granddaughter		
Usher, Mary Claire	4th great-granddaughter	VI	6
Valleran, Magdelaine	Wife of the grandfather		
Veillon, Winnnie Mae	Wife of the 2nd great-grandson		
Venable, Ann-Elyse	5th great-granddaughter	VII	7
Venable, Emily Ann	4th great-granddaughter	VI	6
Venable, Felicia Marie	4th great-granddaughter	VI	6
Venable, Sarah Kate	4th great-granddaughter	VI	6
Venable, Theobert George, Jr.	5th great-grandson	VII	7
Venable, Theobert George, Sr.	Husband of the 4th great-granddaughter		
Venable, Vance David	Husband of the 3rd great-granddaughter		
Veneralla, Doyle George	Husband of the 3rd great-granddaughter		
Venerella, Avrien Joseph	4th great-grandson	VI	6
Viator, Catherine	Wife of the 4th great-grandson		
Volk, Living	Wife of the half 3rd great-grandnephew		
Voskamp, Raymond Leonard III	Husband of the 3rd great-granddaughter		
Waggenspack, Agatha	Great-grandniece	V	4
Waggenspack, Allen	Great-grandnephew	V	4
Waggenspack, Alonzo Francois	Great-grandnephew	V	4
Waggenspack, Andre	Grandnephew	IV	3
Waggenspack, Anne(Julia)	Great-grandniece	V	4
Waggenspack, Bertha Eve	Great-grandniece	V	4
Waggenspack, Beth	3rd great-grandniece	VII	6
Waggenspack, Beth, Dr.	3rd great-grandniece	VII	6
Waggenspack, Carmel Anne	2nd great-grandniece	VI	5
Waggenspack, Christopher Paul	4th great-grandson	VI	6
Waggenspack, Clara Ann	Great-grandniece	V	4
Waggenspack, Claude Francis X.	2nd great-grandson	IV	4
Waggenspack, Clay A.,Jr.	2nd great-grandnephew	VI	5
Waggenspack, Clay, Sr.	Great-grandnephew	V	4
Waggenspack, Clinton	Great-grandnephew	V	4
Waggenspack, Dawn	3rd great-grandniece	VII	6
Waggenspack, Dean	3rd great-grandnephew	VII	6
Waggenspack, Emma Irma	Grandniece	IV	3
Waggenspack, Ernest	Grandnephew	IV	3
Waggenspack, Esther Ann, (Tay-Tay)	2nd great-granddaughter	IV	4
Waggenspack, Euphemie	Great-grandniece	V	4
Waggenspack, Felicie	Grandniece	IV	3
Waggenspack, Felix Andre, Sr.**	Grandnephew	IV	3
Waggenspack, Felix, Jr.	Great-grandnephew	V	4
Waggenspack, Florine Mary	Great-grandniece	V	4
Waggenspack, Floyd G.	2nd great-grandnephew	VI	5
Waggenspack, Francis Benoit	2nd great-grandson	IV	4
Waggenspack, Gaston Jean Pierre	Great-grandnephew	V	4
Waggenspack, Guy J.	2nd great-grandnephew	VI	5
Waggenspack, Harold	2nd great-grandnephew	VI	5
Waggenspack, Hector	Great-grandnephew	V	4
Waggenspack, Hilton	Great-grandnephew	V	4
Waggenspack, Inez	Great-grandniece	V	4
Waggenspack, Irwin Anthony, (Finny)	2nd great-grandnephew	VI	5
Waggenspack, Jacque Rene, **	Great-grandnephew	V	4
Waggenspack, James Berlin, (Bill)	2nd great-grandson	IV	4
Waggenspack, James Joseph	3rd great-grandson	V	5
Waggenspack, Jan Marie	3rd great-granddaughter	V	5

Kinship of Jean Robért, *-***

Name	Relationship with Jean Robért	Civil	Canon
Waggenspack, Janie	3rd great-grandniece	VII	6
Waggenspack, Jeanne	Great-grandniece	V	4
Waggenspack, Jeannette Marie, (Non-e)	2nd great-granddaughter	IV	4
Waggenspack, Joan	3rd great-grandniece	VII	6
Waggenspack, Joan	3rd great-grandniece	VII	6
Waggenspack, John	3rd great-grandnephew	VII	6
Waggenspack, John Robert	2nd great-grandson	IV	4
Waggenspack, Joseph Leo	Grandnephew	IV	3
Waggenspack, Judy Ann	3rd great-granddaughter	V	5
Waggenspack, Juliette Theresa,(Ye-Yet)	2nd great-granddaughter	IV	4
Waggenspack, Katie Marie	4th great-granddaughter	VI	6
Waggenspack, Kay Marie	3rd great-granddaughter	V	5
Waggenspack, Kevin Joseph	4th great-grandson	VI	6
Waggenspack, LaMarylis Ann	3rd great-granddaughter	V	5
Waggenspack, Laville Louis	2nd great-grandnephew	VI	5
Waggenspack, Leah Arthemise	Great-grandniece	V	4
Waggenspack, Lee Jude	3rd great-grandson	V	5
Waggenspack, Lenny	3rd great-grandnephew	VII	6
Waggenspack, Leo André	Great-grandnephew	V	4
Waggenspack, Linden Gaspard	2nd great-grandnephew	VI	5
Waggenspack, Lori	3rd great-grandniece	VII	6
Waggenspack, Luke	Great-grandnephew	V	4
Waggenspack, Mark	3rd great-grandnephew	VII	6
Waggenspack, Mark	3rd great-grandnephew	VII	6
Waggenspack, Mary Laville	3rd great-grandniece	VII	6
Waggenspack, Mazie	2nd great-grandniece	VI	5
Waggenspack, Melvin	2nd great-grandnephew	VI	5
Waggenspack, Mott (Batatier)	Great-grandnephew	V	4
Waggenspack, Nita	2nd great-grandniece	VI	5
Waggenspack, Olga	Great-grandniece	V	4
Waggenspack, Owen John	2nd great-grandnephew	VI	5
Waggenspack, Patricia	2nd great-grandniece	VI	5
Waggenspack, Paul John	3rd great-grandson	V	5
Waggenspack, Pauline Marie	2nd great-granddaughter	IV	4
Waggenspack, Percy Paul	2nd great-grandson	IV	4
Waggenspack, Raymond	Great-grandnephew	V	4
Waggenspack, Rene Anthony, (Beebe)	2nd great-grandson	IV	4
Waggenspack, Rose Mary	2nd great-grandniece	VI	5
Waggenspack, Ruffin Joseph, (2-D)	2nd great-grandson	IV	4
Waggenspack, Sarah M.	Great-grandniece	V	4
Waggenspack, Scott Joseph	4th great-grandson	VI	6
Waggenspack, Sherlee	3rd great-grandniece	VII	6
Waggenspack, Sidney	Great-grandnephew	V	4
Waggenspack, Sully(Edward)	Great-grandnephew	V	4
Waggenspack, Susan	3rd great-grandniece	VII	6
Waggenspack, Susan Marie	4th great-granddaughter	VI	6
Waggenspack, Thelma C.	2nd great-grandniece	VI	5
Waggenspack, Therése	Great-grandniece	V	4
Waggenspack, Vickie Lene	3rd great-grandniece	VII	6
Waggenspack, Vincent, (Coo)	2nd great-grandnephew	VI	5
Waggenspack, Warren	2nd great-grandnephew	VI	5
Waggenspack, Wilbert J.	2nd great-grandnephew	VI	5
Waggenspack, Wilda	2nd great-grandniece	VI	5
Waggenspack, Willis Jean	Great-grandnephew	V	4
Waguespack, Aaron Marie	5th great-granddaughter	VII	7

Kinship of Jean Robért, *-***

Name	Relationship with Jean Robért	Civil	Canon
Waguespack, Adam Duval	Grandnephew	IV	3
Waguespack, Adele, (Waggenspack)	Great-grandniece	V	4
Waguespack, Adrian Charles	4th great-grandson	VI	6
Waguespack, Adrian Jade	5th great-grandson	VII	7
Waguespack, Alcee	Great-grandson	III	3
Waguespack, Alfred	Great-grandnephew	V	4
Waguespack, Alice Marie	Great-granddaughter	III	3
Waguespack, Alice Marie	4th great-granddaughter	VI	6
Waguespack, Alidor	Great-grandnephew	V	4
Waguespack, Alidor	Grandnephew	IV	3
Waguespack, Alidore Joseph	2nd great-grandson	IV	4
Waguespack, Almanza	2nd great-grandniece of the wife		
Waguespack, Amanda Lynn	5th great-granddaughter	VII	7
Waguespack, Amedee	Grandnephew	IV	3
Waguespack, Amedee	Half 2nd great-grandnephew	VI	5
Waguespack, Amelia	2nd great-grandniece	VI	5
Waguespack, Amelia	Great-grandniece of the wife		
Waguespack, Amelie<Emily>, **	Grandniece	IV	3
Waguespack, Amy Marie	4th great-granddaughter	VI	6
Waguespack, Amy Marie	5th great-granddaughter	VII	7
Waguespack, Anaize	2nd great-grandniece of the wife		
Waguespack, André	Grandnephew	IV	3
Waguespack, Andre Bienvenue	Grandnephew	IV	3
Waguespack, André Evariste	Nephew	III	2
Waguespack, André Louis, **	Brother-in-law		
Waguespack, André M.	Great-grandson	III	3
Waguespack, Andrea	2nd great-granddaughter	IV	4
Waguespack, Angela	Great-grandniece	V	4
Waguespack, Angele	Great-grandniece	V	4
Waguespack, Anna Mae	3rd great-granddaughter	V	5
Waguespack, Anne Marie	3rd great-granddaughter	V	5
Waguespack, Anne Valerie	Wife of the great-grandson		
Waguespack, Annette	2nd great-grandniece of the wife		
Waguespack, April Marie	4th great-granddaughter	VI	6
Waguespack, Arlene Lucy	4th great-granddaughter	VI	6
Waguespack, Arthur Anthony, Sr.	Husband of the great-grandniece		
Waguespack, Arthur Antoine, (Waggenspack)	Grandnephew	IV	3
Waguespack, Aubert	Great-grandnephew of the wife		
Waguespack, Aubert Florian	Grandnephew of the wife		
Waguespack, Aubin Moise	Great-grandnephew of the wife		
Waguespack, August J.	2nd great-grandnephew	VI	5
Waguespack, Aurelie	2nd great-granddaughter	IV	4
Waguespack, Author Anthony, Jr.	2nd great-grandniece	VI	5
Waguespack, Ayme	Great-grandniece	V	4
Waguespack, Barbara Rita	3rd great-granddaughter	V	5
Waguespack, Barry Joseph	4th great-grandson	VI	6
Waguespack, Benoit James	Half 2nd great-grandnephew	VI	5
Waguespack, Benoit Joseph	Half 3rd great-grandnephew	VII	6
Waguespack, Bernard Joseph	4th great-grandson	VI	6
Waguespack, Bernie Noel	3rd great-grandson	V	5
Waguespack, Bertha	2nd great-grandniece of the wife		
Waguespack, Bessie Marion	3rd great-granddaughter	V	5
Waguespack, Bonnie Ann	4th great-granddaughter	VI	6
Waguespack, Brad A.	5th great-grandson	VII	7
Waguespack, Brad Michael	4th great-grandson	VI	6

Kinship of Jean Robért, *-***

Name	Relationship with Jean Robért	Civil	Canon
Waguespack, Brandon Michael	5th great-grandson	VII	7
Waguespack, Brenda Ann	3rd great-granddaughter	V	5
Waguespack, Brett Charles	5th great-grandson	VII	7
Waguespack, Brian Patrick	5th great-grandson	VII	7
Waguespack, Brooke Nicole	5th great-granddaughter	VII	7
Waguespack, Camille	Grandnephew	IV	3
Waguespack, Carl	3rd great-grandson	V	5
Waguespack, Carolyn	2nd great-granddaughter	IV	4
Waguespack, Casey Lynn	5th great-granddaughter	VII	7
Waguespack, Catherine	Sister-in-law		
Waguespack, Catherine	4th great-granddaughter	VI	6
Waguespack, Catherine Adele	Niece	III	2
Waguespack, Cathy Marie	3rd great-granddaughter	V	5
Waguespack, Cecile Ruth, (infant)	3rd great-granddaughter	V	5
Waguespack, Cecilia	3rd great-granddaughter	V	5
Waguespack, Chad Anthony	4th great-grandson	VI	6
Waguespack, Christi Lynn	4th great-granddaughter	VI	6
Waguespack, Cidalise	2nd great-grandniece of the wife		
Waguespack, Claire Marie	4th great-granddaughter	VI	6
Waguespack, Clarence Anthony	2nd great-grandson	IV	4
Waguespack, Clyde Paul	3rd great-grandson	V	5
Waguespack, Clyde Paul, Jr.	4th great-grandson	VI	6
Waguespack, Connie Theresa, (infant)	4th great-granddaughter	VI	6
Waguespack, Corin Marie	6th great-granddaughter	VIII	8
Waguespack, Cynthia (Cindy)	3rd great-granddaughter	V	5
Waguespack, Cyril	2nd great-grandnephew	VI	5
Waguespack, Dal Jeremy	4th great-grandson	VI	6
Waguespack, Dana Marie	4th great-granddaughter	VI	6
Waguespack, Daniel	3rd great-grandson	V	5
Waguespack, Daniel Joseph	5th great-grandson	VII	7
Waguespack, Daren Michael	5th great-grandson	VII	7
Waguespack, Daryl Joseph	3rd great-grandson	V	5
Waguespack, David	Grandnephew	IV	3
Waguespack, Dawn Marie	4th great-granddaughter	VI	6
Waguespack, Deborah Lee	4th great-granddaughter	VI	6
Waguespack, Delia Philomene	2nd great-granddaughter	IV	4
Waguespack, Delphine Eve	Great-grandniece of the wife		
Waguespack, Denise Marie	2nd great-granddaughter	IV	4
Waguespack, Denise Marie	4th great-granddaughter	VI	6
Waguespack, Dennis	3rd great-grandson	V	5
Waguespack, Devon Michele	4th great-granddaughter	VI	6
Waguespack, Donna	3rd great-granddaughter	V	5
Waguespack, Donna Marie	4th great-granddaughter	VI	6
Waguespack, Donovan	4th great-grandson	VI	6
Waguespack, Drasin Telesphore	Grandnephew	IV	3
Waguespack, Duane Joseph	4th great-grandson	VI	6
Waguespack, Durward Gerald	4th great-grandson	VI	6
Waguespack, Dwain	Half 4th great-grandnephew	VIII	7
Waguespack, Edgar Joseph	2nd great-grandson	IV	4
Waguespack, Edgar Joseph, Jr.(E.J.)	3rd great-grandson	V	5
Waguespack, Edmire	Grandnephew	IV	3
Waguespack, Edmond Pierre	Great-grandnephew of the wife		
Waguespack, Edourard	Great-grandnephew	V	4
Waguespack, Edward	2nd great-grandnephew of the wife		
Waguespack, Edwin	Half 2nd great-grandnephew	VI	5

Kinship of Jean Robért, *-***

Name	Relationship with Jean Robért	Civil	Canon
Waguespack, Eglantine	Niece	III	2
Waguespack, Elda Augustine	2nd great-granddaughter	IV	4
Waguespack, Eleanore Pamela	Grandniece	IV	3
Waguespack, Eleonore	Niece of the wife		
Waguespack, Eleonore	Grandniece	IV	3
Waguespack, Elgie Mae	3rd great-granddaughter	V	5
Waguespack, Elise Rita	4th great-granddaughter	VI	6
Waguespack, Eliska	Great-grandniece	V	4
Waguespack, Ella Haydel	Great-grandniece of the wife		
Waguespack, Elodie	Grandniece	IV	3
Waguespack, Eloise	2nd great-grandniece	VI	5
Waguespack, Emelia	Great-grandniece	V	4
Waguespack, Emerante	Niece	III	2
Waguespack, Emerante	Grandniece	IV	3
Waguespack, Emerante	Grandniece of the wife		
Waguespack, Emile T.	Husband of the 2nd great-granddaughter		
Waguespack, Emily Claire	5th great-granddaughter	VII	7
Waguespack, Ernest	Grandnephew	IV	3
Waguespack, Ernestine	Great-grandniece	V	4
Waguespack, Ethelyn Marie	3rd great-granddaughter	V	5
Waguespack, Eugenie	Grandniece	IV	3
Waguespack, Eugenie Esther Therese	Great-grandniece of the wife		
Waguespack, Euphemie	Great-grandniece of the wife		
Waguespack, Eusebe	Great-grandnephew	V	4
Waguespack, Eva Louise	Great-grandniece of the wife		
Waguespack, Eve Palmyre	Grandniece of the wife		
Waguespack, Evelina	Half 2nd great-grandniece	VI	5
Waguespack, Eveline Marian, (Waggenspack)	Great-grandniece	V	4
Waguespack, Felician	Grandnephew of the wife		
Waguespack, Felicie, (Waggenspack)	Great-grandniece	V	4
Waguespack, Felix	Grandnephew	IV	3
Waguespack, Felonise	2nd great-grandniece of the wife		
Waguespack, Firmin Stanislaus	Grandnephew	IV	3
Waguespack, Florent	2nd great-grandnephew of the wife		
Waguespack, Florestan	Grandnephew	IV	3
Waguespack, Florestant	Grandnephew of the wife		
Waguespack, Fran Cabrini	4th great-granddaughter	VI	6
Waguespack, Francis	Husband of the 2nd great-granddaughter		
Waguespack, Francois	Nephew	III	2
Waguespack, Francois	Grandnephew	IV	3
Waguespack, Francois	Grandnephew	IV	3
Waguespack, Francois Oseme	Great-grandnephew	V	4
Waguespack, Froisin	Great-grandnephew of the wife		
Waguespack, Frumence Hubert	2nd great-grandson	IV	4
Waguespack, Galyn Thomas	3rd great-grandson	V	5
Waguespack, Gayle Anne	3rd great-granddaughter	V	5
Waguespack, Genevieve	3rd great-granddaughter	V	5
Waguespack, Genevieve Emelie	Niece	III	2
Waguespack, George	2nd great-grandson	IV	4
Waguespack, George	2nd great-grandnephew	VI	5
Waguespack, George David	3rd great-grandson	V	5
Waguespack, George Henry, Sr.	Husband of the 3rd great-granddaughter		
Waguespack, George Keith	4th great-grandson	VI	6
Waguespack, George Nicholas	5th great-grandson	VII	7
Waguespack, George Nicholas, (Gee)	2nd great-grandson	IV	4

Kinship of Jean Robért, *-***

Name	Relationship with Jean Robért	Civil	Canon
Waguespack, George Ann	3rd great-granddaughter	V	5
Waguespack, Georgene Marie	4th great-granddaughter	VI	6
Waguespack, Georgette Marie	2nd great-granddaughter	IV	4
Waguespack, Gerald	4th great-grandson	VI	6
Waguespack, Gerald Jude	4th great-grandson	VI	6
Waguespack, Gerald M., Jr.(infant)	4th great-grandson	VI	6
Waguespack, Gerald Marie	3rd great-grandson	V	5
Waguespack, Gerard	Great-grandnephew of the wife		
Waguespack, Gerri Lynn	5th great-granddaughter	VII	7
Waguespack, Gertrude Ann	3rd great-granddaughter	V	5
Waguespack, Gladys	3rd great-grandniece of the wife		
Waguespack, Glenn Michael	3rd great-grandson	V	5
Waguespack, Godfrey Joseph	3rd great-grandson	V	5
Waguespack, Godfrey Joseph, Jr	4th great-grandson	VI	6
Waguespack, Harriet	2nd great-grandniece	VI	5
Waguespack, Heloise Marie	2nd great-granddaughter	IV	4
Waguespack, Heneretta	2nd great-grandniece of the wife		
Waguespack, Heno <Enougle> J.	Great-grandson	III	3
Waguespack, Henriette Melanie	Great-grandniece	V	4
Waguespack, Hilton	Great-grandnephew	V	4
Waguespack, Hollis Mark	4th great-grandson	VI	6
Waguespack, Honorine	3rd great-granddaughter	V	5
Waguespack, Horace	2nd great-grandnephew	VI	5
Waguespack, Horistine Henry	2nd great-grandnephew	VI	5
Waguespack, Hortense	Great-grandniece	V	4
Waguespack, Hubert Jean Baptiste,***	Grandnephew of the wife		
Waguespack, Hubert Jean Louis	Grandnephew	IV	3
Waguespack, Hubert, Jr	Grandnephew of the wife		
Waguespack, Hubert, Sr. ***	Nephew of the wife		
Waguespack, Ida	2nd great-grandniece of the wife		
Waguespack, Inez	Half 3rd great-grandniece	VII	6
Waguespack, Irene, (Waggenspack)	Great-grandniece	V	4
Waguespack, Ivy Joseph	3rd great-grandson	V	5
Waguespack, J.Therence, <Waggenspack>, **	Nephew	III	2
Waguespack, Jackie,(infant)	3rd great-granddaughter	V	5
Waguespack, Jacqueline Marie	3rd great-granddaughter	V	5
Waguespack, Jacquelyn,(infant)	3rd great-granddaughter	V	5
Waguespack, Jan	3rd great-granddaughter	V	5
Waguespack, Janel Mary	3rd great-granddaughter	V	5
Waguespack, Jason Paul	4th great-grandson	VI	6
Waguespack, Jean Baptiste	Grandnephew of the wife		
Waguespack, Jean Baptiste Hubert	Husband of the half great-grandniece		
Waguespack, Jean Baptiste Louis	Great-grandnephew	V	4
Waguespack, Jean Jacques, <Waguenspack>	1st cousin of the wife		
Waguespack, Jean Lesin	Great-grandnephew of the wife		
Waguespack, Jean Louis III	Husband of the niece		
Waguespack, Jean Louis IV	Grandnephew	IV	3
Waguespack, Jean Louis, Jr ***	Brother-in-law		
Waguespack, Jean Louis, Sr * ** ***	Father-in-law		
Waguespack, Jean Paul	Great-grandnephew	V	4
Waguespack, Jean Pierre	Uncle of the wife		
Waguespack, Jean Pierrell, <Waguenspack>	1st cousin of the wife		
Waguespack, Jean, (Waggenspack)	Great-grandnephew	V	4
Waguespack, Jeanne Marie	Great-grandniece	V	4
Waguespack, Jennifer Lynn	4th great-granddaughter	VI	6

Direct Descendants of Jean Robért and Marianne Waguespack

Kinship of Jean Robért, *-***

Name	Relationship with Jean Robért	Civil	Canon
Waguespack, Jeri	3rd great-granddaughter	V	5
Waguespack, Jerome, (Jerry)	2nd great-grandson	IV	4
Waguespack, Jessie Jude	4th great-grandson	VI	6
Waguespack, Joanie Lynn	5th great-granddaughter	VII	7
Waguespack, Joel Anthony	3rd great-grandson	V	5
Waguespack, Joell Marie	4th great-granddaughter	VI	6
Waguespack, Johannis, <Vagensbach>	Great-grandfather of the wife		
Waguespack, John Wallis	5th great-grandson	VII	7
Waguespack, Joseph	Great-grandnephew	V	4
Waguespack, Joseph	Grandfather of the wife		
Waguespack, Joseph	Nephew	III	2
Waguespack, Joseph Adam	Grandnephew	IV	3
Waguespack, Joseph Camille	Great-grandnephew	V	4
Waguespack, Joseph Clodimir	Great-grandnephew	V	4
Waguespack, Joseph Fredy	2nd great-grandnephew	VI	5
Waguespack, Joseph III	Grandnephew of the wife		
Waguespack, Joseph Louis, Jr. (Jose)	Nephew of the wife		
Waguespack, Joseph Louis, Sr.	Brother-in-law		
Waguespack, Joseph Rosney	3rd great-grandson	V	5
Waguespack, Joseph Valerie	2nd great-grandnephew	VI	5
Waguespack, Josephine	Half 2nd great-grandniece	VI	5
Waguespack, Josephine Marie, ***	Grandniece of the wife		
Waguespack, Joyce	4th great-granddaughter	VI	6
Waguespack, Judy Marie	4th great-granddaughter	VI	6
Waguespack, Julie	Wife of the grandnephew		
Waguespack, Julie	Wife of the grandnephew		
Waguespack, Julie Eglantine	Grandniece	IV	3
Waguespack, Justine	Grandniece	IV	3
Waguespack, Kade Austin	5th great-grandson	VII	7
Waguespack, Karen Ann	4th great-granddaughter	VI	6
Waguespack, Kassie Leigh	5th great-granddaughter	VII	7
Waguespack, Keith John	5th great-grandson	VII	7
Waguespack, Kelli Jean	4th great-granddaughter	VI	6
Waguespack, Kerry Ann	4th great-granddaughter	VI	6
Waguespack, Kerry Gerard	3rd great-grandson	V	5
Waguespack, Kevin John	4th great-grandson	VI	6
Waguespack, Kim Marie	4th great-granddaughter	VI	6
Waguespack, Kirk Patrick	4th great-grandson	VI	6
Waguespack, Kurt Dominic	4th great-grandson	VI	6
Waguespack, Landry	Great-grandnephew of the wife		
Waguespack, Larry P., Jr.	4th great-grandson	VI	6
Waguespack, Larry Pierre, Sr.	3rd great-grandson	V	5
Waguespack, Laura Ann	4th great-granddaughter	VI	6
Waguespack, Laura Marie	3rd great-granddaughter	V	5
Waguespack, Laure	Half 2nd great-grandniece	VI	5
Waguespack, Laure	2nd great-grandniece of the wife		
Waguespack, Laurence Marie	3rd great-granddaughter	V	5
Waguespack, Lawrence	2nd great-grandnephew	VI	5
Waguespack, Lea	Great-grandniece	V	4
Waguespack, Lenfroi A.	Great-grandnephew of the wife		
Waguespack, Lenora Theresa	3rd great-granddaughter	V	5
Waguespack, Leon	Husband of the 2nd great-granddaughter		
Waguespack, Leonard	2nd great-grandson	IV	4
Waguespack, Leonard James	3rd great-grandson	V	5
Waguespack, Leonard Joseph	Great-grandnephew	V	4

Kinship of Jean Robért, *-***

Name	Relationship with Jean Robért	Civil	Canon
Waguespack, Leonard Omer	Great-grandnephew of the wife		
Waguespack, Leonce Pierre	2nd great-grandnephew	VI	5
Waguespack, Leroy	3rd great-grandson	V	5
Waguespack, Leroy Joseph	3rd great-grandson	V	5
Waguespack, Leroy Joseph, Jr.	4th great-grandson	VI	6
Waguespack, Leslie Ann	4th great-granddaughter	VI	6
Waguespack, Leslie J., Jr.	3rd great-grandson	V	5
Waguespack, Leslie J., Sr.	2nd great-grandson	IV	4
Waguespack, Lilia Catherine	Grandniece	IV	3
Waguespack, Linda Judith	4th great-granddaughter	VI	6
Waguespack, Louis	Nephew	III	2
Waguespack, Louis	2nd great-grandnephew of the wife		
Waguespack, Louis Frederick	Great-grandnephew of the wife		
Waguespack, Louis III	Husband of the grandniece		
Waguespack, Louisa Marie	Great-grandniece	V	4
Waguespack, Louise	Great-grandniece	V	4
Waguespack, Louise	Great-grandniece	V	4
Waguespack, Lucille	2nd great-grandniece	VI	5
Waguespack, Lydia	2nd great-grandniece	VI	5
Waguespack, Lydia Eve	Grandniece	IV	3
Waguespack, Lydia, (Waggenspack)	Great-grandniece	V	4
Waguespack, Madeleine	3rd great-granddaughter	V	5
Waguespack, Majel Ann	3rd great-granddaughter	V	5
Waguespack, Mandie Lee	5th great-granddaughter	VII	7
Waguespack, Marcial	2nd great-grandnephew	VI	5
Waguespack, Margariet	2nd great-grandniece	VI	5
Waguespack, Marguerite	Aunt of the wife		
Waguespack, Marguerite	Sister-in-law		
Waguespack, Marguerite	3rd great-granddaughter	V	5
Waguespack, Marian	3rd great-granddaughter	V	5
Waguespack, Marianne, (minor)*- ***	Wife		
Waguespack, Marie Agnes, (Waggenspack)	Great-grandniece	V	4
Waguespack, Marie Anaise	Grandniece of the wife		
Waguespack, Marie Antoinette	2nd great-granddaughter	IV	4
Waguespack, Marie Aurelie	2nd great-granddaughter	IV	4
Waguespack, Marie Azelise	Grandniece	IV	3
Waguespack, Marie Catherine	Aunt of the wife		
Waguespack, Marie Delphine	Grandniece of the wife		
Waguespack, Marie Edith, (Waggenspack)	Great-grandniece	V	4
Waguespack, Marie Elisa	Grandniece	IV	3
Waguespack, Marie Elmira	Grandniece of the wife		
Waguespack, Marie Euphemie	Great-grandniece	V	4
Waguespack, Marie Eveline	Wife of the grandnephew		
Waguespack, Marie Eveline	Great-grandniece of the wife		
Waguespack, Marie Floresca	2nd great-grandniece of the wife		
Waguespack, Marie Josepha	Niece of the wife		
Waguespack, Marie Julie	Grandniece	IV	3
Waguespack, Marie Leontine	Great-grandniece	V	4
Waguespack, Marie Louise	Great-grandniece	V	4
Waguespack, Marie Louise	Half 2nd great-grandniece	VI	5
Waguespack, Marie Madelaine	Sister-in-law		
Waguespack, Marie Marcelite	Niece	III	2
Waguespack, Marie Melina	2nd great-grandniece	VI	5
Waguespack, Marie Nezile (Inezile)	Grandniece	IV	3
Waguespack, Marie Roseline	Wife of the nephew		

Kinship of Jean Robért, *-***

Name	Relationship with Jean Robért	Civil	Canon
Waguespack, Marie Sidonie	2nd great-grandniece of the wife		
Waguespack, Marie Turselia	Grandniece	IV	3
Waguespack, Marie Zeolide	Grandniece	IV	3
Waguespack, Marie Antoinette	Great-granddaughter	III	3
Waguespack, Marjorie Mary	Wife of the 2nd great-grandson		
Waguespack, Marjorie Mary	4th great-granddaughter	VI	6
Waguespack, Martha	2nd great-grandniece of the wife		
Waguespack, Martha Adele	Grandniece	IV	3
Waguespack, Martha, (Waggenspack)	Great-grandniece	V	4
Waguespack, Marvin Peter	4th great-grandson	VI	6
Waguespack, Mary Grace	3rd great-granddaughter	V	5
Waguespack, Mathilde	2nd great-grandniece	VI	5
Waguespack, Mathilde	Grandniece of the wife		
Waguespack, Mathilde Folse	Grandniece	IV	3
Waguespack, Mathilde Therese	3rd great-granddaughter	V	5
Waguespack, Mathurin	Brother-in-law		
Waguespack, Mathurin	Grandnephew	IV	3
Waguespack, Maxime	Grandniece	IV	3
Waguespack, Melissa Stephens	5th great-granddaughter	VII	7
Waguespack, Merancia Marguerite	2nd great-grandniece	VI	5
Waguespack, Mercedes Ann	3rd great-granddaughter	V	5
Waguespack, Michael Curtis	4th great-grandson	VI	6
Waguespack, Michele Clare	Wife of the 2nd great-grandson		
Waguespack, Michelle Marie	4th great-granddaughter	VI	6
Waguespack, Mildred	2nd great-grandniece	VI	5
Waguespack, Monica Ann	4th great-granddaughter	VI	6
Waguespack, Monique	5th great-granddaughter	VII	7
Waguespack, Morris	2nd great-grandson	IV	4
Waguespack, Myrtile Arthemise	Great-granddaughter	III	3
Waguespack, Myrtle Marie	3rd great-granddaughter	V	5
Waguespack, Nanette	3rd great-granddaughter	V	5
Waguespack, Nanette Marie	4th great-granddaughter	VI	6
Waguespack, Neal Anthony	4th great-grandson	VI	6
Waguespack, Nelda Ann	4th great-granddaughter	VI	6
Waguespack, Nevil Ann	4th great-granddaughter	VI	6
Waguespack, Nicole	4th great-granddaughter	VI	6
Waguespack, Nicole Lenore	5th great-granddaughter	VII	7
Waguespack, Noemie	Great-grandniece of the wife		
Waguespack, Noilee	2nd great-grandniece	VI	5
Waguespack, Nolan Joseph	3rd great-grandson	V	5
Waguespack, Octave Pierre	2nd great-grandson	IV	4
Waguespack, Octavie	Grandniece	IV	3
Waguespack, Odile Delphine	Niece of the wife		
Waguespack, Ola Mae Rita	3rd great-granddaughter	V	5
Waguespack, Olesiphore	Grandnephew	IV	3
Waguespack, Olive	2nd great-grandniece	VI	5
Waguespack, Olympe	Great-grandniece	V	4
Waguespack, Ozelia	Great-grandniece	V	4
Waguespack, Palmyre E.	Great-grandniece of the wife		
Waguespack, Paul	2nd great-grandson	IV	4
Waguespack, Paul	Nephew	III	2
Waguespack, Paul	2nd great-grandnephew of the wife		
Waguespack, Paul Elysse	Grandnephew	IV	3
Waguespack, Paula Ann	4th great-granddaughter	VI	6
Waguespack, Phelonise Cecile Therese	Great-granddaughter	III	3

Kinship of Jean Robért, *-***

Name	Relationship with Jean Robért	Civil	Canon
Waguespack, Philip Brent	5th great-grandson	VII	7
Waguespack, Phillip	2nd great-grandnephew of the wife		
Waguespack, Pierre Aurelian	Grandnephew	IV	3
Waguespack, Pierre Edmond, Jr.	2nd great-grandnephew of the wife		
Waguespack, Pierre Edmond, Sr.	Great-grandnephew of the wife		
Waguespack, Pierre Norbert	Great-grandnephew of the wife		
Waguespack, Prudent	Husband of the great-granddaughter		
Waguespack, Randy Paul	5th great-grandson	VII	7
Waguespack, Raphael Stanislaus	Great-grandnephew	V	4
Waguespack, Raymond Joseph	Great-grandnephew of the wife		
Waguespack, Raymond Leonard	Grandnephew	IV	3
Waguespack, Rebecca Eve	Great-grandniece	V	4
Waguespack, Rebecca Marie	4th great-granddaughter	VI	6
Waguespack, Regina Victoria	2nd great-granddaughter	IV	4
Waguespack, Rene Ferdinand	Great-grandnephew of the wife		
Waguespack, Rhonda Faye	4th great-granddaughter	VI	6
Waguespack, Richard	Great-grandnephew	V	4
Waguespack, Richard	3rd great-grandson	V	5
Waguespack, Richard	2nd great-grandnephew	VI	5
Waguespack, Richard P., Jr. (Woody)	4th great-grandson	VI	6
Waguespack, Ricky Lee	5th great-grandson	VII	7
Waguespack, Rita Marie	Great-grandniece	V	4
Waguespack, Rita Marie	Half 2nd great-grandniece	VI	5
Waguespack, Rita Olympe	2nd great-grandniece	VI	5
Waguespack, Robért	Grandnephew	IV	3
Waguespack, Robert Gregoire	Great-grandnephew	V	4
Waguespack, Roberta Therese	4th great-granddaughter	VI	6
Waguespack, Rodney John	4th great-grandson	VI	6
Waguespack, Romana	3rd great-granddaughter	V	5
Waguespack, Rosa	Great-grandniece	V	4
Waguespack, Roseline	Grandniece	IV	3
Waguespack, Rosine, (Waggenspack)	Great-grandniece	V	4
Waguespack, Rosney, (Waggenspack)	Great-grandnephew	V	4
Waguespack, Rudy Paul Antoine	3rd great-grandson	V	5
Waguespack, Ryan Joseph	4th great-grandson	VI	6
Waguespack, Sandry (Sandy)	3rd great-granddaughter	V	5
Waguespack, Saturinn	Great-grandnephew of the wife		
Waguespack, Seraphine	Grandniece	IV	3
Waguespack, Seymour Raymond	3rd great-grandson	V	5
Waguespack, Seymour Raymond, Jr.	4th great-grandson	VI	6
Waguespack, Shane Anthony	4th great-grandson	VI	6
Waguespack, Shane Joseph	5th great-grandson	VII	7
Waguespack, Sharon Ann	4th great-granddaughter	VI	6
Waguespack, Shirley Philomine	3rd great-granddaughter	V	5
Waguespack, Sidney Jean	Husband of the great-grandniece		
Waguespack, Stanford John	3rd great-grandson	V	5
Waguespack, Stanislas J.	2nd great-grandnephew of the wife		
Waguespack, Stanislaus	Great-grandnephew	V	4
Waguespack, Stanley Paul	2nd great-grandson	IV	4
Waguespack, Stanley Paul, (Da-Da)	3rd great-grandson	V	5
Waguespack, Stephen	2nd great-grandson	IV	4
Waguespack, Steve Paul	4th great-grandson	VI	6
Waguespack, Susan Mary	4th great-granddaughter	VI	6
Waguespack, Tanya Ann	4th great-granddaughter	VI	6
Waguespack, Telesphore	Nephew	III	2

Kinship of Jean Robért, *-***

Name	Relationship with Jean Robért	Civil	Canon
Waguespack, Theophile	Great-grandnephew	V	4
Waguespack, Theresa	Great-grandniece	V	4
Waguespack, Theresa	Great-grandniece of the wife		
Waguespack, Therese Elmira	Grandniece	IV	3
Waguespack, Thomas Christopher	5th great-grandson	VII	7
Waguespack, Timothy	2nd great-grandson	IV	4
Waguespack, Tobie Mikael	5th great-granddaughter	VII	7
Waguespack, Tony Jude	5th great-grandson	VII	7
Waguespack, Trudi Marie	4th great-granddaughter	VI	6
Waguespack, Tyler Michael	5th great-grandson	VII	7
Waguespack, Ulger	Nephew	III	2
Waguespack, Ulger	Grandnephew	IV	3
Waguespack, Ulger Eugene	Husband of the niece		
Waguespack, Ulgere	Grandnephew	IV	3
Waguespack, Valentine	Great-grandniece	V	4
Waguespack, Valerie	Great-grandniece	V	4
Waguespack, Valsin	Nephew	III	2
Waguespack, Vickie Ann	4th great-granddaughter	VI	6
Waguespack, Victoire	2nd great-granddaughter	IV	4
Waguespack, Victor Lovincie,***	Husband of the great-granddaughter		
Waguespack, Virginie Leonise	Great-grandniece	V	4
Waguespack, Vivian	2nd great-granddaughter	IV	4
Waguespack, Wallis J., Jr.	3rd great-grandson	V	5
Waguespack, Wallis J., III	4th great-grandson	VI	6
Waguespack, Wallis Jean	2nd great-grandson	IV	4
Waguespack, Wendy	3rd great-granddaughter	V	5
Waguespack, Westley Paul, Jr.	5th great-grandson	VII	7
Waguespack, Westley Paul, Sr.	4th great-grandson	VI	6
Waguespack, Wilhelm Jean	Great-grandson	III	3
Waguespack, Wilhelm John	Great-grandnephew of the wife		
Waguespack, Wilson	2nd great-grandson	IV	4
Waguespack, Wilson Pierre	Great-grandson	III	3
Waguespack, Winna	Great-granddaughter	III	3
Waguespack, Zephius Drossin	Great-grandnephew of the wife		
Waguespack, Zulima	Grandniece	IV	3
Walker, Stephanie Ann	Wife of the 4th great-grandson		
Walker, Theodorine Marie	Wife of the grandnephew		
Wallace, Ashley	Wife of the 5th great-grandson		
Ware, Chandler Halliburton	5th great-grandson	VII	7
Ware, George Halliburton III	Husband of the 4th great-granddaughter		
Ware, Grayson Paul	5th great-grandson	VII	7
Washer, Karen Ann	Wife of the 4th great-grandson		
Webre, Frank Burcard	Husband of the great-grandniece		
Webre, Joseph Benoit	2nd great-grandnephew	VI	5
Webre, Vivian	2nd great-grandniece	VI	5
Wegner, Mary	Wife of the 5th great-grandson		
Weimer, Eric Charles	Husband of the 4th great-granddaughter		
Weimer, Randy	Husband of the 4th great-granddaughter		
Wesele, Veronica	Great-grandmother of the wife		
Whatley, Jan Reneau	Wife of the 3rd great-grandson		
Whatley, Lindsay	4th great-granddaughter	VI	6
Whatley, Scarlett	4th great-granddaughter	VI	6
Wheat, Mary Frances Woods	Wife of the 3rd great-grandson		
White, Kristina Ellen	Wife of the 4th great-grandson		
Wiche, Bernard	Great-grandfather of the wife		

*Kinship of Jean Robért, *-****

Name	Relationship with Jean Robért	Civil	Canon
Wiche, Marguerite	Grandmother of the wife		
Wilcher, Cynthia Renée	Wife of the 4th great-grandson		
Wilde, Joey	Husband of the 4th great-granddaughter		
Wilhoite, Melissa Tullier	Wife of the 3rd great-grandson		
Williams, Brett	Husband of the 4th great-granddaughter		
Williams, Kelli	Wife of the 3rd great-grandson		
Williamson, Kayla	Wife of the 4th great-grandson		
Wilson, Stacie Elise	Wife of the 4th great-grandson		
Wiltz, Violet	Wife of the 2nd great-grandnephew		
Wintz, Necia	Wife of the 2nd great-grandnephew		
Witt, Lynn Janice	Wife of the 4th great-grandson		
Wonnacott, Joseph	3rd great-grandnephew	VII	6
Wonnacott, Linda	3rd great-grandniece	VII	6
Wonnacott, Mark	3rd great-grandnephew	VII	6
Wonnacott, Patricia	3rd great-grandniece	VII	6
Wonnacott, Richard	3rd great-grandnephew	VII	6
Wonnacott, Richard F.	Husband of the 2nd great-grandniece		
Wonnacott, Tommye	3rd great-grandnephew	VII	6
Wood, Martha	Wife of the half 4th great-grandnephew		
Woosley, John Stanley	Husband of the 3rd great-granddaughter		
Woosley, Michael J.	4th great-grandson	VI	6
Wright, Allie Marie	4th great-granddaughter	VI	6
Wright, Amy Lee	4th great-granddaughter	VI	6
Wright, Chad Michael	Husband of the 3rd great-granddaughter		
Wright, Chase Michael	4th great-grandson	VI	6
Wright, Deanie	Wife of the 4th great-grandson		
Young, Chet David	4th great-grandson	VI	6
Young, Lance Michael	4th great-grandson	VI	6
Young, Rae Michelle	4th great-granddaughter	VI	6
Young, Sloan Lloyd	Husband of the 3rd great-granddaughter		
Zatarain	Husband of the 3rd great-granddaughter		
Zeller, Adelina	Wife of the 2nd great-grandson		
Zeller, Melanie	Daughter-in-law		
Zeringue, Albert Paul	Husband of the 2nd great-granddaughter		
Zeringue, Alce Ann	4th great-granddaughter	VI	6
Zeringue, Aline Cecile	3rd great-granddaughter	V	5
Zeringue, Andre Alfred	Half grandnephew	IV	3
Zeringue, Annette	3rd great-grandniece	VII	6
Zeringue, Barbara Ann	Wife of the 3rd great-grandson		
Zeringue, Beatrice	2nd great-grandniece	VI	5
Zeringue, Brent	3rd great-grandnephew	VII	6
Zeringue, Brian	3rd great-grandnephew	VII	6
Zeringue, Bruce	3rd great-grandnephew	VII	6
Zeringue, Carol	3rd great-grandniece	VII	6
Zeringue, Charles	Grandnephew of the wife		
Zeringue, Charles	Great-grandnephew of the wife		
Zeringue, Cherie	3rd great-grandniece	VII	6
Zeringue, Clelie, (BeBel)	2nd great-granddaughter	IV	4
Zeringue, Cleona	2nd great-granddaughter	IV	4
Zeringue, Craig	Husband of the 4th great-granddaughter		
Zeringue, Craig	3rd great-grandnephew	VII	6
Zeringue, Dennis Paul	3rd great-grandnephew	VII	6
Zeringue, Didier Sydney	Husband of the half 2nd great-grandniece		
Zeringue, Dionne	3rd great-grandniece	VII	6
Zeringue, Doris	3rd great-granddaughter	V	5

Kinship of Jean Robért, *-***

Name	Relationship with Jean Robért	Civil	Canon
Zeringue, Eldridge Paul	2nd great-grandnephew	VI	5
Zeringue, Ellen	3rd great-grandniece	VII	6
Zeringue, Emily Michelle	5th great-granddaughter	VII	7
Zeringue, Estelle	Half grandniece	IV	3
Zeringue, Felicity Myrtille	Half grandniece	IV	3
Zeringue, Florence	3rd great-grandniece	VII	6
Zeringue, Forestal Hubert	Great-grandnephew of the wife		
Zeringue, Francois Joseph	Husband of the great-granddaughter		
Zeringue, Fuicy	2nd great-grandson	IV	4
Zeringue, Gaile	3rd great-grandniece	VII	6
Zeringue, Glynn Joseph	Husband of the 4th great-granddaughter		
Zeringue, Herman J.	2nd great-grandnephew	VI	5
Zeringue, Hermina	Great-grandniece of the wife		
Zeringue, Irene	3rd great-grandniece	VII	6
Zeringue, James	3rd great-grandnephew	VII	6
Zeringue, John	Great-grandnephew of the wife		
Zeringue, Johnny Joseph	Husband of the 4th great-granddaughter		
Zeringue, Joseph	Half grandnephew	IV	3
Zeringue, Joseph	Husband of the great-grandniece		
Zeringue, Joseph	Husband of the half niece		
Zeringue, Joseph Anatole	Half grandnephew	IV	3
Zeringue, Joseph Author	Husband of the 2nd great-granddaughter		
Zeringue, Joseph Brou	2nd great-grandnephew	VI	5
Zeringue, Josepha Marie	2nd great-granddaughter	IV	4
Zeringue, Lance Michael	5th great-grandson	VII	7
Zeringue, Leah	2nd great-grandniece of the wife		
Zeringue, Lena Marie	Wife of the 2nd great-grandson		
Zeringue, Leon	2nd great-grandson	IV	4
Zeringue, Leon Alonzo	Half grandnephew	IV	3
Zeringue, Leonard	2nd great-grandnephew	VI	5
Zeringue, Leopold Jean	Husband of the 2nd great-granddaughter		
Zeringue, Lisa Marie	4th great-granddaughter	VI	6
Zeringue, Living	3rd great-granddaughter	V	5
Zeringue, Living	Wife of the 4th great-grandson		
Zeringue, Louis	Great-grandnephew of the wife		
Zeringue, Louis Honore	Grandnephew of the wife		
Zeringue, Louis Joseph	Husband of the 3rd great-granddaughter		
Zeringue, Louis Roch	Half grandnephew	IV	3
Zeringue, Louisa Marie	3rd great-granddaughter	V	5
Zeringue, Lynette	4th great-granddaughter	VI	6
Zeringue, Marie	3rd great-grandniece	VII	6
Zeringue, Marie	Grandniece of the wife		
Zeringue, Marie Eleonore	Wife of the half 2nd great-grandnephew		
Zeringue, Marie Euphemie	Great-grandniece of the wife		
Zeringue, Marie Genevieve	Great-grandniece of the wife		
Zeringue, Marie Josephine	Half grandniece	IV	3
Zeringue, Marie Therese	3rd great-grandniece	VII	6
Zeringue, Marie Honorine	Wife of the great-grandson		
Zeringue, Marjorie Cecilia	Half 4th great-grandniece	VIII	7
Zeringue, Mark	4th great-grandson	VI	6
Zeringue, Maureen	4th great-granddaughter	VI	6
Zeringue, Natalie	Half grandniece	IV	3
Zeringue, Nathalie	Wife of the grandson		
Zeringue, Nemour	Great-grandnephew of the wife		
Zeringue, Noe	Great-grandnephew of the wife		

Kinship of Jean Robért, *-***

Name	Relationship with Jean Robért	Civil	Canon
Zeringue, Noellis	Great-grandniece of the wife		
Zeringue, Norbert	Grandnephew of the wife		
Zeringue, Norman	3rd great-grandnephew	VII	6
Zeringue, Norman Peter, (Tom)	2nd great-grandnephew	VI	5
Zeringue, Octavie	Wife of the half 2nd great-grandnephew		
Zeringue, Oneida	2nd great-granddaughter	IV	4
Zeringue, Paul	Husband of the great-grandniece		
Zeringue, Paul Aubert	Grandnephew of the wife		
Zeringue, Pearl	Wife of the 2nd great-grandson		
Zeringue, Prudhomme	Half grandnephew	IV	3
Zeringue, Ralph Jerome	2nd great-grandnephew	VI	5
Zeringue, Rene Joseph	2nd great-grandnephew	VI	5
Zeringue, Rene Victor	Husband of the great-grandniece		
Zeringue, Renée Ann	3rd great-grandniece	VII	6
Zeringue, Roland	3rd great-grandson	V	5
Zeringue, Sarah Elizabeth	5th great-granddaughter	VII	7
Zeringue, Sharon	3rd great-grandniece	VII	6
Zeringue, Thelma	3rd great-grandniece	VII	6
Zeringue, Therese Marie	3rd great-granddaughter	V	5
Zeringue, Thomas	3rd great-grandnephew	VII	6
Zeringue, Vicky	3rd great-grandniece	VII	6
Zeringue, Victor Joseph	Half 3rd great-grandnephew	VII	6
Zeringue, Victor Norbert	Husband of the half 2nd great-grandniece		
Zeringue, Windy	3rd great-grandniece	VII	6
Zimmerman, Amanda Gwen	Wife of the 3rd great-grandson		

Bibliography of Sources

Abstract of Civil Records of St. John the Baptist Parish.
Archdiocese of New Orleans Sacramental Records.
Diocese of Baton Rouge Catholic Church Records.
Glenn R. Conrad, *Abstract of Civil Records of St. Charles Parish.*
Lafourche Parish, Marriages 1820-1900.
Louisiana State Death Index.
Nicholas Russell Murray, *St. John the Baptist Parish Marriage Records.*
Ruth Robert, *Robert Family Book II.*
Social Security Death Index.
St. Charles Borromeo Catholic Church, Destrehan, Louisiana.
St. Charles Parish Records 1771-1900, Marriage Records.
St. James Parish Marriage Book.
St. James Parish Marriage Records in Conveyance.
St. James Parish Records.
St. John the Baptist Parish Civil Records.
St. John the Baptist Parish Marriages.
St. Louis Cathedral Church Records, New Orleans, Louisiana.
St. Phillip Catholic Church Records, Vacherie, Louisisna.

Source Usage Report

Source: Abstract of Civil Records of St. Charles Parish
Jean Robért, *-***
    Died: 15 July 1815, St. Charles Parish, Louisiana

Source: Abstract of Civil Records of St. John the Baptist Parish
Jean Robért II
    Divorce #1: 28 August 1820, SJBED,M3,37
Mathieu Robért, *- **- ***
    Died: Btn. 20 July - 06 October 1777, St. Charles Parish, Louisiana, USA
Ursin Robért
    Died: 29 August 1855, St. John the Baptist Parish, Louisiana
Hubert Jean Baptiste Waguespack,***
    Born: 12 May 1830, St. John the Baptist Parish, Louisiana
Josephine Marie Waguespack, ***
    Born: 18 November 1832, St. John the Baptist Parish, Louisiana

Source: Archdiocese of New Orleans Sacramental Records
Delia Felonise Faucheux
    Died: 15 March 1862, St. Charles Parish, Destrehan, Louisiana
Myrtille Antoinette Faucheux
    Born: 17 June 1816, Louisiana
    Died: 04 July 1860, St. John the Baptist Parish, Louisiana
Delia Marie Robért
    Born: 08 May 1853, St. John the Baptist Parish, Louisiana
Edna Marie Robért
    Born: 05 November 1900, Kenner, Jefferson Parish, Louisiana
Elmira Marie Robért
    Born: 19 December 1876, Wallace, St. John the Baptist Parish, Louisiana
Etienne Robért
    Born: December 1836, St. John the Baptist Parish, Louisiana
    Died: 29 June 1838, St. John the Baptist Parish, Louisiana
Jean Paul Robért, *
    Born: 26 July 1855, Wallace, St. John the Baptist Parish, Louisiana
Jean Ursin Robért
    Born: 14 June 1868, St. John the Baptist Parish, Louisiana
Marie Evelina Robért
    Born: 16 May 1873, St. John the Baptist Parish, Louisiana
Mathieu Robért, Jr. (Yen-Yen)
    Name: Mathieu Robért, Jr. (Yen-Yen)
    Born: 16 January 1835, St. John the Baptist Parish, Louisiana
Mathieu Robért, Sr. *- ***
    Born: 1811, St. Charles Parish, Louisiana
    Died: 12 September 1855, St. John the Baptist Parish, Louisiana
Octave Pierre Robért
    Born: 22 August 1894, Wallace, St. John the Baptist Parish, Louisiana
Palmire Marie Robért
    Born: 31 August 1848, St. John the Baptist Parish, Louisiana
Pierre Amedee Robért
    Born: 20 September 1851, St. John the Baptist Parish, Louisiana
Remy Paul Robért
    Born: 02 July 1892, Wallace, St. John the Baptist Parish, Louisiana
Rene Benoit Robért, (Ne-Nall)
    Born: 21 February 1897, Wallace, St. John the Baptist Parish, Louisiana

Roland Jacques Robért, Sr. (Pan-Am)
> **Born:** 15 April 1900, Tchoupitoulas Plantation, Jefferson Parish, Louisiana

Willis Louis Mathieu Robért
> **Born:** 10 July 1865, St. John the Baptist Parish, Louisiana

Catherine Charlotte Schexnayder
> **Born:** 21 September 1741, St. Charles Parish, Louisiana (SCB B1-12)

Jean George Albert Schexnayder
> **Born:** 10 September 1746, St. Charles Parish, Louisiana

Jean Henry Albert Schexnayder
> **Died:** 08 September 1778, St. John the Baptist , Louisiana

Marie Lucie Schexnayder
> **Born:** 13 December 1748, St. Charles Parish, Louisiana (SCB, B1,55)

Albert Simon Schexnaydre
> **Born:** 1874, Edgard, St. John the Baptist Parish, Louisiana

Jacque Rene Waggenspack, **
> **Born:** 09 December 1867, Raceland, Lafourche Parish, Louisiana

Thérése Waggenspack
> **Born:** 27 April 1878, Houma, Terrebonne Parish, Louisiana

Marie Nezile (Inezile) Waguespack
> **Name:** Marie Nezile (Inezile) Waguespack
> **Born:** 18 March 1838, Thibodaux, Lafourche Parish, Louisiana

Octave Pierre Waguespack
> **Born:** 04 March 1898, Edgard, St. John the Baptist Parish, Louisiana

Marriage of Jean Robért II and Eleanor Toups
> **Marriage:** 28 August 1820, St. Charles Borromeo Catholic Church, Destrehan, Louisiana

Marriage of Norbert Robért and Amanda Leocadie Toledano
> **Marriage:** 20 March 1843, St. Louis Cathedral, New Orleans, Orleans Parish, Louisiana

Marriage of Emilien Schexnayder and Nathalie Zeringue
> **Marriage:** 02 June 1855, New Orleans, Orleans Parish, Louisiana

Marriage of Jacque Rene Waggenspack, ** and Elmira Marie Robért
> **Marriage:** 11 January 1902, St. Mary Catholic Church,Kenner, Louisiana

Marriage of Epiphany <Tiffany> Schexnayder, Jr. and Marianne Melanie Robért
> **Marriage:** 05 November 1821, St. John the Baptist Catholic Church, Edgard, Louisiana

Source: Diocese of Baton Rouge Catholic Church Records

Amedee Jean Robért
> **Born:** 29 February 1880, Vacherie, St. James Parish, Louisiana

Joseph Olide Robért, (Do-Doot)
> **Born:** 25 November 1880, Wallace, St. John the Baptist Parish, Louisiana

Leona Theresa Robért, (Na-Na)
> **Born:** 15 October 1882, Wallace, St. John the Baptist Parish, Louisiana

Marie Octavie Robért, ***
> **Born:** 22 August 1869, St.James Parish, Louisiana

Marie Palmyre Robért, (Tee-Nannan)
> **Born:** 18 April 1876, Vacherie, St. James Parish, Louisiana

Martha Philomene Robért, (Bot)
> **Born:** 28 February 1890, Wallace, St. John the Baptist Parish, Louisiana

Paula Cecile Robért, (Tow-Tow)
> **Born:** 22 November 1878, Wallace, St. John the Baptist Parish, Louisiana

Raoul Matthew Robért
> **Born:** 31 March 1885, Wallace, St. John the Baptist Parish, Louisiana

Wallace Jean Robért, Sr.
> **Born:** 27 February 1874, Vacherie, St. James Parish, Louisiana

Source: Lafourche Parish, Marriages 1820-1900

Marriage of Jean Paul Robért, * and Marie Octavie Brou, *
> **Marriage:** 05 February 1876, Thibodaux, Lafourche Parish, Louisiana

Direct Descendants of Jean Robért and Marianne Waguespack

Marriage of Mathieu Robért, Jr. (Yen-Yen) and Marie Nezile (Inezile) Waguespack
Marriage: 08 October 1866, Lafourche Parish, Louisiana
Marriage of Augustine Dardard and Anatole Robért
Marriage: 14 September 1895, Lafourche Parish, Louisiana

Source: Louisiana State Death Index
Mathieu Robért, Jr. (Yen-Yen)
Died: 16 November 1920, Darrow, Ascension Parish, Louisiana

Source: Robert Family Book II
Anne Marie Robért, (Grand-Fille)
Born: 05 December 1912, Moll Plantation, (Remy) St.John the Baptiste Parish, Louisiana

Source: Social Security Death Index
Erin Lynn Gagen
Died: 05 November 1995, Orlando, Orange County, Florida
Jean Omér Robért, Jr. (Noon)
Died: 28 February 2004, New Orleans, Orleans Parish, Louisiana

Source: St. Charles Borromeo Catholic Church, Destrehan, Louisiana
Marriage of Jean Louis Robért and Isabelle Arceneaux
Marriage: 05 November 1821, St. Charles Borromeo Catholic Church, Destrehan, Louisiana

Source: St. Charles Parish Records 1771-1900, Marriage Records
Marriage of Mathieu Robért, Jr. (Yen-Yen) and Delia Felonise Faucheux
Marriage: 05 January 1856, St. Charles Parish, Louisiana
Marriage of Honore Augustin Brou, (Tee Parrain) and Marie Palmyre Robért, (Tee-Nannan)
Marriage: 18 February 1896, St. Rosaire Catholic Church, St.Charles Parish, Louisiana
Marriage of Jean Baptiste Bertrand, Jr. and Camille Robért
Marriage: 17 January 1832, St. Charles Parish, Louisiana
Marriage of Hubert Robért, Sr. and Julie Faucheux
Marriage: 09 February 1829, St. Charles Borromeo Church, Destrahan, Louisiana
Marriage of Louis Robért and Adelaide Belsome
Marriage: 20 March 1854, St. Charles Parish , Louisiana

Source: St. James Parish Marriage Book
Marriage of André Evariste Waguespack and Arthemise Faucheux
Marriage: 25 January 1820, St. James, St. James Parish, Louisiana
Marriage of Willis Louis Mathieu Robért and Albertine Brou, (Tante Bat)
Marriage: 04 April 1893, St. James Catholic Church, St. James, Louisiana
Marriage of Marcellin G. Schexnayder and Elia Falgoust
Marriage: 29 July 1914, St. James Parish, Louisiana
Marriage of Marcellin O Schexnayder and Marie Francesca (Frances) Torres
Marriage: 06 October 1908, St. James Parish, Louisiana

Source: St. James Parish Marriage Records in Conveyance
Marriage of Hubert Jean Baptiste Waguespack,*** and Josephine Marie Waguespack, ***
Marriage: 09 April 1849, St. James Parish, Louisiana

Source: St. James Parish Records
Marriage of Wallis Jean Waguespack and Edna Marie Decareaux
Marriage: 07 April 1915, St. James Parish, Convent, Louisiana

Source: St. John the Baptist Parish Civil Records
Jeanne Clelie Robért
Born: 24 November 1869, St. John the Baptist Parish, Louisiana
Ursin Robért

Born: 14 September 1840, St. John the Baptist Parish, Louisiana

Source: St. John the Baptist Parish Marriage Records
Marriage of Albert Simon Schexnaydre and Cesaire Eva Haydel
    Marriage: 12 February 1898, Edgard, St. John the Baptist Parish, Louisiana
Marriage of Jean Frumence Robért, *** and Euphrasie Froiselee Bouy, (Tante Pay-Pay), ***
    Marriage: 21 February 1867, Edgard, St. John the Baptist Parish, Louisiana
Marriage of Wallace Jean Robért, Sr. and Zelia Hymel
    Marriage: 26 April 1900, Edgard, St. John the Baptist Parish, Louisiana
Marriage of Alidor Waguespack and Delia Marie Robért
    Marriage: 16 April 1873, St. John the Baptiste Parish, Edgard, Louisiana
Marriage of Septime Louis Robért, Sr. and Marie Schexnayder
    Marriage: 26 January 1861, Edgard, St. John the Baptist Parish, Louisiana
Marriage of Jean Ursin Robért and Euphrosine Brou
    Marriage: 08 April 1893, St. John the Baptist Parish, Louisiana
Marriage of Rene Francois Brou, Sr. and Myrtile Mathilde Marie Robért
    Marriage: 16 April 1898, St.John the Baptist Parish, Edgard, Louisiana
Marriage of Floribert Pierre Schexnaydre, * and Marie Antoinette Robért
    Marriage: 23 November 1867, Edgard, St. John the Baptist Parish, Louisiana
Marriage of Francois Joseph Zeringue and Jeanne Clelie Robért
    Marriage: 07 April 1894, St. John the Baptist Catholic Church, Edgard, Louisiana
Marriage of Henry Joseph Schexnaydre, Sr * and Marie Antoinette Waguespack
    Marriage: 09 August 1894, Edgard, St. John the Baptist Parish, Louisiana
Marriage of Omèr Jean Robért, Sr. and Marie Louise Borne, < Borise>
    Marriage: 09 April 1891, Edgard, St.John the Baptiste Parish, Louisiana
Marriage of Prudent Waguespack and Marie Evelina Robért
    Marriage: 18 May 1893, St. John the Baptist Parish, Louisiana

Source: St. John the Baptist Parish Marriages
Marriage of Mathieu Robért, Sr. *- *** and Myrtille Antoinette Faucheux
    Marriage: 15 July 1833, Edgard, St. John the Baptist Parish, Louisiana
Marriage of Albert Schexnayder and Heloise Robért
    Marriage: 30 October 1826, Edgard, St. John the Baptist Parish, Louisiana

Source: St. Louis Cathedral Church Records, New Orleans, Louisiana
Catherine Marie Menard, *- **- ***
    Born: 22 April 1750, St. Charles Parish, Louisiana, USA
Marriage of Pierre Louis Bertrand and Marie Octavie Schexnayder
    Marriage: 14 February 1831, St. Louis Cathedral, New Orleans, Orleans Parish, Louisiana

Source: St. Phillip Catholic Church Records, Vacherie, Louisisna
Marriage of Victor Lovincie Waguespack,*** and Marie Octavie Robért, ***
    Marriage: 17 May 1887, St. Philip Catholic Church, Vacherie, Louisiana

Index of Individuals

273

Marie Delphine: 204
Octavie F.: 204
Pierre Louis: 204, 270
Pierre Louis II: 204
Theodore: 204
Theogene: 204
Thomas Leo: 204

Best -
John: 129, 204

Betty -
Unnamed: 204

Bianchini -
Anne: 123

Bienvenu -
Alden: 37, 204

Bihm -
Tommy Vincent: 157, 204

Binder -
Joseph Victor: 91, 204

Birdsall -
Susane Bercell: 204

Birdsong -
Amy Elizabeth: 132, 204
Edmond Ker: 132, 204
Frank Allen ,Jr.: 132
John Taylor: 132, 204
Joseph Allen: 132, 204
Samuel Ker: 132, 204

Bishop -
Anne Marie: 161, 204
David Nolan: 161, 204
Julie Frances: 161, 204

Blackwell -
Randy: 84, 204

Blades -
Abraham Eligh: 84
Glenda Ann: 84, 204

Blanchard -
Aimee Lynn: 172, 204
Cathy J.: 92, 204
Christine Theresa: 128, 204
Clay Michael: 173, 204
Constance Anne: 102, 172, 204
Courtney Marie: 128, 191, 204
Donna Marie: 102, 172, 204
Jennifer Marie: 173, 204
Joseph S.: 61
Joseph , III: 172, 204
Julie Therese: 102, 173, 204
Lauren Claire: 102, 173, 204
Laurie Elizabeth: 172, 204

Lillian Theresa: 61, 128, 191, 192, 204
Living: 75, 204
Madeline Marie: 61, 128, 192, 204
Marvin Clay: 102, 173, 204
Nedra: 143
Raymond Francois: 102, 204
Rebecca Anne: 172, 205
Robert Courtland , Jr.: 61, 127, 128, 191, 205
Robert Courtland , Sr.: 61, 205

Blood -
Leisa Gay: 150, 205

Blue -
Amy Elizabeth , (Divorced 2007): 184, 205
M.D. Kenneth M. , Jr.: 184

Blum -
Kaysie Christine Nordby Anderson: 187, 205
Sam Monette: 187, 205

Boltin -
Sherry: 158, 205

Bondi -
Anne Antionette: 138

Bonvillian -
Jo Ann: 87, 205

Borne -
Betty: 102, 205
Edward Maurice , Sr.: 87
Marie Louise , < Borise>: 17, 205, 270
Shirlie: 87, 205

Bouchereau -
Lori: 205

Boudreaux -
Brad Thomas: 159, 205
Bret Patrick: 152, 205
Daisy: 21, 205
Darlene: 153, 205
Dawn Michelle: 159, 205
Gayle: 152, 205
Jaime Ann: 159, 205
Jazenette: 134
Melvin: 114, 205
Michael Shane: 152, 205
Newell Roy: 113, 114, 205
Rob: 80, 205
Roy Thomas: 159, 205
Tilda: 114, 205
Troy Jude: 159, 205

Boulanger -
Chantal Marthe: 137, 205

Toue: 119, 214
Foster -
Claude: 112
Debra Ann: 166, 214
Frankie: 112, 214
Nellie: 81
Fournet -
Anne Elizabeth: 94, 214
Fournier -
Helen Mae: 36, 214
Foxworth -
Emmet Allen: 97, 215
Emmett Allen , Sr.: 96, 97, 215
Steven Glen: 97, 215
Tammy Ann: 97, 215
Francais -
Solange Gabrièlle: 137
Francebois -
John Litaire: 130
Franchebois -
Sydney Lee: 130, 215
Frederic -
Patrick Jude: 113, 215
Frederick -
Angelique Alice: 215
Freeze -
Hugh Alphonso: 77, 215
Fremin -
Dale Joseph , Jr.: 103, 215
Friche -
Nomie: 57
Friloux -
Adonia: 35
Calamire Selvince Celina: 36
Celamire: 14
Clorinne: 36
Dennis J.: 14, 37, 74, 215
Edgar Joseph: 36, 215
Florent: 14
George J.: 14, 74, 215
Lucia: 13, 215
Winfield Joseph: 37, 215
Froisy -
Marie Adele: 128
Fryoux -
Raymond Anthony , Jr.: 128, 215
Fuselier -
Gerald Anthony: 63, 215

G

Gabor -
Virginia: 215
Gadel -
Ann Marie: 115, 215
Warren Charles: 115
Gagen -
Erin Lynn: 269
Gallagher -
Kristy: 108, 215
Gant -
Debra: 164, 215
Garner -
Edna: 113
Garrison -
Mary Elizabeth: 107
Gaspard -
Lee Roy F.: 215
Vina: 71
Gaubert -
Ambrose: 74
Eunice: 74, 215
Gaudet -
Charles Francois: 215
Charles Myrtile: 215
Hortense Aimee: 215
Gaughan -
Francis Terrance: 170
John Martin: 170, 215
Gauthier -
Cedric Alexandre: 192, 215
Everett Paul , Jr.: 128, 215
Everett Paul , III (Rett): 128, 192, 215
Everett Paul , Sr.: 128
Lindsey Marie: 128, 215
Philippe Rene: 128, 215
Samuel Everett: 192, 215
Gautreau -
Brittni Nicole: 183, 215
Christen: 169, 215
Gay: 195
Henry Wilton: 58, 100
Laurie: 147
Mildred: 58, 215
Myrtle Marie: 100, 215
Gautreaux -
Bessie: 128
Catherine: 149
Craig: 109, 215
George -
Samantha Vondel: 190, 215
Sarah Marie: 140, 215

H

Hacker -
Kimberly Georgia: 186, 216
Merritt: 186
Hammel -
Dianne Rose: 134
Hanson -
Belvas Lynn: 78, 216
Harelson -
Donald Ray: 106, 216
Gary Paul: 106, 216
Glen Thomas: 106, 216
Jacob Charles: 175, 216
Jennifer Lynne: 175, 216
Jody Robért: 106, 216
Jonathan Hebert: 175, 216
Wade Anthony: 106, 175, 216
Hargrave -
Mildred: 86, 216
Harlan -
Eric Hampton: 135, 216
Leo: 135
Robért Scott: 135, 217
Stephen Joseph: 135, 217
Harp -
Bruce: 117
Lettie: 117, 217
Myrtis: 77
Harper -
Jody: 217
Harvey -
Benjamin Gayle: 151, 217
Brittney Nichole: 150, 217
Bryan Taylor: 151, 217
Caberial Alexandria: 150, 217
Courtney Ann: 150, 217
George Brian: 72, 151, 217
Jesseca Lee Ann: 151, 217
Kathryn Olivia: 151, 217
Lainey Cait: 151, 217
Lauren Rene: 151, 217
Lynsey Nicole: 151, 217
Macey Elise: 150, 217
Meghan Elizabeth: 150, 217
Monique Antonia: 150, 217
Morgan Elizabeth: 150, 217
Robert Doyle: 72, 150, 217
Valerie Ann: 72, 151, 217
Woodson III: 72, 150, 217
Woodson , Sr.: 72
Woodson ,Jr.: 72, 217
Wynn Traylor: 72, 150, 151, 217

Wynn Traylor II: 151, 217
Haydel -
Achille: 22, 217
Antoine Ernest: 45, 99, 100, 217
Ashley Anne: 168, 217
Cesaire Eva: 22, 217, 270
Chris , Rev.: 100, 217
Craig David: 100, 217
Damien Dale: 154, 217
Ernest: 45, 217
Faith Elizabeth: 154, 217
Genevieve Ambroise: 2
George J. , Sr: 31, 217
Jennie Marie: 45, 99, 217
Jessie Joseph: 45, 99, 168, 217
Kenneth: 99, 168, 217
Kenneth James , Jr.: 168, 217
Laurance: 217
Lucy: 2
Marie Antonia: 217
Marie Azelie: 5, 217
Pierre: 5
Pierre Stanley: 45
Rita Theresa: 45, 217
Sam: 18, 217
Sandy Lee: 154, 217
Hayes -
Margaret: 192, 217
Hebert -
Alex Joseph , Jr: 139
Alexander Paul: 139, 217
Annette Marie: 24, 217
Austin Gregory: 144, 217
Bessie: 62
Brenen: 107, 217
Cameron Michael: 144, 217
Catherine: 175, 217
Catherine Marie: 144, 217
Celeste Marie: 139, 217
Cleo J. , Sr.: 68
Cleo Joseph , Jr.: 68, 217
Cliff Michael: 69, 144, 218
Colin Gregory: 144, 218
Curtis Joseph: 160, 161, 218
David Ryan: 144, 218
Dean Gregory: 68, 144, 218
Edna: 218
Emilie Marie: 139, 218
James Philip: 139, 218
Jeffery Paul: 69, 218
Kaitlyn Renée: 191, 218
Kaycee Lynn: 161, 218

Linda M.: 222
Linda Marie: 222
Lloyd Lawrence: 123
Lori Therese: 110, 222
Loyce Clare: 73
Lydia Ann: 110, 222
Marcia Leigh: 110, 222
Marie Louise: 43, 222
Melanie Marie: 191, 222
Michael Joseph: 192, 222
Michael Paul: 42
Michael Paul: 43, 223
Michelle Annette: 128, 192, 223
Nicole Monique: 128, 192, 223
Patsy Ruth: 223
Robert: 76, 223
Robért J. , (Cap): 223
Robért J. , Jr.: 223
Rosemary: 43, 223
Ruffin Joseph: 110, 223
Shirley P.: 223
Susan: 76, 223
Troy Michael: 128, 191, 223
Vicki Lyn: 79, 223
Viola: 120
Waldon Charles , Sr.: 61, 64, 223
Waldon , Jr.: 223
Wharton Armand: 76, 223
Wharton Armand , Jr.: 76, 223
LeBouef -
Emma Dell Marie: 53, 223
LeDoux -
Richard L.: 131
Suzanne Angelique: 131, 223
Lee -
Byan Andrew: 141, 223
David Michael: 141, 223
Gary Wayne , Jr.: 141, 223
Gary Wayne , Sr.: 141
Katherine Grace: 141, 223
Madeline Ruth: 141, 223
Neva Helen: 139
Lefort -
Kenneth: 85, 223
Matilda: 223
Legendre -
Eugene E.: 182
Reine Ann: 182, 223
Leglue -
Randell Clement: 78, 223
Lejeune -

Sylvestre , (Legendre): 223
Leloup -
Anne: 223
Lemoine -
Dana Lynn: 155, 223
Dave Paul: 155, 223
Lacey Michelle: 155, 223
Tiffany Anne: 155, 223
Lessard -
Mercedean Marie: 104, 223
Letulle -
Glory Mary: 51, 52, 223
Lewis -
Jeffrey Dean: 110, 223
Liddell -
Debra Ann: 159, 223
Little -
William Charles , (Divorced): 146, 223
Living -
Unnamed: 53
Longanecker -
Lisa Lené: 182, 223
Wilson R.: 182
Longmire -
Ruphena: 76
Lopinto -
Tinna: 111, 223
Lorio -
Lucien: 36
Sadie: 36, 223
Loupe -
Phyllis Yvonne: 141
Seraphine , <Loup>: 223
Louque -
Pam: 155, 223
Louviere -
Edmond: 22, 223
Luce -
Jana Reneé: 184, 223
John Raymond: 184
Luquette -
Cynthia: 223

M
MacFarland -
Rose: 170
MacKensie -
Ian Rome: 130, 223
Louis Lee: 130
Michael William: 130, 223

Ryan Rome: 130, 223
Sean Rome: 130, 223

Madatic -
John Richard: 184
Marci Reneé: 184, 223

Maddock -
Hazel: 85, 223

Madere -
Antoine Sidney , Jr.: 94, 223
Antoine Sidney , Sr.: 94, 223
Denise: 129, 224
Fernand: 128
Joan Ann: 93, 224
John Williams: 93, 224
Judith Ann: 94, 224
Julie: 129, 224
June Mary: 93, 224
Lee: 128, 129, 224
Lynn Terese: 93, 224
Marlene Ann: 93, 224
Mary Elizabeth: 94, 224
Mitzie: 129, 224
William Joseph: 94, 224

Maggiore -
August John: 99, 224
Ernest Joseph: 99, 224
John August: 99, 224

Magill -
George: 81
Paul Pierre: 81, 224
Victoria Ann: 81, 224
William Medford: 81, 224

Magill. -
Medford William: 81, 224

Mahler -
Denis John: 88, 224

Maillard -
Eugenie: 3, 224
Genevieve: 224

Major -
Beverly: 171

Malliard -
Jacques: 224
Jacques Pere ,(Mayard): 224
Louis: 224
Paul: 224

Manguna -
Vivian Theresa: 167, 224

Manley -
Susan: 127, 224

Manuel -

Bertha Lee: 131

Many -
Barry: 224
Brent: 224
Donna: 224
J.Timothy: 224
Karen: 224
Warren J.: 224

Marchand -
Antoine: 224
Catherine: 224
Charles Nicolas: 224
Ellen: 29
Helene: 224
Nicolas: 224

Margaret -
Unnamed: 18, 224

Margiotta -
Marie Mary: 36, 224

Marino -
Rita Lynn: 78, 224

Maris -
Kellie Lynn: 186, 224

Marix -
Louis Hill: 78, 224

Marlowe -
Betty: 140

Marshall -
Lily Brooke: 127

Martin -
Allen: 83
Barbara Ann: 83, 224
Benoit Wilson: 121
Brenda Ann: 121, 224
Dorothy Lea: 83, 224

Martine -
Agnes Lillian: 50, 224
Marie: 55

Martinez -
Adam Ozay: 32
Agalice: 49
Marie Ursuline , (Seline): 32, 56, 224

Matherne -
Andrew Paul: 89, 224
Craig Michael: 94, 224
Eugenie Laura: 224
Kevin: 93, 224

Matranga -
Joseph Salvadore: 69
Marcia , (Divorced): 69, 224

Maurin -

296

Salvadore: 242

Salas -
Victor: 103, 242

Salaun -
Cheryl Lynn: 177, 242
James George: 177

Salvail -
Christopher Michael: 145, 242
Lanie Elizabeth: 145, 242
Luke Michael: 145, 242
Patrick: 145

Sanders -
Jack: 71
Jeannie Arlene: 71, 242

Sandoz -
Tosy: 43, 242

Saucier -
Edgar Anthony , Jr.: 134
Edgar Anthony , III: 134, 242
Lauren Day: 134, 242
Steven Paul: 134, 242

Saurage -
Susie: 167, 242

Savoie -
Blake D.: 177, 242
Caroline Elizabeth: 177, 242
Daniel Nicholas: 118, 177, 242
Eunice Norma Marie: 37, 242
Felix , Sr.: 117
Jon Anthony: 117, 242
Jon Anthony ,Jr: 118, 176, 242
Kelsey Nicole: 177, 242
Leslie Ann: 176, 242
Lisa Marie: 117, 176, 242
Michelle Ann: 118, 177, 242
Michelle Marie: 176, 242
Nicholas J.: 177, 242
Pamela Joan: 118, 178, 242
Sarah Elizabeth: 176, 242
Stephanie Jo: 118, 177, 242

Savoy -
Brady Michael: 152, 242
Brian: 151, 152, 242
Dawn Marie: 133, 134, 242
Doris: 145
Laura Ashley , (Adopted): 152, 242
Leza Delano , Jr.: 131, 242
Leza Delano , Sr.: 131
Nolan: 133
Seth Brian: 152, 242
Tina Lynn: 131, 242

Say -
Alexander Douglas: 183, 242
George Douglas: 183, 242
Harrison George: 183, 242
Parker Robert: 183, 242
Robert Leo: 183
Whitney Estelle: 183, 242

Scallon -
Rita: 242

Schexnayder -
Alan Manuel: 242
Albert: 1, 242, 270
Alherry Joseph: 5, 242
Alice Margaret: 32
Amanda: 197, 242
Amy Marie: 165, 242
Antoinette: 21, 242
Azelie: 11, 242
Benjamin Louis , *: 8
Catherine Charlotte: 268
Cecila: 10, 31, 242
Charles Joseph: 160, 243
Claire: 74, 243
Clara Belle: 74, 243
Claude: 33, 243
Clemence: 243
Edgar Joseph III: 243
Edgar Joseph , Sr.: 243
Edgar , Jr.: 243
Edwin Joseph: 11, 32, 243
Edwin Joseph , Jr.: 32, 243
Elodie: 21, 243
Emilien: 243
Emilien: 2, 5, 10, 31, 243, 268
Emilien Joseph: 5, 11, 32, 73, 243
Epiphany (Etienne) , Sr.: 2, 243
Epiphany <Tiffany> , Jr.: 1, 2, 243, 268
Ethel: 49, 243
Furcy: 243
Gary: 243
Genevieve: 33, 243
Gerrard (Jerry): 74, 243
Gilbert: 5, 11, 12, 243
Hubert Joseph: 5, 243
Inette: 33, 243
Jean George Albert: 268
Jean Henry Albert: 268
Jean Marcellin , (Zoot): 11, 32, 33, 73, 243
Kalli Anne: 160, 243
Kelley: 73, 243
Kent: 73, 243

304

Kevin Mark: 73, 243
Kim: 73, 243
Louis: 6
Louis Bartholomu: 5, 10, 31, 243
Madeline Marie: 243
Marcelin: 243
Marcelin Ursin: 243
Marcellin: 2, 5, 10, 11, 32, 73, 74, 243
Marcellin G.: 12, 243, 269
Marcellin O: 11, 243, 269
Marie: 6, 24, 243, 270
Marie Beatrice: 32, 56, 73, 243
Marie Lucie: 268
Marie Marcelline: 11, 243
Marie Octavie: 243, 270
Marie Azelino: 5, 243
Marie Donna: 32, 243
Mary Ann: 74, 243
Odile: 21, 51, 243
Optime Joseph: 5, 10, 11, 32, 73, 243
Orenia: 11, 243
Phedlise: 243
Philomine: 243
Pierre Roman: 11, 243
Robin: 243
Romain , (Wa-Watt): 49
Rosa T.: 21, 243
Rose: 74, 243
Sidney , Jr.: 21, 243
Simon Joseph: 33, 73, 74, 243
Susie: 244
Victor Arnold: 32, 73, 244
Victor Joseph ,Sr.: 11, 32, 56, 73, 244
Willis: 11, 244
Zoe Suzanna: 21, 244

Schexnaydre -
Ada: 22, 244
Agnes: 22, 244
Alan Joseph: 166, 244
Albert Simon: 8, 22, 52, 53, 113, 114,
    244, 268, 270
Alceé: 22, 244
Alicia Marie: 167, 244
Andrew: 166, 244
Angela Ann: 109, 244
Anne: 23, 244
Antonia , (ya-ya): 8, 244
Bernadette Marie: 22, 52, 244
Bertha M.: 21, 244
Berthile Joseph , Jr. (Bert): 50, 98, 110,
    166, 167, 169, 244
Berthile Joseph , Sr. *: 21, 50, 51, 98,

109-112, 166, 167, 176, 244
Bertin , (Boo Boo): 23, 244
Bianca: 50, 244
Blaine Thaddeus: 110, 244
Boyd Joseph: 99, 244
Brian Thomas: 111, 169, 244
Carmen Ann: 111, 244
Cecile Marie: 22, 53, 244
Chris Michael: 111, 244
Clara: 23, 244
Clint Michael: 112, 244
Clyde Thaddeus: 50, 110, 244
Connie Theresa: 52, 113, 244
Craig Joseph: 98, 166, 244
Crystal Michelle: 113, 244
Dale Anthony: 111, 244
Dayton: 50, 111, 244
Delia: 21, 244
Dennis Thomas: 22, 244
Diane Marie: 111, 244
Dirk P.: 113, 244
Dolores Edith ,(Doe-Doe): 50, 244
Earl Joseph: 50, 244
Edith Marie , (Bo-Boot): 50, 111, 244
Effie: 22, 244
Elaine Rita: 51, 244
Elise Marie: 23, 244
Ellen Claire: 109, 244
Ferducie F.: 22, 244
Floribert Pierre , *: 8, 23, 244, 270
Francois: 244
Guy Grancis: 111, 244
Henry Joseph , Sr *: 8, 21, 23, 50-52, 109-
    113, 166, 167, 176, 244, 270
Henry , Jr.: 22, 244
Imelda: 21, 244
Ione Theresa: 50, 110, 244
Iris Joan: 109, 244
James Maurice: 109, 245
Jay Michael: 113, 245
Jeffery Joseph: 99, 167, 245
Jody Lynne: 166, 245
Julian Pierre , Sr. (Zoo): 22, 51, 52, 113,
    245
Julian Pierre ,Jr.: 52, 113, 245
Katheleen: 50, 245
Kenneth , (Ke-Ken): 50, 245
Kent Alan: 109, 176, 245
Kim Marie: 98, 166, 167, 245
Kim Marie: 167, 245
Kip J.: 113, 245
Lamar: 109, 245

Waguespack -

Rebecca Marie: 80, 152, 153, 260
Regina Victoria: 16, 40, 41, 260
Rene Ferdinand: 260
Rhonda Faye: 101, 170, 196, 260
Richard: 260
Richard: 46, 100, 170, 171, 196, 197, 260
Richard: 260
Richard P. , Jr. (Woody): 101, 260
Ricky Lee: 158, 260
Rita Marie: 260
Rita Marie: 260
Rita Olympe: 260
Robért: 260
Robert Gregoire: 260
Roberta Therese: 100, 169, 196, 260
Rodney John: 97, 260
Romana: 32, 260
Rosa: 260
Roseline: 260
Rosine , (Waggenspack): 260
Rosney , (Waggenspack): 31, 260
Rudy Paul Antoine: 43, 260
Ryan Joseph: 80, 153, 260
Sandry (Sandy): 54, 260
Saturinn: 260
Seraphine: 260
Seymour Raymond: 45, 98, 115, 164, 165, 260
Seymour Raymond , Jr.: 98, 260
Shane Anthony: 106, 260
Shane Joseph: 153, 260
Sharon Ann: 80, 152, 260
Shirley Philomine: 53, 260
Sidney Jean: 260
Stanford John: 45, 90, 97, 159, 260
Stanislas J.: 260
Stanislaus: 260
Stanley Paul: 18, 260
Stanley Paul , (Da-Da): 45, 97, 164, 260
Stephen: 24, 260
Steve Paul: 98, 260
Susan Mary: 80, 153, 260
Tanya Ann: 98, 164, 260
Telesphore: 260
Theophile: 261
Theresa: 261
Theresa: 261
Therese Elmira: 261
Thomas Christopher: 164, 261
Timothy: 24, 261
Tobie Mikael: 170, 196, 261
Tony Jude: 158, 261

Trudi Marie: 104, 174, 261
Tyler Michael: 170, 261
Ulger: 261
Ulger: 261
Ulger Eugene: 261
Ulgere: 261
Valentine: 261
Valerie: 261
Valsin: 261
Vickie Ann: 104, 174, 261
Victoire: 16, 261
Victor Lovincie ,***: 18, 38, 55, 261, 270
Virginie Leonise: 261
Vivian: 25, 54, 114, 261
Wallis J. , Jr.: 45, 97, 164, 261
Wallis J. , III: 97, 164, 261
Wallis Jean: 18, 44, 45, 90, 97-99, 110, 159, 164, 165, 167, 261, 269
Wendy: 55, 114, 115, 261
Westley Paul , Jr.: 164, 261
Westley Paul , Sr.: 97, 164, 261
Wilhelm Jean: 9, 261
Wilhelm John: 261
Wilson: 25, 54, 261
Wilson Pierre: 9, 24, 53, 54, 114, 261
Winna: 9, 261
Zephius Drossin: 261
Zulima: 261

Walker -
Cynthia Brightwell: 187
Stephanie Ann: 187, 261
Theodorine Marie: 261
Wallace -
Ashley: 196, 261
Ware -
Chandler Halliburton: 181, 261
George Halliburton III: 181, 261
George Halliburton , Jr.: 181
Grayson Paul: 181, 261
Washer -
Karen Ann: 162, 261
Webre -
Frank Burcard: 261
Joseph Benoit: 261
Vivian: 261
Wegner -
Mary: 197, 261
Weimer -
Eric Charles: 82, 261
Randy: 109, 261
Wesele -